Foreword

序

Thank you for buying this book. I am confident that the guidance, practice and advice you will find between these covers will be a great help towards achieving the IELTS score you need.

As the representative of the IELTS partners in China, I wish you every success in your IELTS test and trust that your IELTS score will be instrumental in opening doors upon new educational and career opportunities in the future.

With very best wishes,

感谢您购买《雅思考试官方指南》。我相信本书所提供的指导、练习和建议将帮助您取得理想的雅思成绩。

作为雅思考试主办方在中国的代表，我衷心地祝愿您雅思考试一切顺利，并通过雅思考试开启学业和事业的新契机！

致以最美好的祝愿！

Greg Selby　葛思斌

Director Examinations, East Asia　考试部东亚区业务总监

British Council　英国文化协会

Introduction
前　言

《雅思考试官方指南》及其配套光盘针对考生在雅思考试中发挥出最佳水平所需的技能提供解析、建议和练习。本书是英国文化协会专为中国雅思考生推出的第一部官方出版物，其中精心挑选了相关提示和例题，帮助你尽可能取得最佳成绩。

本书内容

本书包含四套完整的学术类雅思试题和两套培训类阅读和写作试题。

听力与阅读试题配有全面的答案解析，不仅提供正确答案，而且说明答案为何正确，在适当的情况下还提供错误答案分析。

你还将获得针对雅思考试听力、阅读、写作、口语四个部分的提示与考试解析。在每个部分，你都能：

- 了解该部分考试的内容和形式
- 练习需要了解和运用的知识和技能
- 获得如何应对考试本身的具体建议

本书内容专为中国雅思考生而设计，因此你将获得：

- 中英双语提示和考试解析
- 针对中国雅思考生的建议
- 中国考生中口语和写作任务 2 高分考生的答题范例

如何使用本书

如果你有数月时间备考，你应从考试解析、提示和练习入手，然后看配套多媒体光盘中的内容。光盘中包含：

- 介绍雅思考试四个部分的短片，特别是口语与写作部分的各项评分标准
- 中国考生口语考试实况，附有得分与评议
- 中国考生写作任务 2 的答题实例，附有得分与评议

最后，做测试题。对时间的把握十分重要，因为雅思考试中并不是每道题都有答题用时提示。本书中没有誊写答案的地方，因此你需要自备答题纸。

如果你的备考时间有限，则应先做一套测试题。与老师或熟悉雅思考试的人讨论你的答案和得分，了解自己在四个部分的长处和短处，然后针对最薄弱的方面进行重点练习。如果时间允许，再阅读了解其他部分。

除本书外，你还可以使用“雅思之路”的在线备考资源，其中包含针对雅思考试四种能力的逾 300 个互动练习、英国文化协会的专家提供雅思考试建议的短片以及计时雅思练习测试与参考答案。

准备雅思考试的任一部分都没有单一的最佳方式。不同的老师、书籍和网站会为你提供不同的建议、方法和技巧，其中不乏有用的内容，不过有些建议虽然用心良苦但未必真正有益。因此，我们建议你听取官方信息，保持开放心态，寻找最适合自己的备考方式。

英国文化协会

英国文化协会与剑桥大学考试委员会外语考试部、IDP 教育集团共为雅思考试主办方。

英国文化协会为英国和世界各国人民创造国际机遇，积极构建英国与各国人民之间的相互信任。我们称之为文化关系工作。我们在 100 多个国家实地开展工作。

英国文化协会于 1943 年在中国成立了第一个办公室。如今，我们每年与来自中国 50 多个城市的逾 2500 万英语学习者进行交流，与 10000 名英语教师进行合作。通过提供雅思考试以及其他学术与职业资格考试，我们已帮助数以十万计的中国人获得国际教育与职业发展的机会。本书的编写融入了我们对中国、中国考生的认识和理解。

雅思考试

雅思考试（国际英语语言测试系统）是高等教育与移民领域在全球最受欢迎的英语水平测试，去年共有超过 200 万人次参加了雅思考试。

雅思考试由世界领先的语言测评专家开发，具有一流的国际声誉，获得全球超过 9000 所机构的认可，包括学校、大学、雇主、移民当局与专业机构。

雅思考试是英语交际能力的测试，对英语能力进行全方位考查——阅读、写作、听力和口语，它的设计意图是要反映你在国外新的生活环境中使用英语进行学习、工作和休闲的能力。雅思考试评分的不同等级意义如下：

分数	语言水平	说明
9 分	专家水平	具有完全自如的英语运用能力。使用英语恰当、准确、流利，并能完全理解语言。
8 分	优秀水平	能自如运用英语，偶有不准确和使用不当。在不熟悉的语境下可能出现误解，可将复杂细节的争论掌握得相当好。
7 分	良好水平	能有效运用英语，虽然偶尔出现不准确、不恰当的运用和误解。整体而言对复杂的英语掌握得不错，能够理解详细的推理。
6 分	合格水平	大致能有效运用英语，虽然时有不准确、不恰当的运用和误解发生。能够使用并理解比较复杂的英语，特别是在熟悉的语境下。
5 分	基础水平	可以部分运用英语，在大多数情况下可明白大致意思，虽然经常出现错误。在经常涉及的领域能够应付基本的沟通。
4 分	有限水平	只在熟悉的语境下有基本的运用能力，在理解与表达上常出现问题，无法使用复杂的英语。
3 分	极有限水平	在极熟悉的情况下也只能进行一般沟通，频繁发生沟通障碍。
2 分	初学水平	在理解书面英语和口语方面存在很大困难。
1 分	不懂英语	除少数几个单词以外，基本上没有能力使用英语。
0 分	未参加测试	未能回答问题。

更多信息请浏览：https://www.chinaielts.org/guide/band_descriptors_introdction.shtml#

2012 年在中国参加雅思考试的考生的平均得分如下：

听力	阅读	写作	口语	总分
5.8	5.9	5.2	5.3	5.6

信息来源：http//www.ielts.org/researchers/analysis-of-test-data/test-taker-performance-2012.aspx

要想在雅思考试中取得佳绩，关键是要提升使用英语进行沟通的水平。这也应该成为你备考的目标与目的。

希望你既要重视本书前四部分以及测试部分中与考试相关的练习，也要重视日常生活中的综合练习，例如听或读英语新闻。

大幅提高英语水平没有秘诀或特别技巧。最好加强日常练习，找到提高自己语言水平的最佳学习方法。

最后，我们希望本书能够帮助你使用英语更好地进行交流，并在雅思考试中发挥出最佳水平。祝你考试成功，未来在你使用英语的领域好运常伴！

This book and its accompanying DVD provide explanations, advice, and practice in the skills you will need to perform to the best of your ability in the IELTS test. This is the first official publication produced by the British Council which is specifically targeted at Chinese test-takers, with tips and samples which have been carefully selected to help you achieve your best possible score.

Content of this book

The book includes four complete IELTS Academic practice tests combined with two General Training Reading and Writing papers.

The practice tests come with comprehensive answer key analysis for the Listening and Reading papers, which not only tells you what the correct answers are but also shows you why these are correct, and where appropriate, why other answers are incorrect.

You will also find tips and commentary on the four sections which make up the IELTS test: Listening, Reading, Writing and Speaking. In each section you will:

- learn what to expect in the test
- practise what you need to know and do
- get advice on exactly how you need to approach the test itself

We have prepared this content especially for Chinese test-takers, so you will find:

- bilingual tips and commentary sections
- advice specifically for Chinese test-takers
- high-scoring samples of Speaking and Writing Task 2 produced by Chinese candidates

How to use this book

Assuming you have a few months to prepare, you should start with the commentary, tips and practice activities. Then look at the contents of the accompanying DVD. In the DVD you will find:

- videos explaining the four sections of the test, and in particular each of the assessment criteria used for the Speaking and Writing papers
- examples of Chinese candidates sitting Speaking tests, with scores and explanatory comments
- examples of Chinese candidates written responses, all addressing the same Task 2 question, with scores and explanatory comments

Finally, do the practice tests. Monitoring your timing is important here, since you will not always be told how much time to spend on individual questions during the IELTS test. There is no space in the book for you to write answers and so you will need to prepare your own answer sheets.

If preparation time is limited, do a practice test first. Discuss your answers and results with a teacher or someone who is familiar with the test, and get a sense of your strengths and weaknesses over the four papers. Then focus on the practice activities for those papers where you show the most significant weaknesses. If time permits, go on to look at the other areas.

In addition to this book, you can also use the online content of *Road to IELTS*, which has over 300 interactive activities for the four IELTS skills, videos of British Council experts giving IELTS advice and timed IELTS practice tests with model answers.

There is no single perfect way to approach any of the IELTS papers. Different teachers, books and websites will give you different advice, methods and techniques. Many of these might be useful. Some advice, though well-intentioned, may not really be helpful. So listen to official sources, have an open mind, and see what works best for you.

Who are the British Council?

The British Council is a joint owner of the IELTS test, along with IDP: IELTS Australia and Cambridge English Language Assessment.

The British Council creates international opportunities for the people of the UK and other countries and builds trust between them worldwide. We call this work cultural relations. We are on the ground in over 100 countries.

The British Council was established in China in 1943. Each year, we now engage with more than 25 million English language learners from more than 50 cities across China, and also work with 10,000 English teachers. Through the delivery of IELTS, as well as other academic and professional exams, we have facilitated access to international education and professional careers for hundreds of thousands of Chinese people. We have used our knowledge and understanding of the Chinese context, and Chinese test-takers, in producing this book.

The IELTS test

The International English Language Testing System (IELTS) is the world's most popular English language proficiency test for higher education and global migration, with over 2 million tests taken in the past year.

The IELTS test is developed by some of the world's leading experts in language assessment. It has an excellent international reputation, and is accepted by over 9,000 organisations worldwide, including schools, universities, employers, immigration authorities and professional bodies.

IELTS is a test of communicative ability. IELTS assesses all of your English skills – reading, writing, listening and speaking, and is designed to reflect how you will use English at study, at work and at play, in your new life abroad. The IELTS results mean:

Band	Skill level	Definition
Band 9	Expert user	You have a full operational command of the language. Your use of English is appropriate, accurate and fluent, and you show complete understanding.
Band 8	Very good user	You have a fully operational command of the language with only occasional unsystematic inaccuracies and inappropriate usage. You may misunderstand some things in unfamiliar situations. You handle complex detailed argumentation well.

Band	Skill level	Definition
Band 7	Good user	You have an operational command of the language, though with occasional inaccuracies, inappropriate usage and misunderstandings in some situations. Generally you handle complex language well and understand detailed reasoning.
Band 6	Competent user	Generally you have an effective command of the language despite some inaccuracies, inappropriate usage and misunderstandings. You can use and understand fairly complex language, particularly in familiar situations.
Band 5	Modest user	You have a partial command of the language, and cope with overall meaning in most situations, although you are likely to make many mistakes. You should be able to handle basic communication in your own field.
Band 4	Limited user	Your basic competence is limited to familiar situations. You frequently show problems in understanding and expression. You are not able to use complex language.
Band 3	Extremely limited user	You convey and understand only general meaning in very familiar situations. There are frequent breakdowns in communication.
Band 2	Intermittent user	You have great difficulty understanding spoken and written English.
Band 1	Non-user	You have no ability to use the language except a few isolated words.
Band 0	Did not attempt the test	You did not answer the questions.

More information: https://www.chinaielts.org/guide/band_descriptors_introdction.shtml#

These are the average scores for IELTS candidates in China for 2012.

Listening	Reading	Writing	Speaking	Overall
5.8	5.9	5.2	5.3	5.6

Produced from http://www.ielts.org/researchers/analysis-of-test-data/test-taker-performance-2012.aspx

If you want to do well in the IELTS test, the key factor you need to address is your proficiency in using English to communicate. This should be your goal and purpose in your preparation for the test.

We encourage you to focus on both the exam-related practice we have set out in the first four sections and the practice test section of this book, and also general practice in your everyday life, such as listening to or reading the news in English.

There are no secret methods or special techniques that will lead to a dramatic improvement in your performance. It is better to focus on regular practice and identifying the style of learning which best improves your language proficiency.

Finally, we hope you find this book useful and that it helps you both communicate better in English and perform to the best of your ability in the IELTS test. Good luck in the test and in whatever you use your English for in the future!

Contents 目录

IELTS Listening Test

Overview
of the Listening Test

Format

- The Listening module takes about 30 minutes to complete.
  - At the end, candidates are allowed 10 more minutes to transfer answers to an answer sheet.
- The Listening module is the same for both the Academic and the General Training versions of the test.
- There are 4 sections, each with 10 questions.
- Each section has one or more of various task types.
- The test gets progressively more difficult.
- All instructions are printed on the question booklet.
- 听力部分用时约 30 分钟。
  - 听力部分播放完毕时，会另给考生 10 分钟时间将答案誊写到答题纸上。
- 学术类与培训类的听力考试内容相同。
- 听力考试包括 4 部分，每部分 10 道题。
- 每部分涉及一种或多种不同的题型。
- 试题难度递增。
- 所有指令均印在试卷上。

Audio Recording

- You will hear a variety of accents (e.g. British, American, Australian).
- Answer the questions as you listen because the recording is played once only.
- Some time is allowed during the recording to preview the questions.
- Answers are in the same order as the information on the recording.
- If you missed an answer, guess because wrong answers are not penalised.
- 你会听到多种口音（如：英式、美式、澳大利亚式）。
- 录音只播放一次，所以你需要边听边答题。
- 录音播放的过程中会留出一些时间供考生预览问题。

- 答案与录音中信息出现的顺序一致。
- 如果你错过了某个答案，可以猜测作答，答错不扣分。

Marking

- A mark is given for each correct answer.
- Answers can be written in either upper or lower case; both are acceptable.
- The use of punctuation, like commas, hyphens or apostrophes in answers, is not necessary.
- Spelling is important. A spelling mistake counts as a wrong answer.
    - Both American and British English spelling are accepted but be consistent.
    - A hyphenated word (e.g. absent-minded) counts as one word.
- Grammar is important, e.g. if you write a singular instead of a plural noun, it counts as a wrong answer.
- Write answers clearly. Illegible handwriting will result in a wrong answer.
- Word limits set in the instructions need to be observed, otherwise answers will automatically be marked incorrect.

- 每个正确答案得一分。
- 答案可用大写也可用小写，两种方式均可。
- 作答时无需使用标点符号，例如逗号、连字符或撇号。
- 拼写很重要。拼写错误会被计为错误答案。
    - 使用美式拼写或英式拼写均可，但要保持一致。
    - 含有连字符的词（如：absent-minded）计为一个单词。
- 语法很重要，例如：如果误将复数名词写成单数名词，会被计为错误答案。
- 书写答案须清晰。字迹难以辨认的会被计为错误答案。
- 须遵循指令中的词数限制，否则将自动被计为错误答案。

Advice for Chinese candidates

When you receive the Listening test booklet, do not immediately open it. Do not open it until you are instructed to do so, otherwise it can be considered a breach of IELTS test rules.

拿到听力试卷后，不要立即打开，听到打开试卷的指令后才能打开，否则会被视为违反雅思考试纪律。

Section 1

What to Expect

- Section 1 deals with social needs and everyday topics.
- It consists of a conversation or interview between two people.
- It is important to listen for specific information (e.g. names, numbers, common objects, places).
- At the beginning of this section, there is an example which you will hear repeated.
- You will also have time to read through the questions.
- 第一部分的话题为社交需求和日常生活。
- 这部分是一段两人间的对话或采访。
- 注意听具体信息（例如：姓名、数字、常见物体、地点）。
- 在本部分的开头，会播放一个例子，这个例子会在接下来的录音中重复出现一次。
- 录音中会留出时间供考生浏览问题。

Task Type 1: Form Completion

- Fill in the gaps on a form.
- The instructions tell you how many words and/or numbers you can use.
- Writing more than the stated number of words counts as a wrong answer.
- Write the exact words you hear on the recording.
- Listen for names of people or places (which will be spelt for you).
- Listen for other specific information, e.g. dates, times, measurements.
- 在表格里填空作答。
- 指令会说明可以填写多少个单词和/或数字。
- 词数超过规定，会被计为错误答案。
- 要用录音中使用的原词作答。
- 注意听人名或地名（录音中会拼读出来）。
- 注意听其他具体信息，例如日期、时间、度量衡。

Activity 1

TIP: Spelling

- Familiarise yourself with the letters of the alphabet and practise the ones that cause difficulty for you (e.g. 'i' and 'e'; 'g' and 'j').
- 要熟悉字母表中的字母，并练习对你来说较困难的字母（如："i" 和 "e"，"g" 和 "j"）。

01 **1.1** *Listen and repeat the letters of the alphabet.*

02 **1.2** *Listen and write down the groups of letters you hear.*

1 ....

2 ....

3 ....

4 ....

03 **1.3** *Listen and fill in the gaps with the words that are spelt out on the recording.*

1 Name: Suzanne ....

2 Address: 139 ....

3 Town: ....

4 Company: .... Publishing House

5 Website: www. .... .com

Advice for Chinese candidates

Be careful when following spelling in the Listening test. For instance, some candidates confuse a 'w' for 'uu'. Double-check your spelling in the transfer time to identify errors of this kind.

听力考试中，听拼读时要格外仔细。例如，有些考生会将"w"拼写成"uu"。誊写答案时要再次检查拼写，以辨别类似错误。

TIP: Spelling

- These occur in many different forms, e.g. street numbers, phone numbers[1], prices[2], dates[3], times or measurements[4]. Sometimes there is a combination of letters and numbers as in a passport, car registration, or the serial number of an appliance.
- 数字会以各种各样的形式出现，例如街道门牌号、电话号码[1]、价格[2]、日期[3]、时间或度量衡[4]。有时还会出现数字和字母结合的形式，例如护照号、汽车牌照号或电器序列号。

Note 1: The 0 in phone numbers may be pronounced as 'oh' or 'zero'.

Note 2: Learn to write the symbols for pound (£), dollar ($) and euro (€) – if the symbol is not given on the paper, you will have to write it as part of your answer. Note also: If you hear 'nine pounds fifty', you write '£9.50'; 'five euros forty-five' = '€5.45'; 'two dollars twenty' = '$2.20', etc.

Note 3: There are different ways of writing the date: both American and British English styles are accepted. 'The thirtieth of November' = '30th November' or '30 November' or 'November 30(th)'.

Note 4: Standard abbreviations are accepted, e.g. you can write 50 kilogrammes/kilograms or 50 kg; 100 metres/meters or 100 m; 42 kilometres/kilometers or 42 km.

注释 1: 电话号码中的数字 0 可读作 "oh" 或 "zero"。

注释 2: 学会写英镑（£）、美元（$）和欧元（€）的符号——如果试卷上没有给出相应的符号，你需要写出来，将其作为答案的一部分。还需注意：如果你听到 "nine pounds fifty"，应写作 "£ 9.50"，同理，"five euros forty-five" = "€ 5.45"，"two dollars twenty" = "$ 2.20" 等。

注释 3: 日期有不同的书写方式：美式和英式均可。"The thirtieth of November" = "30th November" 或 "30 November" 或 "November 30(th)"。

注释 4: 可以使用标准的缩写，例如：你可以写 50 kilogrammes/kilograms 或者 50 kg；100 metres/meters 或者 100 m；42 kilometres/kilometers 或 42 km。

04 **1.4** *Listen and fill in the gaps with the numbers you hear.*

1 Date of departure: ....

2 Room number: ....

3 Price per night: ....

4 Breakfast: .... per day

5 Storage for case: .... in weight

6 Late check-out time: ....

7 Parking: Car registration No.: ....

Task Type 2: Short-answer Questions

- Read a question to which you have to write a short answer.
- The instructions tell you how many words and/or numbers you can use.
- Sometimes the question asks you to list 2 or 3 points (for one mark).
- You will listen for concrete facts and specific information.
- Before you listen, use the question words (who, where, why, etc.) to **predict** possible answers – this will help you recognise the answer when you hear it.

- 阅读简答题的问题。
- 指令会说明可以使用多少个单词和 / 或数字。
- 有时一个问题会要求你列出 2 或 3 个题点（共计一分）。
- 要注意听具体事实和细节性信息。
- 听之前，利用疑问词（who，where，why 等）**预测**答案。这样，听录音时，一旦答案出现便能识别。

Activity 2

05 *Listen and answer the questions below. Write* ***NO MORE THAN THREE WORDS AND/OR A NUMBER*** *for each answer.*

1 What colour is the car? ....

2 What time did the owner park the car? ....

3 Where was the owner when the car was stolen? ....

Test Practice

*On the next page is a sample Listening Section 1. You will practise **form completion** and **short-answer questions** tasks. Other task types are possible in this section of the test.*

TIPS

- This is the first section and also the easiest. You should be able to get a high score on this section – it is important to be relaxed and calm so that you don't miss any answers. Practise some deep breathing or other relaxation exercises that you can use on the exam day to help you settle quickly.
- Listen to the introduction (which sets the scene) and use the time given to look at the first set of questions. You are then less likely to miss an answer.
- It is important to keep up with the recording. If you do miss an answer, don't stop. Move on to the next question. Later you can guess an answer for the missed one.
- Part-way through Section 1, time will be given for you to look at the next set of questions.
- At the end of Section 1, you will be given time to check your answers. Use this time wisely – check spelling, words that may need final 's', and make guesses if you have to. There is no penalty for a wrong answer.

- 这是听力的第一部分，也是难度最低的部分。你应该能够在这一部分获得高分，所以要放松心情，保持镇静，以免错过答案。平时可以练习一些深呼吸或其他放松活动，考试当日可用这些活动帮你快速进入状态。
- 注意听录音中的开篇介绍（介绍中会说明场景），利用所给的时间阅读第一组问题。这样可以降低错过答案的可能。
- 一定要跟上录音的进度。如果错过了一个答案，不要停下来。继续听下一个问题。稍后你可以对错过答案的问题猜测作答。
- 第一部分进行过程中，会给你一些时间阅读下一组问题。
- 第一部分结束时，会给一些时间检查答案。合理利用这段时间：检查拼写；检查可能需要在末尾添加“s”的单词；如有必要，猜测答案。错误答案不会被扣分。

06

SECTION 1 *Questions 1–10*

Questions 1–6

Complete the form below.

Write ***NO MORE THAN TWO WORDS AND/OR A NUMBER*** *for each answer.*

EASTSIDE LIBRARY APPLICATION FORM for *VISITOR'S MEMBERSHIP*	
Example Purpose of visit:	*Answer* exchange
Family name:	Sunderland
First name:	**1** ....
Nationality:	**2** ....
Address:	**3** .... Road, Winton
Proof of address:	**4** ....
Telephone number:	0405 492 451
Date of proposed departure:	**5** ....
Passport number:	**6** ....

Questions 7–10

Answer the questions below.

Write ***NO MORE THAN TWO WORDS AND/OR A NUMBER*** *for each answer.*

7 How many items may a visitor member borrow at one time?

....

8 How long is the loan period for a 'hot book'?

....

9 How much is the deposit to borrow a laptop to use in the library?

---

10 Name **ONE** method of renewing items on loan.

Advice from Chinese candidate

即便在浏览网页时也开着 BBC 广播，不求听懂，只为置身于英式英语的感觉。

——雅思高分考生　王茜

Advice for Chinese candidates

If you have any problems hearing the audio of the Listening test clearly, put your hand up to alert the invigilator immediately.

如果无法听清录音，应马上举手向监考人员示意。

Section 2

What to Expect

- Section 2 deals with a topic of general interest.
- It consists of a monologue (one speaker), e.g. a talk, a radio broadcast.
- You will listen for **factual information** and **select relevant** and **appropriate** information to answer the questions.
- 第二部分为大众性话题。
- 这部分是一段独白（一个说话者），例如：一段讲话或一段广播。
- 要留意听**事实性信息**并**选择相关**且**合适**的信息来作答。

Task Type 3: Matching Information

- Choose answers from a box of options (labelled A, B, C, etc.).
- Write down the letter of the answer (A, B, C, etc.) next to the numbered questions which will be a list (names of people, places, events, objects, etc.).
- Use the time given to preview both the options and the list of questions.
- The options in the box will NOT be in the same order as the recording.
- The questions follow the order of the recording.
- Choose **one** option for each question (there may be more options than you need).
- Listen for **synonyms** or words and phrases of similar meaning – it is unlikely that you will hear the exact words in the questions.
- 从选项框中选择正确的答案（选项以 A，B，C 等标记）。
- 问题标有序号并以列表的形式呈现（如一列人名、地点、活动、物体等），把代表答案的字母（A，B，C 等）写在问题序号旁。
- 利用所给时间预览选项和问题列表。
- 框中的选项顺序不会与录音中出现的顺序相同。
- 问题的顺序与录音内容的出现顺序相同。
- 每个问题只能选择**一个**答案（答案选项可能会多于所需）。
- 注意听**同义词**或意思相近的词和短语，录音中一般不会出现与问题中完全相同的词。

Activity 3

07 *Study the questions (1–3) and think of other ways in which these ideas can be expressed. Then listen and complete the exercise.*

Which team will carry out each of the following tasks?

*Choose **THREE** answers from the box and write the correct letter, **A–D**, next to Questions 1–3.*

Teams
A black caps
B blue caps
C green caps
D red caps

1 collecting entrance tickets ....

2 acting as messengers ....

3 working in the kitchen ....

Task Type 4: Multiple Choice

- This task type may be presented in different ways.
- It may be a question followed by three possible answers or the beginning of a sentence followed by three possible sentence endings – choose one correct answer, A, B, or C.
- Sometimes there is a longer list of possible answers and you have to choose more than one (e.g. two out of five possible answers).
- Read each question carefully to check how many answers are required.
- This task type may test **detailed understanding of specific points** or **overall understanding of the main points.**
- Study the questions and underline **key words** but remember these ideas may be expressed by **synonyms**[5] in the recording.
- Only the questions (not the options) follow the order of the Listening text.
- 这种题型可能以不同方式呈现。
- 可能给出一个问题后面跟着三个可能的答案，也可能给出一个句子的开头后面跟着三种可能的结尾，你需要在选项 A，B，C 中选择一个正确的答案。
- 有时答案选项会稍多一些，你需要从中选择不止一个答案（例如：从五个答案选项中选择两个）。

- 仔细阅读每个问题，确定要求选择几个答案。
- 这种题型或考查**对具体要点的细致理解**，或考查**对主旨大意的整体理解**。
- 仔细阅读问题，在**关键词**下画线标记，但要记住，这些词的意思在录音中可能会用**近义词**[5]来表达。
- 只有问题（而不是答案选项）的顺序与录音中的内容顺序相同。

Note 5: Listen also for antonyms or ways of expressing similar meaning by using a different word with a negative (e.g. sick = not well).

注释 5: 还要注意听反义词，或用一个不同的词加上否定词来表达相似意思的表达方式（例如：sick = not well）。

Activity 4

TIP

- Speakers rarely use exactly the same words as in the questions; therefore, it is important to listen for other ways of expressing the same idea.
- 录音中的说话人很少会使用与问题中完全相同的词。因此，要注意听表达同一观点的其他方式。

08

4.1 *Take a moment to think of paraphrases for the underlined words and phrases in the questions below. Then, listen.*

1 You should see the doctor if

A you have a constant headache.

B you have a sick stomach.

C you have a cold.

2 Why is Jason feeling stressed?

A He has money troubles.

B He is overworked.

C He is afraid of losing his job.

3 and **4** Which **TWO** things is Janice worried about?

A finding a part-time job

B having enough money

C keeping up with her studies

D moving away from home

E talking to male students

4.2 *Did you recognise the equivalent expressions? Look at the underlined phrases in the tapescripts.*

4.3 *Now listen again and answer the questions.*

Test Practice

On the next page is a sample Listening Section 2. You will practise ***matching information*** *and* ***multiple choice*** *tasks. Other task types are possible in this section of the test.*

TIPS

- Listen to the introduction and use your time wisely – preview the questions in the time available, underline key words and think about possible **synonyms**.
- There is a break in the recording part-way through Section 2 which gives you time to prepare for the second set of questions.

- **注意听开篇介绍，合理利用时间：在录音提供的时间内预览问题，在关键词下画线标记，想一想有可能出现的同义词。**
- **第二部分录音中会出现一次暂停，这段时间你可以为回答下一组问题做准备。**

09 SECTION 2 *Questions 11–20*

Questions 11–16

Which advantage is mentioned for each of the following holidays?

*Choose **SIX** answers from the box and write the correct letter, **A–H**, next to Questions 11–16.*

Advantages
A a range of prices to choose from
B explore inaccessible places
C go at your own pace
D high-quality meals provided
E no backpack to carry
F not physically demanding
G withdraw at any point
H follow rough tracks

11 freedom walking ....

12 guided walking ....

13 road cycling ....

14 sea kayaking ....

15 sailing ....

16 luxury cruising ....

Questions 17 and 18

*Choose the correct letter **A**, **B** or **C**.*

17 Walking holidays with a guide are currently offered

A all over New Zealand.
B only in the South Island.
C in the South Island and Stewart Island.

18 On rest days, when is entertainment provided?

A when guests request it
B every night
C most nights

Questions 19 and 20

*Choose **TWO** letters, **A–E**.*

Which of the following does a self-catering unit contain?

A a dishwasher

B a fireplace

C an electric stove

D electric blankets

E refrigerator

Advice from Chinese candidate

泛听和精听相结合，勤于练习，熟能生巧。

——雅思高分考生　魏新华

Section 3

What to Expect

- Section 3 deals with a situation set in an educational context.
- It consists of a conversation between two main speakers (although there may be up to four speakers), e.g. students in a discussion or tutorial.
- You will listen for **facts** and **ideas** and how they are connected.
- You may also have to **identify** the **attitudes** and **opinions** of the speakers.
- 第三部分围绕教学场景。
- 这部分是两个主要说话者之间的一段对话（尽管最多可能有四个说话者），例如：学生讨论或学生个别辅导。
- 要注意听**事实**和**想法**，以及它们之间的联系。
- 你也可能需要**辨别**说话者的**态度**和**观点**。

Task Type 5: Plan, Map, Diagram Labelling

- Complete labels on a visual: a diagram (e.g. a piece of equipment), a plan (e.g. of a building), a map (e.g. part of a town).
- Understand the description of a place or object and relate it to the visual.
- Follow language expressing spatial relationships and directions.
- Study the map/plan – think of the language for describing the location of places.
- If the directions north, south, east or west are used in the description, a compass symbol will show where north is (it may only be labelled **N** for north).
- Use your pencil tip to follow the route or object described as you listen.
- Use any places (or parts) already marked on the map (or diagram) to help you.
- Read the instructions carefully – know what to write (words or a letter, A, B, C).
- Letters (A, B, C, etc.) on a map/plan are NOT in the same order as the recording, but the places in the questions follow the recording.
- Write the place names on the map/plan as you listen (abbreviate if necessary).
- Put the letters next to the question numbers at the finish.
- 完成视图中的标记，如（一台设备的）示意图、（一座建筑的）布局图、（一个城市的）地图。

- 理解对地点或物体的描述，并将其与视图内容进行关联。
- 理解对空间关系及方向方位的语言表述。
- 仔细研究地图 / 布局图，思考描述地点方位的语言。
- 如果描述中出现东、西、南、北的方位，视图中会用指南针的符号标明北方（也可能仅以 N 代表“北方”）。
- 一边听，一边用铅笔标记录音中所描述的路线或物体。
- 利用地图（或示意图）上已经标记出来的地点（或部分）帮助自己作答。
- 仔细阅读指令，明确如何作答（填单词还是字母 A，B，C）。
- 地图 / 布局图上的字母（A，B，C 等）出现的顺序不会与录音中出现的顺序相同，但问题中地点的出现顺序与录音相同。
- 一边听一边在地图 / 布局图上写下地名（如需要可使用缩写）。
- 最后将正确选项的字母写在对应的题号旁。

Activity 5

10

5.1 *Look at the map below and complete the dialogue with the following phrases, and then listen to the dialogue to check your answers.*

car park	roundabout *(x 2)*
go past	traffic lights
junction	go straight on
turn left *(x 2)*	take the second exit
turn right *(x 2)*	take the first on the left
keep going	take the second on the right

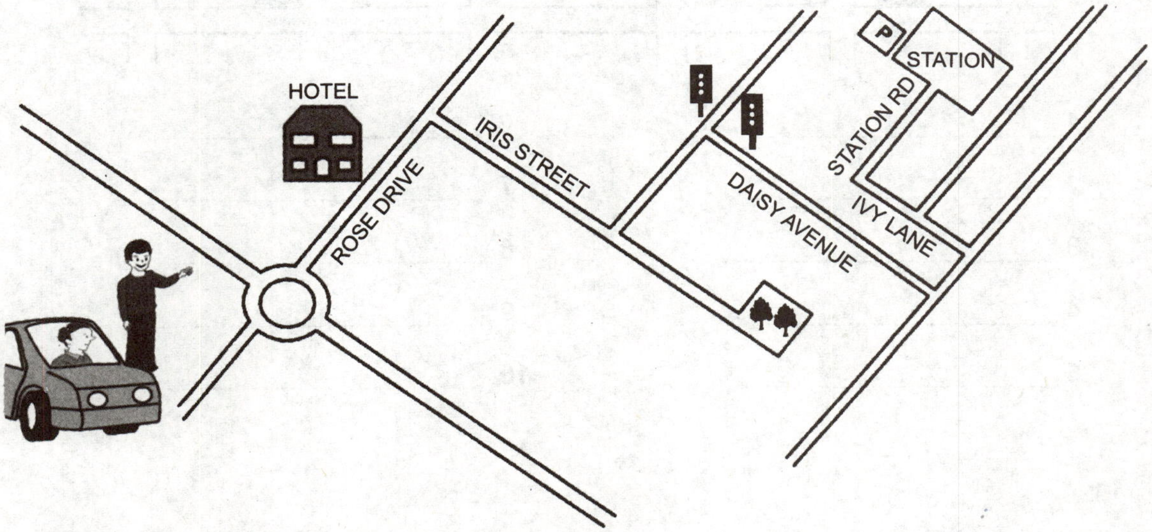

A: Could you tell me the way to the station, please?

B: **1** ________________ until you come to the **2** ________________. At the **3** ________________ **4** ________________ into Rose Drive. **5** ________________ the hotel on your left and **6** ________________ into Iris Street. Then **7** ________________ and **8** ________________ as far as the **9** ________________ . Then **10** ________________ into Daisy Avenue. At the next **11** ________________ **12** ________________. Then **13** ________________ again into Ivy Lane and **14** ________________. This is Station Road and the station is right at the end. You'll see the **15** ________________ adjacent to it.

11

5.2 *Look at the map below. Listen to the questions and write down your answers.*

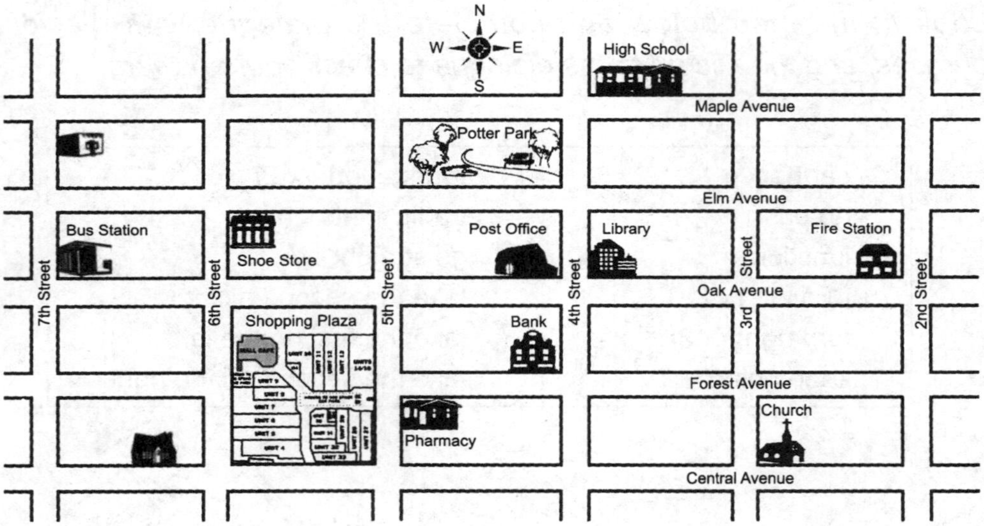

1 ________________ **6** ________________

2 ________________ **7** ________________

3 ________________ **8** ________________

4 ________________ **9** ________________

5 ________________ **10** ________________

Task Type 6: Sentence Completion

- Read a set of sentences which summarise key information.
- Complete a gap in each sentence using a word or words from the Listening text.
- A word limit is given, so read the instructions carefully.
- The limit will be one, two or three words (and/or a number).
- Identify **key information** and understand **functional relationships** (e.g. cause and effect).
- The completed sentence must be grammatically correct – this is one way you can check whether you have the right answer.

- 阅读一组总结关键信息的句子。
- 使用录音中的一个或多个单词完成句子填空。
- 所填词数是有限制的，因此要仔细阅读指令。
- 词数限制为一个、两个或三个单词（和/或数字）。
- 识别**关键信息**，理解信息之间的**功能关系**（例如因果关系）。
- 填写完成的句子必须符合语法规范。这也可作为检查答案是否正确的一个方法。

Activity 6

12 *Complete the sentences below. Write* ***ONE WORD ONLY*** *for each answer.*

1 Ivan wants to know if Maria is finding her .... more difficult.

2 Maria says that, because she knows the vocabulary now, the .... is not so heavy.

3 Ivan correctly assumes that the .... is much the same as what she studied before.

Advice for Chinese candidates

Be careful with singular and plural nouns – these are common incorrect answers, for instance, especially 's' making plural where not needed.

注意名词的单复数形式。这是非常常见的错误，特别是在不需要的情况下使用"s"把单词变为复数形式。

Test Practice

The following is a sample Listening Section 3. You will practise ***labelling a plan*** *and* ***a diagram*** *and* ***sentence completion*** *tasks. Other task types are possible in this section of the test.*

TIP

- Section 3 is a discussion in an academic situation.
- 第三部分是学术情境性讨论。

13

SECTION 3 *Questions 21–30*

Questions 21–24

Label the plan below.

Write the correct letter, ***A–J****, next to Questions 21–24.*

THE PUBLIC LIBRARY

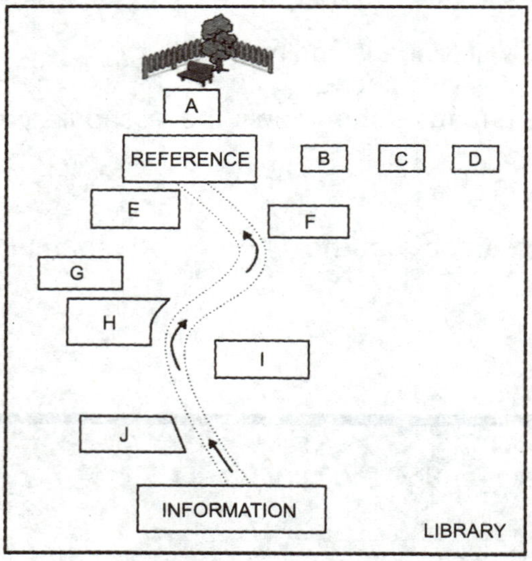

21 Multimedia room ....

22 Junior fiction ....

23 Journals & Magazines ....

24 Café ....

Questions 25–27

Label the diagram below.

Choose **THREE** *answers from the box and write the correct letter,* **A–E**, *next to Questions 25–27.*

A anchorage
B catwalks
C chain-link fence
D deck
E main span

The Mackinac Suspension Bridge

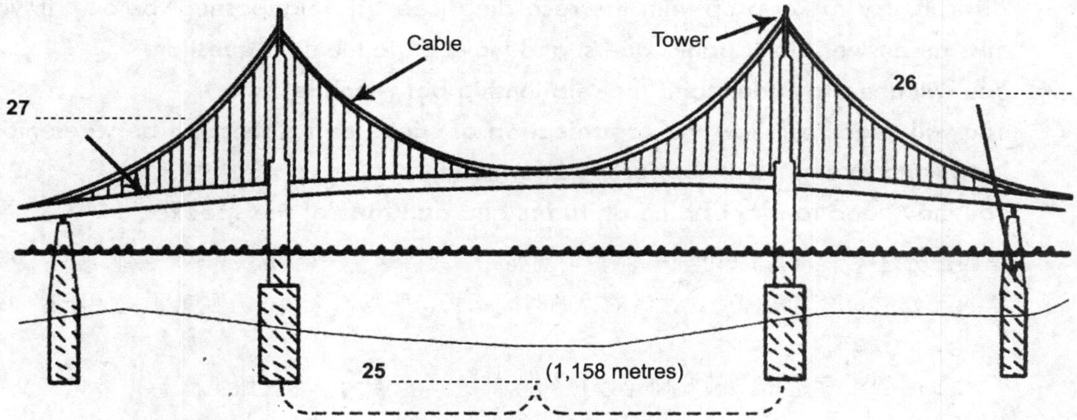

Questions 28–30

Complete the sentences below.

Write **NO MORE THAN THREE WORDS** *for each answer.*

28 Zoe suggests they should not include too many .... in their presentation.

29 Gary says the design of suspension bridges since 1940 makes allowances for wind, ... and weight.

30 Zoe explains that the Mackinac Bridge could move considerably but this would only occur in ....

Section 4

What to Expect

- Section 4 is a monologue (e.g. a talk, presentation or lecture) on an academic subject.
- There is **no break** in the middle of Section 4: the speaker only pauses for a moment so you must preview **all** the questions (31–40) at the beginning.
- The test gets progressively harder so you can expect this section to be the most difficult. Try to keep up with the recording (see 'TIP: Signposting' below). If you miss an answer, don't panic, guess, and move on to the next question.
- You will need to understand the relationship between **ideas.**
- You will need to follow the **organisation of ideas** and distinguish between main ideas and examples or supporting information.
- You may need to **identify** the **attitudes** and **opinions** of the speaker.
- 第四部分是关于某个学科的一段独白（例如：一段讲话、一个报告或一个讲座）。
- 第四部分中间没有**暂停**：说话者的停顿时间不长，所以你必须一开始就预览完**所有**问题（第 31~40 题）。
- 听力试题的难度递增，因此你可以预知本部分难度最大。尽量跟上录音（参见下文的"TIP: Signposting"部分）。如果你错过了某个答案，不要慌张，猜测答案，然后进入下一个问题。
- 你需要理解**论点**之间的关系。
- 你需要跟上**论点的组织思路**，并将主要论点与例子或论据信息加以区分。
- 你可能需要**辨明**说话者的**态度**和**观点**。

Activity 7

TIP: Signposting

- 'Signposts' or verbal signals help you follow a long talk. Listen for them as they guide you through the structure of the talk. Some common types of signposts are ways of:

a **introducing** the topic or a new phase of the talk

b **adding** information or developing the topic

c giving an **example**

d stating **cause**

e stating **effect**

f concluding or **referring back**

- "指示语"或话语信号词可以帮助你理解篇幅较长的讲话。它们能引导你理清讲话的结构，因此要注意听这些词。常见的指示语用于：

a **引出**讲话的主题或开启下一部分内容

b **添加**信息或展开主题

c 列举**事例**

d 表述**原因**

e 表述**结果**

f 总结或**回指**

14

Listen to the recorded expressions and decide what kind of signposts they are.[6]

Note 6: Some may fit into more than one category.

注释 6： 有些指示语可能属于多个类别。

Task Type 7: Notes, Table, Flow Chart, Summary Completion

- In this type of question, you fill in gaps in an outline of part or all of the Listening text.
- The outline will focus on the **main ideas** or facts in the text.
- A set of **notes** is used to summarise information using the layout to show how different items are related (very similar to the **form completion** you did in Section 1).
- A **table** is used to summarise information which falls into clear categories.
- A **flow chart** summarises a process which has clear stages – the direction of the process is shown by arrows.

- A **summary** takes the form of complete sentences so your answer must fit the sentence grammatically. If it does not, it's not the correct answer.
- You select answers from a list **OR**
- You identify the missing words from the recording. Check the word limit and do not change the words from the recording in any way.
- 这种题型要求对录音中部分或全部内容的概要进行填空。
- 概要的内容侧重于录音中的主要观点或事实。
- **笔记题**用于总结录音中的信息，并通过一定的格式展示不同项目之间的相互关系（与第一部分中的 form completion 题型十分相似）。
- **表格题**用于总结可以清晰归纳为不同类型的信息。
- **流程图题**用于总结具有清晰步骤的某一过程，过程的发展方向用箭头表示。
- **总结题**以完整句子的形式出现，因此你的答案必须符合句子的语法规范。如果不符合，则不是正确答案。
- 你需要从选项列表中选择答案，或者
- 从录音中辨别出所缺单词。检查词数限制，不要对录音中的词做任何改变。

Activity 8: Table Completion

TIPS

- Check the instructions – what is the word limit for each gap?
- Read the heading – this tells you the broad topic or subject.
- Read the column headings.
- Look at each row and think about the kind of information you will need to fill the gaps.
- Use the information that is given to help you predict the kind of answer you need.
- Be sure to locate each question number – it's easy to miss one in a large table!
- 核对指令：每个题空的词数限制是多少？
- 阅读表格的标题：标题会揭示大致话题或学科。
- 阅读表格中的列标题。
- 浏览表格中每行的内容，思考需要填写何种信息。
- 利用表格中已提供的信息预测所需答案的类型。
- 确保找到每个问题的题号，因为在一个复杂的表格里容易漏题！

15 *Complete the table below. Write **ONE WORD ONLY** for each answer.*

URBAN vs SUBURBAN LIVING		
	Advantages	**Disadvantages**
Urban	▪ Action – clubs, cafés, etc. ▪ **1** ______________ ▪ Arts & culture – museums, etc. ▪ Close to work	▪ Noise ▪ More **2** ______________ and pollution ▪ Price of housing
Suburban	▪ Peace & quiet ▪ Greener environment ▪ Better for children ▪ Homes larger with more **3** ______________ – back yard, etc.	▪ Cost of **4** ______________ ▪ Time lost in daily commute

Activity 9: Flow Chart Completion

TIPS

- Check the instructions – do you choose answers from a list or from the recording?
- If it is a list, you will write a letter (A, B, C, etc.) as your answer.
- If you have to write down words you hear in the recording, note the word limit.
- Look at the heading to see what the topic is.
- If a list is given, think about how the words in the box might fill the gaps.
- Use the other information in the chart to help you predict likely answers.
- Read ahead and use the arrows to guide you through the development of the talk.

- 核对指令：是从选项列表中还是从录音中选择答案？
- 如果从选项列表中选择，需要写下字母（A，B，C 等）来作答。
- 如果需要写下录音中听到的词，要注意词数限制。
- 阅读标题，确定所听内容的主题。
- 如果给出了一个选项列表，思考如何将选项框里的词用于填空。
- 利用流程图中的其他信息帮助预测可能的答案。
- 提前阅读问题，利用箭头来引导你跟上讲话的进展。

16

Complete the flow chart below. Write ***NO MORE THAN TWO WORDS*** *for each answer.*

THE PROCESS OF BUYING A HOME

Find a property you like

↓

Make a **1** ....

↓

Agree to terms of sale

↓

Sign a **2** ....

↓

Pay a **3** ....

↓

Sale becomes unconditional and binding

↓

If settlement date is postponed,
4 .... must be paid on remainder of purchase price

Activity 10: Summary Completion

TIPS

- When you fill in the gaps, you are completing sentences which must be grammatically correct.
- When you preview the questions, think about the grammar of the missing word(s) – are you listening for a noun (singular or plural?), a verb or an adjective?
- 'a' before the gap would indicate a singular noun beginning with a consonant; 'an' would indicate a singular noun starting with a vowel sound.
- If the gap is followed by a plural verb, you need a plural subject.
- Before you listen, try to predict the part of speech (e.g. noun, adjective, participle) that will go in the gap.

- Look at the context – the surrounding words, the heading (if there is one), the meaning – and think about what suitable words might fit.
- A summary will be a condensed version of what you hear – just the main ideas.
- It looks as if the answers come close together but, remember, a lot of detail has been left out.
- 填空时，所完成的句子必须符合语法规范。
- 预览问题时，思考所缺单词的语法要求：你需要注意听的是名词（单数还是复数）、动词还是形容词？
- 题空前若出现不定冠词“a”，说明答案是以辅音开头的单数名词，而“an”则说明答案是以元音开头的单数名词。
- 如果题空后为复数形式的动词，则需要一个复数形式的主语。
- 在录音开始之前，尽量预测题空所需单词的词性（如名词、形容词、分词）。
- 观察上下文——周围的词、标题（如果有）、意思，思考可能适合填入什么词。
- 总结是所听内容的浓缩——仅仅是大意。
- 答案看似集中出现，但要记住：题中省略了录音中的很多细节。

17 *Look at the summary below. Before you listen, try to predict the answers. Write your predictions in the gaps in pencil. Use the notes to help you.*

Write ***ONE WORD ONLY***[7] *for each answer.*

The Red Cross[8]

The Red Cross is an **1** ....[9] that helps the needy. During wartime it delivers aid to **2** ....[10] but it is also active in peacetime bringing **3** ....[11] relief to survivors of accidents and **4** ....[12] of all kinds. **5** ....[13] attention is given to the injured; food and water is delivered; and **6** ....[14] is provided for the homeless.

Now listen and check your answers.

Note 7: The instruction is very helpful – you know to listen out for just one word to fill each gap.

注释 7： 指令很有帮助——通过指令你知道需要注意听其中的一个单词来完成每个填空。

Note 8: Read the title and try to recall everything you know about the topic – this will help your prediction.

Note 9: The grammar will tell you that a singular noun starting with a vowel is required here: 'an ...' (e.g. apple, egg, index, ox, ultra). The context tells you the word will probably have a general meaning. Any guesses?

Note 10: Probably a plural noun – the context is a big help here!

Note 11: The gap occurs just before a noun so you want an adjective (remember also that nouns can be used in front of other nouns as adjectives) – what kind of 'relief' is given after an accident?

Note 12: Two nouns joined by 'and': 'accidents and ...' – a plural noun with a similar meaning. Can you guess?

Note 13: What kind of 'attention' is given to injured people? Think of an appropriate adjective.

Note 14: The following verb 'is' tells you this must be a singular noun – uncountable because there is no article (a/an). Not too hard to guess – what do the homeless need?

注释 8: 读标题，尽力回忆你对这一话题的全部所知——这可以帮助你进行预测。

注释 9: 因为题空前有"an"，所以本题在语法上要求填一个以元音开头的单数可数名词（例如：apple，egg，index，ox，ultra）。上下文语境则提示你所需单词可能具有泛指含义。猜一猜是什么？

注释 10: 本题可能需填一个复数名词——上下文语境在这里有很大帮助！

注释 11: 本题空出现在名词前，所以你需要填一个形容词（还需记住：名词也可以放在另一个名词前充当形容词）——在事故之后提供的是什么样的"relief"呢？

注释 12: 两个名词通过"and"连接在一起："accidents and ..."——应该填一个与 accidents 意思相近的复数名词。你能猜出来吗？

注释 13: 提供给伤者的是什么样的"attention"？想出一个合适的形容词。

注释 14: 后面的单词"is"提示你这里必须是一个单数名词——而且这个名词不可数，因为这里没有冠词（a/an）。并不是很难猜——无家可归的人需要什么？

Test Practice

*The following is a sample Listening Section 4. You will practise **notes**, **table** and **summary completion** tasks. Other task types are possible in this section of the test.*

TIP

- Section 4 is an academic talk of some kind.
- 第四部分是一个学术方面的讲话。

18

SECTION 4 *Questions 31–40*

Questions 31–33

Complete the notes below.

*Write **NO MORE THAN ONE WORD** for each answer.*

Effects of introduced species on the New Zealand environment:

- NZ as part of Gondwanaland – ancient species of flora
- After separation – more species of flora arrived
- Vegetation untouched until humans came, then damaged by **31** .... and introduced animals and plants

Human arrivals:

1st.	Polynesians, brought one kind of **32** .... and rat
2nd.	Captain Cook, European sealers & whalers, brought rats and **33** ....
3rd.	European settlers, brought most introduced species (some from Australia)

Questions 34–37

Complete the table below.

*Write **NO MORE THAN TWO WORDS** for each answer.*

REASON	INTRODUCED MAMMAL
Utility	possum; **34** ____________; feral goat; feral pig; Pacific rat
Sport	hare; wallaby; Himalayan thar; chamois; **35** ____________
Escapees	feral sheep; feral **36** ____________; feral horse; feral cat
Biological control	**37** ____________; ferret; stoat; weasel
Stowaway	black rat

Questions 38–40

Complete the summary below.

Write ***NO MORE THAN TWO WORDS*** *for each answer.*

Economic impact and methods of control

The introduction of animals into the New Zealand environment has important **38** ____________ and financial consequences. Rabbits affect sheep farming; deer damage forests and possums have wide-ranging effects, not only on vegetation but on the **39** ____________ because they spread disease. These 'pests' do have some economic benefits for the fur and meat trade, tourism, and the export of health products. Feral farm animals could be useful for **40** ____________ but many herds have already been eradicated.

Advice for Chinese candidates

Remember when you transfer your answers from the Listening test booklet to write on the correct side of the answer sheet – we continuously see candidates write Listening test answers on the Reading side of the answer sheet.

从试卷上誊写答案时，记住要写在答题纸上正确的那一面——我们常见到考生将听力答案写在答题纸阅读部分的那一面上。

IELTS Reading Test

Overview of the Reading Test

Format

- The Reading module takes one hour to complete.
    - At the end, there is **no** extra time to transfer answers to the answer sheet.
- The Reading module is not the same for the Academic and General Training versions of the test.
- **Task types** are the **same** for Academic and General Training but the **test format and content** is a **little different.**
- For both modules:
    - There are 3 sections with a total of 40 questions in all.
    - Each section has one or more of various task types.
    - All instructions are printed on the question booklet.
- 阅读考试用时一小时。
    - 考试结束后**不**另给时间将答案誊写到答题纸上。
- 学术类与培训类的阅读考试不同。
- 学术类和培训类的**题型相同**，但**考试形式和内容略有不同**。
- 两类阅读考试：
    - 都包括 3 部分，共计 40 道题。
    - 每部分涉及一种或多种不同的题型。
    - 所有指令均印在试卷上。

Marking

For both modules:

- A mark is given for each correct answer.
- Answers can be written in either upper or lower case; both are acceptable.
- The use of punctuation, like commas, hyphens or apostrophes in answers, is not necessary.
- Spelling is important. A spelling mistake counts as a wrong answer.

  - Both American and British English spelling are accepted but be consistent.
  - A hyphenated word (e.g. absent-minded) counts as one word.
- Grammar is important: e.g. writing a singular instead of a plural noun counts as a wrong answer.
- Write answers clearly. Illegible handwriting counts as a wrong answer.
- Word limits set in the instructions need to be observed; otherwise answers will automatically be marked incorrect.
- Answer the questions as you read and transfer to the answer sheet immediately.

两类阅读考试均采用下列评分标准：

- 每个正确答案得一分。
- 答案可用大写也可用小写，两种方式均可。
- 作答时无需使用标点符号，例如逗号、连字符或撇号。
- 拼写很重要。拼写错误会被计为错误答案。
  - 使用美式拼写或英式拼写均可，但要保持一致。
  - 含有连字符的词（如：absent-minded）计为一个单词。
- 语法很重要。例如，如果误将复数名词写成单数名词，会被计为错误答案。
- 书写答案须清晰。字迹难以辨认的会被计为错误答案。
- 须遵循指令中的词数限制，否则将自动被计为错误答案。
- 边读边作答，直接把答案誊到答题纸上。

Advice from Chinese candidates

做阅读练习的时候一定要掐着点儿做，尽量控制在50至55分钟之间。

——雅思高分考生　王茜

Advice for Chinese candidates

Learn from your experience, especially from your mistakes. Read the answer key explanation we provide in this book carefully and see where you went wrong, and then apply this learning in future practice.

从经验中学习，尤其要从错误中学习。仔细阅读本书提供的答案解析，研究自己做错的地方，并把所学内容运用到以后的练习中。

General Training
Reading Module

- The texts are taken from notices, advertisements, timetables, leaflets, newspapers, instruction manuals, books and magazines.
- There are three sections of increasing difficulty.
  - **Section 1** (14 questions)
    - contains texts relevant to basic linguistic survival in English ('social survival');
    - provides mainly general, **factual** information;
    - may contain 2 or 3 short texts or several shorter texts (e.g. advertisements).
  - **Section 2** (13 questions)
    - focuses on the **work** context ('workplace survival') ;
    - two texts with more complex language (e.g. job descriptions, contracts).
  - **Section 3** (13 questions)
    - **general** context ('general reading');
    - one long text (e.g. from magazines, fictional and non-fictional book extracts);
    - most likely descriptive or instructive.

- 培训类的阅读文本取材于通知、广告、时间表、宣传单、报纸、说明书、书籍和杂志。
- 三个部分难度递增。
  - **第一部分**（14 道题）
    - 材料为涉及基本生存（"社会生存"）英语的文本；
    - 主要提供一般性、**事实性的**信息；
    - 可能包括两三篇文本，或者多篇更短的文本（例如：广告）。
  - **第二部分**（13 道题）
    - 侧重**工作**场景（"职场生存"）；
    - 包括两篇文本，语言更为复杂（如：职位描述、合同）。
  - **第三部分**（13 道题）
    - **一般性**场景（"一般性阅读"）；
    - 一篇较长的文本（如：来自杂志、小说或非小说图书的摘录）；
    - 最可能的体裁是记叙文或说明文。

Academic
Reading Module

- There are three reading passages taken from journals, books, magazines and newspapers that have been written for a non-specialist audience.
- Topics are of general interest and at an appropriate level for candidates entering university courses or seeking professional registration.
- There are three sections:
    - **Section 1** = passage 1, 13 questions
    - **Section 2** = passage 2, 13 questions
    - **Section 3** = passage 3, 14 questions
- 学术类的阅读文本包括三篇选自期刊、图书、杂志和报纸的阅读文章，文章都是针对非专业读者而写的。
- 话题为大众普遍感兴趣的内容，水平适合将要申请大学课程或职业注册的考生。
- 共包括三个部分：
    - **第一部分** = 文章 1，13 道题
    - **第二部分** = 文章 2，13 道题
    - **第三部分** = 文章 3，14 道题

Reading

Strategies: Overview

- Before you start, quickly look through the whole test so you **know what to expect**.
- **Time management** is extremely important – do not spend more than the recommended time (20 minutes) on each passage. Limit yourself to one or 1½ minutes at most per question. If you don't have an answer, guess, and move on. Write your answers directly onto the answer sheet – no extra time is given for this.
- **Read instructions carefully** so you know what to do and how to answer the questions.
- **Skim** the passage to get an idea of what it is about.[1]
- **Scan** the text to find the specific information required to answer the question.[2]
- **Read carefully** to make sure this is the right answer.[3]
- 开始阅读前，快速浏览整个试卷，以便**对考试内容心中有数**。
- **时间控制**极为重要：每篇文章不要超出建议时间（20 分钟）。回答每道题的时间控制在 1 分钟或最多 1 分半钟。如果找不到答案，猜测作答，然后继续。将答案直接写在答题纸上，阅读考试没有额外时间誊写答案。
- **仔细阅读指令**，明确你要做什么、如何作答。
- **略读**文章，了解文章主要内容。[1]
- **扫读**文本，寻找作答所需的具体信息。[2]
- **仔细阅读**，确保答案正确。[3]

Note 1: Skimming is done very quickly – read the title of the passage, read the subheading (if there is one), then skip from paragraph to paragraph looking for the main idea – look at the content words (nouns and verbs) which carry the meaning of the sentence. Only look at the main clause of each sentence. Ignore relative clauses and adverbial clauses – they add extra information and details about the main idea. Do not stop to think about unfamiliar vocabulary.

注释 1: 略读要迅速——阅读文章标题、副标题（如果有的话），然后从一个段落跳读至另一段落，寻找大意——要看传达句子含义的实词（名词和动词）。只看每句话的主句部分，忽略关系从句和状语从句——它们只是为文章大意补充额外的信息和细节。遇到不熟悉的词不要停止阅读去思考词汇。

Note 2: Again, it is not necessary to read or understand everything – your eyes should move quickly just looking for key words.

注释 2: 同样没有必要阅读或理解所有内容——眼睛应迅速移动以寻找关键词。

Note 3: After you have located what you think is the answer, read every word in the sentences that come both before and after it to fully understand the meaning.

注释 3: 定位了你认为的答案之后，逐词仔细阅读答案前后的句子，完全理解其含义。

Reading
Task Types

Task Type 1: Short-answer Questions

- Answer questions which relate to factual information and detail.
- Write answers in words or numbers on the answer sheet.
- Use only words from the text.
- Read instructions carefully to find out how many words/numbers to use.
- If you write more words/numbers than the limit, no mark is given.
- Numbers can be written as figures or words (e.g. '200' or 'two hundred').
- A hyphenated word counts as one word (e.g. 'mother-in-law' = one word).
- The questions are in the same order as the information in the text.[4]

- 这种题型的问题涉及事实性的信息和细节。
- 在答题纸上填写单词或数字。
- 只能使用文章中出现的词。
- 仔细阅读指令，明确可以使用多少个单词 / 数字。
- 如果填写的单词 / 数字超出词数限制，则不能得分。
- 数字可写作阿拉伯数字或单词形式（例如："200" 或 "two hundred"）。
- 带有连字符的单词计作一个单词（例如："mother-in-law" 为一个单词）。
- 问题的顺序与信息在文中出现的顺序相同。[4]

Note 4: If you have found the answers to No. 2 and No. 4, you know the answer to No. 3 is somewhere in between.

注释 4： 如果你找到了第 2 题和第 4 题的答案，则可得知第 3 题的答案位于两者之间的某处。

TIP: Scanning

- For short-answer questions you need to **scan** for facts and details. This means **not** reading every word but moving your eyes **quickly** over the text just looking for the relevant fact or detail. You don't need to understand every word – just enough to answer the question. The answers to 'wh-' type questions are often numbers or proper nouns (starting with a capital letter) so they should be relatively easy to find. Read the questions first so you know what to look for. (Is it a number? a place? a name? etc.)
- 回答简答题，需要通过**扫读**寻找事实和细节，即**不要**逐词阅读，而要在文字间**迅速**移动眼睛，仅寻找相关的事实或细节。无需理解每一个单词，只要理解到足以回答问题即可。特殊疑问句的答案一般是数字或专有名词（以大写字母开头），因此比较容易找到。首先阅读问题，明确要寻找的目标。（是一个数字、地点还是姓名，等等？）

Activity 1: Short-answer Questions

*In this activity you will practise **short-answer** questions based on an excerpt from a General Training Reading Section 1 text.*

NB *Short-answer questions appear in the Academic as well as the General Training Reading module. Skills and strategies needed to approach this task type are the same for both modules. This is not the only task type that you might find in General Training Reading Section 1 – other task types are possible.*

Early Morning Blaze

Four firemen suffered minor burns early this morning after the local fire brigade answered a call-out to a menswear store. The alarm went off at 2.40 a.m. but the fire was not brought under control for several hours. The flames were finally extinguished at 5.15 a.m. The injuries occurred when the roof collapsed trapping several firefighters inside the building. The fire chief said the fire originated in the kitchenette at the back of the store. The cause of the fire is still under investigation but an initial examination of the scene suggests defective wiring might be at fault.

Questions 1–6

Answer the questions below.

Choose ***NO MORE THAN THREE WORDS AND/OR A NUMBER*** *for each answer.*

Write your answers in Boxes 1–6 on your answer sheet.

1 How many firefighters were injured?

2 Where did the fire occur?

3 When was the fire put out?

4 How did the men get hurt?

5 In which room did the fire start?

6 What is thought to be the cause of the fire?

Task Type 2: Identifying Information [TFNG]

- Recognise particular points of information.
- Answer questions about a number of statements.
- Write the answer 'true', 'false', or 'not given' on the answer sheet.[5]
- The questions are in the same order as the information in the text.[6]
- 这种题型需要判断特定的信息点。
- 题中含多个陈述，要对这些陈述判断作答。
- 将答案"true""false"或"not given"写在答题纸上。[5]
- 问题的顺序与信息在文中出现的顺序相同。[6]

Note 5: Write 'true', 'false' or 'not given' **according to the text** (not your personal knowledge).

Note 6: If you have found the answers to No. 2 and No. 4, you know the answer to No. 3 is somewhere in between.

注释 5: 根据文章（而非你自己了解的知识）填写"true""false"或"not given"。

注释 6: 如果你找到了第 2 题和第 4 题的答案，则可得知第 3 题的答案位于两者之间的某处。

TIP: Matching Statements: True? False? Not given?

In TFNG-type questions you match two statements: what is stated in the question and what is stated in the passage. You **match meaning**, not particular words or phrases.

- The meaning is the same = True
- The meaning is the opposite = False
- The meaning of the question is neither confirmed (true) nor contradicted (false) in the text = Not Given[7]

在信息判断（正 / 误 / 未给）题中，你要将两种陈述进行比对：一种是问题中的陈述，另一种是文中的陈述。你要比对的是意思，而不是特定的单词或短语。

- 意思相同 = True
- 意思相反 = False
- 问题所表达的意思在文中既未得到肯定（true）也未得到否定（false）= Not Given[7]

Note 7: If you are running out of time, guess – you have a one-in-three chance of being right!

注释 7: 如果时间不够，猜测作答——你有三分之一的答对几率！

Activity 2: TFNG

Read the following extract and answer the questions below.

Procrastination

People often joke about procrastination saying things like 'Why do today what you can put off till tomorrow?' Generally speaking, it is no laughing matter. Occasionally procrastination can have a positive outcome. For example, a problem may solve itself over time or the meeting you haven't prepared for is cancelled. And some people do work faster and more efficiently under time pressure. Most often, though, procrastination turns out to be a serious problem costing big businesses millions of dollars every year.

Surveys have shown that the average worker procrastinates an estimated 20% of the time which amounts to chronic behaviour and it is found in just about every occupation and profession.

Doctors, too, are known for it.

An inability to say no often leads to procrastination. Even executives find it difficult to refuse additional work when they are already overworked. When their superior, or subordinate, makes a request, executives rarely take the trouble to explain that dealing with this particular issue means something else has to be let go.

Do the following statements agree with the information given in the text?

Write

TRUE	*if the statement agrees with the information*
FALSE	*if the statement contradicts the information*
NOT GIVEN	*if there is no information on this*

1 Some people work better at the last minute.

2 Procrastination is usually harmless.

3 Large corporations lose millions of dollars annually because of procrastination.

4 Doctors procrastinate more than other people.

5 Executives who have trouble saying no to their boss do not have trouble saying no to an assistant.

Activity 3: TFNG

Excerpt from General Training Section 2:

*In this activity you will practise **identifying information** [TFNG] questions based on an excerpt from a General Training Reading Section 2 text.*

NB *Identifying Information [TFNG] questions appear in the Academic as well as the General Training Reading module. Skills and strategies needed to approach this task type are the same for both modules. This is not the only task type that you might find in General Training Reading Section 2 – other task types are possible.*

Bullying in the Workplace

When workmates use offensive or intimidating behaviour to humiliate other workers, it is a form of abuse. Bullies are frequently insecure people with low self-esteem (although it may not be obvious). Their targets are usually competent, honest and independent people who get on well with their colleagues – often the very characteristic which bullies feel they lack. Bullies are often most concerned with gaining power and exerting dominance over people by causing fear and distress.

The individual on the receiving end of this behaviour may experience stress, anxiety, excessive worry, loss of concentration, and irritability as a result. The company may suffer, too, by way of a decrease in productivity and morale and higher rates of absenteeism. In some cases, the person being bullied quits his or her job resulting in a high turnover of personnel.

If you believe you are being bullied by someone at work, keep a record of each incident, including dates, and bring it to the attention of your employer, trade union representative, or health and safety officer. If you think you were singled out for abuse because of discrimination against your gender, age, religious beliefs, race or a disability, you could lay a complaint with the Human Rights Commission.

Questions 15–20

Do the following statements agree with the information given in the text?

In Boxes 15–20 on your answer sheet, write

TRUE	if the statement agrees with the information
FALSE	if the statement contradicts the information
NOT GIVEN	if there is no information on this

15 Bullies seldom lack confidence in themselves.

16 Bullies generally focus their unwanted attention on capable, decent individuals.

17 Bullies usually feel powerful when they frighten and upset others.

18 The target of a bully may suffer from insomnia or disrupted sleep.

19 Bullying in the workplace always has a negative effect on the organisation.

20 The Human Rights Commission is obliged to act if you were targeted because of discrimination.

Advice for Chinese candidates

We have noticed that candidates have written answers like 'Talse' (instead of 'False'), 'No Given' (instead of 'Not Given'). These have to be marked INCORRECT. Be careful with your answers!

我们发现有考生把“False”写作“Talse”，把“Not Given”写作“No Given”。这样的答案会被计为错误答案。注意你所填写的答案！

Task Type 3: Sentence Completion

- Scan to locate detail or specific information.
- Use words taken from the text to fill in gaps in sentences.[8]
- The completed sentence must be grammatically correct.[9]
- Underline key words in the sentence – remember to look for synonyms in the text.
- Decide what kind of word you need for the gap (e.g. noun, participle, adjective).
- Find the word(s) in the text and copy exactly onto the answer sheet.

- 这种题型需要扫读文章，定位细节或具体信息。
- 要使用文中的原词进行句子填空。[8]
- 所完成的句子必须符合语法规范。[9]
- 把句子中的关键词用下画线标出来，并记得在文中寻找同义词。
- 判断空格中所需单词的类型（例如：名词、分词、形容词）。
- 从文中找到所需单词，直接填写在答题纸上。

Note 8: Refer back to the advice for "Short-answer Questions".

Note 9: This is one way you can check whether you have the right answer.

注释 8： 参考上文关于"简答题"的建议。

注释 9： 这是一种可以检验答案是否正确的方法。

Task Type 4: Notes, Table, Flow Chart Completion

- Understand details and/or main ideas.
- Complete the gaps in the notes, table or flow chart with information from the text (the instructions will tell you how many words and/or numbers you can use); OR
- Select from a list of answers (there will always be more words than gaps).
- The answers will **not** necessarily occur in the same order as in the text.

- 这种题型需要理解细节和/或大意。
- 使用文中的信息完成笔记、表格或流程图中的填空（指令会说明可以填写多少个单词和/或数字），或
- 从答案选项表中选择答案（选项数目总是多于空格数目）。
- 答案出现的顺序不一定与文中出现的顺序相同。

TIP:
Using Given Information

- Use the title to help you locate the right part of the text. With a table you can use the column headings to narrow down your search. Use the notes or parts of the table or flow chart that have no gaps to help you find the answers and determine how to answer correctly within the word limit.
- 使用标题帮助在文中准确定位。如果是表格，可使用列标题缩小搜索范围。使用没有空格的笔记内容或者表格或流程图的部分内容帮助寻找答案，并决定如何在词数限制内正确作答。

Activity 4: Table Completion

Read the following extract and fill in the gaps in the table below.

The four longest rivers in the world are located in four different continents. That at least is undisputed. However, while most scientists agree on the order, it is difficult to accurately measure the length of such enormous rivers and there is also sometimes disagreement on where a river actually starts and finishes. The Nile, beginning at Lake Victoria, is Africa's longest river, negotiating its 6,650 kilometre journey to the Mediterranean Sea through the land which has been used continuously for over 6,000 years.

The Amazon in South America is the largest but not the longest river, starting high in the Peruvian Andes and flowing for much of its 6,400 kilometre length parallel to and not far from the Equator, eventually emptying into the Atlantic Ocean.

The Yangtze, with its source in the Kunlun Mountains of Tibet, is China's most important internal waterway and travels 6,300 kilometres to the Yellow Sea.

The fourth longest river of the world is the Mississippi-Missouri, the source of which was not discovered until 1832 when it was traced to Lake Itasca in Minnesota. It deposits rich silt in the delta where it ends its 6,275 kilometre journey and flows into the Gulf of Mexico.

Complete the table below.

*Write **NO MORE THAN TWO WORDS** for each answer.*

Top Four Longest Rivers in the World				
River	**Length in kilometres**	**Continent**	**Source**	**End**
Nile	1 ______ [10]	Africa	2 ______ [11]	Mediterranean Sea
3 ______ [12]	6,400	South America	Peruvian Andes	4 ______ [13]
5 ______	6,300	Asia	Kunlun Mountains	6 ______
Mississippi-Missouri	7 ______	North America	8 ______ [14]	Gulf of Mexico

Note 10: Both the column heading and the example in the box below show that you need write the number only (without '*kilometres*').

注释 10: 本列标题和下面单元格中的例子都表明只写数字即可（不用写"kilometres"）。

Note 11: This is an example of answers not occurring in the same order as the text. However, they are often in the same sentence or not too far apart.

注释 11: 这是答案没有与文本中出现的顺序一致的例子。然而，它们一般在同一句话中或离得不远。

Note 12: Although the rivers are referred to in the text as '*the Nile*', etc., follow the example in the box above (write the name without '*the*').

注释 12: 尽管文章中提到河流时用的是"the Nile"等，但要遵循上面单元格中的例子（只写名称，不需加"the"）。

Note 13: If you use 'the' in the answer, you exceed the word limit – notice how the example in the box above is written (without 'the').

注释 13: 如果在答案中用了"the"，则会超出词数限制——注意上面单元格中的例子是如何写的（不加"the"）。

Note 14: '*Lake Itasca in Minnesota*' is too long – notice what was omitted from the name of the source in the box above.

注释 14: "Lake Itasca in Minnesota"过长——注意上面单元格中河流源头名称省略了什么。

Task Type 5: Diagram Label Completion

- Understand a detailed description and relate it to information presented in a diagram.
- Complete labels on the diagram using words from the text (the instructions will tell you how many words and/or numbers you can use).

- The answers will **not** necessarily occur in the same order as in the text.
- 这种题型需要理解细节性的描述，并将其与示意图中呈现的信息相关联。
- 要使用文中的原词完成示意图中的标记（指令会说明可以填写多少个词和/或数字）。
- 答案出现的顺序不一定与文中出现的顺序相同。

Activity 5: Sentence Completion, Flow Chart and Diagram Label Completion

*In this activity you will practise **sentence completion**, **flow chart** and **diagram label completion** questions based on an excerpt from a General Training Reading Section 3 text.*

NB *Sentence Completion, Flow Chart and Diagram Label Completion questions appear in the Academic as well as the General Training Reading module. Skills and strategies needed to approach this task type are the same for both modules. This is not the only task type that you might find in General Training Reading Section 3 – other task types are possible.*

SECTION 3 *Questions 28–40*

Read the text below and answer Questions 28–40.

WRITER'S BLOCK

You have to finish that report for the boss, write an essay or article, or you work in the information economy – the deadline for the current project is looming but you find yourself mindlessly staring at a blank page on the screen and the words just won't come.

Writers' block is not an uncommon experience. The root cause is anxiety. There are many reasons for the writer to feel anxious. Perfectionism is one of them – the writer is too judgemental, viewing her work as inferior in some way. The project itself may be fundamentally misconceived or the writer lacks the experience or ability to complete it. Perhaps the pressure of a tight deadline is paralysing. There are other anxiety-provoking life stresses and deep-seated issues: serious illness, depression, a relationship break-up, not to mention financial difficulties. Sometimes distractions are too great or the writer simply runs out of inspiration.

There are various ways of overcoming the block. Exercise gets the blood moving through the body and brain: a visit to the gym, a walk around the block, a few yoga poses and some deep breathing all help to clear the head, induce relaxation and get the creative juices flowing. The body and brain need to be nourished with healthy food and pure water. Junk food is unlikely to increase mental output. Obviously, distractions have to be completely eliminated – phones turned off, the Internet disconnected, the desk or workspace uncluttered – because good writing needs focus and undivided attention.

Consider also that the subconscious mind is continually problem-solving even while a person is sleeping so writing for twenty minutes prior to bedtime and thinking about the difficult bits before falling asleep might just induce the subconscious to resolve the issue overnight, the writer waking up with a fresh perspective in the morning. The best time for writing is early in the morning; tackle the most complex task first, and the easier stuff should just flow.

A tired writer will accomplish less and is more likely to suffer from a block – a good eight-hour sleep at night is optimal but not always achievable. In this case, the best and most successful remedy is the caffeine nap. Researchers at Loughborough University in the U.K. found that a cup of coffee followed by a fifteen-minute nap is an effective way to re-boot the brain. The recommendation is to imbibe the coffee swiftly and then stretch out immediately and snooze for no more than a quarter of an hour. By the end of this period, the caffeine has had time to take effect and the subject wakes up feeling refreshed and is usually able to resume work without delay. The micro-sleep or power nap, combined with the stimulatory effect of the caffeine, although it sounds paradoxical, is apparently an effective antidote to fatigue.

The effects of a caffeine nap are much more powerful if the coffee is good. A semi-automatic pump espresso machine makes an excellent brew and it is easy to operate. The machine is turned on at the on/off switch at the bottom and, with the portafilter securely in place, allowed to heat for at least 20 minutes. The temperature light on the control panel at the top will indicate when the machine is ready. Then, pre-ground beans are measured into the portafilter, levelled off, and pressure is applied with a tamper to create an even seal. The pump is started by pressing the square button in the middle of the control panel and the water flows through the coffee into the cup. When there is enough espresso in the cup, the pump is shut off by pressing the button again. The portafilter is then removed and the used grinds are banged out. It should be rinsed well and dried before being placed back under the grouphead ready for the next shot.

Questions 28–32

Complete the sentences below.

Choose ***NO MORE THAN TWO WORDS*** *from the text for each answer.*

Write your answers in Boxes 28–32 on your answer sheet.

28 Some writers judge their writing too harshly, thinking it is ....

29 The writing task could be at fault if it has been ....

30 Writers may suffer from complete inaction if there is not enough time to meet a ....

31 All possible forms of disturbance should be ....

32 The .... may sort out a problem when the writer is asleep.

Questions 33–36

Complete the flow chart below.

Choose ***NO MORE THAN TWO WORDS OR A NUMBER*** *from the text for each answer.*

Write your answers in Boxes 33–36 on your answer sheet.

How the Caffeine Nap Works to Ward Off Fatigue

Drink **33** .... quickly
↓
Lie down at once
↓
34 .... for **35** .... minutes while caffeine goes into operation
↓
Get up **36** .... and go straight back to work

Questions 37–40

Label the diagram below.

Choose ***NO MORE THAN TWO WORDS*** *from the text for each answer.*

Write your answers in Boxes 37–40 on your answer sheet.

Semi-Automatic Pump Espresso Machine

Task Type 6: Matching Features

- Recognise relationships and connections between facts.
- Recognise opinions and theories.
- Match a set of statements to a list of options (A, B, C etc.).
- Some options may not be used.
- Some options may be used more than once (read instructions carefully).
- The questions do **not** follow the same order as information in the passage.
- 这种题型需要辨别事实之间的相互关系和联系。
- 需要辨别观点和理论。
- 将一组陈述与一系列选项（A，B，C 等）进行匹配。
- 部分选项可能会用不到。
- 部分选项可能会用到多次（仔细阅读指令）。
- 问题的顺序**不会**与信息在文中的顺序相同。

Activity 6: Identifying Features

Read the extract below and answer the questions.

There are three main kinds of surveys that can be used for collecting data. A census collects information about every unit in a population. The advantage of this method is that the sampling variance is zero because it is calculated using data from the whole population. It also enables detailed information about sub-groups to be gathered. However, it is generally very expensive to carry out a census and it is a protracted procedure with information having to be gained from every member of the target group. A sample survey is not as expensive to conduct because data are collected from only part of the total population. Results are obtained more quickly – because fewer units are contacted, there is less information to be processed. The sampling variance is non-zero – the data may not be as precise coming from just a sample instead of the whole group. A further disadvantage is that the sample may not be large enough to produce information about small sub-groups. The third type of survey consists of administrative data which may be collected as a result of the day-to-day operations of an organisation. The government, for example, will have files on births, deaths, marriages, car registrations and the like. In this type of survey the sampling variance is zero and the information is collected on an on-going basis which allows for trend analysis. It also eliminates the need to design a survey or census saving time and work and there is no additional burden on the respondents because the data have already been collected. There is, however, a certain lack of flexibility as the material gathered is limited to essential administrative information and the data are limited to that part of the population on whom the records are kept.

Classify the following statements as referring to

A a census
B a sample survey
C administrative data

*Write the correct letter, **A**, **B** or **C**, next to Questions 1–5 below.*

NB *You may use any letter more than once.*

1 It does not require subjects to answer questions for the purpose of the survey.

2 It obtains information that may not be entirely exact or accurate.

3 It collects data about each individual in a group.

4 It makes it possible to track changes over time.

5 It is a costly and lengthy practice.

TIP

Many candidates worry about their reading speed – it is true that speed is important with the time limits of the test. The key to speed is using the right reading skill. Think about these situations; are you using the same reading skills?

- You are looking through a magazine or newspaper looking for something interesting to read.
- You are reading an article and want to know a specific fact.

You are not using the same skills here. The first uses skimming skills; the second uses scanning skills. Do you need to read every word to do either of these? No, you do not need to read every word. It is important your eyes move quickly across the text to pick up the key information you need, which might be a general idea of a text or paragraph or it might be a specific detail like the cost of an object. Of course there are times when you need to read for detail, and read very carefully, but hopefully you can do this in a specific paragraph or area because that's where you know the answer should be.

很多考生担心自己的阅读速度——由于考试有时间限制，所以速度的确很重要。提高速度的关键是使用正确的阅读技巧。思考下列情况，你使用的是相同的阅读技巧吗？

- 你在浏览杂志或报纸，寻找有趣的阅读内容。
- 你在阅读一篇文章，想要了解一个具体的事实。

这两种情况下你所使用的阅读技巧是不同的。第一种情况下使用的是略读技巧，第二种则是扫读技巧。在这两种情况下，是否需要阅读每个单词呢？不需要，没必要阅读每个单词。要在文字间迅速移动眼睛挑选出所需要的关键信息，有可能是一段文字或一个段落的大意，或者可能是一个具体细节，例如某件物品的价格。当然，有时你需要非常仔细地阅读以寻找细节，但希望你可以把范围缩小到一个具体的段落或区间，因为你知道答案应该就在这里。

Task Type 7: Matching Information

- Scan for specific information in the lettered paragraphs/sections of the text (e.g. an example, a definition, a reason, a comparison, an explanation, etc.).
- You may not need to find information in every paragraph/section.
- There may be more than one piece of information in a paragraph/section – if so, instructions will say you can use any letter more than once.
- The questions do **not** follow the same order as information in the passage.
- 这种题型需要扫读文中用字母标记的段落/部分，寻找具体信息（例如：一个例子、定义、原因、对比、解释，等等）。
- 可能不需要在每一个段落/部分寻找信息。
- 一个段落/部分中的信息可能会不止一条，在这种情况下，指令会说明可以多次使用任一字母。
- 问题的顺序**不会**与信息在文中出现的顺序相同。

Activity 7

For this task type you need to recognise what the writer is doing: giving an example, stating a definition, giving a reason, making a comparison/contrast, etc. Think of the language that is used to do this.

In the sentences below identify the function and underline the language that shows what the writer is doing.

Example: A sample survey is not as expensive to conduct ... = *comparison*

1 This technique is much more effective than earlier methods of ...

2 Although the population is rising, the birth rate is declining ...

3 The increase in population is mainly due to immigration ...

4 Birds like the kiwi are flightless ...

5 This feature has led to their decline ...

6 The decline in numbers can be attributed to predation by dogs ...

7 Predators such as stoats and rats are unmanageable ...

8 This has contributed to the loss of many native species of ...

9 Biomedical engineering is the application of engineering principles and techniques to the medical field ...

10 In spite of their efforts to save the stranded whales, ...

11 Deforestation refers to the cutting and clearing of rainforest ...

12 As a direct consequence of changes in microclimates ...

Activity 8: Matching Information and Matching Features

In this activity you will practise ***matching information*** *and* ***matching features*** *questions based on an excerpt from Academic Reading Passage 1.*

NB *Matching Information and Matching Features questions appear in the Academic as well as the General Training Reading module. Skills and strategies needed to approach this task type are the same for both modules. This is not the only task type that you might find in Academic Reading Passage 1 – other task types are possible.*

Questions 1–10 are based on Reading Passage 1 below.

Happiness Is ...

According to *Merriam-Webster's Online Dictionary*, the definition of happiness is:

— *A state of well-being and contentment*

— *A pleasurable or satisfying experience*

A 'Happiness' today is investigated as a psychological phenomenon. However, for the Greek philosopher Aristotle (384–322 BC) it had a much broader significance. His theory of *eudaimonia*, 'well-being' or 'happiness', meant living well, enjoying many different aspects of a flourishing life: good health and physical well-being, material prosperity, thriving familial and friendship ties, fulfilment of intellectual and moral needs as well as living in a just and well-ordered society.

B A lot of our current assumptions about happiness have been confirmed by recent studies. Robust romantic relationships, good health, being well-off and enjoyment of a spiritual dimension to life all generate happiness. Our expectations are that positive outcomes in life will make us far happier and negative ones far unhappier than they really do. Harvard psychologist Dan Gilbert explains that over the last two million years human brains have grown and gained a new structure – the pre-frontal cortex. This allows us to simulate experiences but we tend to imagine the outcome of one scenario (for example, passing an exam) as being radically different from another (failing the exam) in terms of impact. Gilbert says, however, the difference is less significant than what we envisage because of our innate ability to synthesise happiness.

C Gilbert claims there are two kinds of happiness: 'Natural happiness is what we get when we get what we wanted, and synthetic happiness is what we make when we don't get what we wanted.' Gilbert maintains that synthetic happiness is just as real and enduring as natural happiness. They might have different origins but they feel the same. He likens the production of synthetic happiness to a psychological immune system – a system of mainly unconscious cognitive processes that facilitate a modification of our view of the world so that we feel better about the situation we find ourselves in. We have the ability to manufacture happiness.

D This inherent coping mechanism minimises our disappointment and allows us to experience happiness even when we do not achieve our desires but Timothy Pychyl (Carleton University, Canada) warns that, when this happens, we minimise the 'perceived distance between our actual self and ideal self'. This 'cognitive dissonance' is an important source of incentive in our lives. For instance, think of an athlete who receives a bronze medal when she expected gold. If happiness is synthesised, she is content but where is the stimulus to improve? Pychyl believes we must learn to recognise synthetic happiness and use the tension caused by the divergence between actual and ideal self to change our behaviour; in the case of the athlete, this discrepancy would provide the impetus for harder training.

E According to Gilbert, if we get what we want, natural happiness ensues. If we don't get what we want, our psychological immune system is activated and synthetic happiness kicks in. However, when we have the liberty to choose from many options, we tend to agonise over squandered opportunities denying ourselves synthetic happiness. He believes synthetic happiness ensues only when people have no alternative.

F However, as Barry Schwartz points out, 'we take choice as the critical sign that we have freedom and autonomy'. Although it may seem counterintuitive, an explosion of choice leads not to heightened feelings of liberation but to paralysis instead. Even if we overcome the paralysis, with proliferation of possibility there is an escalation of expectations and consumers experience regret because they imagine the alternatives might have been better.

G H. A. Simon classified consumers into 'satisficers', who settle for 'good enough', and 'maximisers', who want the best. It is the maximiser's pursuit of perfection amidst an overwhelming array of options that leads to constant dissatisfaction and disappointment. Why? Because they made the choice and therefore they are responsible. Where there is no choice, we tend to blame outside factors. The satisficer's strategy seems practical and sensible but, with more choice, comes more pressure to maximise, making life more difficult and stressful. For many the freedom to choose is no freedom at all.

Questions 1–5

Reading Passage 1 has seven paragraphs, **A–G**.

Which paragraph contains the following information?

*Write the correct letter, **A–G**, in Boxes 1–5 on your answer sheet.*

1 the result of always looking for excellence

2 the distinction between synthetic and natural happiness

3 causes of happiness today

4 a definition of an ancient concept of happiness

5 an example of how synthesised happiness results in lack of motivation

Questions 6–10

Look at the following statements (Questions 6–10) and the list of researchers below.

*Match each statement with the correct researcher, **A–D**.*

*Write the correct letter, **A–D**, in Boxes 6–10 on your answer sheet.*

***NB** You may use any letter more than once.*

6 People can use the conflict between how they really are and how they would like to be to improve performance.

7 People think the power of choice proves they are independent and free.

8 People who seek perfection blame themselves if the outcome is not perfect.

9 Synthetic happiness lasts for the same length of time as natural happiness.

10 Too much choice results in a failure to take action.

List of Researchers

A Gilbert
B Pychyl
C Schwartz
D Simon

Task Type 8: Multiple Choice

- This task type may require a detailed understanding of specific points or overall understanding of the main points.

- Choose the best answer from 4 alternatives (A, B, C, D) or 2 answers from 5 alternatives (A–E) or 3 answers from 7 alternatives (A–G).
- The correct option will either complete a sentence or answer a question that **means the same as something in the text**.
- The questions are in the same order as the information in the text.
- In order to **match meaning** you need to recognise synonyms and paraphrase (see 'TIP: Finding the Answers' below).
- 这种题型可能需要详细理解具体信息点或总体理解主要信息点。
- 从 4 个选项（A，B，C，D）中选择 1 个最佳答案，或从 5 个选项（A~E）中选择 2 个答案，或从 7 个选项（A~G）中选择 3 个答案。
- 正确的选项能将一个句子补充完整，或回答一个**与文中某处内容意思相同**的问题。
- 问题的顺序与信息在文中出现的顺序相同。
- 为了**对意思进行匹配**，需要识别同义词并进行同义转换（见下文的 "TIP: Finding the Answers"）。

Task Type 9: Matching Sentence Endings

- You are given the first half of a sentence based on main ideas in the text.
- Choose the best way to complete it from a list of options.
- There are more options than questions.
- Write the letter of the option you have chosen (A, B, C etc.) on the answer sheet.
- The questions are in the same order as the information in the text.[15]
- The completed answer will **mean the same** as an idea in the text.
- In order to **match meaning** you need to recognise synonyms and paraphrase (see 'TIP: Finding the Answers' below).
- 这种题型中的句子围绕着文章大意，问题给出了句子的前半部分。
- 从选项表中选择最佳方式完成句子。
- 选项的数量多于问题的数量。
- 在答题纸上填写你所选择的选项字母（A，B，C 等）。
- 问题的顺序与信息在文中出现的顺序相同。[15]
- 所完成的答案将与文中的某个**意思一致**。
- 为了**对意思进行匹配**，需要识别同义词并进行同义转换（见下文的 "TIP: Finding the Answers"）。

Note 15: If you have found the answers to No. 2 and No. 4, you know the answer to No. 3 is somewhere in between.

注释 15： 如果你找到了第 2 题和第 4 题的答案，则可得知第 3 题的答案位于两者之间的某处。

TIP: Finding the Answers (matching meaning)

- Underline the key word(s) or phrase in the question or sentence half.
- **Scan** and **locate** it (or something that means the same) in the passage.
- Read **intensively** around it including the sentences that come before and after – sometimes **not all the parts of the key phrase are found close together** (you may have to skim over some interesting but irrelevant facts in between).
- Look for **changes in the order** of the sentence – information in the question could be written in a different order in the passage.
- You may find words that **correspond exactly** (which makes your task easier).
- You may find words with **a similar pattern** (where there is just a different verb, adjective or adverb, e.g. *indigenous* frogs → *native* frogs).
- You may find phrases or sentences that look quite **different** but have the **same** meaning.
- You may be able to guess the meaning of an unfamiliar word from the **context**.[16]

- 把问题或半个句子中的关键词或关键短语用下画线标出来。
- 在文中**扫读**并**定位**关键词/短语（或意思相同的内容）。
- **详细阅读**关键词/短语前后的内容，包括上下文的句子。有时**关键短语的几个部分并不在一起**（你可能需要跳过中间一些有趣但并不相关的事实）。
- 留意句中**顺序的变化**——问题中的信息可能会以不同顺序出现在文中。
- 你有可能遇见**完全一致**的词组（此时作答比较容易）。
- 你有可能遇见具有**相似结构**的词组（只有一个动词、形容词或副词不同，例如：*indigenous* frogs → *native* frogs）。
- 你有可能遇见看似**迥异**但**意思相同**的短语或句子。
- 你有可能从**语境**中猜测生词的意思。[16]

Note 16: Context is dealt with in more detail on Page 68.

注释 16: 关于语境，第 68 页有更详细的讲解。

Compare these pairs of sentences. Notice how the techniques (above) have been used.

1 New Zealand's indigenous frogs have changed very little in 70 million years.

→ *Over the last 70 million years the native frogs of New Zealand have not changed much.*

2 They are small, nocturnal, and difficult to see as they camouflage[17] themselves well.

→ *They are tiny creatures that are active at night and disguise themselves well.*

3 These native frogs are rare, essentially silent and confined to undisturbed native bush.

→ *It is unlikely that you would ever encounter or hear one of these native frogs.*

4 Three species live in shady, moist woodland areas but one is semi-aquatic[18], living on stream edges.

→ *Although one species lives near water, the other three inhabit damp, dark forested regions.*

Note 17: You can guess from context that *camouflage* means 'disguise; conceal' because *they are difficult to see.*

注释17: 你可以从语境中猜测出camouflage的意思是"伪装；隐藏"，因为"它们难以看到"。

Note 18: You can guess the meaning of *semi-aquatic* from context: *living on stream edges*, i.e. near water.

注释18: 你可以从语境中猜测出semi-aquatic的意思："居住在溪水边缘"，即在水畔。

Activity 9: Multiple Choice and Matching Sentence Endings

In this activity you will practise ***multiple choice*** *and* ***matching sentence ending*** *questions based on an excerpt from Academic Reading Passage 2.*

NB *Multiple Choice and Matching Sentence Ending questions appear in the Academic as well as the General Training Reading module. Skills and strategies needed to approach this task type are the same for both modules. This is not the only task type that you might find in Academic Reading Passage 2 – other task types are possible.*

Questions 14–22 are based on Reading Passage 2 below.

The science behind charisma

It has long been known that a small group of people in every society possess a special personality trait that allows them to captivate an audience, inspire devotion among others and lead their communities with an almost effortless flair. Today we call this special ability 'charisma'. Although easily sensed by others, it has long proved difficult to arrive at an exact definition of the term, largely due to the array of diverse criteria encompassed within our understanding of it.

Despite this obstacle, some scholars have turned their attention to the subject and attempted to discover exactly how charisma works and what its fundamental components are. In conducting these investigations they have discovered that the stereotypes of smooth-talking Hollywood film stars and politicians which circulate among the general populace are only partially true, and ultimately fail to penetrate to the core of what really makes charismatic people tick.

Psychology professor Robert Riggio has broken the key elements of charisma down into three key traits: expressivity, control, and sensitivity, and in his opinion the third of these is often underplayed. 'In the late 1970s, I thought a charismatic person was a bubbly, effervescent type that lit up a room,' Riggio notes, adding that he now believes sensitivity is crucial, as it assists the charismatic person in navigating a range of social functions with a measure of tact and understanding. Although sometimes requiring a person to step back from the heart of a social setting and shy away from conflict, in the long run this sensitivity fosters long-standing emotional bonds.

This authentic emotional engagement underpins charisma in its truest sense, and explains why there are limits to the extent to which charisma can be affected for the purpose of deceiving others. Those with an obviously self-interested agenda – sales people and marketers are among the numerous examples frequently cited – may effortlessly adopt the more instrumental components of charisma, such as increased amounts of eye contact and an open body stance, but due to a lack of genuine interest tend to present themselves as smarmy and unappealing.

There is of course, much more to charisma than an earnest intent. Research has shown that charismatic people are natural mimics, easily switching their postures and mannerisms to those of their audience. They tend to speak in a fluid manner, with few gaps or hesitations, and tend to move conversations along at a relatively lively pace. Another find that piqued the curiosity of researchers is that revealing vulnerability can actually enhance charisma by adding a more human touch to the speaker's persona. Too much, however, and the effect is extinguished, as an overarching authority must remain intact. Finally, even when they are the object of attention, charismatic figures generally steer the topic of discussion away from their own lives and accentuate shared passions instead.

As research begins to unpick these elements of charisma, the vital role of charismatic people in society becomes apparent. Far from being automatically vain and power-hungry, they foster social cohesion in their communities and encourage a strong sense of self-esteem among individuals they encounter. Without people doing this work, conflicts both large and small might erupt with a far greater frequency.

This is not to say that charisma has no dark side, however. It is undoubtedly a high-octane personality trait, and as such taxes the social stamina of those who possess it. A highly successful lawyer, for example, may get her way in court, but struggle to keep her friendships alive outside work. Likewise, a political leader who can inspire thousands at a rally may find his marriage unravelling as a result of his need to 'switch off' when he returns home.

Then there are those situations where one charismatic leader has stirred others to action, but for ends that were ultimately calamitous for all involved. This is perhaps where the most valuable contribution of the studies and experiments on charisma is to be made. By developing an awareness of how we can be manipulated into following another person's wishes, it is possible these studies will encourage us to think more critically about our decisions and in doing so avoid the mistakes of the past.

Questions 14–17

*Choose the correct letter, **A**, **B**, **C** or **D**.*

Write the correct letter in Boxes 14–17 on your answer sheet.

14 Charisma is difficult to describe because it

A only exists among a few people in society.
B combines many different qualities.
C has only recently begun to be studied.
D is not easily recognised by most people.

15 Researchers have discovered that

A popular ideas about the nature of charisma are incomplete.
B people with power and fame tend to be the most charismatic.
C charisma is not as mysterious as many people believe it to be.
D not all actors and politicians have charisma.

16 Riggio believes that sensitivity

A improves relationships for brief periods of time.
B is not as important as other aspects of charisma.
C allows people to become the centre of attention.
D helps people to interact appropriately with others.

17 Charisma is difficult to fake because

A the physical aspects of charisma are hard to learn.
B too many people are attempting to learn how to use it.

C it is based on the communication of real feelings.

D vendors and marketers are too selfish.

Questions 18 and 19

Choose ***TWO*** *letters,* ***A–E****.*

Write the correct letters in Boxes 18 and 19 on your answer sheet.

Which **TWO** of the following five statements are true of charismatic people?

A They focus conversations on themselves.

B They copy other people's behaviour.

C They speak slowly with frequent pauses.

D They emphasise differences between people.

E They show some personal weakness.

Questions 20–22

Complete each sentence with the correct ending, ***A–E****, below.*

Write the correct letter, ***A–E****, in Boxes 20–22 on your answer sheet.*

20 Charismatic people are needed because their way of acting

21 Being charismatic can be difficult because it

22 Research on charisma is useful because it

A leads to poor decision making that can harm social well-being.
B keeps people together and makes them feel good about themselves.
C could help people to realise how they are being influenced.
D contributes to the development of charisma in others.
E is not possible to sustain across all relationships in a person's life.

Task Type 10: Matching Headings

- A 'heading' refers to the **main idea** or **theme** of a paragraph or section of text.
- Match headings from a list (i, ii, iii, etc.) to the correct paragraphs (A, B, C, etc.).
- You will not use all the headings – there are more than you need.
- No heading may be used more than once.
- 标题（heading）指的是文中一个段落或一个部分的**大意或主题**。
- 将选择列表中的标题（i，ii，iii 等）与文章段落（A，B，C 等）进行正确匹配。
- 不会用到所有标题，即提供的选项多于所需。
- 任何一个标题都不能重复使用。

TIP: Finding the Answers (matching meaning)

For this task type it is essential to be able to pick out the main idea of a paragraph/section and distinguish the main idea from supporting ones.

- A main idea is the overall fact or idea a writer wants to convey in a paragraph.
- It must be general enough to encompass all of the ideas in the paragraph.
- Look for the topic sentence (which expresses the main idea).
- Often the topic sentence is the first in the paragraph but not always - sometimes the writer begins with specific details or supporting ideas that lead up to the main idea so it may come at the end or even in the middle of the paragraph.
- Sometimes there is no clear topic sentence - you have to read carefully for clues about the main idea (which is implied rather than stated openly).

做这种题型，能够找出一个段落 / 部分的主旨大意并将主旨大意与论述信息加以区分，至关重要。

- 主旨大意指作者在一个段落中想要表达的总体事实或观点。
- 主旨大意的概括性程度要足以包含该段中的所有信息。
- 寻找用于表达主旨大意的主题句。
- 主题句常位于段首，但并非总是如此——有时作者以具体细节或论述信息开头，继而引向主旨大意，所以主题句也可能位于段末，甚至段中。
- 有时没有明显的主题句，必须仔细阅读，领会字里行间所传递的主旨大意（在这种情况下，主旨大意是通过暗示而非直接陈述的方式表达的）。

Activity 10: Recognising the Main Idea

What is the main idea of the following paragraphs?

A It is important to protect all species of animal wildlife. In areas where mountain lions and coyotes have disappeared, herds of deer have grown too large for the available food supply. As a result of this, many deer die of starvation. By allowing seemingly harmful animals to continue their existence, a better balance of nature can be maintained.

- i Coyotes are extinct.
- ii Nature's balance is best.
- iii Food shortages cause animal starvation.

B Iron is the most common metal in today's society. It is used in the construction industry, vehicle manufacturing, machinery, cookware, weapons and tools, to name a few. Think of the surgeon's scalpel, the steel beams in a skyscraper, or even the wire in your spiral notebook. You can find iron, or a form of it, wherever you may be. Iron is not only a very strong material, it also has the ability to be magnetised. Iron in magnets is used in computers, televisions, electric guitars and even toys. Its many uses make iron a valuable commodity.

- i Iron is very plentiful.
- ii Iron is a useful metal.
- iii Steel beams are made of iron.

C In cold weather, people can dress more warmly, stay indoors and turn up the heating. Wild animals, however, must find other ways to survive. Some migrate to warmer climates; others hibernate until the coming of spring. Still others grow thicker coats of fur in the winter. Animals seem well equipped to survive even under conditions of extreme cold.

- i Animals suffer from the cold.
- ii Humans stay inside more in wintertime.
- iii Animals survive winter differently from humans.

Task Type 11: Identifying Writer's Views/Claims [YNNG]

- Recognise opinions or ideas.
- Answer questions about a number of statements.
- Write the answer 'yes', 'no', or 'not given' on the answer sheet.
- The questions are in the same order as the information in the text.[19]

- 这种题型需要判断观点或看法。
- 题中包含多个陈述，要对这些陈述判断作答。
- 将答案"yes""no"或"not given"写在答题纸上。
- 问题的顺序与信息在文中出现的顺序相同。[19]

Note 19: If you have found the answers to No. 2 and No. 4, you know the answer to No. 3 is somewhere in between.

注释 19： 如果你找到了第 2 题和第 4 题的答案，则可得知第 3 题的答案位于两者之间的某处。

TIP: Dealing with Yes/No/Not Given Questions

- Underline key words in the questions.
- Scan to find the relevant part of the text (look for paraphrases of the key words).
- The statement in the question agrees with what the writer says = Yes.
- The writer expresses a view or makes a claim which is the opposite of or disagrees with the statement in the question = No.
- The view or claim in the question is neither confirmed (yes) nor contradicted (no) in the text = Not Given.[20]
- Guess unknown vocabulary using context clues.

- 把问题中的关键词用下画线标出来。
- 扫读寻找文中的相关部分（寻找关键词的同义转换表达）。
- 问题中的陈述与作者表达的内容一致 = Yes。
- 作者表达的观点或提出的主张与问题中的陈述相反或不符 = No。
- 问题中的观点或主张在文中既未得到肯定（yes）也未得到否定（no）= Not Given。[20]
- 根据语境线索猜测生词。

Note 20: If you are running out of time, guess – you have a one-in-three chance of being right!

注释 20： 如果时间不够，猜测作答——你有三分之一的答对几率！

Activity 11: Determining Meaning from Context Clues

You will come across many unfamiliar words in the IELTS Reading Test. Use context to work out possible meanings. The words and ideas that surround a particular word or phrase can help express its meaning.

In the paragraph above, the last sentence explains the meaning of 'context' in the middle sentence. Even if you can't determine the exact meaning of a word, you may be able to work out enough to correctly guess the answer to a YNNG question.

In the sentences below, guess the meaning of the words in bold using context (in italics).

1 The weather this spring has been quite **erratic**. *It's hot and still one day and cold and windy the next.* ____________

2 Imprisonment as a punishment is not working as rates of **recidivism** continue to rise. Most *criminals fall back into crime* soon after they have served their sentence and been released. ____________

3 Everyone *liked* the new apprentice; he was a very **affable** person. ____________

Now try these examples without the help of italics.

4 When we breathe, we draw oxygen into our lungs and it **permeates** our entire body. ____________

5 The spinal cord is the main **conduit** for nerve messages to the brain. ____________

6 If notice of cancellation is given prior to the course starting, fees are refunded in full. However, after commencement date there is no **reimbursement** of fees. ____________

TIP

- Some candidates are concerned they cannot complete Reading tests if they cannot understand all the difficult words. It is not always necessary to understand all the words in a text. You might be able to answer questions even if you do not understand every word.
- 有些考生担心如不理解所有难词就无法完成阅读考试。并非总是需要理解文中的所有单词。即使不理解所有单词，也可回答问题。

Task Type 12: Summary Completion

- Understand details and/or main ideas of a section of the text.
- Answers are selected either from the passage or from a list of answers.
- When taking words from the passage, check instructions for the word limit.
- Answers are not necessarily in the same order as the text.
- 这种题型需要理解细节和/或文中一段文字的大意。
- 从文中选词作答或从答案列表中选择答案。
- 从文中选词作答时，检查指令中的词数限制。
- 答案的顺序不一定与文中出现的顺序相同。

TIP: Dealing with Summary Questions

- A summary consists of connected sentences so your answers must not only fit the context (meaning) but also the grammar of the sentence.
- You can use this to predict the kind of word(s) to look for to fill the gap (a singular/plural noun; verb; adjective, etc.).
- If the summary has a heading, use this information to find the relevant section of the text.
- Then, look for synonyms or paraphrases – it is unlikely that exactly the same words will be used in the summary as in the text.
- 总结由多个相互关联的句子构成，所以答案必须既符合语境（含义）又符合句子的语法规范。
- 可以以此预测需要寻找哪种类型的单词（如一个单数/复数名词、动词、形容词等）用来填空。
- 如果总结有标题，利用这一信息找到文中的相关部分。
- 然后寻找同义词或同义转换表达，总结中不太可能会使用与文中相同的词。

Advice from Chinese candidates

在练习过程中，我会从自己的错误中总结、学习，以提高阅读速度。

——雅思高分考生　路倩

Activity 12: Matching Headings, Identifying Writer's Views [YNNG] and Summary Completion

In this activity you will practise ***matching headings, identifying writer's views*** *[YNNG] and* ***summary completion*** *questions based on Academic Reading Passage 3.*

NB *Matching Headings, Identifying Writer's Views [YNNG] and Summary Completion questions appear in the Academic as well as the General Training Reading module. Skills and strategies needed to approach this task type are the same for both modules. This is not the only task type that you might find in Academic Reading Passage 3 – other task types are possible.*

READING PASSAGE 3

You should spend about 20 minutes on ***Questions 27–40****, which are based on Reading Passage 3 on the following pages.*

Questions 27–31

Reading Passage 3 has five paragraphs, **A–E**.

Choose the correct heading for paragraphs ***A–E*** *from the list of headings below.*

Write the correct number, ***i–viii****, in Boxes 27–31 on your answer sheet.*

List of Headings

- i Long-term effects on cultural expression
- ii Celebrity status achieved very quickly
- iii *Werther* based on author's own life experience
- iv A mix of old and new story-telling elements
- v Goethe resents long-term association with *Werther*
- vi *Werther* still loved by modern-day readers
- vii *Werther* seen as an innovative love story
- viii Fanatical response of youthful male readers

27 Paragraph **A** ....

28 Paragraph **B** ....

29 Paragraph **C** ....

30 Paragraph **D** ....

31 Paragraph **E** ....

'The first bestseller'

A *The Sorrows of Young Werther* was the first major literary work of German writer Johannes Wolfgang von Goethe. It is written in the epistolary form[21] and depicts the deep infatuation of a temperamental young artist for a woman already engaged to another man. Neither the format of the story nor its general narrative arch was especially groundbreaking at the time; epistolary novels had long since reached their zenith in popularity and the notion of a destructive, unrequited love had been explored since around 5 BC, when the Roman poet Ovid counselled young men on how to overcome such desire through his poem *Remedia Amoris* (The Cure for Love). *The Sorrows of Young Werther* nonetheless revolutionised the genre and set a number of new standards, most notable of which being the author's willingness to forgo the broad social fabrics of family and community, and to focus almost exclusively on an individual and his thoughts about himself.

B At the time of the novel's publication, the notion of an 'instant bestseller' was foreign to European society. Most titles emerged from well-regarded authors and were quietly circulated amongst small groups of *literati* before gradually progressing to a wider readership. All this changed with the publication of *The Sorrows of Young Werther.* Although Goethe was virtually unknown at the time of publication – a twenty-four year old with few literary achievements to his name – his novel experienced a meteoric rise to fame and turned him into a literary superstar almost overnight. *Werther* bypassed the traditional gatekeepers and went straight to the target readership – young, sensitive men who would associate themselves with the character of the title's name. As a result of this, some literary historians consider the novel to be the first mass-market bestseller.

C The impact of *Werther* went beyond rapid rise in readership, however. Young men were not content merely to read the novel and discuss it feverishly in salons and other gathering places. Many began to emulate the protagonist Werther by imitating his style of dress, his willingness to pontificate at length on his emotions and – most concerning for the authorities of the day – the character's tendency toward self-destructive expressions of his despair. This phenomenon, termed *Werther-Fieber* (Werther Fever), sparked the observation, backed up by subsequent studies, that human behaviour can be 'contagious' in a similar way to bodily-transmitted diseases.

D Although a sudden literary and popular sensation, *Werther* was no passing fad, either. Goethe's dramatic and overwrought style, embracing the psychological extremes and restless introspection of his lead character, strongly influenced the *Sturm und Drang* movement in Germany, which emerged as a rebellion against prior artistic dictates of serenity, order and reason. The impact of this transformation has been longstanding, and can still be witnessed across a range of literary and social media today: the profusion of confessional song writing, the exaggerated drama of celebrity journalism, and the prolific self-reflection and sharing of emotions propagated by online social networks all owe much to the early example that *Werther* set out.

E In spite of its success, however, Goethe never fully embraced the widespread acclaim and attention he received for publishing *The Sorrows of Young Werther* for a number of reasons. At the time of publication the author openly confessed to the autobiographical nature of the novel, which was inspired by his ardent love for a young woman named Charlotte Buff, and he later regretted having made this youthful infatuation publicly known. Goethe also became frustrated by the extent to which, throughout his career, many in Europe identified him solely with *Werther*, despite the substantial body of literary work he subsequently produced, along with his many other contributions to science and politics. In his later years Goethe saw himself as a serious scholar and classicist, dabbling in fields as diverse as botany and even anatomical studies. Among the general public, however, he remained firmly pegged to *Werther* and his story of passionate young love.

Note 21: A novel composed of a series of documents, such as letters or diary entries.

注释 21: 由一系列文件（比如信件或日记）组成的小说。

Questions 32–37

Do the following statements agree with the views of the writer in Reading Passage 3?

In Boxes 32–37 on your answer sheet, write

YES *if the statement agrees with the views of the writer*
NO *if the statement contradicts the views of the writer*
NOT GIVEN *if it is impossible to say what the writer thinks about this*

32 *The Sorrows of Young Werther* started the trend for epistolary novels.

33 The novel explores human relationships on a large scale.

34 The general public were not familiar with Goethe before he wrote the novel.

35 *Werther* did not receive positive reviews.

36 Some readers attempted to copy aspects of the main character's personality.

37 *Werther* is still a very popular novel today.

Questions 38–40

Complete the summary below.

Choose **NO MORE THAN THREE WORDS** *from the passage for each answer.*

Write your answers in Boxes 38–40 on your answer sheet.

Impact of *Werther's* popularity on society and the author

The Sorrows of Young Werther transformed creative style of the time and was seen as a revolt against the previous artistic fashion of calmness, **38** .... and .... Its influence can still be seen today. Although the novel was hugely successful, its author would have preferred to have been recognised as an academic and **39** .... However, he will always be remembered by ordinary people for his tale of **40** ....

Advice for Chinese candidates

Remember there is no additional time to transfer answers from the Reading question booklet to the answer sheet – we still see many blank Reading answer sheets where students clearly misunderstood how/when to transfer answers.

记住，阅读考试没有额外时间将答案从阅读试卷誊写到答题纸上——我们仍能看到很多空白的阅读答题纸，很明显考生误解了应当如何／何时誊写答案。

IELTS
Writing
Test

Overview
of the Writing Test

Format

- The Writing module takes one hour to complete.
- The **format** is the same for both the Academic and the General Training modules.
    - There are 2 tasks to complete: Task 1 and Task 2.
- The **tasks** are different for the Academic and the General Training versions of the test, as outlined in the table below.

	General Training	**Academic**
Task 1 **(150 words)**	Letter	Report
Task 2 **(250 words)**	Essay	Essay
	(in response to a point of view, argument, or problem)	

- All instructions are printed on the question booklet.

- 写作考试用时一小时。
- 学术类和培训类的写作考试**形式**相同。
    - 都需要完成两个写作任务：任务 1 和任务 2。
- 学术类和培训类的**写作任务**并不相同，下表概括了差异之处。

	培训类	**学术类**
任务 1（**150 词**）	书信	报告
任务 2（**250 词**）	短文	短文
	（针对一个观点、论点或问题进行回应）	

- 所有指令均印在试卷上。

Marking

- You are marked on 4 criteria:
  - task achievement (Task 1) / task response (Task 2)
  - coherence and cohesion
  - lexical resources (vocabulary)
  - grammatical range and accuracy
- These four are equally important to your score, i.e. weight 25% each, and all 4 criteria are assessed in both tasks.
- 写作考试按四个标准来评分：
  - 写作任务完成情况（任务 1）/ 写作任务回应情况（任务 2）
  - 连贯与衔接
  - 词汇多样性
  - 语法多样性与准确性
- 四个标准同等重要，即各占 25% 的比重。两个写作任务都会通过这四个标准进行测评。

TIP

- Spend about 20 minutes on Task 1 and 40 minutes on Task 2 for both the Academic and the General Training Writing modules.
- 无论是参加学术类还是培训类写作考试，建议用 20 分钟完成任务 1，用 40 分钟完成任务 2。

Task 1:
Academic Writing

Task Types

- In **Academic Writing** Task 1, you are asked to write 150 words to describe visual information in your own words. The visual information can include: **bar charts, pie charts, tables, line graphs, diagrams** or **maps.**
- **学术类**写作任务 1 要求考生用自己的语言描述所看到的信息，篇幅为 150 词。所看到的信息可能是：**柱形图、饼状图、表格、曲线图、示意图**或**地图**。

Activity 1

Look at the charts below, and match each one to its type.

Chart 1

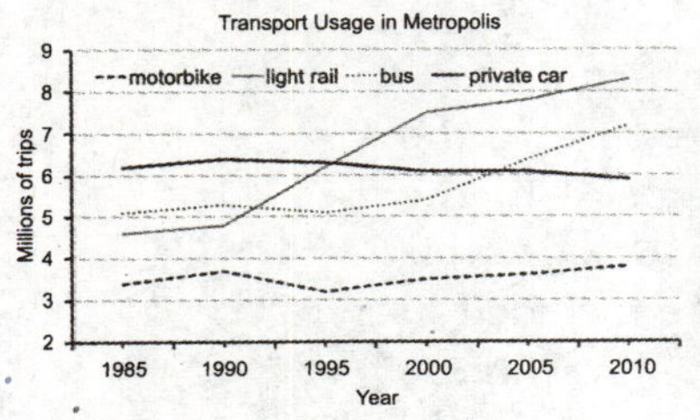

Charts 2 & 3

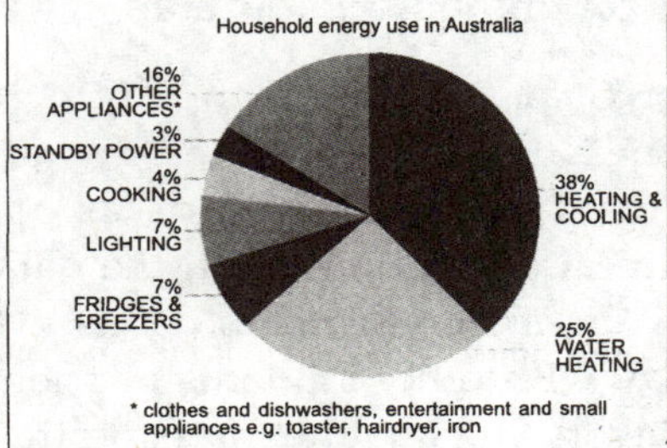

Amount of electricity used in a typical Australian home

Number of people in the house	Electricity used: kilowatt-hours (kWh) per year
1	5,000–6,500
2	6,000–8,000
3	7,500–10,000
6 or more	12,000–16,000

Chart 4

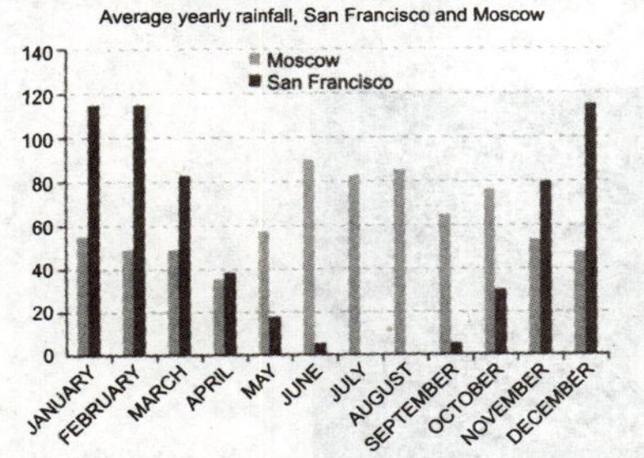

Chart 5

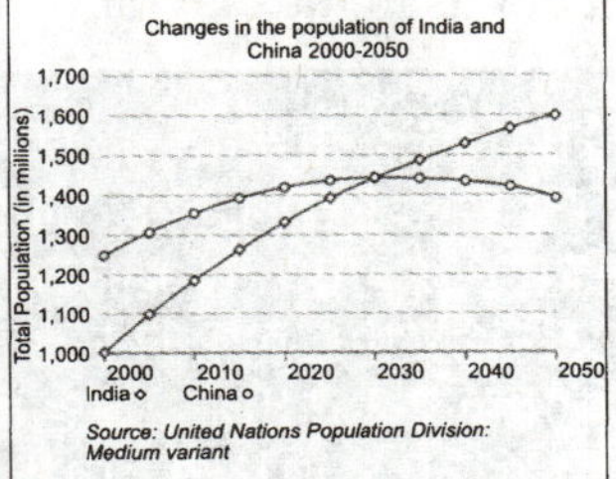

Chart 6

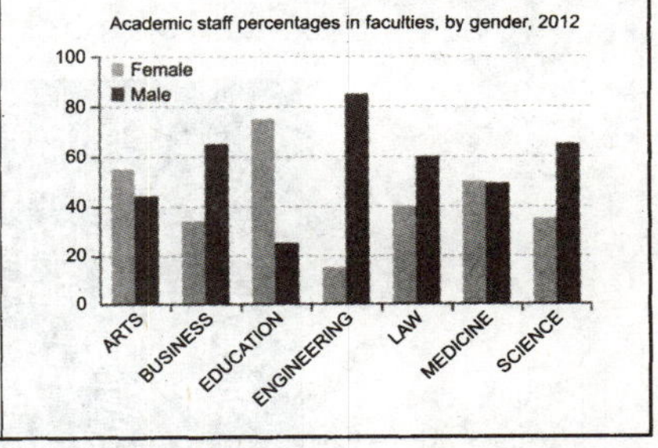

Structure of the Answer

- The best structure for an **Academic Writing** Task 1 response describes:
  1. the topic (in your own words)
  2. the main trends
  3. significant data points which illustrate the main trends (not every detail)
  4. conclusion (optional)
- **学术类写作**任务 1 的回答最好按下列结构进行描述：
  1. 主题（使用自己的语言）
  2. 主要趋势
  3. 表明主要趋势（而非每个细节）的重要数据点
  4. 结论（可选）

TIP

- Your task is to tell the reader the **main ideas or trends** illustrated in the charts, plus **significant** data points. The reader should be able to 'see' the chart in his mind when he reads your answer.
- 你要做的是告诉读者图表中表明的**主要信息或趋势**，以及**重要数据点**。在阅读你的回答时，读者应该可以在脑海中"看见"相应的图表。

Advice for Chinese candidates

It is critical you select the right information – examiners look for those essays identifying the significant and main trends as opposed to the mechanical description of all the data. Practise this skill by discussing the main points to be included in an essay with other students or friends in Chinese before worrying about expressing this in writing in English. Practise looking at different tasks. Spend a few minutes with each question identifying 2-3 main and significant points in the diagram.

选择正确的信息十分重要——考官阅卷时就是在看文章是否找出了重要和主要的趋势，而不是对所有数据进行机械性的描述。练习这一技能的方式：先与其他同学或朋友用中文讨论文中应包含的主要信息，然后再考虑如何在写作中用英文表达出来。拿各种不同的写作任务来练习。每道题花几分钟从图表中找出 2~3 个主要和重要的信息点。

Activity 2

2.1 *Look at Chart 1[1] and its Sample Answer and find out Parts 1–4 above in the Sample Answer.*

Note 1: All Task 1 questions and Sample Answers are also at the back of 'IELTS Writing Test' for ease of reference.

注释 1: 在"IELTS Writing Test"部分后面附有所有任务 1 的问题和范文，以便参考。

2.2 *Answer the following questions about the Sample Answer.*

1 What main trends did the writer describe?

2 Which data points were chosen? Why?

Chart 1

The graph shows the usage of four different types of transport in Metropolis from 1985 to 2010.

Write a report on this graph, describing its main features and comparing and contrasting where appropriate.

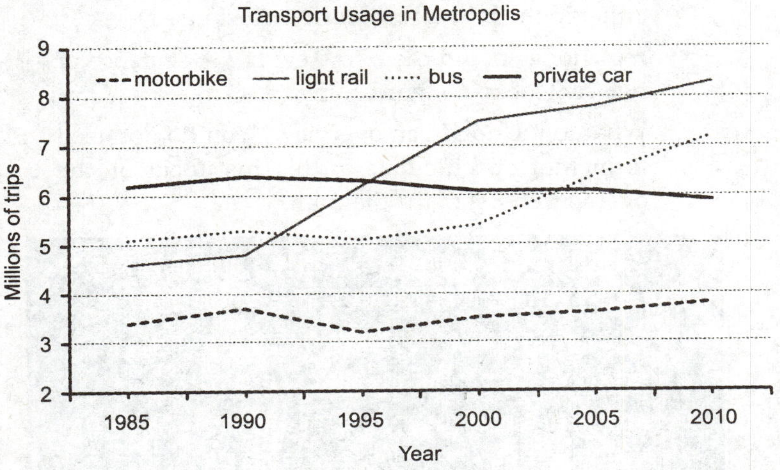

Sample Answer for Chart 1

The line chart illustrates changes in four methods of travel in Metropolis from 1985 to 2010, measured in five-yearly intervals. In general, there was an increase in travel over the period. The use of public transport markedly increased, while private car usage declined slightly.

Light rail and bus usage was approximately the same in 1985, at around 5 million trips, but in 1990 light rail saw a dramatic increase to reach approximately 7.8 million trips by 2000. By 2010, this was the most popular form of transport at just over 8 million trips. Usage of buses remained steady as trains grew in popularity, but in 2000, this also started to grow to a high of just over 7 million trips in 2010.

In 1985, private cars were the most popular form of transport in Metropolis, at just over 6 million trips. However, there was a small but steady decline in car usage to just under 6 million in 2010. Motorbike usage fluctuated, but overall, there was a small increase from about 3.5 million trips in 1985 to just under 4 million in 2010.

Advice for Chinese candidates

An Academic Task 1 must include an **overview** – this is a general statement summarising the main trends of the diagram or data. Some specific tips for this:

✓ Where to write the overview? Best places are either in the introduction or conclusion.

✓ How long should the overview be? A sentence or two sentences, no more.

✓ What to include in an overview? You do not need to include specific data in this, just focus on the overall trend(s) in the diagram.

学术类任务 1 必须包含一个**概述**，即概括图表或数据中主要趋势的总体陈述。以下是一些具体提示：

✓ 概述应写在哪里？最好写在介绍或结论部分。

✓ 概述应写多长？一两句话即可，无需更长。

✓ 概述应包含哪些内容？无需包含具体数据，只需侧重于图表中的（一个或多个）总体趋势。

Skill 1: Planning (Task Achievement, Coherence and Cohesion)

- You should spend approximately 20 minutes planning and writing your Task 1 answer.
- 对于任务 1，应该用大约 20 分钟时间构思并作答。

TIPS

- Before you begin writing your Task 1 response, you need to spend **2–3** minutes **analysing the chart**.
- If you do NOT do this, you may misinterpret the chart, or miss out important main trends or details.
- If you analyse carefully, you help yourself to write a clear, thorough and well-planned answer.

- 开始任务 1 的写作前，需要花 **2~3** 分钟**分析图表**。
- 如果不这么做，你可能会错误解读图表，或遗漏重要的主要趋势或细节。
- 仔细分析有助于写出清晰、透彻、构思缜密的回答。

- Follow these 4 key points:
  1. Read and understand the topic.
  2. Check the time scale and the units of measurement.
  3. Find the main trends.
  4. Choose the significant data points.
- 遵循下列四点：
  1. 阅读并理解题目。
  2. 确认时间标记和计量单位。
  3. 找出主要趋势。
  4. 选择重要的数据点。

TIPS

- Train yourself to follow the SAME procedure EVERY time you see a Task 1 question.
- Practise, practise, practise! Make the process automatic.

- 训练自己每次看到任务 1 的问题时都采用相同的流程作答。
- 练习，练习，再练习！让整个过程不假思索地进行。

Activity 3

3.1 *Look at Charts 2 and 3 and their rubric (written instructions). Answer the following questions. Take your time over this. Remember, you are learning and automating important skills.*

1 What is the topic of this chart?

2 What are the units of measurement?

3 What is the time frame of this chart? Is it past, present and/or future or is it a fact chart (i.e. always true)? What verb tense should you use?

4 What are the main trends?

5 What are the significant data points?

Charts 2 and 3

The pie chart below shows where energy is used in a typical Australian household, and the table shows the amount of electricity used according to the number of occupants.

Summarise the information by selecting and reporting the main features, and make comparisons where relevant.

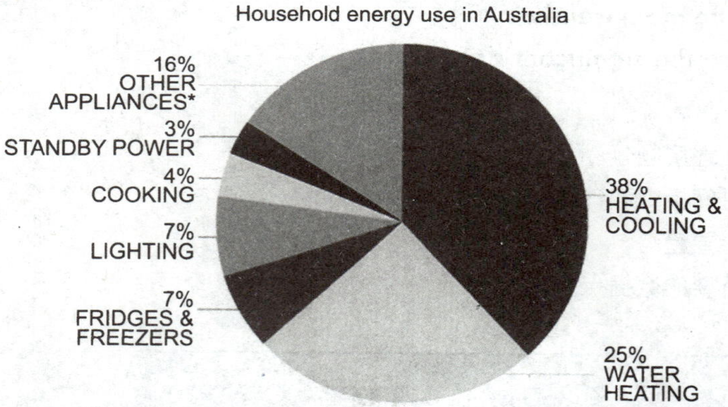

* clothes and dishwashers, entertainment and small appliances e.g. toaster, hairdryer, iron

Amount of electricity used in a typical Australian home	
Number of people in the house	Electricity used: kilowatt-hours (kWh) per year
1	5,000–6,500
2	6,000–8,000
3	7,500–10,000
6 or more	12,000–16,000

3.2 *Now, do the same exercise for all the charts in this book. Try to do this in 2–3 minutes if you can,* ***but*** *it is better to go slowly and get it right while you are learning.*

3.3 *Try this activity for every Task 1 chart that you study while preparing for the IELTS Academic Writing test.*

Skill 2: Writing Topic Sentences and Finding Main Trends

- Your first sentence needs to describe the topic of the chart, and the following sentence(s) should describe the main trends of the chart(s).
- 第一句话要描述图表的主题，之后的句子或句群应描述图表中的主要趋势。

TIPS

- You need to change the words used in the rubric. You can change the grammar or the words. Do **not** copy the chunks of the rubric exactly.
- Remember, your task is to make a **clear** and **accurate** picture for the reader. Writing a **main trend sentence** is an important part of creating a clear picture.
- Main trend sentences should go after your topic sentence. You should write **one or two sentences** about main trends.

- 不要照抄指令中的用词。可以变通语法或单词。**不要**大段重复指令中的原话。
- 记住，你的任务是为读者呈现一个**清晰**、**准确**的描述。想要描述得清晰，写出一个**反映主要趋势的句子**很重要。
- 反映主要趋势的句子应位于主题句之后。应将几个主要趋势用**一两句话**描述出来。

Activity 4

Look at Chart 4 and answer the following questions:

Chart 4

The graph below shows average yearly rainfall in Moscow and San Francisco, measured in millimetres.

Summarise the information by selecting and reporting the main features, and make comparisons where relevant.

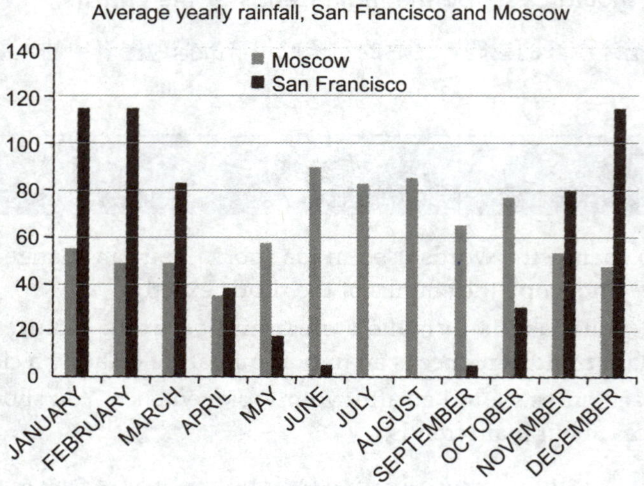

1 Which city has the highest rainfall? (REMEMBER, IELTS Task 1 Writing is NOT a test of maths. Is it a good use of your time to add up all the rainfall numbers to check which city has the highest rainfall?)

2 What is/are the **main difference(s)** in rainfall between Moscow and San Francisco? *Choose one or more below.*

A They have a different amount of annual rainfall.

B They have their most/least rain in different months.

C San Francisco has some months with a much higher rainfall than Moscow does.

D They have a different pattern of rainfall, and San Francisco has a more fluctuating rainfall than Moscow.

Activity 5

5.1 *Choose the best main trend sentence(s) for Chart 4 from the list below and think about why they are the best ones. Notice that, in each case, the topic sentence is a little different.*

A The bar chart illustrates the rainfall each year in San Francisco and Moscow, measured in millimetres per month. Overall, San Francisco has much more rain in December, January and February than Moscow does.

B The graph indicates the rainfall per month over a typical year in both San Francisco and Moscow, measured in millimetres per month. In general, San Francisco has approximately 630 mm of rain per year, whereas Moscow has about 700 mm.

C The bar chart compares the average amount of rain over the year in two cities, San Francisco and Moscow, measured in millimetres per month. Overall, although the two cities have approximately the same annual rainfall, the distribution of this rain over the year is widely different.

D The bar chart compares the average amount of annual rainfall in two cities, San Francisco and Moscow, measured in millimetres per month. Overall, San Francisco has a much more fluctuating annual rainfall than Moscow, and there is a different monthly pattern for that rainfall.

5.2 *Now, write a topic and main trend sentence for Charts 2 and 3 on Page 111. Use the skills you practised in Activities 4 and 5 to do this. Check your answer by reading the Sample Answer provided on Page 116.*

5.3 *Try this activity for every Task 1 chart that you study while preparing for the IELTS Academic Writing test.*

Skill 3: Finding Significant Data Points and Grouping Data

- After you have described the topic and the main trends, you need to write about the details of the chart.
- 在描述完主题和主要趋势后，还需描述图表中的细节。

TIPS

- Candidates who try to describe every data point do not get good scores on Task 1 Writing answers. Remember, you are making a clear picture for the reader. Your job is to select the **significant** data points to do this.
- You also need to **group** the data to help the reader to picture and understand the chart. Grouping the data is key to effective coherence in your writing.

- 力图描述所有数据点的考生在任务1中不会取得高分。记住，你在为读者呈现一个清晰的描述。要做到这一点，你的任务是要选择**重要的**数据点。
- 你还需要将数据**分类**，以帮助读者想象和理解图表。对数据**分类**是有效增强文章连贯性的关键。

Advice from Chinese candidates

坚持每天写一篇真题的作文，并将自己的作文与范文进行比较。

——雅思高分考生　路倩

Activity 6

6.1 *Look at Chart 5, and think about which significant data points you would choose to describe these trends, and why. Choose the best option below.*

A data for starting points, the crossover point and the final projection points, plus language to describe the shape of each line

B data for starting points, and then for each 10-yearly interval thereafter

C data each time the data lines cross one of the horizontal lines

Chart 5

The graph below shows the population of India and China from the year 2000 to the present day with projections for growth to the year 2050.

Summarise the information by selecting and reporting the main features, and make comparisons where relevant.

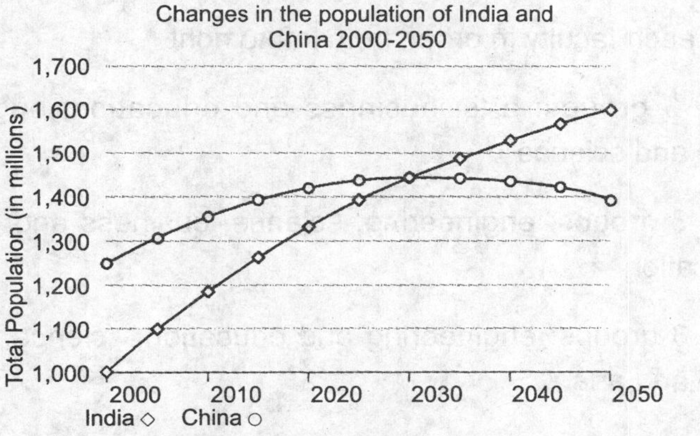

Source: United Nations Population Division: Medium variant

6.2 *Next, read the Sample Answer for Chart 5, and mark on the chart as you do so* ***the significant points*** *that the writer has selected.*

Sample Answer for Chart 5

The graph gives information about population growth in China and India from the year 2000 with predicted changes to 2050.

In 2000, China's population stood at 1.25 billion and this number rose steadily to where it is currently at around 1.35 billion. It is projected to peak at 1.45 billion in 2025, when the number will level off and start to decline. It is expected that by 2050 the population will have dropped slightly to 1.4 billion.

In contrast, although the population of India started at just one billion in 2000, it has increased rapidly to just under 1.25 billion today. The data indicate it will continue its upward surge, overtaking China in 2030 and reaching a peak of 1.6 billion by 2050.

Overall, the major difference between the two population trends is that the number of people in China is forecast to start falling after 2030 whereas the population of India will continue to soar.

Activity 7

7.1 *Look at Chart 6 and think how **you** would group this data. Then consider the different ways to group the bars from the list below.*

1 What are the advantages and disadvantages of each one?

2 What information is each one emphasising?

A describe each faculty in order, from left to right

B describe 3 groups: arts, business and education; engineering and law; medicine and science

C describe 3 groups: engineering, science, business and law; medicine; arts and education

D describe 3 groups: engineering and education; science, law and business; medicine and arts

E describe 4 groups: engineering; science, business and law; medicine; arts and education

Chart 6

The graph below shows the percentage of male and female academic staff members across the faculties of a major university in 2012.

Summarise the information by selecting and reporting the main features, and make comparisons where relevant.

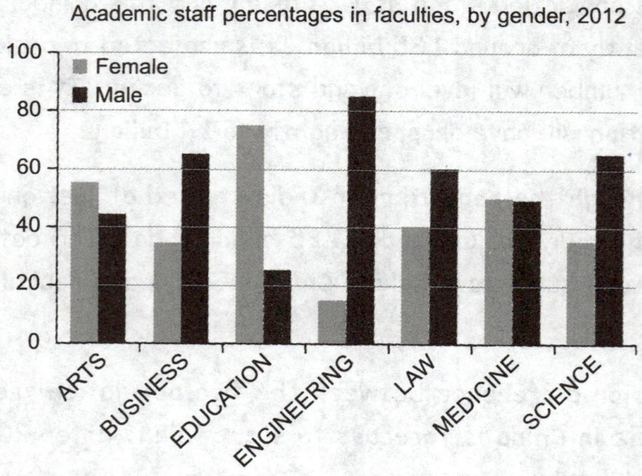

7.2 *Now, read the Sample Answer for Chart 6 and notice how the writer has grouped the data.*

Which option above did he choose?

Sample Answer for Chart 6

The bar chart shows the proportion of men and women who taught in seven different faculties of a particular university in 2012.

There was a large gender disparity in some faculties: engineering was dominated by male academics whereas education had the highest percentage of female academics. Notably, 85% of the engineering teachers were male and only 15% female. Three quarters of the academic staff in education were women, with just 25% males.

However, other faculties were more balanced in their composition. In medicine, gender representation was almost equal, while in arts subjects slightly more than half the academics were female (55%). It is interesting to note that business and science had the same proportions of men and women, with 65% male to 35% female academics in those faculties. Law had a slightly higher percentage of women at 40%.

Although the faculties of engineering, business, science and law were still primarily male-dominated in 2012, women made up half the faculty of medicine and were predominant in education and arts.

7.3 *Look at each chart in 'IELTS Writing Test' and think about grouping the data and choosing significant data points. Read the Sample Answers, and as you do so, mark how the writer has grouped the data and which significant points he/she has selected in his/her answer.*

7.4 *Try this activity for every Sample Answer that you read while preparing for the IELTS Academic Writing test.*

Skill 4: Describing Trends

- In the details paragraphs, you must **summarise** the information shown in the graph. You must **include data,** but also **describe trends** as you do so.
- 在描述细节的段落中，必须总结图表中出现的信息。这些信息必须**包含数据**，但同时你还需要**描述趋势**。

TIPS

- Try to vary your sentence structures and vocabulary. Demonstrating a wide range of grammar and vocabulary, used at the right time and in the right way, is central to getting high scores in these two criteria.
- If you regularly repeat the same vocabulary and grammar, you will not get a high band score.
- 尝试变化句子结构和用词。展现多样化的语法和词汇并且在恰当的时机正确地使用，这是在语法和词汇这两个标准中获得高分的关键。
- 如果多次重复使用相同的词汇和语法，将不会获得高分。

Activity 8

Look at Charts 2 and 3 (on Page 111), and read the two examples below.

These show you the difference between **repetition**, and **varying** structures and vocabulary.

NB *While Answer A below is accurate, and includes* ***more*** *data than Answer B, it gives a* ***less*** *clear picture of the chart. It would also get a poor band score because of the repetition of language structures.*

1 Notice the different sentence structures that are used in Paragraph B.

2 Make a list of all the different ways of expressing 'use'.

A 38% of the total energy is used for heating and cooling, whereas 25% is consumed for water heating. 7% is used for fridges and freezers, and lighting, and 4% is used for cooking. 3% is used for standby power, and 16% is used for all other appliances.

One-person households use 5,000 to 6,500 kWh per year, and two-person households consume 6,000 to 8,000 kWh. Three-person households consume 7,500 to 10,000 kWh, and six- or more-person households use 12,000 to 16,000 kWh per year.

B Well over half the total household energy is used for the two main purposes of heating and cooling, at 38%, and water heating, which consumes 25%. The other uses are all much smaller. The next category is for fridges and freezers and for lighting, each of which accounts for 7% of the total. Cooking and standby power are responsible for 4% and 3% respectively, and then other appliances use 16% all together.

The table shows that energy is used more efficiently in larger households. Whereas one person living alone uses 5,000 to 6,500 kWh per year, a 6-person household consumes only 2 to 3 times of this, at 12,000 to 16,000 kWh.

TIPS

- Research and practise some different vocabulary and sentence structures. For example, Activity 8 has provided you with a list of ways to express the idea of '**using something**'.
- Make your own lists of other useful language by studying other Sample Answers, and refer to these frequently.
- Learn a FEW items **well**. Do **not** try to learn too many structures without knowing how to use them appropriately.

  Examples to look for:
  - Language to describe rising and falling
  - Language to compare and contrast
  - Language to describe average trends and for unusual data points (far higher or lower than average)

- 发掘并练习使用一些不同的词汇和句子结构。例如，上文 Activity 8 中提供了一系列用于表达“using something”的不同方式。
- 通过学习其他范文，自己将其他有用的语言列出来，并经常参照。
- 学习并掌握几个结构。不要贪图学习太多结构却不知道如何正确使用。

  可以留意的例子有：
  - 描述上升和下降的用语
  - 进行比较和对比的用语
  - 描述平均趋势和（远高于或远低于平均数的）不寻常的数据点的用语

Skill 5: Comparing and Contrasting

- Structures for comparing and contrasting are very important when writing good Task 1 answers.
- 在任务 1 的写作中，比较和对比的结构非常重要。

TIPS : Some Useful Key Structures

- Comparative and Superlative Structures
  - By far **the most / the highest / the lowest** ...
  - X is significantly **greater / smaller** than Y.
  - X spent (50% / a great deal) more/less (time/money) on ... than Y.
  - X spent **the least / the most** ... on ...
- Similar
  - **Both** X and Y ...
  - X and Y **show a similar pattern**.
- Opposite
  - ... whereas/while ... **illustrates a different trend**.
  - However, ...
  - In contrast, **only** [emphasis] ...

Activity 9

Look at the Sample Answer for Chart 4 below and highlight the comparative, superlative and contrasting structures.

Sample Answer for Chart 4

The bar chart compares the average amount of rain over the year in two cities, San Francisco and Moscow. Overall, although the two cities have approximately the same annual rainfall, the distribution of rain over the year is widely different.

In general, Moscow has a more even yearly rainfall than San Francisco. Rain averages about 50 mm in the months of January to March, dropping to an annual low of just under 40 mm in April. It then rises steadily to a high of about 90 mm in June, and slightly less in July and August, and from that point on it fluctuates, dropping at the end of the year to about 45 mm in December.

In contrast, San Francisco illustrates a different trend. It has a widely fluctuating rainfall, with significantly greater annual variation. December, January and February are by far the rainiest months, averaging just under 120 mm in each of these months. From March onwards, there is a dramatic drop to less than 10 mm in June, and effectively no rain falls in July or August. Rainfall then increases steadily and evenly to the December high of about 110 mm.

The chart shows us that Moscow has the most rain in July and August, at a time when San Francisco is virtually dry.

Task 1: General Training Writing

Task Type

- In **General Training Writing** Task 1, you are asked to write an informal, semi-formal, or formal letter of at least 150 words, requesting information or explaining a situation. You are told what kind of information to include in the form of 3 bullet points in the question. For example:
- 培训类写作任务 1 要求写一封索取信息或解释某种情况的非正式、半正式或正式信件，篇幅不少于 150 词。答题指令会用三个信息点说明需要涵盖的信息。例如：

> ***You recently moved out of a rental property, which you shared with two other tenants. You forgot an item of value at the property.***
>
> ***Write a letter to the landlord. In your letter***
> - ***describe the item***
> - ***say where it might be***
> - ***explain what action you want the landlord to take.***

Structure of the Answer

- The structure for a **General Training Writing** Task 1 includes:
  1. a greeting (e.g. Dear ...)
  2. two or three body paragraphs related to the bullet points
     - The first paragraph should clearly state your purpose for writing. (Why are you writing this letter?)
     - Make it clear when you are ending the letter. (e.g. I'm looking forward to hearing from you.)
  3. a sign-off (e.g. Yours sincerely)
- It is not necessary to write your address as part of the response.

- 培训类写作任务 1 的作文结构包括：
  1. 称呼（例如：Dear ...）
  2. 针对答题指令所要求的信息点而写的两三个主体段落
     - 第一段应清楚地陈述你写信的目的。（你为什么写这封信？）
     - 用明显的语言结束这封信。（例如：I'm looking forward to hearing from you.）
  3. 结尾（例如：Yours sincerely）
- 作答时无需写自己的地址。

Language of the Answer

- Your task is to respond to common, everyday situations in an **appropriate style** of language.
- 写作任务需采用**得体的语言风格**回应常见的日常情景。

TIPS

- The style depends on the **audience**. For example, an informal style is used for writing to a friend, while a semi-formal or formal style is used to write to a manager, school principal, etc.
- Make sure you adjust the sign-off to match the style required.
- 语言风格取决于**阅读对象**。例如，写给朋友时使用非正式的风格，而写给经理、校长等时则使用半正式或正式的风格。
- 结尾应与信件所要求的风格保持一致。

- Below are some examples to illustrate the difference between formal and informal language:
- 下面举例说明正式与非正式语言之间的不同之处：

	Formal	Semi-formal	Informal
Greeting	Dear Sir, Dear Madam, Dear Sir/Madam,	Dear Mr Smith, Dear Mrs Smith, Dear Ms Smith,	Dear John, Dear Anne, Hi Bob,
Body	I am writing with regard to ... I am interested in receiving ... I am looking forward to hearing from you.		I'm writing about ... Please send me ... Hope to hear from you soon!
Sign-off	Yours faithfully,	Yours sincerely, Sincerely,	Regards, Best regards, Best wishes,

Task 2: Writing

Task Types

- In Task 2 of the Academic Writing module, you are asked to write 250 words on a general topic. You may be asked to
  1. compare advantages and disadvantages
  2. discuss the reasons for something
  3. discuss the results of current problems or issues
  4. suggest some solutions to current problems or issues
  5. evaluate two conflicting opinions and give your ideas
  6. say to what extent (how much) you agree or disagree with an opinion
- In most cases, you will need to express an opinion at the end of your essay.
- Task 2 of the General Training Writing module is very similar, but the topics and the tasks tend to be simpler. All of the information about Academic Writing also applies to the General Training module.
- Each Task 2 question has 2 parts:
  - a **topic:** what you must write about
  - a **task:** usually one or two from the list of tasks above.
- 学术类写作任务 2 要求就一个大众性话题写一篇文章，篇幅为 250 词。你可能需要
  1. 比较优势与劣势
  2. 讨论某事的成因
  3. 讨论当前问题或争议的结果
  4. 就当前问题或争议的解决方案提出建议
  5. 评价两个对立的观点并阐明自己的想法
  6. 表明自己在多大程度上赞同或反对某个观点
- 大多数情况下，你需要在文章末尾表达一个观点。
- 培训类写作任务 2 十分相似，但话题和写作任务通常相对比较简单。此处有关学术类写作的信息对培训类写作同样适用。
- 每个任务 2 均包含两部分：
  - **主题**：写作内容
  - **任务**：通常是上文任务列表中的一两项。

TIP

- You need to **analyse** the topic **carefully**. Identify the specific topic, and find the **task (rubric)**. If you train yourself to do this, you will be sure to write on the correct topic, and you will improve your band score.
- 要**仔细分析**写作主题。确认具体的主题，然后找到**写作任务**（**题目中的指令**）。如能这样进行训练，你肯定能按照正确的主题写作，并提升考试成绩。

Activity 10

10.1 *Look at the following topics. Mark the topic, and the task. Match the task(s) to the list above. Notice that sometimes the* ***same general topic*** *can have* ***different tasks****.*

1 Over the past twenty years there has been a big rise in international tourism. What are some of the advantages and disadvantages of this growth?

2 Many people now travel overseas for their holidays, rather than staying in their own countries. What are some reasons for this change? What problems does the rise in international tourism cause?

3 Tourism is becoming increasingly popular, and this can affect some beautiful natural places. Why does this happen? What can we do to prevent further damage?

4 Some people say that holding huge international events is a great advantage for a country, while others say that this is a costly mistake. Evaluate both of these viewpoints and give your opinion.

5 It is often said that exams are a poor way of evaluating students' ability, and that they cause a great deal of unnecessary stress. To what extent do you agree with this opinion?

10.2 *Try this activity for every Task 2 question that you study while preparing for the IELTS Academic Writing test.*

Skill 1: Topic Analysis, Brainstorming Ideas and Making a Plan

- You should spend approximately 40 minutes planning and writing your Task 2 response.
- 对于任务 2，你应该用大约 40 分钟时间构思并作答。

TIPS

- Before you begin writing your Task 2 response, you need to spend **4–5 minutes analysing the topic** and **the task**, **brainstorming** some **ideas** and **planning** your **answer**.
- If you analyse and plan carefully, you help yourself to write a clear, well-planned answer.
- 开始对任务 2 下笔作答之前，需要花 **4～5 分钟来分析主题和写作任务**，**通过头脑风暴想出一些观点**，**构思好如何作答**。
- 仔细分析和构思有助于写出清晰、构思缜密的回答。

- Follow these 3 key points:
  1. Read and understand the topic and the task.
  2. Write down a few notes for main ideas.
  3. Plan your answer – body paragraphs and your conclusion.
- 遵循以下三个要点：
  1. 阅读并理解写作主题和任务。
  2. 以笔记的形式记下主要思想观点。
  3. 构思回答内容——主体段落和结论。

TIPS

- Train yourself to follow the SAME procedure EVERY time you see a Task 2 question.
- Practise, practise, practise! Make the process automatic.
- 训练自己每次看到任务 2 的问题时都采用相同的流程作答。
- 练习，练习，再练习！让整个过程不假思索地进行。

Activity 11

11.1 *Read the topics, and follow the 3 key points above to create a plan for each one.*

1 In recent years, it has become harder for new graduates to find employment, and many young people struggle to join the workforce. Why do you think this situation has occurred? What can you suggest to solve this problem?

2 It is often said that exams are a poor way of evaluating students' ability, and that they cause a great deal of unnecessary stress. To what extent do you agree with this opinion?

11.2 *Try this activity for every Task 2 question that you study while preparing for the IELTS Academic Writing test. Try to do each one in 4–5 minutes if you can,* ***but*** *it is better to go slowly and get it right while you are learning.*

Advice for Chinese candidates

Some candidates are concerned that the ideas expressed in a Writing Task 2 are more important – in that these ideas should match the examiner's ideas – than how you express these ideas. The relevance of ideas is important in that it must address the question, but **not** whether your ideas match those of the script marker. You are only judged on how well you communicate those ideas through your writing.

有些考生担心写作任务 2 中所表达的思想观点比如何表达这些思想观点更为重要，也就是自己的思想观点应与考官的一致。思想观点切题很重要，在于其必须回应问题，而不在于是否与评卷人员的思想观点一致。评分仅根据你运用语言表达这些观点的能力高低进行评判。

Skill 2: Essay Structure and Thesis Statements (Coherence and Cohesion, Grammar)

- A good Task 2 Writing response follows a clear 'pathway' or structure. You need to explain how your essay will be organised **at the end of the introduction.** This part of the essay is often called the **thesis statement.**
- 一篇优秀的任务 2 回答应遵循清晰的“路径”或结构。**在介绍部分的结尾**，要解释文章将如何组织。文章中这一部分一般被称为**中心句**。

TIPS

- After you have planned your answer, stick to your plan. Do not change your mind! This may affect the coherence of your response.
- However, you do not have to give your opinion in the introduction. You can write your opinion in the conclusion. This has two advantages:
  - It gives you something concrete to write about in the conclusion.
  - It gives you more flexibility and time to think as you are writing.
- 构思好回答之后，按照构思进行写作。不要改变主意！这有可能会影响回答的连贯性。
- 但是，无需在介绍部分表明自己的观点，可以在结论部分表明观点。这有两个好处：
  - 让你在结论中有具体的内容可写。
  - 让你在写作过程中有更多的灵活度和思考时间。

Activity 12

12.1 *Look at these thesis statements. Remember, these come* ***after*** *the topic sentence. For each one, decide if the writer* ***has*** *or* ***has not*** *given his opinion. Which thesis statements allow the writer more flexibility in his response?*

1 Despite its disadvantages, international tourism has significant advantages, because of the money it brings to a country.

2 This essay will discuss the advantages and disadvantages of international tourism.

3 I will discuss the problems that our ageing population is causing for our society, and suggest some solutions for these problems.

4 Our ageing population is causing problems for the health system and for the younger generation, and we need to spend more money to develop better facilities for older people.

12.2 *Write a* ***brief*** *outline to match each thesis statement above.*

Activity 13

13.1 *Write TWO thesis statements for each of these essay topics. Write one that gives the writer's opinion, and one that does not give the writer's opinion.*

1 Some feel that young people today have many possessions and a lot of money, while others say that they have a harder life than ever before. Evaluate both these ideas and give your opinion.

2 Solar energy is becoming more and more popular as a source of household energy in many countries around the world. Why is this? What are the advantages and disadvantages of solar energy?

13.2 *Practise writing a thesis statement for every Task 2 question that you study while preparing for the IELTS Academic Writing test.*

Skill 3: Expanding Your Ideas

- After you have planned the topic of each paragraph, you need to expand your ideas by giving examples, details or reasons.
- 构思好每段的主题后，要通过举例、给出细节或原因来展开你的思想观点。

TIPS

- Each paragraph should have **one** main idea, expanded with examples, details or reasons. If you want to start a new idea, start a new paragraph. There is no rule about the number of paragraphs you must have in your Task 2 response.
- Avoid 'shopping lists' where you list many ideas and do not expand any of them. It is better to give a few reasons and develop them than to write many ideas without development.

- 每段应该有一个中心思想，通过例子、细节或原因把中心思想展开。如果要开始谈一个新的问题，应另起一段。雅思考试对任务 2 作答的段落数量没有规定。
- 避免以“购物清单”的方式列举很多观点却不对任何一个加以展开。与其列举很多观点却不展开论述，不如提供几个论据并展开论述。

Advice for Chinese candidates

You can extend your points by using explanations, examples, or personal experience.

可以使用解释、例子或个人经历来展开论述你的观点。

Activity 14

Read the sample paragraph below about the advantages of solar energy.

1 Highlight each new idea, and the extra information that extends the idea.

2 Write the plan that this paragraph was based on.

The main advantage of solar energy is that after the initial installation it is entirely free and renewable, so there are no extra costs involved in producing the energy. Solar energy is silent and environmentally friendly as well – it does not destroy or poison the ecosystem. This is because the raw material, sunshine, does not need to be extracted or refined, so there are no pollutants or toxic residue produced. Another major advantage is that it is produced where it is needed so there is no energy wasted on transport. This decentralisation of the power source not only leads to savings on transmission, but also to more self-reliant communities – the ability to produce their own power is a significant advantage for remote populations. There are also employment opportunities in the design and development, manufacture, installation and maintenance of the new technology for solar panels, which are consequently becoming less expensive, more available and much more efficient.

Activity 15

Write the paragraph plan below into whole paragraphs, expanding the ideas, OR choose your own plan to do this.

In recent years, it has become harder for new graduates to find employment, and many young people struggle to join the workforce. Why do you think this situation has occurred? What can you suggest to solve this problem?

Para 2 - Reasons -
- more tertiary institutions, so more graduates
- ageing workforce, and global recession, so few vacancies
- high, sometimes unrealistic, expectations of graduates

Para 3 - Solutions -
- career guidance and counselling
- encourage young people into growing employment areas
- get some work experience and be prepared to start at the bottom

Skill 4: Linking Ideas

- Linking ideas together has two parts:
  - Linking the whole essay and each paragraph to the thesis statement.
  - Linking ideas together inside each paragraph.
- Linking devices can be:
  - The **adverbial expressions and conjunctions** that you are familiar with: as a result, because, so, however, while, whereas, on the other hand, in addition ...
  - **Referencing expressions**: because of this, these ideas, ...
  - **Repetition of words or the use of synonyms** (words with similar meanings) to link ideas together.
  - Sentences or phrases to **link the paragraphs to the thesis statement and the conclusion.**
- 连接涉及两个部分：
  - 将整篇文章以及每个段落都与中心句连接起来。
  - 将每个段落内部的思想观点连接起来。
- 连接手段包括：
  - 你所熟悉的**副词性词语和连词**：as a result，because，so，however，while，whereas，on the other hand，in addition ...
  - **指称性表达**：because of this，these ideas ...
  - 通过**重复单词或使用同义词**把观点连接起来。
  - 运用句子或短语将**各个段落与中心句和结论**连接起来。

TIP

- Learn and practise some useful linking structures for beginning paragraphs and for linking ideas within paragraphs.
- 学习并练习使用一些有用的连接性结构，这些结构可用于段落开头，或用于连接段内的观点。

Advice for Chinese candidates

Use linking devices accurately and carefully – not EVERY sentence needs a linking word! It is better to understand and accurately use a few words or expressions than to try to use many devices only partially understood.

使用连接手段要准确、小心：不是所有句子都需要使用连接词！与其使用很多连接手段但对使用方法一知半解，不如理解并准确使用几个单词或表达。

Activity 16

Most people accept that we now live in a globalised world but not everyone agrees that this is beneficial.

To what extent is globalisation a positive or negative development?

Look at the sample Task 2 essay below, and identify some of the linking devices. There are MANY linking devices in this essay. Use the list of linking devices above to identify each type of linking.

Globalisation is here to stay, driven by advances in information technology and resulting in scientific, technological and economic progress and increased international trade and investment. It has had wide-ranging positive and negative effects on employment and economic development, scientific research, language and culture, global health and the environment.

One positive result of globalisation is the global distribution of labour. It is now much easier to move to other countries to find work, and this leads to better employment prospects for individuals and to more diverse workplaces. In addition, capital and industrial resources have migrated to developing countries, thus providing local jobs and boosting local economies. It has also resulted in greater contact between different cultures, as travel has become relatively safer and less expensive than it used to be. Ease of communication has encouraged an unprecedented level of global scientific research and cooperation, and a subsequent explosion of knowledge and information.

A downside of this global economy is that when a catastrophe occurs, as (NB: Example, NOT reason) in the recent global financial crisis that started in the

USA, this affects the whole world. Similarly, when a virus emerges in one region of the world, it spreads rapidly, threatening worldwide health. Globalisation affects culture and language, too; minority languages are dying out because of the necessity of learning English for international business, and indigenous cultures are being rejected in favour of a dominant, often USA-based, culture. Finally, levels of pollution are rising as (NB: Reason, NOT example) countries strive for economic growth and a competitive edge in the global market.

In conclusion, globalisation is a double-edged sword that has created jobs and promoted international cooperation but has led to cultural losses, more environmental damage, increased health risks and exposure to economic crises. However, our world will continue to shrink as technology expands, and we need to accept globalisation as a fact of life in the 21st century.

Skill 5: Using Complex Sentence Structures

- In both Task 1 and Task 2 of the IELTS Writing test, you are likely to improve your band score for grammar by using a **variety** of **complex structures. Some common examples of complex structures are:**
    - **Complex sentences with subordinating clauses**
      e.g. Whereas many people accept the need for exams, others are less convinced.
    - **Complex noun phrases**
      e.g. The most important reason for this problem is lack of resources and infrastructure.
    - **Reduced relative clauses**
      e.g. Finally, they should consider assisting families in looking after elderly relatives in their own homes, which would be a cheaper option than putting them into care.
    - **Complex verb structures which include modals**
      e.g. It is important to be able to use some of the structures listed here.
- These complex structures can be combined in many ways.
- 在雅思写作考试的任务 1 和任务 2 中，使用**多样化的复杂结构**将有助于提高在语法方面的得分。**一些常见的复杂结构有：**
    - **带有从句的复合句**
      例句：Whereas many people accept the need for exams, others are less convinced.
    - **复杂的名词短语**

例句：The most important reason for this problem is lack of resources and infrastructure.

- 简化的关系从句

  例句：Finally, they should consider assisting families in looking after elderly relatives in their own homes, which would be a cheaper option than putting them into care.

- 带有情态动词的复合动词

  例句：It is important to be able to use some of the structures listed here.

- 这些复杂结构可以通过多种方式组合使用。

TIPS

- You need to become aware of and practise these structures in different contexts.
- Try to develop patterns that you can use and then practise substituting different vocabulary into the structure.
- 要有意识地在不同语境中练习使用这些结构。
- 尝试发掘一些自己可以使用的句型，然后练习用不同的词语替换句型中的用词。

Advice from Chinese candidate

长短句杂糅，不要刻意使用很生僻的单词和所谓的模板。

——雅思高分考生　李鉴鹏

Activity 17

Read the sample Task 2 essay below, and underline as many complex structures as you can.

In many countries throughout the world, young people are pushed into careers that they have no aptitude for, or do not want to do, and there are two main reasons for this situation.

The first reason is lack of tertiary study options. In some countries, such as China, there are limited places available for tertiary study, and those who do not manage to earn a place at the institution of their choice often find themselves studying a subject which does not interest them, or which is a poor match for their skills and aptitudes. The other main reason, which is closely aligned to the former point, is parental aspirations. Many parents push their children into a limited set of career options because these choices represent social success, security and money in later life. In many cases, the skills and needs of the children are ignored, as their parents encourage them to earn places in prestigious, if inappropriate, institutions and to study subjects that are acceptable to their friends and extended family.

Some of those children who do manage to jump through all the required hoops find that they are trapped in a career which does not suit their needs or abilities, and that they can see no escape from the life sentence imposed by the well-meaning family. This can have both personal and social consequences. Firstly, unsatisfied workers can suffer from job stress, which drains human potential and may lead to physical and psychological illness. Dissatisfaction and distress also impacts on their chosen profession and on society as a whole, as unhappy and disaffected workers tend not to give their best, and this affects the quality of their work.

Skill 6: Making Conclusions

- The last part of the Task 2 essay is the conclusion. This should:
    - summarise your main ideas
    - give your opinion
- 任务 2 文章中最后一个部分是结论。这部分应该：
    - 总结你的主要思想
    - 表明你的观点

TIPS

- Your conclusion must match your introduction and the body of your essay. For example, if you have argued that sport at school has many advantages, the conclusion must not state that it has mostly disadvantages!
- Some Task 2 essay rubrics ask you to state your opinion, but your conclusion does not need to state a strong opinion for one side or the other. In this case, you can say that both sides are balanced. This kind of essay is often easier to write.

- 结论部分必须与介绍部分以及文章的主体相符。例如，如果前文已经论述了学校体育活动有很多好处，结论绝对不能说它弊大于利！
- 有些任务 2 的答题指令要求表明你的观点，但结论部分不需要强烈表示支持一方或另一方。在这种情况下，可以说两方的观点都有道理。这种文章写起来一般比较容易。

Activity 18

Read the conclusions.

1 Underline the places where the writer has summarised his ideas.

2 Does the conclusion include the writer's opinion?

3 If so, does it state a strong opinion for one side of the topic, or is it balanced?

A In short, I wholeheartedly disagree with the statement that arts subjects should not be taught. I suggest that every student should have instruction in philosophy, history or other arts subjects, even if they elect to major in the sciences, because learning critical thinking skills, and developing a wide background knowledge, will benefit them enormously in later life. In addition to this general training, we need specialist graduates in arts subjects to make their contribution to a well-rounded society.

B In conclusion, a person who is pushed into uncongenial work because of social constraints or family pressure is not likely to be a productive and happy member of society. We need to ensure that individual talents and skills are recognised and catered for if we are to have a harmonious and well-developed society.

C In my view, the government needs to take immediate and drastic action to improve public well-being by legislating against the proliferation of fast food businesses, raising taxes on fast food, removing tax from fruit and vegetables and banning all advertising of food with no or low nutritional value. Appropriately resourced PE and fitness programmes must also be compulsory in all schools. A multifaceted approach, which combines schools and public initiatives, is the best way to improve public health.

Sample Charts
for Task 1 Writing

Chart 1

The graph shows the usage of four different types of transport in Metropolis from 1985 to 2010.

Write a report on this graph, describing its main features and comparing and contrasting where appropriate.

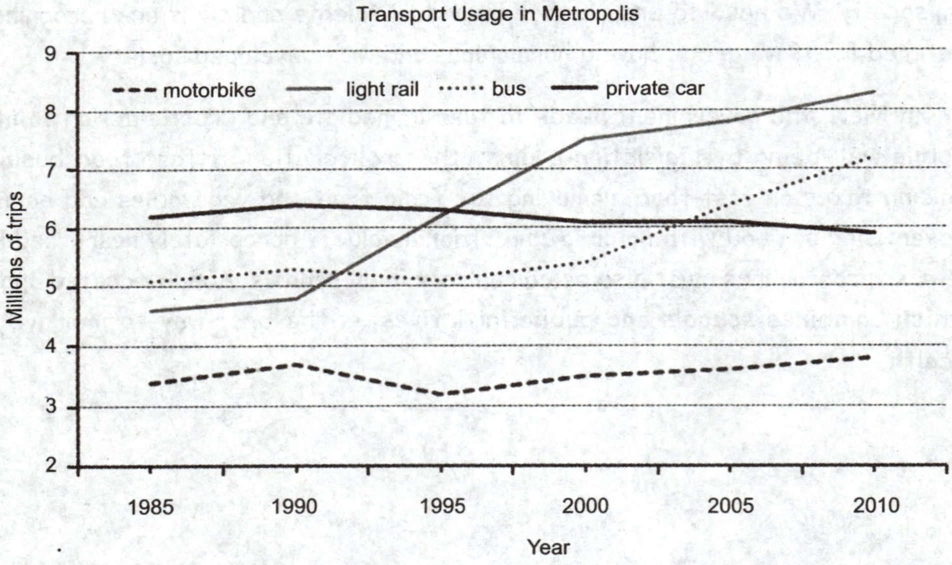

Charts 2 and 3

The pie chart below shows where energy is used in a typical Australian household, and the table shows the amount of electricity used according to the number of occupants.

Summarise the information by selecting and reporting the main features, and make comparisons where relevant.

Household energy use in Australia

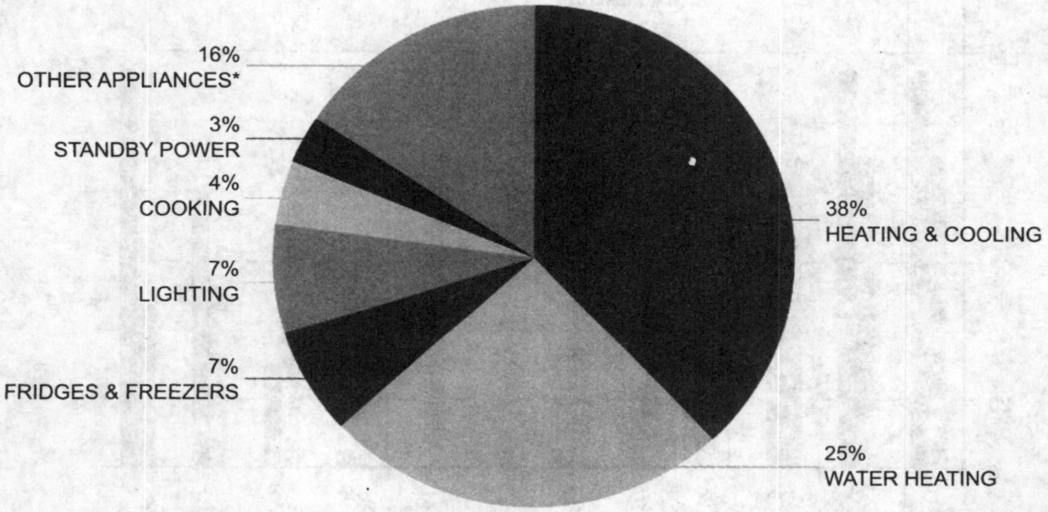

*clothes and dishwashers, entertainment and small appliances e.g. toaster, hairdryer, iron

Amount of electricity used in a typical Australian home

Number of people in the house	Electricity used: kilowatt-hours (kWh) per year
1	5,000–6,500
2	6,000–8,000
3	7,500–10,000
6 or more	12,000–16,000

Chart 4

The graph below shows average yearly rainfall in Moscow and San Francisco, measured in millimetres.

Summarise the information by selecting and reporting the main features, and make comparisons where relevant.

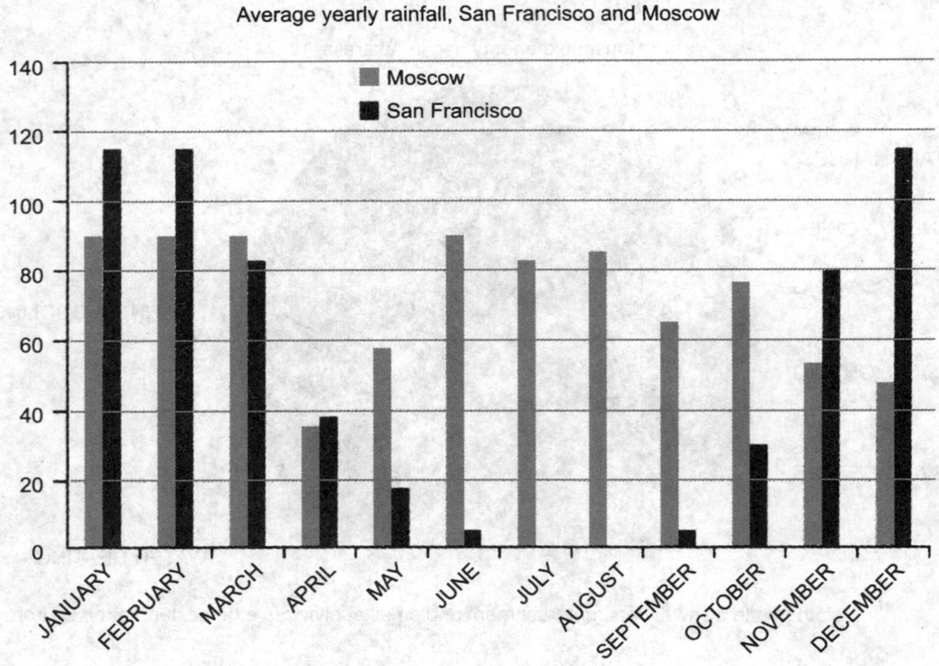

Chart 5

The graph below shows the population of India and China from the year 2000 to the present day with projections for growth to the year 2050.

Summarise the information by selecting and reporting the main features, and make comparisons where relevant.

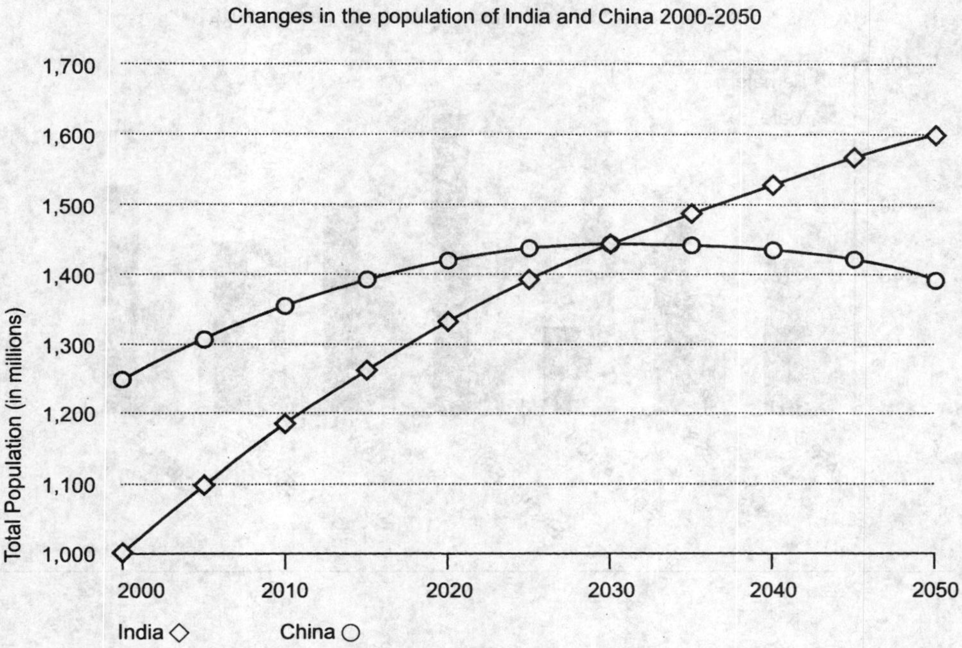

Source: United Nations Population Division: Medium variant

Chart 6

The graph below shows the percentage of male and female academic staff members across the faculties of a major university in 2012.

Summarise the information by selecting and reporting the main features, and make comparisons where relevant.

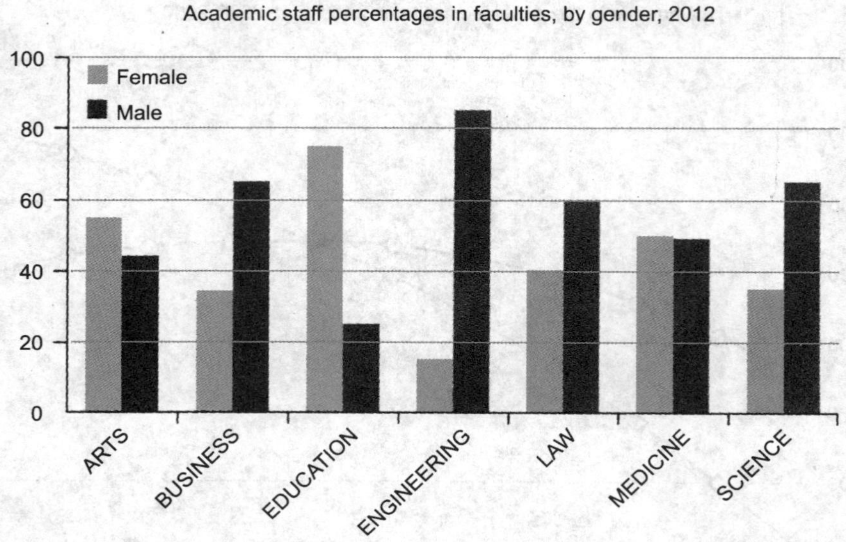

Sample Answers
for Charts

Sample Answer for Chart 1

The line chart illustrates changes in four methods of travel in Metropolis from 1985 to 2010, measured in five-yearly intervals. In general, there was an increase in travel over the period. The use of public transport markedly increased, while private car usage declined slightly.

Light rail and bus usage was approximately the same in 1985, at around 5 million trips, but in 1990 light rail saw a dramatic increase to reach approximately 7.8 million trips by 2000. By 2010, this was the most popular form of transport at just over 8 million trips. Usage of buses remained steady as trains grew in popularity, but in 2000, this also started to grow to a high of just over 7 million trips in 2010.

In 1985, private cars were the most popular form of transport in Metropolis, at just over 6 million trips. However, there was a small but steady decline in car usage to just under 6 million in 2010. Motorbike usage fluctuated, but overall, there was a small increase from about 3.5 million trips in 1985 to just under 4 million in 2010.

Sample Answer for Charts 2 and 3

The pie chart illustrates the proportion of energy consumed by different appliances in an average Australian home. In general, the pie chart shows that temperature control, both for heating and cooling, is the major user, followed by water heating, and the table shows that energy consumed per capita drops as household size increases.

Heating and cooling devices account for almost 40% of total energy, and water heating consumes a quarter of total household power. Other appliances, such as dishwashers, televisions and smaller items, make up 16% of energy consumption. Slightly less than half that amount (7%) is used for both refrigeration and lighting. Standby power comprises a remarkable 3% compared with stoves, ovens and other cooking equipment that expend only 4% of household energy.

The table shows that a single person's electricity usage is 5,000 to 6,500 kWh per annum, whereas two people use a similar amount or not much more. A three-person Australian household typically uses about the same as two people (6,000-8,000) or perhaps up to 10,000 kWh. Six people or more living in the same house only double the consumption of a two-person household.

In summary, all forms of heating and cooling - air temperature, water, refrigeration and cooking - are major consumers of energy in Australian houses, and it is more economical to live in a larger household.

Sample Answer for Chart 4

The bar chart compares the average amount of rain over the year in two cities, San Francisco and Moscow. Overall, although the two cities have approximately the same annual rainfall, the distribution of rain over the year is widely different.

In general, Moscow has a more even yearly rainfall than San Francisco. Rain averages about 50 mm in the months of January to March, dropping to an annual low of just under 40 mm in April. It then rises steadily to a high of about 90 mm in June, and slightly less in July and August, and from that point on it fluctuates, dropping at the end of the year to about 45 mm in December.

In contrast, San Francisco illustrates a different trend. It has a widely fluctuating rainfall, with significantly greater annual variation. December, January and February are by far the rainiest months, averaging just under 120 mm in each of these months. From March onwards, there is a dramatic drop to less than 10 mm in June, and effectively no rain falls in July or August. Rainfall then increases steadily and evenly to the December high of about 110 mm.

The chart shows us that Moscow has the most rain in July and August, at a time when San Francisco is virtually dry.

Sample Answer for Chart 5

The graph gives information about population growth in China and India from the year 2000 with predicted changes to 2050.

In 2000, China's population stood at 1.25 billion and this number rose steadily to where it is currently at around 1.35 billion. It is projected to peak at 1.45 billion in 2025, when the number will level off and start to decline. It is expected that by 2050 the population will have dropped slightly to 1.4 billion.

In contrast, although the population of India started at just one billion in 2000, it has increased rapidly to just under 1.25 billion today. The data indicate it will continue its upward surge, overtaking China in 2030 and reaching a peak of 1.6 billion by 2050.

Overall, the major difference between the two population trends is that the number of people in China is forecast to start falling after 2030 whereas the population of India will continue to soar.

Sample Answer for Chart 6

The bar chart shows the proportion of men and women who taught in seven different faculties of a particular university in 2012.

There was a large gender disparity in some faculties: engineering was dominated by male academics whereas education had the highest percentage of female academics. Notably, 85% of the engineering teachers were male and only 15% female. Three quarters of the academic staff in education were women, with just 25% males.

However, other faculties were more balanced in their composition. In medicine, gender representation was almost equal, while in arts subjects slightly more than half the academics were female (55%). It is interesting to note that business and science had the same proportions of men and women, with 65% male to 35% female academics in those faculties. Law had a slightly higher percentage of women at 40%.

Although the faculties of engineering, business, science and law were still primarily male-dominated in 2012, women made up half the faculty of medicine and were predominant in education and arts.

IELTS Speaking Test

Overview
of the Speaking Test

Format

- The Speaking module lasts for 11–14 minutes, and consists of an introduction section plus three parts.
- The Speaking module is the same for both the Academic and the General Training versions of the test.
- The linguistic challenge of the test increases with each part.
- 口语考试用时 11~14 分钟，包含一个介绍环节和三个主体部分。
- 学术类和培训类的口试内容相同。
- 各部分的语言难度递增。

PART 部分	TIMING 时间	CONTENT 考试内容
INTRODUCTION 介绍环节	30 secs 30 秒	• Name, nationality, ID check • 姓名、国籍、证件查验
PART 1 INTERVIEW 第一部分 问答	3.5–4.5 mins 3.5~4.5 分钟	• 2 or 3 unrelated, short, simple conversations about your personal preferences or experience • 就考生的个人爱好和经历进行两三个互不相关的简短对话
PART 2 LONG TURN 第二部分 长段陈述	3–4 mins 3~4 分钟	• 1 minute of preparation time • 1–2 minutes' talk on a topic which draws on your personal experience • There may be one or two follow-up questions. • 1 分钟的准备时间 • 根据自己的经历，针对一个话题进行 1~2 分钟的陈述 • 可能会有一两个后续问题
PART 3 DISCUSSION 第三部分 讨论	4–5 mins 4~5 分钟	• A discussion in more depth, related to the topic from the Part 2 long turn • 围绕第二部分长段陈述中的话题，进行更深入的讨论

Marking

- You are marked on four criteria
    - fluency and coherence
    - lexical resources (vocabulary)
    - grammatical range and accuracy
    - pronunciation
- These four are equally important to your score, i.e. weight 25% each, and all four criteria are assessed throughout the interview.
- 口语考试按四个标准来评分：
    - 流利性与连贯性
    - 词汇多样性（词汇使用）
    - 语法多样性与准确性
    - 语音
- 这四个标准同等重要，即各占25%的比重。整个口试过程都会根据这四个标准进行测评。

TIPS

- Make sure you arrive early for the Speaking test. Arriving at the last minute means you might be more stressed, this will not help you perform to the best of your ability. Worse still, arriving later than your scheduled interview time might mean you miss your slot altogether.
- Before the test starts, the examiner records a brief introduction, including the date, the location of the test, your name, and his/her name. Use this opportunity to relax and get used to the examiner's voice.
- Give brief replies to the introduction and ID check questions.
- Do not get upset or worried if the examiner stops you from making a long answer during the introduction section. This part is intended to be a brief settling down time, and it is not the time to give a long talk.
- Remember, this test is a conversation. It is acceptable to use an informal speaking style. You do not have to give formal, academic replies to every question.

- 参加口语考试时，要确保提前到场。最后一刻才到达考场，你可能会更紧张，这不利于你发挥出最好的水平。更糟糕的是，如果迟到，你可能无法参加考试。
- 考试正式开始之前，考官会录一段简短的介绍，包含考试日期、考试地点、你的姓名，以及考官的姓名。你应该利用这个机会放松下来并熟悉考官的声音。
- 简要回答这一环节中有关介绍和证件查验的问题。
- 如果考官在介绍环节打断你的长篇回答，无需沮丧或担心。设置这一环节的意图是让考生很快进入状态，而不是长篇作答。
- 记住：口语考试是对话的形式。可以使用非正式的说话方式。不必对每个问题都给予正式的、学术性的回答。

Advice for Chinese candidates

Despite what some people have suggested, your appearance, body language or handshake makes no difference to your score. You are only judged on your communicative ability, so do not worry about those irrelevant factors and focus on the key – communicative ability. If you know someone that did well in their test, they did well because they showed their ability, not because they wore the right clothes.

有人认为个人形象、肢体语言或握手方式对成绩有影响，但事实并非如此。考试只对你的沟通能力进行评估，因此不必担心那些无关的因素，而要专注于考试的关键——沟通能力。你可能认识某个考得不错的人，考得不错是因为他们展现了自己的能力，而不是因为穿戴得体。

Part 1

What to Expect

- In Part 1 of the Speaking test, you will have 2 or 3 short, simple conversations about everyday life.
- The topics of these conversations will not be related to each other.
- 在口语考试的第一部分，会进行两三个关于日常生活的简短对话。
- 这几个对话的主题互不相关。

Topics

Typical **topics** are:

- your house, street or city
- your job or study
- your daily routines: shopping, sleeping, work ...
- things you did when you were a child: school, leisure, helping in the house ...
- things you own: car, bicycle, cell phone, computer ...
- things you do: gardening, sport, reading ...

常见**话题**包括：

- 你所居住的房子、街道或城市
- 你的工作或学习
- 你每天的日常活动：购物、睡觉、工作……
- 你童年时做过的事情：上学、休闲、帮着做家务……
- 你拥有的物品：汽车、自行车、手机、电脑……
- 你做的事情：园艺、体育运动、阅读……

TIP

- Expect the examiner to change the topic two or three times during Part 1 of the test. Listen carefully for each topic. You can ask the examiner to repeat a question if you did not hear clearly.
- 在第一部分考试中，考官会变换两三次话题。仔细听清每一个话题。如果没有听清，你可以要求考官重复问题。

Advice for Chinese candidates

The list of possible topics IELTS might cover is potentially endless, so do not worry about covering everything. These are all everyday topics, and you are not expected to demonstrate expert knowledge in any of these topics. If you practise naturally talking – not memorising answers – about a broad range of topics, developing your skills in fluency and coherence, you will have the confidence and flexibility to adapt to other topics.

雅思口语考试可能出现的话题数不胜数，所以不必担心不能准备得面面俱到。这些都是日常话题，不期望你对任何话题展现出具备专家级的知识。如果能针对广泛的话题练习自然地说话——而不是背诵答案，提高流利性与连贯性的技能，你就会有信心灵活应对其他话题。

Question Types

Typical question types are:

- have you ever ...? (ridden a bike, baked a cake, been to a sports match ...)
- did you ... (learn to play sport, watch TV, live in the country ...) when you were a child?
- which do you prefer? (tea or coffee, night-time or daytime, wet or dry weather ...)
- do you like ...? (playing sport, sleeping, listening to music, shopping for clothes ...)
- do you think that ...? (children should have a pet, the news is important ...)
- when did you ...? (start learning English, go to your first movie ...)

常见问题类型包括：

- 你曾经（做过……）吗？（骑过自行车，烤过蛋糕，参加过体育比赛……）
- 你小时候（做过……）吗？（学过体育运动，看过电视，在农村住过……）
- 你更喜欢哪个？（茶还是咖啡，晚上还是白天，湿润的天气还是干燥的天气……）
- 你喜欢……吗？（参加体育运动，睡觉，听音乐，买衣服……）
- 你认为……吗？（儿童应该养宠物，这条消息重要……）
- 你是什么时候……的？（开始学英语，第一次去看电影……）

TIPS

- Listen carefully to the questions and try to answer what you were asked.
- Don't worry if the examiner's next question does not follow your previous answer. In Part 1, the examiner must ask the questions written on the paper; he cannot change his questions according to your answers.
- If your answer is negative, for example you have never ridden a bike, or you don't like cooking, or you can't remember when you first started doing something, don't worry. This is a test of English conversation, not a test of your experiences and opinions! A negative answer is just as good as a positive one. In both cases, **give a reason** for your answer.
- In general, your answers in Part 1 should be 2 or 3 sentences. One- or two-word answers are not sufficient, and equally the examiner may interrupt you if you give a very long answer. Aim for something in between.

- 仔细听问题，尽量就问题作答。
- 如果考官提出的下一个问题与你前面的回答没有关联，不必担心。在第一部分中，考官必须按照试卷上的问题提问，不能根据你的回答改变问题。
- 如果你的回答是否定的——例如你从未骑过自行车，不喜欢烹饪或不记得第一次做某事是什么时候，不必担心。这是英语对话考试，而不是个人经历和看法考试。否定的回答与肯定的回答效果相同。无论是肯定还是否定，都要在回答中**提供理由**。
- 总体来说，第一部分考试中的回答长度应为两三个句子。一两个单词的回答不够充分。同理，如果回答太长，考官可能会打断你。应避免出现这两种极端情况。

Advice for Chinese candidates

Be careful of basic grammar mistakes. Too many of these and your speaking score will be limited, for instance:

1 I'*m* still keep in contact with them (correction = 'I still keep in ...')

2 ... in *recently* two years (correction = '... in the last two years')

3 I cannot *found* it (correction = '... cannot find it')

Polish you knowledge on aspects of grammar – this resource can help you:

http://learnenglish.britishcouncil.org/

注意基础性语法错误。过多的这类错误会影响口语成绩，例如：

1 I'*m* still keep in contact with them（正确的说法："I still keep in ..."）

2 ... in *recently* two years（正确的说法：“... in the last two years”）

3 I cannot *found* it（正确的说法：“... cannot find it”）

增强语法方面的知识，下面的学习资源可以为你提供帮助：http://learnenglish.britishcouncil.org/

Strategies for Improving Answers

Strategy 1: Extending Answers

Activity 1

1.1 *Match the questions and the answers. Look carefully to see how the speaker has extended his or her answers.*

1	Have you ever cooked a meal for your family?	**A**	Well, I suppose we do, but I think it's OK as long as we make sure we get exercise as well. I think we're all probably too sedentary nowadays.
2	Which do you prefer, getting an email or a text message?	**B**	Oh yes, I LOVE it! It's my favourite free time activity. I think I spend far too much money, though, and I'd spend more if I had it!
3	When did you watch your first movie in a cinema?	**C**	Oh, I prefer emails, because I work in front of a computer all day so this is easy for me. I'm not very good at texting. I know I'm a bit old-fashioned.
4	Do you like shopping for clothes?	**D**	Well, I haven't actually. My mum tends to do all the cooking in our house. But I did bake some biscuits once. They were terrible! No-one would eat them.
5	Do you think that we spend too much time sitting in front of computers?	**E**	I can't really remember; it was so long ago. But I **do** remember very clearly going to see *Teenage Mutant Ninja Turtles*. I was so scared that my mum had to take me out of the movie.

1.2 *Match each of the answers in Activity 1.1 to a strategy from this list. Some answers may include more than one strategy.*

1	Extending the answer by giving a reason or an example	
2	Telling a story about a personal experience	
3	Adding a personal opinion	
4	Buying thinking time at the start of the answer	
5	Adding emphasis to the answer	
6	Telling a joke or a funny story	

Strategy 2: Pronunciation

TIPS

- 25% of your score for IELTS Speaking is for pronunciation. It is very hard to change your first language phonemes (sounds) and accent, but here are a few items to think about.
    - **Speed** – Not too slow, BUT **not too fast**! You will be penalised if you speak too slowly, as this is an indicator of a lack of fluency. Equally be aware that speaking too quickly might affect the clarity of your speech. Try to speak naturally and at a steady pace.
    - **Pausing and word stress** – Use pauses and stressed words to break up your speaking. You will **not** be penalised if you pause occasionally; in fact, you **will** be penalised if there are **no** pauses in your speaking. Check the correct word stress in a dictionary where you are unsure. Making errors in word stress can cause confusion for a listener.
    - **Intonation** (voice going up and down) – Try to **vary** your intonation. If you want to stress something, speak louder and use a rise/fall intonation. (e.g. It was **lovely!**)
    - **Sentence stress** is another way to add meaning to what you say. You can say the same sentence in different ways but change the meaning by stressing different words. Think about the difference between these sentences:
        - *I said she might consider a NEW car.*
        - *I said she might consider a new CAR.*
- **Accent** is not directly assessed. It is only a factor if your accent affects how intelligibly or clearly you speak. There is no preference for a specific accent, for example British or American accent. Any is acceptable.

- 语音占雅思口语评分比重的 25%。要改变母语的音位（发音）和口音是很难的，但可以考虑从以下几方面进行提高。
    - **语速**——不要太慢，但也**不要太快**！语速太慢表明缺乏流利性，将被扣分。同理，要明白语速太快可能会影响话语的清晰度。要尽量说得自然、匀速。
    - **停顿与单词重音**——使用停顿与重读单词将话语切分成段。如果偶尔出现暂停，**不会**被扣分。实际上，如果在表述过程中**没有**任何停顿，**将会**被扣分。如果不确定单词重音的位置，应查词典。单词重音读错会让听者困惑不解。
    - **语调**（声音的高低变化）——要尝试着**变化**语调。如果要强调某一点，提高音量并使用升调/降调。（例如：It was **lovely!**）
    - **句子重音**也能为说话内容增添含义。你可以用不同的方式说同一个句子，但强调不同的单词便改变了句子的意思。思考下列句子的不同：
        - *I said she might consider a NEW car.*
        - *I said she might consider a new CAR.*
- **口音**不是雅思口试的直接测评因素，除非你的口音影响到了表述的可辨性与清晰度。考试不偏向任何一种口音，例如英式或美式口音。任何口音均可。

Advice for Chinese candidates

When you are speaking and learning new words, make sure you get the basic sounds right – not paying attention to the sounds can lead to errors that can confuse meaning. For instance,

1 'My city is famous for the snakes we eat.' – should this be 'snakes' or 'snacks'?
2 'Near my flat is a park. It is a nice place to work.' – should this be 'work' or 'walk'?
3 'It is very quiet at net.' – should this be 'net' or 'night'?

在说话和学习新单词时，要注意基本读音的正确。不注意发音可能会造成错误，产生歧义。例如：

1 "My city is famous for the snakes we eat."——应该是"snakes"还是"snacks"？
2 "Near my flat is a park. It is a nice place to work."——应该是"work"还是"walk"？
3 "It is very quiet at net."——应该是"net"还是"night"？

Activity 2

🎧 001 *Listen to the recording of Part 1 of the Speaking test.* ***NB:*** *the introduction and identification part is* ***not*** *included in this recording.*

2.1 *Listen the first time without reading the transcript.*

What questions did the examiner ask? How did the candidate extend his answers?

2.2 *Listen a second time. Read the transcript this time if you wish to. Tick each of the strategies from the list above that the candidate has used to extend his answers. Mark those places on the transcript.*

Can you add any more strategies to the list in Activity 1.2?

2.3 *Listen a third time, and read the transcript as you listen. On the transcript, mark some of the words that the speaker has* ***stressed****, and some of the places where he has* ***paused****.*

Advice from Chinese candidates

建议有条件一定要跟老外练练。另外推荐大家看看经典的流行美剧。

——雅思高分考生　王　茜

Part 2

What to Expect

- In Part 2 of the Speaking test, you will be given 1 minute to prepare a 1–2 minutes' talk on a topic. This topic will be related to your personal experience or your dreams for the future.
- After your long turn, the examiner will ask one or two rounding off questions.
- 在口语考试第二部分中，会给你 1 分钟时间来就某个话题准备 1~2 分钟的陈述。这个话题可能是你的个人经历或是你未来的梦想。
- 你做完长段陈述后，考官会问一两个问题来结束本部分考试。

Topics

Typical **topics** are:

- ... (a book, movie, TV programme ...) you like / have watched
- a time when you ... (got some help from someone, worked very hard to achieve a goal, gave someone some advice ...)
- ... (a place, building) you have visited / **would like to visit**
- a sports event, family occasion, happy day ...
- a person who ... (you like, admire, **would like to meet,** is important to you ...)
- an object / a thing ... (you really like, you bought recently, you **would like to own** ...)

常见**话题**包括：

- 你喜欢 / 看过的……（一本书，一部电影，一个电视节目……）
- 一次你……（获得别人帮助，为了达到某个目标而努力，给别人建议……）的经历
- 你参观过 / **想参观的**……（一个地方，一座建筑……）
- 一次体育赛事，一个家庭的重要时刻，愉快的一天……
- 一个……（你喜欢，你钦佩，**你想见**，对你来说很重要……）的人
- （你非常喜欢，你最近购买，**你想拥有**）的一件东西 / 事情

TIP

- Read your topic carefully: most topics ask you to talk about your past experience, but some of them ask you to talk about your future dreams or plans (see the **bolded** topics above). This will affect the verb tenses (time references) in your response.
- 仔细阅读题目：大部分题目要求谈论你的过往经历，但有些要求谈论你的未来梦想或计划（参见上文**加粗的**题目）。这将影响你在回答中所使用的动词时态（即时间参照）。

Advice for Chinese candidates

There is a lot of focus on an examiner's facial expression and gestures to tell whether he/she likes what you're saying and will award a positive score. Do not be concerned with this. An examiner's apparent friendliness or detachment means nothing about the score you will be given. They are trained not to give feedback, encouragement or signals of this nature. Just focus on performing your best.

很多人关注考官的面部表情和手势，以此判断考官是否满意自己所说的内容，是否会给予正面的评分。不要顾虑这一点。考官表现出来的友善或冷漠与你的得分无关。考官受过培训，不会给予反馈、鼓励或类似的示意。你只需集中精力发挥出自己的最佳水平。

Strategies for Improving Answers

Strategy 1: Using Your Planning Time

- The topic card will include some cue questions to help you to plan your answer. These cue questions typically ask 'wh' questions (when, where, why ...) and then there will be a final, opinion cue question at the end.
- 话题卡上会包含几个提示性问题，以帮助你组织自己的回答。这些提示性问题通常是特殊疑问句（什么时间，什么地点，什么原因……）。最后会用一个收尾的提示性问题来询问你的观点。

Example Topic Card:
Achieving a Goal

Talk about a time when you had to work very hard to achieve a goal.

You should say:

- What the goal was
- When this happened
- What you did to achieve the goal

And talk about why the goal was important for you.

TIPS

- If you don't understand a word on the topic card, or you want to check the task, ask immediately. The examiner will give you a brief answer to help you to understand. Don't waste time wondering what the topic means!
- The cue questions on the topic card are included to help you to prepare your answer. However, you will **not** be penalised if your talk does not follow all the cues on the card. It is more important to talk fluently and to keep going for 2 minutes than to cover all the points on the topic card.
- Remember, this is a test of speaking, not of your experience! Do not panic if you have no experience with the topic. For example, you can talk about someone else's experience instead of your own, or say that you can't remember a funny movie, but you do remember a sad one.
- Do not worry if the examiner stops you. You are allowed to speak for only 2 minutes.

- 如果不明白话题卡上的某个单词，或者想要明确陈述任务，应马上提问。考官会做简短回答帮助你理解。不要在弄清题目意思上浪费时间！
- 话题卡上的提示性问题旨在帮助你准备作答。但是，如果你的陈述没有全部按照卡上的提示来作答，**不会**被扣分。流利、不间断的两分钟作答要比把话题卡上的信息点说完更重要。
- 记住：这是口语考试，而不是个人经历考试！如果没有与话题相关的经历，不必慌张。例如，你可以谈一谈别人而不是自己的经历，或者告诉考官你想不起一部有趣的电影，但倒记得一部伤感的电影。
- 如果考官打断你，不要担心。只给你 2 分钟的陈述时间。

Activity 3

Topic Card 1

Talk about a time when you had to work very hard to achieve a goal.

You should say:

- What the goal was
- When this happened
- What you did to achieve the goal

and talk about why the goal was important for you.

Topic Card 2

Talk about a story in the news that made a big impression on you.

You should say:

- where you read or heard this story
- what the story was about
- when the story happened

and talk about why the story made such an impression on you.

Topic Card 3

Talk about a city you would like to visit one day.

You should say:

- which city this is
- who you would like to go with
- what you would like to do there

and talk about why you would choose this city to visit.

Topic Card 4

Talk about a person you know who you admire very much.

You should say:

- who this person is
- what he/she works at, or studies
- when and where you met him/her

and talk about why you admire him/her so much.

3.1 *Look at the sample topic cards above, and for each one, think about the following questions:*

1 Is this topic asking me about:

A my past experience or a past event?

B what I do every day, or facts about someone?

C my future dreams or plans?

2 What verb tenses or time references should I use?

3 What stories or events in my life relate to this topic?

3.2 *Then spend 1 minute (time yourself!) planning each topic. Write down a few key words to help you remember your plan.*

Strategy 2: Extending Answers

- Some candidates struggle to speak for 2 minutes, while others have so much to say that they have barely begun when the time is up! Part of this is your personality; some people like talking more than others. However, everyone should try to speak for 2 minutes in the IELTS Speaking test.
- 有些考生难以说够 2 分钟，而有些考生要说的话很多，时间结束时还未进入话题。部分原因与个人性格有关，有些人比较健谈，有些人则不。然而，每位考生在雅思口语考试中都应尽量陈述 2 分钟。

TIPS

- The best way to expand your answer in Part 2 is to give more **details** or **extra stories** about each part of the topic.
- Remember that you do NOT have to cover all of the points on the topic card, so if you run out of time before you cover everything, or you miss something out, you will not be penalised for this.
- Remember coherence is important – this is the logical flow and structure of what you are saying. Introduce each new bullet point before you address it, in different ways, so your listener knows what you are talking about. Linking words and expressions are important here.
- Use the preparation time effectively. Practise noting down ideas, key vocabulary, likely tenses and possible linking expressions – this might seem a lot but practise making notes, not complete sentences, and make sure these are easy to read. Mind maps help to make notes easy to follow.

- 在第二部分考试中，展开回答最好的方式是就话题的各个部分提供更多的细节或额外的叙述。
- 记住，无需涵盖话题卡上所有的信息点，因此如果时间结束时未能涵盖所有内容或有所遗漏，你不会因此被扣分。
- 记住，连贯性十分重要，这是指话语的逻辑性与结构。在谈每个新的信息点前应先以不同的方式进行介绍，这样听者能够了解你打算谈论的内容。关联词语在这里十分重要。
- 有效利用准备时间。练习记录想法、关键词语、可能用到的时态及关联词语。这些内容看似很多，但要练习做笔记而不是写下完整的句子，并且所做的笔记应该便于阅读。思维导图有助于让笔记易于阅读。

Activity 4

4.1 *Look again at the topic card about achieving a goal. Here is an example of some notes that someone made for that topic:*

Candidate Notes:
Achieving a Goal

Goal:

- What - a 4-day walk in the mountains
- When - last year, March
- What I did - walked every day, swam, took long walks sometimes, increased the speed and distance
- Why - great holiday with my husband, wanted to enjoy it, personal achievement

4.2 *Now look at the 2 monologues, which are both based on the notes above about a personal goal. In Response B, mark all the places where the speaker has extended her answers, and notice* ***how*** *she did this.*

A One of my recent goals was to go on a 4-day walk in the mountains in the South Island. This happened in March of last year. To prepare for this goal, I did a lot of exercise. I walked every day, and I gradually increased the speed and the distance I was walking. Some days we did quite long walks. I also went swimming three times a week.

This was an important goal for me because I wanted to have a great holiday with my husband, and I wanted to enjoy the walk and not be too tired. It was also a personal achievement for me.

B One of my recent goals was to go on a 4-day walk in the mountains in the South Island. This is one of the famous walks in our country, and it is a very beautiful walk round some bays by the ocean. We planned to stay in hotels each night, so it was going to be a great holiday for my husband and me, but I needed to get fit enough to enjoy it first!

I did lots of exercise and training to prepare for this goal. When I started, I was reasonably fit, but I knew I needed to get a lot fitter, so I did a lot of walking. At first, the 8 km circle route near my house was really hard for me, and it took about 2 hours, but by the end I could do it easily in a much shorter time. On the weekends I went for longer walks with my husband. We used to walk to the Botanical Gardens, which was a long way, but we got to have lunch in a café when we got there, so that was fun! In fact, preparing for the goal was generally a lot of fun, and I found that I had much more energy as I got fitter, too. My feet and legs started to hurt with all the exercise, so I went to swimming classes three times a week. I had to get up at 6 am for this! But it was worth it. It really improved my balance and stamina, and it helped those sore muscles, too.

This goal was important because I really wanted to go on this holiday with my husband. Reaching it also gave me a great sense of personal achievement. I was very proud of myself! And of course I was a lot fitter by the end of the training. I resolved to keep up my level of fitness, but unfortunately, I haven't managed to do that. Still, at least I know that I can do it again if I want to, now.

Activity 5

5.1 *Read the topic card below and the notes that the candidate took about the topic.*

5.2 *Listen to the recording of Part 2 of the Speaking test. As you listen, think about the ways that the speaker has extended his notes to make a full answer.*

5.3 *Now, listen again, and mark:*

- Some of the places where the candidate used **pauses** to make a natural break in the story
- Some of the places where the candidate **varied his intonation** (his voice went up or down). What is the effect of this?

Topic Card: Movie

Describe a movie that you watched that you really enjoyed.

You should say:

- What the movie was called
- When and where you saw the movie
- Who you saw it with

And talk about why you enjoyed it so much.

Candidate Notes: Movie

- *Avatar*
- watched twice – 2D and 3D
- with my kids
- story – blue people, humans try to take over the planet
- production – visual effects – plants, floating islands
- story – the message – people living with nature vs greedy humans

Advice for Chinese candidates

Many candidates try to memorise their answers for the Speaking test, particularly for Part 2. We do not recommend this approach. Examiners are trained to identify this. Focus on producing your genuine performance. Use your 1-minute preparation time as effectively as possible. Plan your ideas using bullet points as above, or using a mind map.

很多考生试图背诵口语考试的答案，特别是第二部分的答案。我们并不推荐这种备考方式。考官受过培训，可以识别这种情况。应注重表现出自己的真实水平。尽可能有效地利用 1 分钟的准备时间。整理思路时可使用如上所示的项目符号，亦可使用思维导图。

TIP

- There are times when you are speaking that you will not be able to remember the specific word you want to use. This is natural. This happens to everyone. DO NOT GIVE UP if this happens. Try to explain what you mean, even if you cannot remember the specific word. This is an important skill called paraphrasing. You could use phrases like this:
  - It's like a ...
  - It's something you use to ...
  - It's a way of ...
  - It's a place that ...
  - It's a kind of ...
- 表述过程中有时会记不起自己想用的某个单词。这很正常。每个人都会遇到。如果这种情况发生，不要放弃。尽量解释你要表达的意思，即使不记得这个具体的单词。这是一种十分重要的技能，叫作同义转换。可以使用下列表达：
  - It's like a ...
  - It's something you use to ...
  - It's a way of ...
  - It's a place that ...
  - It's a kind of ...

Strategy 3: Using Appropriate and Idiomatic Vocabulary

- 25% of your score for IELTS Speaking is for vocabulary. Extending your vocabulary will help you to get a better score in the Speaking test.
- 口试中词汇占总分的 25%。扩展词汇量有助于在口试中取得更好的分数。

Advice for Chinese candidates

Many candidates have been told to use advanced high-level words or profound vocabulary – this is misleading advice. Most candidates who follow this advice usually use these words in an inappropriate way. Focus instead on precise meaning. Think about the difference in these two sentences:

1 David is a good **teacher** at work. I have learnt a lot from him.

2 David is a good **mentor** at work. I have learnt a lot from him.

The meaning of these two sentences is very similar, but which sentence provides a more specific description of the relationship with David?

很多考生被告知要使用高级的复杂单词或深奥的词汇。这种建议是误导。大多数采用这一建议的考生使用这些词汇的方式通常并不恰当。考生应注重词义的精确性，而不是一味追求用高级词汇。思考下面两个句子的不同之处：

1 David is a good **teacher** at work. I have learnt a lot from him.

2 David is a good **mentor** at work. I have learnt a lot from him.

这两句话的意思非常相近，但哪一句能更具体地表述说话人与David的关系呢？

TIPS

- Having a larger vocabulary will help you to express your ideas more clearly and accurately, and this will also improve your score for fluency and coherence.
- However, you should not try to sound like a dictionary! Remember, this is a test of conversation, and your vocabulary needs to be **appropriate** as well as varied.
- It is better to record and learn vocabulary by topic or theme, as opposed to long random lists. Try to regularly brainstorm vocabulary on specific topics, or perhaps you can use mind maps to do this.
- **Idiomatic language** is more appropriate than formal, written language. This is a useful website for idiomatic expressions: www.bbc.co.uk/worldservice/learningenglish/language/theenglishwespeak/

- 拥有较大的词汇量将有助于更清晰、准确地表达想法，也有助于提高在流利性与连贯性方面的得分。
- 然而，要避免让自己听起来像词典一样！记住，这是一项对话测试，你所使用的词汇既要多样也应**恰当**。
- 最好按照话题或主题记录和学习词汇，而不是使用冗长而任意的词汇表。尝试定期运用头脑风暴或者可以用思维导图针对一些具体话题进行词汇练习。
- 相对于正式、书面用语，**习语**更为得当。以下网站有助于学习习语：www.bbc.co.uk/worldservice/learningenglish/language/theenglishwespeak/

Advice for Chinese candidates

Be careful to use vocabulary correctly – think about the correct choice from word families and collocation. For instance, can you see the errors here?

1 It's a kind of remember.
2 The result of studying abroad means a problem about financial.
3 The weather is not very well.

You should notice:

1 'Remember' was used incorrectly instead of 'memory'.
2 The wrong choice from the word family was chosen; 'finances' fits better than 'financial'.
3 'Weather' collocates with 'good' so this should be 'The weather is not very good.'

注意正确使用词汇：想想如何从同族词中选择正确的词以及词的搭配。例如，你能发现下文中的错误吗?

1 It's a kind of remember.
2 The result of studying abroad means a problem about financial.
3 The weather is not very well.

你应该意识到了：

1 "Remember"的用法不对，应改为"memory"。
2 从同族词中选择了错误的词，"finances"更恰当。
3 "Weather"应该与"good"搭配，所以应该是"The weather is not very good."

Activity 6

6.1 *Choose the better of the following responses.*

A I would like to visit Rome for three reasons. Firstly, it is a prestigious city because of its ancient architecture and its cultural significance as the centre of the Roman Catholic religion. Secondly, the city is prominent because of its alluring art works including the majestic Sistine Chapel. Finally, it enjoys distinction for its cuisine and its wine. ...

B A city I'd like to visit is Rome. I've always wanted to go there, mainly because of the architecture. I'd really like to see the Coliseum. The idea of those ancient gladiators fighting in the arena really captures my imagination. And, of course, like everyone else, I'd want to visit the famous art works, especially the Sistine Chapel. The photos I've seen of that are awe-inspiring, and the food and the wine are a big drawcard, too. I'd have to try ...

6.2 *Read the two answers again, and underline the idiomatic language that the speaker uses in Answer B.*

02 **6.3** *Listen to and read the transcript of the* ***sample Part 2 Speaking test*** *again, and underline the idiomatic language that the candidate uses in this Part 2 talk.*

TIP

- In Activity 6 you will have noticed a technique for sequencing ideas, that is, using 'firstly', 'secondly' and 'finally'. This is a common technique, so perfectly acceptable, but do not overuse this. There are other techniques to consider to help link ideas effectively and to avoid repeating the same words. Techniques such as:
  - **Referencing**, using various pronouns. For example, 'I was very happy to receive this award, and I thanked my colleagues. Without ***them*** I would not have been considered for ***this***.'
  - **Signposting**, using various expressions. For example, ***'Yes, I agree, because*** ...' Or 'In my view ***there are probably 2 main differences*** ...'
  - Using **synonyms** or **substitution**. For example, 'I think famous people deserve a private life. But the fact is ***celebrities*** also sell newspapers.'
- 在上文 Activity 6 中，你应该已经注意到了一种罗列观点的技巧，即使用"firstly""secondly"和"finally"。这是一种常用的技巧，因此完全可以接受，但不要过度使用。要有效连接多个观点，还有其他技巧可供考虑，以避免重复使用相同的词。这些技巧包括：
  - 使用不同的代词进行**指代**。例如，"I was very happy to receive this award, and I thanked my colleagues. Without ***them*** I would not have been considered for ***this***."
  - 使用不同的表达方式进行**指示**。例如，"***Yes, I agree, because*** ..." 或者 "In my view ***there are probably 2 main differences*** ..."。
  - 使用**同义词或替代词**。例如，"I think famous people deserve a private life. But the fact is ***celebrities*** also sell newspapers."

Advice for Chinese candidates

Remember demonstrating a range of grammar is one of the key factors in hoping for a high score. Look back at the topic card in Activity 5, think about what difference tenses might be used in an answer for this. Possible tenses:

✓ Past simple: *I went to the cinema to see this 3 years ago.*

✓ Past continuous: *I was studying at university at the time.*

✓ Present perfect: *I have seen it at least 10 times now.*

✓ Present simple: *I like the mix of humour and emotions; I always cry when I watch this.*

记住：要取得高分，展现语法的多样性是其中一个关键因素。回顾上文 Activity 5 中的话题卡，思考对此卡作答时可能用到哪些不同的时态。可能用到的时态：

✓ 一般过去时：*I went to the cinema to see this 3 years ago.*

✓ 过去进行时：*I was studying at university at the time.*

✓ 现在完成时：*I have seen it at least 10 times now.*

✓ 一般现在时：*I like the mix of humour and emotions; I always cry when I watch this.*

Advice from Chinese candidates

多阅读国外的新闻，要出声读，培养出好的语感。

——雅思考分考生　刁小芸

Part 3

What to Expect

- In Part 3 of the Speaking test, you will have a conversation related to the Part 2 topic.
- Part 3 of the Speaking test is the most challenging, and it is here that higher-level candidates have the opportunity to communicate more complex ideas and use a wider range of language structures and vocabulary to express general, rather than personal, ideas.
- 口语考试的第三部分，是针对第二部分话题的相关内容展开的对话。
- 口语考试第三部分是难度最大的。正是在这一部分，高水平的考生有机会表达更复杂的想法，使用更多样化的语言结构和词汇来表达普遍的而不是个人的观点。

TIP

- If you are aiming for a higher-level score above Band 6, you need to focus much of your preparation time on managing the challenges in Part 3 of the test.
- 如果你的目标分数是6分以上，你应该把大量备考时间着重用于应对第三部分考试的挑战。

Topics

- The topic in Part 3 will be related to the topic of your long turn (Part 2). The long turn is a personal story, and in Part 3 you will be asked to have a general discussion on a related topic.
- 第三部分中的话题与你长段陈述（即第二部分）的话题有关。长段陈述是关于个人的故事，而在第三部分中你将就一个相关的话题进行综合性讨论。

Activity 7

Match each long turn topic with the Part 3 discussion topics.

1	a movie you enjoyed	A	education styles; changes in education
2	your ideal job	B	fashion and the fashion industry
3	a time when you learned something new	C	the place of movies in our lives; changes in movie watching
4	a person you admire	D	employment and careers; planning for a career
5	a piece of clothing that you enjoy wearing	E	personal qualities that others admire; personal reputation

TIP

- It is important to listen carefully to the question that the examiner uses to open the Part 3 discussion, and then to answer that question.
- 要注意听考官开始第三部分讨论时所提的问题，然后针对问题作答。

Question Types

Questions in Part 3 may ask you to:

- List items – this is often the opening question
- Compare – older vs younger people, men vs women, the past vs the present ...
- Speculate about future changes – in technology, in communication ...
- Give your opinion – some people think that ..., do you agree with this?
- Give reasons for your opinion ...

第三部分的问题可能会要求你：

- 罗列事物——这种问题常用于第一个问题
- 进行比较——老年人与年轻人，男性与女性，过去与现在……
- 推测未来的变化——在技术方面，在通讯方面……
- 表明你的观点——有人认为……，你同意这种观点吗?
- 给出你持这种观点的理由……

Advice for Chinese candidates

Candidates are sometimes worried about expressing an opinion in the IELTS Writing or Speaking that the examiner might not agree with, and as a result give them a lower score. Do not worry about this. Examiners are only interested in your language and your ability to communicate. That is all they are assessing and judging. Express your opinions, talk about your interests and give examples from your experience.

有时考生担心在雅思写作或口语考试中考官可能不赞同自己表达的观点，并因此打分较低。无需担心这一点。考官只关注你的语言和沟通能力，这是他们评估和判断的所有内容。表达你的观点，谈论你的兴趣，从个人经历中举例说明。

TIPS

- Be ready to share your opinions. Keeping up to date with current affairs can help you with ideas for things to say. Follow news channels like the BBC or Voice of America, which can help you keep up to date and also help broaden your vocabulary.
- The examiner will listen to your responses, and will guide the discussion according to what you say. He or she may say something like 'You've talked about ... Can you give another example?' OR 'Why do you think this?'

- 要为分享观点而做好准备。紧跟时事有助于提供谈论的内容。关注类似 BBC 或美国之音的新闻频道，有助于及时了解新闻，也有助于扩大词汇量。
- 考官将听你作答，并根据你的回答引导讨论。例如，考官可能会说 "You've talked about ... Can you give another example?" 或 "Why do you think this?"

Activity 8

- Here are some of the language functions that are tested in Part 3 of the test:

i.	List	iv.	Give opinions
ii.	Compare	v.	Talk about changes
iii.	Speculate	vi.	Give reasons

- 下面是口语考试第三部分测试的一些语言功能：

i.	列举	iv.	表明观点
ii.	比较	v.	谈论变化
iii.	推测	vi.	提供理由

Advice for Chinese candidates

In Part 3 of the Speaking test it is especially important to try to extend your answers:

✓ Answer the question directly.
✓ Ask yourself why or how (and explain in detail).
✓ Share some evidence or give an example.
✓ Perhaps mention an alternative or opposite answer.
✓ If it's relevant, share some of your experience too.

在口语考试的第三部分中，尽力拓展回答尤为重要：

✓ 直接回答问题。
✓ 自问“为什么”或“怎么样”（给出详细解释）。
✓ 分享一些论据或举例说明。
✓ 可能提及一个不同选择或相反答案。
✓ 如果相关，同时分享一些个人经历。

For example:

Examiner: Who do you think should take responsibility for helping homeless people in China?

Candidate: That's a big question, and a big responsibility. There are various groups involved already, like charities, and obviously government agencies. The government is perhaps best placed to do this. They might do more to arrange temporary housing options.

8.1 *Read the excerpt from a Part 3 discussion below.*

- Use the list above to indicate the examiner's questions – what is the candidate being **asked to do**?
- Think about **language** – what language is the candidate using to compare, give opinions, qualify his/her ideas and speculate?

- Think about **vocabulary** – what useful words or expressions can you find in this sample? Look for **idiomatic** expressions. Remember that idioms in English are often very short and simple, e.g. put someone else first, or look up to someone.

8.2 *Now read the transcript again, and notice how the examiner has guided the candidate to give more details or to extend his/her answers. Notice how the candidate's language has become more complex towards the end of the test.*

Excerpt from Part 3

Examiner: We've been talking about a person who you admire, and now we're going to have a more general discussion about this. Let's think about personal qualities. What qualities make a person admirable?

Candidate: Oh, well, um ... first of all, I think honesty is a very important quality that most people admire, oh, and also, kindness. My friend was very kind to me, and I think that being kind is one of the most admirable qualities in a friend, or in anyone, really. Sometimes it's very hard to put other people first, especially if it is inconvenient, and people who are prepared to do that are very rare and special people.

Examiner: I see. Can you think of any other qualities that are considered admirable?

Candidate: Well, I suppose that competence is always admirable.

Examiner: Yes, can you tell me any more about that?

Candidate: Most people look up to those who do things well. Successful people are usually admired, aren't they? It doesn't really matter what they have succeeded in. Oh, and I suppose that hard work is part of that, so being hard-working can make you an admirable person.

Examiner: Do you think that men and women tend to respect different qualities?

Candidate: Oh, I'm not sure. I think that men probably admire competence more than women do, and maybe women prefer personal qualities, such as kindness.

Examiner: Why do you think that is?

Candidate: Well I suppose it's because of their traditional roles. You know, women traditionally looked after the children and men worked to earn the money, so they grew to admire different qualities. Oh, and I think women are more prepared to acknowledge their feelings, so maybe that's why they admire those qualities. But I also think this is changing and that men and women are becoming more similar in their work and attitudes.

Examiner: Right, let's move on to think about the media and admirable people. Do you think that the media has a big influence on the qualities that people admire?

Candidate: Oh, yes, I do. I think it has a huge influence, especially with people like sports stars and movie actors.

Examiner: Why is that?

Candidate: Well, we see them all the time, and we read about them on the Internet, and so we're all encouraged to admire the same people, in fact to think the same way.

Examiner: OK, and do you think this will continue to change in the future?

Candidate: Yes, I'm sure it will. With the growth of social media websites, I think it's going to become harder and harder to be an individual, and to have your own opinions, unless you cut yourself off altogether of course. I think it could become quite a serious problem, if the media is able to control and influence global opinions and attitudes.

Activity 9

03 *Now listen to the recording of Part 3 of a sample Speaking test.*

9.1 *Listen the first time, without the transcript, and notice:*

- The link in topic between Part 2 and Part 3.
- The language functions that the examiner is testing – use the list from Activity 8 to help you.
- How the examiner guides and extends the candidate's responses.

9.2 *Now, listen again, and read the transcript as you do so. Highlight:*

- The examiner's questions – what is the candidate being asked to do?
- Language – the language the candidate is using to compare, give opinions, qualify his ideas and speculate.
- Useful vocabulary and idiomatic expressions.
- The places where the examiner has guided the candidate.

Advice for Chinese candidates

If the examiner asks you to discuss a topic you are not familiar with, do not be afraid to say this is a topic you have not thought about before. Do this and then try to think through the topic from different perspectives – what are the causes, the effects, the possible solutions, etc. IELTS is not a test of your knowledge. It is a test of your communicative ability. The test isn't necessarily assessing **what** you say (though it must be relevant to the question), but **how** you say it.

如果考官要求你讨论一个并不熟悉的话题，不要担心，可以直接说这个话题你没有思考过，然后尽量从不同的角度思考这一话题——原因、影响、可能的解决方案是什么等。雅思考试测试的不是你的知识面，而是沟通能力。考试不一定评估你的**表达内容**（但必须与问题相关），而是评估你的**表述方式**。

Again, consider this example:

Examiner: Some people choose to have a guide when they go to an unfamiliar place. Do you think this improves the quality of the experience?

Candidate: I have not travelled anywhere so I do not have any experience of a guide. I think it will be useful as guides generally have more knowledge of a specific area, and the special places within that region. But I have heard that sometimes guides can take visitors to specific shops or hotels that they can earn money from. This can create a negative experience of a place so you have to find reliable people to be a guide.

Activity 10

04 *Listen again to the recording of the entire Speaking test and consider these questions:*

1 What are my best skills in speaking?

2 What parts of this test will I find easier?

3 Which area is my weakest?

A fluency and coherence

B grammar

C vocabulary

D pronunciation

4 What can I do to help myself to improve in this area?

Advice for Chinese candidates

Record yourself speaking. This will help you understand your strengths and weaknesses better. Practise answering some IELTS-related questions. Listen to the recording and transcribe it, word for word. Analyse what you said carefully, try to identify any errors in grammar, vocabulary or pronunciation and ways in which you could say something more effectively, i.e. use more effective grammar or vocabulary. Ask someone else to check it if possible too.

对自己的讲话进行录音。这将有助于更好地了解自己的优势与不足。练习回答与雅思考试有关的问题。播放录音，把录音内容逐词写出来。仔细分析你的讲话，尽量找出语法、词汇或发音方面的错误以及更有效的表述方式——即更有效的语法形式或词汇。如有可能，请他人协助检查。

Practice Tests

Academic Test 1

LISTENING

SECTION 1 *Questions 1–10*

Complete the notes below.

Write **NO MORE THAN TWO WORDS AND/OR A NUMBER** *for each answer.*

MARINA RESTAURANT AND RECEPTION ROOMS

Example	*Answer*
• Internet advertisement for	casual staff

- Jobs available: **1** ....
- Duties: wash dishes
  help the chef
  2 prepare .... and other cold food
- Availability: **3** Saturday, Sunday and .... nights
- Hourly adult rate: **4** $ ....
- Start time: **5** at .... p.m. (meal provided beforehand)
- Uniform: (own) strong shoes, shirt, trousers;
  6 (supplied) apron and ....
- Start date: **7** 14th ....
- Appointment: **8** Lola .... 4.30 p.m. Thursday
- Bring: **9** CV and ...., if available
  10 passport and .... number

SECTION 2 *Questions 11–20*

Questions 11 and 12

*Choose the correct letter, **A**, **B** or **C**.*

11 The zoo site was gifted to the city in

A 1950.
B 1902.
C 1860.

12 The zoo was originally designed for

A the preservation of endangered animals.
B scientific research.
C entertainment.

Questions 13–16

Label the map below.

*Write **NO MORE THAN TWO WORDS** for each answer.*

Zoo

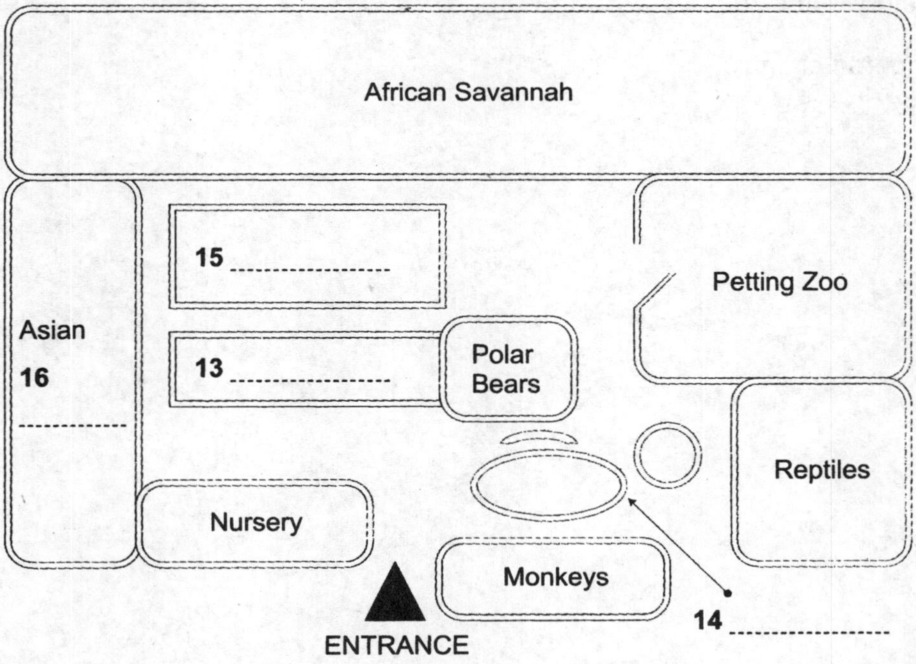

Questions 17–19

*Choose **THREE** letters, **A–G**.*

Which **THREE** animals can be found in the children's petting zoo?

A cats

B goats

C hens

D pigs

E rabbits

F sheep

G dogs

Question 20

*Choose the correct letter, **A**, **B** or **C**.*

The DVD will show

A the young zoo animals.

B the history of the zoo.

C endangered animals.

SECTION 3 *Questions 21–30*

Questions 21 and 22

*Choose the correct letter, **A**, **B** or **C**.*

21 June is with the counsellor because

A she is under stress from course work.
B she didn't do well in her exams.
C she is struggling with course assessment.

22 The counsellor suggests that the purpose of exams is

A to test students' personal ability.
B to test students' self-control.
C to assist students in the outside world.

Questions 23 and 24

*Choose **TWO** letters, **A–E**.*

June should make summaries of which **TWO** of the following sources?

A PowerPoint presentations

B lecture notes

C information from the Internet

D journal articles

E explanations and examples

Questions 25–30

Complete the notes below.

Write **NO MORE THAN TWO WORDS** *for each answer.*

To prepare for exams:

- make summaries of summaries
- begin revising before lectures end
- attend **25** .... (prepare **26** .... beforehand)
- set goals (50% pass in everything)
- focus on **27** ....
- get exam schedule & make study plan for each day but also plan time for **28** ....
- familiarise myself with the **29** .... of each exam

NB Multiple choice relies on recognition, not **30** .... , so study the subject extensively, not intensively.

SECTION 4 *Questions 31–40*

Questions 31–34

Complete the summary below.

Write ***NO MORE THAN TWO WORDS*** *for each answer.*

A feral animal lives in the wild after coming from a **31** .... environment. Camels were brought to Australia primarily for transport. They carried people, supplies and construction **32** .... into the arid inland areas. The camels were imported from China, Mongolia, Arabia and India. Because of their size and strength, the Indian ones were used specifically for transporting **33** ....

Eventually, the camels were replaced by trains and cars and so they were released into the wild. Now they are very common in **34** ....

Questions 35–40

Complete the notes below.

Write ***NO MORE THAN TWO WORDS OR A NUMBER*** *for each answer.*

Problems caused by feral camels

– roam over large areas eating all kinds of plant material

– can drink enormous amounts of water: **35** .... litres in 3 minutes

– damage sensitive areas and threaten the survival of native species

– damage water holes that are **36** .... for Aboriginals

– enter **37** .... and destroy domestic facilities such as bores and tanks

– damage farm property, e.g. fences, **38** .... and water troughs

– carry disease and cause accidents

– produce methane

Feral camels as a resource

Camel meat is exported and also used by the **39** .... trade.

They can be captured, domesticated and used in tourism for **40** ....

READING

READING PASSAGE 1

*You should spend about 20 minutes on **Questions 1–13**, which are based on Reading Passage 1 below.*

Making sense

Recent research suggests that gender affects how we see the world and how we operate within it.

A According to the results of new research into vision carried out at the City University of New York (CUNY), there are marked differences in the way that men's and women's brains process visual data. Israel Abramov of CUNY stated that the experiments relate to specific sets of thalamic neurons in the brain's primary visual cortex, which appear to be gender related. The development of these neurons is influenced by the male sex hormones during foetal growth early in pregnancy. Although Abramov can successfully explain the process that leads to the difference, he is at a loss to know what evolutionary motive there might be for the variance.

B These results should not surprise us, as there are also differences in the senses of hearing and the olfactory system. Previous studies have revealed that in women, these senses are more sensitive to various stimuli in the environment than in men. Women can hear higher-pitched sounds and, when listening, they show activity in the temporal lobe across their whole brain, whereas men generally show activity exclusively in the left hemisphere of the brain. Likewise, research indicates that odours activate a larger region of the brain in females, and they are more sensitive to and are able to differentiate and categorise subtle distinctions in aromas better than males, although the structure of the nose is the same and they have the same number of receptors.

C At CUNY, when subjects with 20/20 sight and normal colour vision were asked by researchers to describe different colours, it was discovered that the males needed a slightly longer wavelength of a colour to detect the same shade as females, and that men were not as good at discriminating between shades. Also, in measuring sensitivity to contrast, the volunteers were shown images of light and dark bars of varying widths that alternated in colour so that they seemed to flicker. The men were better at recognising images that changed faster and were composed of thinner bars.

D Earlier studies carried out at the University of Southern California revealed that males and females focus differently as well. The researchers discovered that when focussing on a speaker, a man will fixate on the lips of the person, but he is liable to divert his focus to any action taking place behind the person, for instance a passing pedestrian or vehicle. Women, however, seem to alternate between looking at the other person's eyes and body, and they are apt to be distracted by other people. Why the difference? Former studies showed that women are better able to interpret nonverbal communication; it stands to reason that, by taking in more of the body with their eyes, they can garner more information about the speaker. It could be said that women pay more attention to the social nature of the setting whereas men are more drawn to shifts in motion and speed. The fact that men do not discern, or have trouble decoding, nonverbal cues leads to each sex constantly misconstruing the other's signals. A man may read a friendly smile as a piece of coquetry, for example, whereas a woman might wrongly identify a furrowed brow as a sign of anger rather than as an expression of concentration.

E It has been known for some time that men's and women's brains are wired differently. Back in the 1980s, however, it was thought that boys and girls were born with the same brains but the environment they grew up in would determine any differences. It is true that boys and girls are still socialised differently, but psychologist Diane Halpern believes that many of the cognitive differences are biologically innate. For instance, even looking at different age groups and cultures, it has been proved that men have better visual-spatial skills – such as rotating an object in their minds, judging angle orientation, and navigating by points of the compass.

F On the other hand, it is also acknowledged that women are more fluent verbally, and they are better at remembering objects and therefore navigate by landmarks. Halpern is at pains to point out that having different skills is not the same as having different levels of intelligence. She will not be drawn into a debate over whether one gender is smarter than or superior to the other. In fact, there are a fair few myths out there with regard to gender differences. You might have heard it said that boys are better at mathematics, but Halpern explains that any difference is context dependent. In more gender-equal societies, 'the male advantage in math disappears', she says. Social context, economics and other environmental influences all have a bearing.

G If the playing field is level and neither gender is more gifted, how do we account for the fact that more than ninety per cent of CEOs are men and more than ninety per cent of secretaries are women? Halpern explains that women do most of the nurturing in society, such as looking after children and taking care of the elderly; therefore, they tend to opt for paid jobs that require less investment of time. As she sees it, this results in both a loss of talented women in the workplace and a loss of capable men on the domestic scene, as fathering is very important and many men would make great caregivers. Halpern puts it in plain words: 'We can't have equality in work, if we don't have equality in the home.'

Questions 1–4

Complete the summary below.

Choose **NO MORE THAN THREE WORDS** *from the passage for each answer.*

Write your answers in Boxes 1–4 on your answer sheet.

Existing research

Experimental evidence from studies of gender differences in vision shows that the **1** .... that control vision in the brain are different in men and women. These differences happen very early in life, and are affected by **2** .... In addition, women's hearing and smell generally respond more to **3** .... in their surroundings. Whereas women use their entire brain to process noise, most men use **4** .... to do this.

Questions 5–11

Classify the following traits as being

A more common among men

B more common among women

C equally common among men and women

Write the correct letter, **A**, **B** *or* **C**, *in Boxes 5–11 on your answer sheet.*

5 They can tell the difference between similar smells.

6 They are able to identify minor variations in colour.

7 They are more easily distracted when listening to someone.

8 They focus on body language and what it means.

9 They misunderstand the intention of simple gestures.

10 They can see something from all sides without touching it.

11 They have the potential to excel at mathematics.

Questions 12 and 13

*Choose **TWO** letters, **A–F**.*

Write the correct letters in Boxes 12 and 13 on your answer sheet.

Which **TWO** of the following claims are made by Diane Halpern in Reading Passage 1?

A Intelligence is related to the ability to work well with numbers.

B Gender differences in the brain lead to different sets of skills.

C Men are not as good as women at taking care of children.

D Men usually work longer hours in their jobs than women.

E The same skills are required for employment and housework.

READING PASSAGE 2

*You should spend about 20 minutes on **Questions 14–26**, which are based on Reading Passage 2 below.*

THE ROMANTIC MOVEMENT

A Romanticism was an artistic and cultural movement that swept through Europe during the nineteenth century, reshaping everything from arts to politics to personal lifestyles as it flourished. Contrary to a commonly held misconception, Romanticism had little to do with 'romance' in the modern, popular sense of the word, and Romantics of the nineteenth century were generally not concerned with questions of infatuation and heartbreak. What interested them more was a different kind of Romantic vision, one that rebelled against caution and reason and praised the intensity and ferocity of wild landscapes and reckless human emotion.

B Like many popular movements, Romanticism emerged as a reaction to the ideas that preceded it. Europe in the 1700s was dominated by the ideals of the Enlightenment, which were firmly grounded in reason and logic, the scientific method, mastery over nature, and a belief that polite intellectual discourse in such institutions as coffee houses and debating societies constituted the most sophisticated expression of humanity's capacity for development. Enlightenment thinkers loathed the expression of emotion, particularly of fiery, uncontrollable feeling, perceiving it to be a threat to order and democracy. They also fought against irrationality and dogmatism of all kinds, having witnessed how despotic kings and other manipulative leaders used folk wisdom and superstition to stir discontent and gain power in their countries.

C Romantic artists resisted the Enlightenment fixation with calmness, order and reason, although the nature of their rebellion varied from one art form to another. Romantic poets, for example, dismissed the sculpted, austere prose of their forebears, favouring styles that focussed on the role of ordinary people and their language. As interest in governance and civic affairs waned, writers began to reject the once-respected literary format of satire. Instead, they turned their attention to those areas of human life that were previously downplayed or taboo. In *Wuthering Heights*, for example, Emily Brontë describes the effects of intense, destructive emotions such as jealousy and vengeance. Elements of the supernatural are introduced in the short stories of Edgar Allan Poe.

D Composers and soloists reached new levels of prominence during the Romantic Movement. This was partly because, freed from the constraints of the Enlightenment era, music was perceived to be the ideal form through which to explore the Romantic notion of a free spirit. Economic shifts also facilitated music's newfound dominance. Whereas musicians had hitherto been required to source financial support from a wealthy patron (usually from the royal court), they now earned their living by performing for burgeoning middle-class audiences. With this transition came the birth of the pop star musician, perhaps best exemplified by the Hungarian pianist Franz Liszt, who would tour cities performing for these crowds with brilliance and flair.

E Romanticism also made its mark on painting, in two notable ways. The first change can be seen in landscape representations. In Enlightenment-era paintings, nature was usually neglected in favour of human subjects. Where nature was shown, it was typically in the form of manicured hedges and lawns, as in the style of estates and palaces of the time. Romantic artists, however, depicted nature as a violent force, rather than as something to beautify gardens and walkways. Windswept mountaintops, dense bush and fogs, and stormy, dark red skies were all popular with such artists.

F The Romantics also revolutionised the painting of human subjects. Previously considered a staid, sedate form of painting, whose principle objective was simply to achieve a lifelike representation of the subject, portraits became a vehicle for examining the darker side of the human experience. Théodore Géricault, for example, chose to paint a series of portraits of psychiatric patients toward the end of his life, depicting his subjects' eyes as being tormented and unsettled. This was strongly divergent from the traditional portrait – a member of royalty or the royal court, festooned with jewellery and wearing their finest clothes.

G By the mid-nineteenth century, Romanticism had hugely influenced every art form with the exception of sculpture, which remained stubbornly impervious to Romantic influences due to the practical constraints of the discipline. Its influence had extended far beyond the arts; scientists reconfigured their ideas about nature, and educators reconsidered their curriculum priorities. Most significantly, nationalist political movements were proliferating across Europe, inspired by the celebration of folklore and indigenous customs in many Romantic art works.

H Toward the end of the nineteenth century, however, Romanticism's dominance waned considerably. What was once revolutionary and provocative began to seem phony and melodramatic. Many authors and artists turned toward Realism, a newer movement that advocated artistry without exaggeration or contrivance. Others saw a need to begin taking social and political affairs seriously again, and sought to retrieve some of the values of the Enlightenment, such as the need for dialogue and reasoned debate. Romanticism never faded away completely, however. Dramatic movie soundtracks and plotlines in which men fight adversity to achieve great triumphs show that the Romantic spirit remains with us to the present day.

Questions 14–16

*Choose the correct letter, **A**, **B**, **C** or **D**.*

Write the correct letter in Boxes 14–16 on your answer sheet.

14 19th century Romantics celebrated

A emotions related to love between men and women.
B careful limits and logical thinking.
C unrestrained feelings and environments.
D rebellion against all forms of state power.

15 The exchange of ideas in a public forum was important in the Enlightenment because

A it helped society to reach its full potential.
B it was the highest form of human conversation.
C it encouraged popular interest in science.
D it provided a safe place for political discussion.

16 According to the writer, Enlightenment thinkers

A believed that kings made the best rulers.
B had strongly held religious beliefs.
C disliked people showing their feelings.
D disapproved of the rule of law in society.

Questions 17–23

Complete the table below.

Choose **NO MORE THAN THREE WORDS** *from the passage for each answer.*

Write your answers in Boxes 17–23 on your answer sheet.

ROMANTICISM IN THE ARTS	
Literature	Poets prefer to use regular spoken language. Writers are less interested in politics. As a result, **17** .... is not as popular as before. New topics are explored, such as harmful feelings and **18** ....
19	The most appropriate art form for the expression of Romantic ideas. No longer paid for by rich individuals, but by **20** .... who wanted to see their favourite artists perform.
Painting	Nature is shown to be **21** .... through depictions of extreme weather and landscapes. **22** .... are used to show more unpleasant aspects of human life.
23	Not affected by the Romantic movement.

Questions 24–26

Complete the sentences below.

Choose **NO MORE THAN THREE WORDS** *from the passage for each answer.*

Write your answers in Boxes 24–26 on your answer sheet.

Peak, decline & legacy

24 The Romantic Movement brought about changes in science and education, and led to the growth of ....

25 Even as Realism grew in popularity, some artists felt that ideas from .... were still relevant.

26 Romantic ideas are currently used in ...., and also in stories of people overcoming problems in their lives.

READING PASSAGE 3

*You should spend about 20 minutes on **Questions 27–40**, which are based on Reading Passage 3 below.*

The Upside of Feeling Down

A Over the past couple of decades, public imagination has been captured by the notion of 'happiness' in an unprecedented way. There is now a *Journal of Happiness Studies*, a burgeoning field of study known as 'happiness economics', and everyone from self-help gurus to sociological researchers to public policy makers is trying to understand what happiness is and how everyone can get more of it. The mania shows no sign of abating – during a three-month period this year, over one thousand books on the subject were released. In our frantic pursuit of good feelings, however, some researchers worry that we may have overlooked the flipside of the coin – sadness. By framing sadness as solely a negative condition, a fetter to free ourselves from, these scholars believe that we may be neglecting an important facet of the human experience.

B Much evidence suggests that sadness plays an important and constructive role in our lives. Firstly, in some very fundamental respects, humans perform better at a range of functions when they're feeling down. In a University of New South Wales study, Professor Joe Forgas discovered that people experiencing negative moods are less gullible, and less likely to make judgemental errors than their happy counterparts. He also found that sad people had better recall of past events and feelings, were better able to communicate their thoughts, and were less likely to judge someone based solely on their appearance. Why would this be so? Primarily, because moods are linked with our evolutionary needs – they effectively tell us how to process any information we receive. Forgas notes that a positive mood indicates comfort and familiarity, whereas a negative mood alerts the brain to be vigilant. As a result, he believes, sadness encourages a 'more attentive and externally focused, information-processing style' whereas happiness prompts us to switch off, making us prone to deception. In other words, bliss is ignorance.

C In other contexts, sadness allows us to cope with traumatic occurrences and, ultimately, move on from them. Unlike other negative emotions such as anger or fear, which temporarily spike energy levels and impel the person experiencing them to act decisively, sadness drains energy. In doing so it draws the sufferer away from the activities of other people and encourages them to reflect on their feelings and the importance of what caused them. This process, known as grief, serves an important role in helping humans to adjust to loss and to integrate it into their lives. In an editorial in the esteemed medical journal *The Lancet*, deputy editor Dr Astrid James warned that psychiatrists are in danger of pathologising normal human experiences by prescribing anti-depressant pills instead of acknowledging the superior role of prolonged sadness in naturally rehabilitating sufferers.

D Aside from acting as a coping mechanism, sadness may also play a more proactive role in encouraging people to improve their lives. According to Jerome Wakefield, clinical social worker at New York University, 'one of the functions of intense negative emotions is to stop our normal functioning, to make us focus on something else for a while'. In this way, the memory of sadness – and of taking time out to be sad – imprints itself on our mind as a psychological deterrent for the future. One can see how, for example, young adults learn to become more guarded and less cavalier with everything from their money to personal relationships after suffering one agonising loss too many. Without the prodding of sadness upon our memory of these situations, we might endlessly repeat these follies with no reason to alter our behaviour.

E Finally, what of the notion that sadness is powerfully linked with great artistic expression? Some evidence suggests this is far from a cultural myth. A researcher from Harvard University, Modupe Akinola, experimented with the connection between depression and creativity. She asked depressed people to perform creative tasks and gave them feedback that was designed to reinforce their negative feelings. Akinola speculates that this feedback encouraged research participants to dwell on their negativity, and this unearthed hidden feelings and bolstered their creative output. Laura Young, a researcher at Boston College, has found that adolescents or young adults who participate in arts programmes are more likely to experience sadness than their peers, a finding that is also true for older adult artists. Young emphasises, however, that painting and drama are not themselves catalysts for depression. Rather, she suggests, they are a chance for some people to vocalise their anger and can provide a therapeutic space for those with emotional troubles.

F With an array of studies indicating that sadness plays a constructive and significant role in human affairs, what are we to make of the current fervour surrounding the pursuit of happiness? Are we being led toward an illusion by false prophets of positivity? According to Steven Hayes, a psychology professor at the University of Nevada, we are. He believes we need to set aside the idea of happiness altogether, or at least any notion of 'pursuing' it. 'What people mean by happiness is feeling good,' Hayes says. '[But] there are many ways to feel good. And many of the ways we feel good actually limit the possibilities for living the way we want to live our lives.' What is more important than experiencing the transient flush of happy feelings, he suggests, is moving through life in accordance with our core values. This expanded notion of good living does not limit itself to happiness, but embraces sadness, and at times, fear, anger and suffering too.

Questions 27–34

Look at the following statements (Questions 27–34) and the list of people below.

Match each statement with the correct person, ***A, B, C, D, E*** *or* ***F****.*

List of People

A Joe Forgas
B Astrid James
C Jerome Wakefield
D Modupe Akinola
E Laura Young
F Steven Hayes

Write the correct letter, ***A, B, C, D, E*** *or* ***F*** *in Boxes 27–34 on your answer sheet.*

27 Modern ideas about happiness are not helpful.

28 Medication is being used unnecessarily.

29 Sad people can remember things better.

30 Art can help teenagers to express their feelings.

31 Sad people are more careful and alert than happy ones.

32 People should focus on what is important to them.

33 Sadness can stop us repeatedly making bad decisions.

34 Thinking about sadness can help people produce original material.

Questions 35–40

Do the following statements agree with the views of the writer in Reading Passage 3?

In Boxes 35–40 on your answer sheet, write

YES *if the statement agrees with the views of the writer*
NO *if the statement contradicts the views of the writer*
NOT GIVEN *if it is impossible to say what the writer thinks about this*

35 People are becoming less interested in happiness.

36 Sadness is an undesirable state.

37 Sadness makes it easier to deal with events that cause psychological pain.

38 People feel more energetic when they are sad.

39 Grief is not experienced very often in most people's lives.

40 Sadness is a necessary and important part of human experience.

WRITING

WRITING TASK 1

You should spend about 20 minutes on this task.

The graph below shows average yearly rainfall in Moscow and San Francisco, measured in millimetres.

Summarise the information by selecting and reporting the main features, and make comparisons where relevant.

Write at least 150 words.

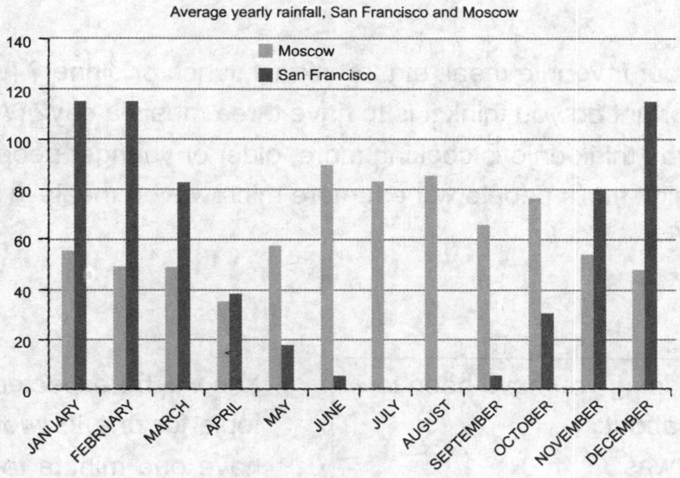

WRITING TASK 2

You should spend about 40 minutes on this task.

Some people believe that the best way to improve the general well-being of schoolchildren is to make physical education compulsory in all schools. Others, however, think that this would have little effect on overall health and that other measures are needed.

Discuss both these views and give your own opinion.

Give reasons for your answer and include any relevant examples from your own knowledge or experience.

Write at least 250 words.

SPEAKING

PART 1

Initial questions about name, where live, work or studies, and other personal topics.

Money

- Is money important? [Why / Why not?]
- Do people in your country save their money? [Why / Why not?]
- What sort of things do young people spend their money on? [Why?]
- How do you feel when you don't have enough money to buy something you want? [Why?]

Food and meals

- What is your favourite meal, e.g. breakfast, lunch or dinner? [Why?]
- How important do you think it is to have three meals a day? [Why?]
- Who do you think enjoys cooking more, older or younger people? [Why?]
- Do you think more people will eat more microwaved meals in the future? [Why / Why not?]

PART 2

Talk about a wedding you have been to.
You should talk about:
- where it was
- when it was
- who you met there

and explain why this wedding was important to you.

You will be expected to talk about the topic for one to two minutes. You will have one minute to think about what you are going to say in advance. You can make some notes to help you if you wish.

PART 3

Weddings and marriage in general

- What is the best age for a person to get married?
- What kinds of things should young people do before they get married? [Why?]
- Do you think people should get married again if their first marriage is not successful?

Marriage and society

- The roles of men and women are changing. How has this impacted on how people view marriage in your culture?
- The media often highlights celebrity marriages and contracts that are agreed on before marriage. Is this practical attitude towards marriage?
- Changes in attitudes to marriage and family responsibilities have resulted in increasing numbers of single parent families. How will this impact on society in future?

General Training Reading and Writing Test 1

READING

SECTION 1 *Questions 1–14*

Read the table below and answer ***Questions 1–6***.

This is an advertising brochure for residential short classes in English plus different sporting activities.

ENGLISH WITH A DIFFERENCE

Combine learning English with coaching in sport!

	Sport combo package	Price[1]	Length of course	Class times	Comments	Transport to & from sporting facility
A	**English with surfing** *A unique opportunity.*	$800 per week (equipment hire extra)	12 weeks	Sport 7–11 a.m. English 1–5 p.m.	Must prove ability to swim before enrolment. Surfboards for hire. Note: this package is not available during winter months.	Only 1 block from the beach – walk in 5 minutes
B	**English with golf** *Mixes well with business.*	$700 per week (equipment hire extra) Packed lunch included	8 weeks	English 8 a.m.–noon Sport 1.30–5.30 p.m.	Golf clubs for hire. Take *Business English* instead of *General English* at no extra cost.	½ hour by minibus to golf course ($2 each way)
C	**English with tennis** *Learn to play like a pro!*	$650 per week Packed lunch can be purchased at the venue	8 weeks	Sport 7–9 a.m. English 10 a.m.–2 p.m. Sport 3–5 p.m.	Must provide own racquets.	5 minutes by (free) bus or ½ hour on foot to tennis courts

[1] Price includes 20 hours' classroom tuition + 20 hours' coaching per week

Questions 1–3

*Look at the three learning packages, **A**, **B** and **C**, on the previous page.*

For which sport combo package are the following statements true?

*Write the correct letter, **A**, **B** or **C**, in Boxes 1–3 on your answer sheet.*

1 This package does not cater for people who can't swim.

2 This package requires you to supply your own equipment.

3 This package involves a travel cost.

Questions 4–6

Answer the questions below.

*Choose **NO MORE THAN THREE WORDS** from the text for each answer.*

Write your answers in Boxes 4–6 on your answer sheet.

4 When will one of the packages not be offered?

5 Which is the faster way to get to the tennis facility?

6 Which package offers a meal at no extra cost?

Read the text below and answer ***Questions 7–14***.

Atlantic Private Day Hospital

Patient Information

Welcome and thank you for choosing Atlantic Private Day Hospital.

We hope that your stay with us will be as comfortable and pleasant as possible.

Pre-Admission Information

Pre-Admission is an important part of your hospital care. To ensure that we can confirm your admission and financial and other arrangements, we ask that you complete the following forms in full and return them to the hospital immediately:

- consent forms
- patient history form
- patient pre-admission forms

You can do this:

- in person at Reception (Open Mon–Fri 6 a.m.–5 p.m.)
- by fax on (09) 6665 4326
- by post to arrive ASAP

If your account is subject to Private Insurance Cover, forward full details of the claim including a letter from your insurance company accepting liability for this admission to our Pre-Admission Office at least 48 hours prior to your procedure.

Your doctor will notify the hospital of the date of your procedure/operation and inform you of the day of admission. The doctor will also explain your procedure or operation and complete the consent form with you.

On the Day of Admission

Please ensure that you bring the following with you to the hospital:

- health insurance card if applicable
- medicare card if applicable
- credit card or cash card
- current x-rays
- phone number or email of the person taking you home

Do not

- eat or drink anything for 6 hours before admission time
- smoke cigarettes or chew gum
- wear jewellery
- wear make-up
- bring any valuables with you

Please

- shower the day prior to coming to the hospital
- wear garments that are comfortable and easy to remove
- arrange with a relative or friend to pick you up
- report to Reception on level 1

Discharge Information

- You must arrange for someone to escort you home.
- You must not drive a car until at least 24 hours following your operation.
- You must check with your doctor about medication and follow-up appointments.
- Do not forget to collect any x-rays brought with you on admission.

Questions 7–14

Classify the following events as something

A you must do before admission day

B you must do on admission day

C you must do on the day you leave hospital

D you must not do on the day you leave the hospital

E your doctor must do

*Write the correct letter, **A**, **B**, **C**, **D** or **E**, in Boxes 7–14 on your answer sheet.*

7 drive a car

8 fill out a patient history form

9 tell the hospital which day you will have your operation

10 have the contact details of your driver

11 talk to your doctor about any pills you need

12 give insurance details to the hospital

13 take a shower

14 take off any expensive watches or rings

SECTION 2 *Questions 15–21*

Read the text below and answer ***Questions 15–21****.*

SETTING UP A SAFE HOME WORK BASE FOR TELECOMMUTING

Working from home can be a flexible and money-saving option for modern businesses, but a company may be legally liable for any injury sustained by the home-based employee.

Before arranging to work from home, telecommuters must identify any potential health and safety issues by following these steps:

- Identify hazards that could harm those who visit, live or work in your home. Imagine your home as an office environment and examine lighting, ventilation, tripping or electrical hazards.
- Minimise the risk – falls are the most common household accident but are easily prevented. Start with the floor: shift chairs, desks or cabinets that impede progress from one area to another, and make sure that, as far as possible, all work desks and other items are arranged round the edges of the space.
- Get rid of loose floor coverings such as small carpets, or use only those with a non-slip backing. If possible, use non-slip mats under office chairs to avoid the possibility of unwanted movement. Pick up any objects that are on the floor (books, shoes, boxes, etc.).
- Carefully examine your workplace environment, and ensure that lamp, telephone or extension cords and computer leads are off the floor to avoid the chance of tripping and falling. Taping these along the edge of the wall above the skirting board and over doorways is one option, or alternatively, you may need to employ an electrician to install more outlets.
- Next, look at the stairs and steps both inside and outside your home. Keep steps and stairs clear; fix any steps that are loose or not level; if carpeted, ensure the carpet is firmly attached, or attach non-slip rubber treads to uncarpeted steps; where there are loose or absent handrails, install new ones; ensure stairs and steps are well lit (change to more powerful wall lighting than normal).
- Create a comprehensive inventory of necessary repair work and/or new installations and follow through on your risk controls.
- Hold a forum with your household members to promote safety consciousness and hazard awareness and run through safety drills; get household members' compliance on issues of tidiness, cleanliness, etc.

Both parties must remember that health and safety obligations apply the same way to work performed in a home-based workplace as they do in the office. After the risk assessment and fixes have been completed, the workplace manager must inspect the workplace with the employee and both should sign off on the findings of the inspection.

Questions 15–21

Complete the summary using the list of words and phrases, ***A–P****, below.*

Write the correct letter, ***A–P****, in Boxes 15–21 on your answer sheet.*

To make the home a safer place to work in, any **15** .... that restricts freedom of movement should be moved. Any **16** .... and items that clutter floor space should be removed. Attach **17** .... to the wall in the work area. Where steps and stairs are concerned, have **18** .... repaired, and get new handrails fitted if any are missing or not firmly attached. Make a **19** .... before arranging for all needed repairs.

It is also important to have a family conference to encourage **20** .... and observance of the rules for a clean and tidy house. Finally, arrange a check with your **21** ....

A electrical cables
B furniture
C handrails
D health issues
E financial plan
F uncarpeted stairs
G rugs
H checklist
I employer
J repair man
K safety awareness
L safety obligations
M finder
N non-slip rugs
O uneven steps
P ventilation system

Read the text below and answer ***Questions 22–27****.*

STARTING A NEW BUSINESS

A There are a few simple principles to ensure success when you are starting up your own business:

B Firstly, you must be able to offer something unique that people want. Why unique? Well, if you are simply following the trends, there is no reason for people to buy from your new business. Be creative – design or discover something that is exceptionally good or different in a specific domain or sector rather than going down the same track as all the other vendors. What you offer could be a product or service, a method of trading, or some aspect of your business that is new, attractive and appealing in some way.

C Before you begin, you have to identify what people want and whether and how much they would be prepared to pay for it. Customer questionnaires, or surveys, are an often-used method of testing the market, but be sure to get some professional help with your design or some training in constructing your survey so that it gives useful and valid information. Badly designed questionnaires can lead to poor marketing decisions. Some people say that the best survey should contain fewer than 20 questions, or that all questions should be answerable with one or two words, but each business is different and you need to tailor the size and format of a survey to your own situation.

D Finally, to ensure the success of your enterprise, you must have a passion for what you are doing and a certain expertise or particular strength in that field.

START-UP VENTURES BY OLDER PEOPLE

E If you have got what it takes to compete in the modern world, maturity is a plus; your experience and accumulated wisdom counts for a lot. Older people often have the self-assurance and confidence that enables them to forge trusting bonds. Positive rapport and connections with staff, partners, colleagues and potential clients and suppliers are the fundamentals of good business.

F Older people are also more likely to recognise the true extent of their capabilities. They know their strengths and weaknesses, and they are capable of patience. Although they are not often credited with this, older people are actually very good at adjusting to changing circumstances and at problem solving, as they generally have faith in their own decisions.

START-UP VENTURES BY YOUNG PEOPLE

G If you are still a bit wet behind the ears, can you start a new business? Of course you can! The basic principles of doing what you excel at and working to your strengths apply no matter what age you are. Young people are full of fresh ideas; they have vision combined with energy; and they are often highly motivated. Lack of experience can be a problem, and one way to overcome this is to use the services of a business mentor. This person could be a paid professional or a family friend, but in either case their suggestions are likely to be invaluable in helping the young entrepreneur to succeed.

Questions 22–27

Do the following statements agree with the information given in the text above?

In Boxes 22–27 on your answer sheet, write

TRUE	*if the statement agrees with the information*
FALSE	*if the statement contradicts the information*
NOT GIVEN	*if there is no information on this*

22 Successful businesses generally copy from previous ideas.

23 Good surveys can use a variety of styles and sizes.

24 Training in business management is important for success.

25 Older people can cope with change because they are confident.

26 Older people are more likely to succeed than younger people.

27 It is best for young people to pay someone for business advice.

SECTION 3 *Questions 28–40*

Questions 28–33

*The text on the following pages has six paragraphs, **A–F**.*

*Choose the correct heading for Paragraphs **A–F** from the list of headings below.*

*Write the correct number, **i–xi**, in Boxes 28–33 on your answer sheet.*

List of Headings

- **i** Relationship with Italy
- **ii** How the governance system works
- **iii** Agricultural produce
- **iv** The currency of San Marino
- **v** Historical background
- **vi** Climate in the enclave
- **vii** The economy
- **viii** Geography
- **ix** Natural life
- **x** The people of San Marino
- **xi** Current and future problems

28 Paragraph **A**

29 Paragraph **B**

30 Paragraph **C**

31 Paragraph **D**

32 Paragraph **E**

33 Paragraph **F**

Serenissima Repubblica di San Marino

(The Most Serene Republic of San Marino)

A The Republic of San Marino is a landlocked microstate or enclave, the third smallest state in Europe, situated on the Italian peninsula. Its total area is no more than 61 square kilometres of rugged terrain (there is no natural level ground at all) completely surrounded by Italy with a border just thirty-nine kilometres long. The climate is typically Mediterranean with warm, sunny summers and mild, sometimes cool, winters. Although it is a small state with a small population, estimated to be 32,448 in July 2013, it has a very long history.

B San Marino is perhaps the world's oldest constitutional republic, founded in the year 301 AD by a stonemason fleeing religious persecution. The stonecutter, Marinus (from whom the settlement derived its name), came from the Roman colony of Arba, which is an island off the coast of present-day Croatia. A community was established which managed to flourish and maintain its sovereignty over the many succeeding centuries, even surviving a potential invasion from Napoleon's army in the 18th century and the period of Italian political unification in the 19th century.

C San Marino today is a multi-party democratic republic, but political parties have to align themselves with one of the two opposing coalitions: the right or the left. Twice a year, the legislature, known as the Grand and General Council, elects two Heads of State. These heads, or Captains Regent as they are called, are selected one from each opposing alliance in order to keep a balance of power. After their six-month term in office is up, if the people are unhappy with their performance in any way, they may lodge a complaint within three days, and if any of their grievances are justified, the ex-heads of state will be held to account. This system of government, as unusual as it may seem to many of us today, originates from the principles of the ancient Roman Republic. The Council performs the role of the Roman Senate and the Captains Regent are comparable to the consuls of early Rome.

D Modern-day San Marino belongs to the Council of Europe and the United Nations but is not a member of the European Union although it is permitted to use the euro as its legal tender; it is even allowed to have its own designs on the national side of the euro coins. Before moving to the euro, it used the San Marino lira for money, and this was linked in value and exchangeable with the Italian lira. Because limited numbers of both the euro and lira coins are/were minted, they are eagerly sought by coin collectors around the world. Likewise, philatelists are keen collectors of San Marino's postage stamps, which are only valid within the state itself. The sale of both coins and stamps to foreign collectors supplements the economy of the country.

E Chief sources of income arise from the industries of tourism, banking, ceramics and electronics together with the manufacture and export of furniture, paints, fabrics and wearing apparel. About a third of San Marino's GDP comes from the manufacturing industry but tourism is the key player and the government makes substantial returns from the taxes and customs imposed on the two to three million annual visitors, who also provide income for many local businesses. Only about sixteen per cent of land in San Marino is arable and primary agricultural products mainly consist of some wine and cheese (most food is imported from Italy); farmers do, however, raise sheep, cows and pigs and produce fruit and grain for local consumption. In the face of the current global financial crisis, it is surprising to note that there is almost no national debt and even a budget surplus.

F For such a tiny, geographically inhospitable country with few natural resources, apart perhaps from building stone, residents of San Marino nevertheless enjoy a relatively high standard of living equivalent to that of Danes or Germans. Unlike many other European nations, the citizens of San Marino experience a very low level of unemployment. The population is predominantly urban (94%); however, the rate of urbanisation is putting pressure on existing rural farmlands, which is an environmental issue of some concern to the inhabitants along with air pollution. Although the natural features of the state may be harsh and forbidding, the pleasant climate and the general affluence of the populace undoubtedly have an impact on life expectancy, which is amongst the highest in the world, the average lifespan of females in San Marino being in excess of eighty-five years and the average male expecting to reach the age of eighty.

Questions 34 and 35

Complete the sentences below.

Choose **NO MORE THAN TWO WORDS** *from the text for each answer.*

Write your answers in Boxes 34 and 35 on your answer sheet.

34 If the people of San Marino make .... , the Heads of State are answerable.

35 The Grand and General Council is the equivalent of the old ....

Questions 36–40

Choose the best answer for each question below:

36 Which of the following does NOT describe San Marino?

A It is very hilly.
B It has many beaches.
C It is an old state.
D It has pleasant weather.

37 In Paragraph B we are told that

A San Marino was established to start a new religion.
B the original founder came from Rome.
C there were two threats to San Marino's independence.
D the Italian army wanted to invade San Marino.

38 Paragraph D states that

A nowadays, San Marino uses its own currency.
B San Marino uses the Italian euro coins.
C there are a great many San Marino coins.
D many collectors want to buy San Marino coins.

39 The main source of overseas income in San Marino comes from

A agriculture.
B tourism.
C manufacturing.
D taxes.

40 Which of the following best describes San Marino's people?

A Most people have enough money and live a long time.
B Most people are of Danish or German origin.
C It is hard to find a job because San Marino is so small.
D The population mostly lives in the country, not the towns.

WRITING

WRITING TASK 1

You should spend about 20 minutes on this task.

You are planning a family holiday at a seaside hotel.

Write a letter to the hotel manager. In your letter

- ***describe what kind of accommodation you want***
- ***make a reservation***
- ***find out what facilities the hotel offers***

Write at least 150 words.

You do **NOT** need to write any addresses.

Begin your letter as follows:

Dear Sir or Madam,

WRITING TASK 2

You should spend about 40 minutes on this task.

School age children and teenagers usually like to do the same things as their friends but parents often have a different idea about what their children should be doing.

Should parents always decide how children spend their free time?

Give reasons for your answer and include any relevant examples from your own knowledge or experience.

Write at least 250 words.

Academic Test 2

LISTENING

SECTION 1 *Questions 1–10*

Questions 1–8

Complete the notes below.

Write ***NO MORE THAN TWO WORDS AND/OR A NUMBER*** *for each answer.*

Horizon Hotel

Example	*Answer*
Guest name:	Sandra MacKay

Date of arrival: **1** ………………… December

Date of departure: **2** ………………… December

Room number: **3** 502 and …………………

Room rate: **4** $ …………………

Deposit: **5** Paid …………………

Receipt

- In name of: **6** Zoe …………………

Contact details

- Address: **7** ………………… , Morning Town
- Phone: 439 4829

Booking number: **8** …………………

Questions 9 and 10

Choose the correct letter, ***A, B*** *or* ***C.***

9 The room will be cleaned at around

A 11 a.m.
B 1 p.m.
C 2 p.m.

10 Room service for dinner is available from

A 6 p.m. to 2 a.m.
B 6 p.m. to 10.30 p.m.
C 9 p.m. to 11 p.m.

SECTION 2 *Questions 11–20*

Questions 11–16

Complete the table below.

*Write **ONE WORD OR A NUMBER** for each answer.*

Venue	Event	Date	Time	Admission Price
Gallery 1	Regional Art exhibition – all works for sale	4 March – 10 April	11 a.m. to 4 p.m. **11**	No charge
Gallery 2	**12** '............ of the 21st Century' exhibition – by students	10 March – 4 April	10 a.m. to 3 p.m. Mon, Wed, Fri & weekends	No charge
Theatre 1	Shakespeare's *Romeo & Juliet*	5 March – 3 April	Daily at 8 p.m.	Adult **13** $ .... Senior $20
The **14**	Shannon Keel – folk/pop/country	1 April	**15** .... p.m.	$12.50
The Showroom	Class Act – **16** .... music & cabaret	1–30 April	11 a.m. Fridays only	$14 Concession $12

Questions 17 and 18

*Choose the correct letter, **A**, **B** or **C**.*

17 Michael's home country is

A Canada.
B Ireland.
C the USA.

18 Michael has been singing for

A 15 years.
B 18 years.
C 20 years.

Questions 19 and 20

Complete the sentences below.

*Write **ONE WORD ONLY** for each answer.*

19 Michael's father went .... to work.

20 Michael's .... was also a singer, and was an inspiration for him.

SECTION 3 *Questions 21–30*

Questions 21–25

Complete the sentences below.

*Write **NO MORE THAN TWO WORDS** for each answer.*

21 Jan suggests doing their joint .... on copyright or IP law.

22 Steve's suggested topic is ....

23 A database may collect statistics on your date of birth, income, legal history, previous jobs, ... or health record.

24 Inaccurate facts may be recorded by data company ....

25 Incorrect information about a .... led to his unfair dismissal.

Questions 26–30

Complete the table below.

*Write **NO MORE THAN TWO WORDS** for each answer.*

Jan's comments	**Steve's comments**
Search engines collect data by analysing people's Internet **26**	Data collecting companies want to collect extra data to expand business and increase their **27** ....
Getting consent could be the main **28** .... in the presentation.	Not legal in Europe to make money from using someone's private details without their direct consent
Annoying to have to buy your own credit reports to ensure accuracy	People writing blogs and Twitter comments should be careful or they may face **29** ....
The 'free information' nature of the Internet has led to this problem.	Browser companies may solve the problem by introducing a **30** .... system.

SECTION 4 *Questions 31–40*

Questions 31–35

*Choose the correct letter, **A**, **B** or **C**.*

31 Which place has been termed 'a living laboratory'?

A the Ross Sea
B the Antarctic Sea
C the Southern Ocean

32 What is said to be the worst form of pollution that fishing boats might cause?

A rubbish dropped overboard
B fuel leaked overboard
C sewage leaked overboard

33 What was the country of registration of the boat which was stuck in thick ice?

A Korea
B New Zealand
C Russia

34 In the case of the *Sparta* repair mission, what does the speaker term 'a miracle'?

A No fishermen died.
B The weather was not stormy.
C An oil spill was avoided.

35 What does the term 'total allowable catch' refer to?

A the amount any boat in the Antarctic can catch
B the amount all the legal boats can catch
C the amount all the boats (legal and illegal) can catch

Questions 36–40

Complete the summary below.

Write ***NO MORE THAN ONE WORD AND/OR A NUMBER*** *for each answer.*

The Antarctic Toothfish

These are big fish, which live in freezing Antarctic waters at depths of 200 to 2,000 metres. They have a life span of roughly **36** .... years, and develop only slowly. Little is known about the early stages of life for this fish including the kinds of **37** .... that feed on the young. Since 1996, the December–February fishing season has resulted in catches of about 100,000 fish per year – although recent catches have declined because of **38** .... Industry spokesmen claim that the Antarctic toothfish industry is **39** .... but it has been estimated that fish numbers in the Ross Sea have already been reduced by at least a fifth, if not more. A plea has been made by several well-known marine scientists for a **40** .... on catching fish in the Ross Sea.

READING

READING PASSAGE 1

*You should spend about 20 minutes on **Questions 1–13**, which are based on Reading Passage 1 below.*

A BAR AT THE FOLIES

(Un bar aux folies)

A One of the most critically renowned paintings of the 19th-century modernist movement is the French painter Edouard Manet's masterwork, *A Bar at the Folies*. Originally belonging to the composer Emmanuel Chabrier, it is now in the possession of The Courtauld Gallery in London, where it has also become a favourite with the crowds.

B The painting is set late at night in a nineteenth-century Parisian nightclub. A barmaid stands alone behind her bar, fitted out in a black bodice that has a frilly white neckline, and with a spray of flowers sitting across her décolletage. She rests her hands on the bar and gazes out forlornly at a point just below the viewer, not quite making eye contact. Also on the bar are some bottles of liquor and a bowl of oranges, but much of the activity in the room takes place in the reflection of a mirror behind the barmaid. Through this mirror we see an auditorium, bustling with blurred figures and faces: men in top hats, a woman examining the scene below her through binoculars, another in long gloves, even the feet of a trapeze artist demonstrating acrobatic feats above his adoring crowd. In the foreground of the reflection a man with a thick moustache is talking with the barmaid.

C Although the Folies (-Bergère) was an actual establishment in late nineteenth-century Paris, and the subject of the painting was a real barmaid who worked there, Manet did not attempt to recapture every detail of the bar in his rendition. The painting was largely completed in a private studio belonging to the painter, where the barmaid posed with a number of bottles, and this was then integrated with quick sketches the artist made at the Folies itself.

D Even more confounding than Manet's relaxed attention to detail, however, is the relationship in the painting between the activity in the mirrored reflection and that which we see in the unreflected foreground. In a similar vein to Diego Velazquez' much earlier work *Las Meninas*, Manet uses the mirror to toy with our ideas about which details are true to life and which are not. In the foreground, for example, the barmaid is positioned upright, her face betraying an expression of lonely detachment, yet in the mirrored reflection she appears to be leaning forward and to the side, apparently engaging in conversation with her moustachioed customer. As a result of this, the customer's stance is also altered. In the mirror, he should be blocked from view as a result of where the barmaid is standing, yet Manet has repositioned him to the side. The overall impact on the viewer is one of a dreamlike disjuncture between reality and illusion.

E Why would Manet engage in such deceit? Perhaps for that very reason: to depict two different states of mind or emotion. Manet seems to be conveying his understanding of the modern workplace, a place – from his perspective – of alienation, where workers felt torn from their 'true' selves and forced to assume an artificial working identity. What we see in the mirrored reflection is the barmaid's working self, busy serving a customer. The front-on view, however, bears witness to how the barmaid truly feels at work: hopeless, adrift, and alone.

F Ever since its debut at the Paris Salon of 1882, art historians have produced reams of books and journal articles disputing the positioning of the barmaid and patron in *A Bar at the Folies*. Some have even conducted staged representations of the painting in order to ascertain whether Manet's seemingly distorted point of view might have been possible after all. Yet while academics are understandably drawn to the compositional enigma of the painting, the layperson is always likely to see the much simpler, more human story beneath. No doubt this is the way Manet would have wanted it.

Questions 1–5

Reading Passage 1 has six paragraphs, **A–F**.

Which paragraph contains the following information?

*Write the correct letter, **A–F**, in Boxes 1–5 on your answer sheet.*

1 a description of how Manet created the painting

2 aspects of the painting that scholars are most interested in

3 the writer's view of the idea that Manet wants to communicate

4 examples to show why the bar scene is unrealistic

5 a statement about the popularity of the painting

Questions 6–10

Answer the questions below.

*Choose **NO MORE THAN THREE WORDS** from the passage for each answer.*

Write your answers in Boxes 6–10 on your answer sheet.

6 Who was the first owner of *A Bar at the Folies*?

7 What is the barmaid wearing?

8 Which room is seen at the back of the painting?

9 Who is performing for the audience?

10 Where did most of the work on the painting take place?

Questions 11–13

*Complete each sentence with the correct ending, **A–F**, below.*

*Write the correct letter, **A–F**, in Boxes 11–13 on your answer sheet.*

11 Manet misrepresents the images in the mirror because he

12 Manet felt modern workers were alienated because they

13 Academics have re-constructed the painting in real life because they

A	wanted to find out if the painting's perspective was realistic.
B	felt they had to work very hard at boring and difficult jobs.
C	wanted to understand the lives of ordinary people at the time.
D	felt like they had to become different people.
E	wanted to manipulate our sense of reality.
F	wanted to focus on the detail in the painting.

READING PASSAGE 2

*You should spend about 20 minutes on **Questions 14–26**, which are based on Reading Passage 2 on the following pages.*

Questions 14–19

Reading Passage 2 has six paragraphs, **A–F**.

*Choose the correct heading for Paragraphs **A–F** from the list of headings below.*

*Write the correct number, **i–ix**, in Boxes 14–19 on your answer sheet.*

List of Headings

- **i** A legacy is established
- **ii** Formal education unhelpful
- **iii** An education in two parts
- **iv** Branching out in new directions
- **v** Childhood and family life
- **vi** Change necessary to stay creative
- **vii** Conflicted opinions over Davis' earlier work
- **viii** Davis' unique style of trumpet playing
- **ix** Personal and professional struggles

14 Paragraph **A**

15 Paragraph **B**

16 Paragraph **C**

17 Paragraph **D**

18 Paragraph **E**

19 Paragraph **F**

MILES DAVIS

***Icon and iconoclast*[1]**

A At the age of thirteen, Miles Davis was given his first trumpet, lessons were arranged with a local trumpet player, and a musical odyssey began. These early lessons, paid for and supported by his father, had a profound effect on shaping Davis' signature sound. Whereas most trumpeters of the era favoured the use of vibrato (a wobbly quiver in pitch inflected in the instrument's tone), Davis was taught to play with a long, straight tone, a preference his instructor reportedly drilled into the young trumpeter with a rap on the knuckles every time Davis began using vibrato. This clear, distinctive style never left Davis. He continued playing with it for the rest of his career, once remarking, 'If I can't get that sound, I can't play anything.'

B Having graduated from high school in 1944, Davis moved to New York City, where he continued his musical education both in the clubs and in the classroom. His enrolment in the prestigious Julliard School of Music was short-lived, however – he soon dropped out, criticising what he perceived as an over-emphasis on the classical European repertoire and a neglect of jazz. Davis did later acknowledge, however, that this time at the school was invaluable in terms of developing his trumpet-playing technique and giving him a solid grounding in music theory. Much of his early training took place in the form of jam sessions and performances in the clubs of 52nd Street, where he played alongside both up-and-coming and established members of the jazz pantheon such as Coleman Hawkins, Eddie 'Lockjaw' Davis, and Thelonious Monk.

C In the late 1940s, Davis collaborated with nine other instrumentalists, including a French horn and a tuba player, to produce *The Birth of Cool,* an album now renowned for the inchoate sounds of what would later become known as 'cool' jazz. In contrast to popular jazz styles of the day, which featured rapid, rollicking beats, shrieking vocals, and short, sharp horn blasts, Davis' album was the forerunner of a different kind of sound – thin, light horn-playing, hushed drums and a more restrained, formal arrangement. Although it received little acclaim at the time (the liner notes to one of Davis' later recordings call it a 'spectacular failure'), in hindsight *The Birth of Cool* has become recognised as a pivotal moment in jazz history, cementing – alongside his 1958 recording, *Kind of Blue* – Davis' legacy as one of the most innovative musicians of his era.

D Though Davis' trumpet playing may have sounded effortless and breezy, this ease rarely carried over into the rest of his life. The early 1950s, in particular, were a time of great personal turmoil. After returning from a stint in Paris, Davis suffered from prolonged depression, which he attributed to the unravelling of a number of relationships, including his romance with a French actress and some musical partnerships that ruptured as a result of creative disputes. Davis was also frustrated by his perception that he had been overlooked by the music critics, who were hailing the success of his collaborators and

---

[1] An iconoclast is somebody who challenges traditional beliefs or customs.

descendants in the 'cool' tradition, such as Gerry Mulligan and Dave Brubeck, but who afforded him little credit for introducing the cool sound in the first place.

E In the latter decades of his career, Davis broke out of exclusive jazz settings and began to diversify his output across a range of musical styles. In the 1960s, he was influenced by early funk performers such as Sly and the Family Stone, which then expanded into the jazz-rock fusion genre – of which he was a frontrunner – in the 1970s. Electronic recording effects and electric instruments were incorporated into his sound. By the 1980s, Davis was pushing the boundaries further, covering pop anthems such as Cyndi Lauper's *Time After Time* and Michael Jackson's *Human Nature,* dabbling in hip hop, and even appearing in some movies.

F Not everyone was supportive of Davis' change of tune. Compared to the recordings of his early career, universally applauded as linchpins of the jazz *oeuvre*, trumpeter Wynston Marsalis derided his fusion work as being 'not true jazz', and pianist Bill Evans denounced the 'corrupting influence' of record companies, noting that rock and pop 'draw wider audiences'. In the face of this criticism, Davis remained defiant, commenting that his earlier recordings were part of a moment in time that he had no 'feel' for anymore. He firmly believed that remaining stylistically inert would have hampered his ability to develop new ways of producing music. From this perspective, Davis' continual revamping of genre was not merely a rebellion, but an evolution, a necessary path that allowed him to release his full musical potential.

Questions 20–26

Do the following statements agree with the views of the writer in Reading Passage 2?

In Boxes 20–26 on your answer sheet, write

YES	if the statement agrees with the views of the writer
NO	if the statement contradicts the views of the writer
NOT GIVEN	if it is impossible to say what the writer thinks about this

20 Davis' trumpet teacher wanted him to play with vibrato.

21 According to Davis, studying at Julliard helped him to improve his musical abilities.

22 Playing in jazz clubs in New York was the best way to become famous.

23 *The Birth of Cool* featured music that was faster and louder than most jazz at the time.

24 Davis' personal troubles had a negative effect on his trumpet playing.

25 Davis felt that his contribution to cool jazz had not been acknowledged.

26 Davis was a traditionalist who wanted to keep the jazz sound pure.

READING PASSAGE 3

*You should spend about 20 minutes on **Questions 27–40**, which are based on Reading Passage 3 below.*

A In the early days of mountaineering, questions of safety, standards of practice, and environmental impact were not widely considered. The sport gained traction following the successful 1786 ascent of Mont Blanc, the highest peak in Western Europe, by two French mountaineers, Jacques Balmat and Michel-Gabriel Paccard. This event established the beginning of modern mountaineering, but the sole consideration over the next hundred years was the success or failure of climbers in reaching the summit and claiming the prestige of having made the first ascent.

B Toward the end of the nineteenth century, however, developments in technology spurred debate regarding climbing practices. Of particular concern in this era was the introduction of pitons (metal spikes that climbers hammer into the rock face for leverage) and the use of belaying[①] techniques. A few, such as Italian climber Guido Ray, supported these methods as ways to render climbing less burdensome and more 'acrobatic'. Others felt that they were only of value as a safety net if all else failed. Austrian Paul Preuss went so far as to eschew all artificial aids, scaling astonishing heights using only his shoes and his bare hands. Albert Mummery, a well-known British mountaineer and author who climbed the European Alps, and, more famously, the Himalayas, where he died at the age of 39 attempting a notoriously difficult ascent, developed the notion of 'fair means' as a kind of informal protocol by which the use of 'walk-through' guidebooks and equipment such as ladders and grappling hooks were discouraged.

C By the 1940s, bolts had begun to replace pitons as the climber's choice of equipment, and criticism surrounding their use was no less fierce. In 1948, when two American climbers scaled Mount Brussels in the Canadian Rockies using a small number of pitons and bolts, climber Frank Smythe wrote of their efforts: 'I still regard Mount Brussels as unclimbed, and my feelings are no different from those I should have were I to hear that a helicopter had deposited its passenger on the summit of that mountain just so that he could boast that he had trodden an untrodden mountain top.'

D Climbing purists aside, it was not until the 1970s that the general tide began to turn against bolting and pitons. The USA, and much of the western world, was waking up to the damage it had been causing to the planet, and environmentalist campaigns and new government policies were becoming widespread. This new awareness and sensitivity to environmental issues spilled over into the rock climbing community. As a result, a stripped-down style of rock climbing known as 'clean climbing' became widely adopted. Clean climbing helped

① fastening or controlling of a climber's rope by wrapping it around a metal device or another person preserve rock faces and, compared with older approaches, it was much simpler to practise. This was partly due to the hallmark of clean climbing – the use of nuts – which were favoured over bolts because they could be placed into the rock wall with one hand while climbers maintained their grip on the rock with the other.

E Not everyone embraced the clean climbing movement, however. A decade later, debates over two more developments were erupting. The first related to the practice of chipping, in which climbers chip away pieces of rock in order to create tiny cracks in which to insert their fingers. The other major point of contention was a process that involves setting bolts in reverse from the top of the climb down. Rappel bolting makes almost any rock face climbable with relative ease, and as a result of this new technique, the sport has lost much of its risk factor and sense of pioneering spirit; indeed, it has become more about muscle power and technical mastery than a psychological trial of fearlessness under pressure. Because of this shift in focus, many amateur climbers have flocked to indoor climbing gyms, where the risk of serious harm is negligible.

F Given the environmental damage rock climbing can cause, this may be a positive outcome. It is ironic that most rock climbers and mountaineers love the outdoors and have great respect for the majesty of nature and the impressive challenges she poses, but that in the pursuit of their goals they inevitably trample sensitive vegetation, damaging and disturbing delicate flora and lichens which grow on ledges and cliff faces. Two researchers from a Canadian university, Doug Larson and Michelle McMillan, have found that rock faces that are regularly climbed have lost up to 80% of the coverage and diversity of native plant species. If that were not bad enough, non-native species have also been inadvertently introduced, having been carried in on climbers' boots.

G This leaves rock climbing with an uncertain future. Climbers are not the only user group that wishes to enjoy the wilderness – hikers, mountain bikers and horseback riders visit the same areas, and more importantly, they are much better organised, with long-established lobby groups protecting their interests. With increased pressure on limited natural resources, it has been suggested that climbers put aside their differences over the ethics of various climbing techniques, and focus on the effect of their practices on the environment and their relationship with other users and landowners.

H In any event, there can be no doubt that the era of the rock climber as a lone wolf or intrepid pioneer is over. Like many other forms of recreation, rock climbing has increasingly come under the fold of institutional efforts to curb dangerous behaviour and properly manage our natural environments. This may have spoiled the magic, but it has also made the sport safer and more sustainable, and governing bodies would do well to consider heightening such efforts in the future.

Questions 27–32

Reading Passage 3 has eight paragraphs, **A–H**.

Which paragraph contains the following information?

*Write the correct letter, **A–H**, in Boxes 27–32 on your answer sheet.*

27 examples of the impact of climbers on ecosystems

28 an account of how politics affected rock climbing

29 a less dangerous alternative to climbing rock faces

30 a recommendation for better regulation

31 a reference to a climber who did not use any tools or ropes for assistance

32 examples of different types of people who use the outdoors for recreation

Questions 33–39

Complete the flow chart below.

Choose **NO MORE THAN THREE WORDS** *from the passage for each answer.*

Write your answers in Boxes 33–39 on your answer sheet.

A rock climbing time line

Late 19th century

Some climbers discuss whether pitons and ropes should only be considered **33** .... **34** .... calls for guidelines based on unwritten rules which discourage climbing aids.

↓

1940s

New equipment becomes controversial. Frank Smythe says that Mt Brussels is effectively **35** .... because of the techniques that were used in order to scale the mountain.

↓

1970s

36 .... is more environmentally friendly. **37** .... are introduced as a climbing aid.

↓

1980s – today

Climbers discuss the merits of new techniques for making hand holds, and also of **38** .... Many say that climbing is now a test of physical strength and **39** .... rather than of courage.

Question 40

Choose the correct letter, ***A, B, C*** *or* ***D****.*

Write the correct letter in Box 40 on your answer sheet.

Choose the most appropriate title for the reading passage.

A A history of rock climbing

B Ethics and issues in rock climbing

C Current trends in rock climbing

D Sport climbers versus traditional climbers

WRITING

WRITING TASK 1

You should spend about 20 minutes on this task.

> ***The graph below shows the percentage of male and female academic staff members across the faculties of a major university in 2012.***
>
> ***Summarise the information by selecting and reporting the main features, and make comparisons where relevant.***

Write at least 150 words.

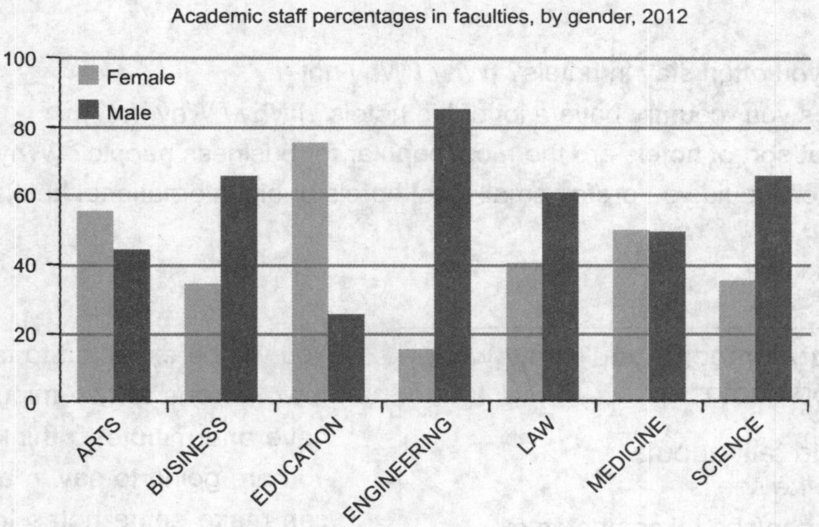

WRITING TASK 2

You should spend about 40 minutes on this task.

Write about the following topic:

> ***Solar energy is becoming more and more popular as a source of household energy in many countries around the world.***
>
> ***Why is this?***
>
> ***What are the advantages and disadvantages of solar energy?***

Give reasons for your answer and include any relevant examples from your own knowledge or experience.

Write at least 250 words.

SPEAKING

PART 1

Initial questions about name, where live, work or studies and other personal topics.

Sports centres

- Are there a lot of sports centres where you live? [Why / Why not?]
- Is it important to have near where people live? [Why / Why not?]
- Do you think people spend enough time doing sport in your country? [Why / Why not?]
- Are most people in your country more interested in sport than in the past? [Why / Why not?]

Hotels

- Do you often stay in hotels? [Why / Why not?]
- Does your country have a lot of big hotels? [Why / Why not?]
- What sort of hotels are the most popular for business people? [Why?]
- Which would you prefer, small local hotels or big international hotels? [Why?]

PART 2

Talk about someone you know who takes good photos.

You should talk about:

- who he/she is
- what he/she takes photos of
- what he/she does with his/her photos

and explain why you think he/she is a good photographer.

You will be expected to talk about the topic for one to two minutes. You will have one minute to think about what you are going to say in advance. You can make some notes to help you if you wish.

PART 3

Photos in general

- Do you think people today take more photos than they used to?
- What kinds of photos do most people like to keep or send to other people?
- Do you think people should take lessons to learn how to take professional photos?

Media and photography

- What are some of the differences between a written news story and a news story with photos?
- Is it a positive development that news stations ask people to send in their own photos of news events as they are happening?
- Has journalism changed since photos can be sent immediately from one side of the world to the other within minutes?

General Training Reading and Writing Test 2

READING

SECTION 1 *Questions 1–14*

Read the text below and answer ***Questions 1–7****.*

What to expect from your Delta Bank Credit Card

Lost/stolen cards

To report a lost or stolen card, phone the 24-hour toll-free number, 0800 700 007.
To order a replacement card, call in at your local branch of the Delta Bank.

Daily limits

Cash advances at an ATM	$1,000
Cash advances across the counter	Up to your available credit[①]
Purchases	Up to your available credit

Rates and fees	Charging time	Amount
Interest rate	Charged on the statement production date	18.5%
Card fee	Charged six-monthly	$25 per half year $3 per half year for each additional card on the account
Card replacement fee	Charged on the day the card is ordered	$25 per card
Statement reprint fee	Charged on the day the reprinted statement is ordered	$5.50 per statement
Inactivity fee	Charged after 12 weeks of no card activity	$12.50
Credit limit excess fee	Charged when the limit is exceeded	$25
Cash advance fee – across the counter	Charged on the day the cash advance is made	$3 per advance

① Please note: available credit on this account is $5,000.

Continued

Rates and fees	Charging time	Amount
Late payment default fee	Charged 7 days after the payment due date	$25
Credit card insurance	Charged monthly on the statement presentation date when applicable	Calculated at the rate of 75 cents for every $100 owing on your monthly statement. No fee is charged if the monthly statement balance is zero.

Questions 1–7

Do the following statements agree with the information given in the text above?

In Boxes 1–7 on your answer sheet, write

TRUE *if the statement agrees with the information*
FALSE *if the statement contradicts the information*
NOT GIVEN *if there is no information on this*

1 You must report a lost or stolen credit card within 24 hours.

2 To get a new card, you should appear in person at the bank.

3 You cannot buy more than $5,000 worth of goods in one day using your card.

4 If you lose your card, you must pay $25 for a new one.

5 If you don't use your card for 3 months, the card will be cancelled.

6 There is no charge for withdrawing cash using your card at an ATM.

7 Credit card insurance is always charged each month.

Read the texts below and answer ***Questions 8–14****.*

A

Health Care Assistant

We are looking to recruit health care assistants for our rest home facility for the aged.

- *This is a full-time position with immediate start.*
- *Relevant work experience an advantage*

If you are honest and reliable and comfortable around old people, this job is for you.

To apply please contact Miss Bridges on 02 566 2805

B

Cleaner

We are looking for an energetic person to work night shifts from 11.30 p.m. to 7.00 a.m. Sunday evenings through to Friday mornings.

Phone Mr Simpson 027 456 987

C

Supremo Cleaning Products

Due to on-going growth of our company, we require an experienced salesperson; approx. 12-15 hours per week – flexible – can be worked around school hours. To fulfil this role you will need:

- *experience in sales*
- *excellent communication skills*

Call in at the Supremo office, 15 Fairview Road, anytime between 9 a.m. and 5 p.m. to pick up an application form.

D

Café Central in the CBD

Requires an assistant manager

- *reliable*
- *able to cope under pressure*

Regular rostered hours for Saturdays and Sundays – from 7.30 a.m. to 6 p.m.

E

Café Kitchen Assistant required for the summer

No previous kitchen experience necessary but must be a clean worker willing to learn.
We are open every day 7.30 a.m. – 9 p.m.
Apply in person – Teapot Café, the Strand.

F

Night Duty Manager

Full-time, permanent manager required
Minimum 3 years' experience in the restaurant trade
Excellent wages, meals provided
Phone Jake on 02 724 4798 at the Night Owl Restaurant after 7 p.m.

G

Café Express

Kitchen assistant wanted with experience in baking, cabinet food and short orders - must be able to work in an organised and safe manner.
We are looking for someone who has a passion for food and the right attitude towards the workplace.
If you are that person, and can commit to a five-hour working day, early start at 6 a.m., please send your CV and a reference to:
The Manager, Café Express, 78 Providence Place

H

Tower Office Suite in the CBD

Reliable cleaner required for the above.
Hours of work (2.5 hours Mon–Fri) flexible but must take place inside office hours.
$15.00 per hour
Phone Mabel 025 262 3655

Questions 8–14

*Look at the eight job advertisements, **A–H**, on the previous pages and read the descriptions of job seekers below.*

Which is the most suitable job for each person?

*Write the correct letter, **A–H**, in Boxes 8–14 on your answer sheet.*

8 a person with school-age children who used to sell cosmetics in a department store

9 a student looking for work over the long vacation

10 an ex-baker with some cooking experience who wants a job that finishes before 3.30 p.m. so that she can pick up her children after school

11 a mother with school-age children who only wants to work a few hours per week

12 a person with ten years' experience in the restaurant business who is looking for a well-paid permanent position

13 an active parent who wants afternoons and weekends free to spend with his young children

14 a person who has spent the last five years looking after her elderly parents but is now eager to get back into the workforce

SECTION 2 *Questions 15–27*

Questions 15–20

The text on the following page has seven paragraphs, **A–G**.

*Choose the correct heading for Paragraphs **B–G** from the list of headings below.*

*Write the correct number, **i–x**, in Boxes 15–20 on your answer sheet.*

List of Headings

- **i** Be tidy
- **ii** Use visual communication
- **iii** Remember your manners
- **iv** Maintain good personal hygiene
- **v** Show courtesy when eating
- **vi** Use appropriate meeting etiquette
- **vii** Respect other people's property
- **viii** Be punctual
- **ix** Adhere to the dress code
- **x** Be trustworthy

Example	*Answer*
Paragraph **A**	**v**

15 Paragraph **B**

16 Paragraph **C**

17 Paragraph **D**

18 Paragraph **E**

19 Paragraph **F**

20 Paragraph **G**

OFFICE PROTOCOL

This is a set of rules or guidelines for appropriate behaviour in the office. Although they are often implicit, they should still be respected.

A Never consume food at your desk; use assigned areas only and avoid pungent foods with strong odours (garlic and curry, for example), as these may be offensive.

B You will get along better with your colleagues if you show consideration, courtesy and respect. Greet fellow workers every day by making eye contact and saying 'Hello' or 'Good morning'. Be polite – say 'please'. Be appreciative – say 'thank you'. Apologise if you have to interrupt someone; say 'sorry' if you make a mistake.

C To assist the smooth running of the workplace, be sure to get to work early or on time and never arrive late for a scheduled meeting.

D Rules about appropriate attire may be unwritten, even unspoken, but rest assured there will be some. Ask if you are not sure, and only wear office outfits that are neat, clean and pressed.

E To maintain a pleasant working atmosphere amongst your colleagues, ask permission before borrowing any item from another person's desk, no matter how small or insignificant; and, most importantly, return it immediately you have finished with it.

F Keep your work area and communal areas orderly and uncluttered. This applies to common rooms like the kitchen, as well. Clean up after yourself and wipe down surfaces in the interests of both hygiene and collegial cooperation.

G Take a shower and clean your teeth before work but avoid wearing overpowering deodorants, scents or aftershaves. Be discreet if you need to re-apply makeup, adjust your clothing or blow your nose – the privacy of the bathroom is the best place for this.

Read the text below and answer ***Questions 21–27***.

Staying positive in the workplace

A There are many reasons why workers are discontented in the workplace. There are also many reasons why they should strive to be more positive. On average, people spend about a third of their lives at work. That's a lot of time to be miserable or depressed. These days, there is often a general atmosphere of anxiety and despondency at work because of insecurity: the economy is depressed and many companies are downsizing, restructuring and making redundancies.

B Staying positive despite this is a challenge but it is important not to develop a negative attitude at work, especially if you already have a stressful workload. Beware: chronic negativity may lead to long-term psychological and physical ill health. On the other hand, optimists have a greater sense of self-worth and are thus more likely to experience job satisfaction through an appreciation of their own achievements and productivity. If workplace tension is getting you down, it is time to take stock of the situation and establish a more positive outlook.

C Firstly, take care of your physical health with a wholesome diet, exercise and sufficient sleep. If work has taken over your life, find a balance: find and nurture friendships outside of work and do something in your free time that is totally unrelated to your job. Remember also to take care of your appearance and dress well to boost your self-esteem in the workplace.

D Avoid negative co-workers if possible; if not, try to put a more positive spin on what they say, tell a joke, or just remain neutral. Focus on the good things rather than the bad, and smile more often – your affirmative attitude may rub off on your colleagues. If it is possible, listen to light, uplifting music if you feel it helps – as long as it does not distract you from your work.

E If job security is causing anxiety, developing professional competence is essential. Expand your skill set – take a course, become familiar with a new computer programme, tackle new tasks – and consider shouldering more responsibility if you are not already overworked. Perhaps it is time to set new goals, even minor ones. Being pro-active and creative will not only keep you focussed, motivated and more in control of your work life but also prepare you for the job market if the worst should happen.

Questions 21–27

Complete the summary below.

Choose ***NO MORE THAN TWO WORDS*** *from the text for each answer.*

Write your answers in Boxes 21–27 on your answer sheet.

In general, people spend around 30% of their lifetime at work but often they are unhappy because of financial **21** .... It may be difficult to stay positive but physical and mental illness can result from **22** .... In contrast, **23** .... feel better about themselves and enjoy their work more.

It is essential to eat well, get enough rest and **24** .... Developing friendships and taking part in leisure activities are also important.

Try to always be positive: your **25** .... could have a good effect on fellow employees.

Learning new skills and taking on more responsibility will improve your **26** .... , which will not only give you more expertise in your current job but also set you up for the **27** .... if you need to seek new employment.

SECTION 3 *Questions 28–40*

Read the text below and answer ***Questions 28–40****.*

Esperanto

One man's vision for world peace

A If English is not your native language but you are reading this article, then you have learnt English at some stage in your life. Why? If you have made an English-speaking country your home, the answer is obvious, but even those who do not need English to communicate in their daily lives may still need to learn it. Despite its eccentric grammar, complex sentence structure and bizarre spelling, English is the nearest thing the world has to a worldwide language; and in order to belong to and fully participate in the new 'global village', you have to learn the dominant language. English is the common language of science and technology, medicine, the aeronautical industry, banking and investment, movies and music, not to mention the Internet, where over 80% of the websites are in English. The argument for learning English would therefore seem quite compelling, but some believe that the predominance of English and its associated culture and attitudes is endangering, if not destroying, other customs and cultures. Wouldn't it be wonderful if there was an easy, politically non-aligned and culturally unbiased tongue that could serve as the medium of international communication?

B In fact, there has been such a language in existence for over a hundred years. Esperanto was conceived and created by a Polish physician, Ludovic Zamenhof. In 19th-century Poland, Zamenhof saw many violent ethnic clashes and decided that language was the root of the problem. He observed that whenever people of different ethnicities tried to communicate, the native speakers of the language in use inevitably had an advantage. He had the grand vision of bringing peace to the world by giving people of different ethnic and linguistic backgrounds a standard, neutral language to converse in. His first thoughts were to restore Latin or classical Greek as a lingua franca, but he soon decided that both these languages were too complex and difficult to learn, and thus he embarked upon the project of developing an entirely new language.

C In 1887, Zamenhof launched his new language, Esperanto, which was constructed specifically to make it simple to learn and easy to pronounce; the grammar was very straightforward, the verbs were all regular and the spelling was phonetic. A sample of the grammar shows us that all common nouns in the singular end in *-o*, adjectives in *-a*, adverbs derived from them in *-e*, while all verbs in the present tense end in *-as*. When it comes to pronunciation, the stress is on the penultimate (second to last) syllable, although there can be exceptions in poetry. Compared with English, this artificial language is simplicity itself. The vocabulary mainly draws on European languages that originated from Latin (for example, French, Spanish and

Italian) but some words also come from German and a few from Slavic languages and Greek. Zamenhof originally published a list of 900 root words which could be increased to make many thousands of words by using prefixes and suffixes and joining words together to make compounds. What is more, because the main aim of Esperanto is to make communication uncomplicated and easy, there are very few idiomatic expressions or slang words. Research carried out in Germany shows that students who spend 1500 hours studying English can reach the same level of proficiency in Esperanto after studying for only 150 hours! In some countries, it has been found that studying Esperanto as a first foreign language accelerates the acquisition of other languages, possibly because of its grammatical simplicity and its cultural impartiality and adaptability.

D Given its logical design, ease of acquisition and lack of bias, it is surprising that Esperanto has not become a dominant global language; after all, its main advantage is that people of different backgrounds can connect and converse on an equal footing, thus reducing tensions and improving relationships. Its detractors would say that its lack of success is due to the fact that it is an artificial or made-up language. However, all languages have some artificial content. Think of all the new words that have come into English, or your own language – words which have been borrowed or invented to describe discoveries in science and technology, for instance. Another common objection to Esperanto is that, despite Zamenhof's laudable intentions, his invented language is Eurocentric, in that it is based only on a small set of world languages. Thus, it can still be accused of being culturally biased and narrow in its vocabulary, structures and pronunciation.

E Historically, Esperanto has had its ups and downs. Initially it was well received but certain totalitarian regimes became suspicious that people learning the language might be a subversive influence, and consequently Esperanto groups and materials were banned in those countries. After the Second World War, Esperanto was accepted and encouraged in East European and Asian countries that were looking for a common language and that wanted to avoid English because of its association with American ideology. It is thought that up to five million people may have learnt the language back then, but since the 1970s far fewer people have learned the language, and it is now not commonly used. Recently, there has been a suggestion that Esperanto should become the official language of the European Union. However, this has not yet come to pass.

F Esperanto has made an appearance from time to time in popular culture such as novels and films, usually when the author or director has wanted to introduce a foreign language without denoting a specific ethnic or national group. There have even been a couple of feature films made completely in the language of Esperanto but mostly the language is used in futuristic productions. There are also lively Esperanto conferences and meetings around the world. Could Esperanto really become the universal language of the future? Although, ideologically appealing, it is doubtful whether Esperanto could ever challenge the supremacy of English as a world language now or in the future.

Questions 28–34

The text on the previous pages has six paragraphs, **A**–**F**.

Which paragraphs contain the following information?

*Write the appropriate letter, **A–F**, in Boxes 28–34 on your answer sheet.*

NB *You may use any letter more than once.*

28 the story of the decline of Esperanto as a world language

29 examples of the international use of English

30 two reasons why people do not like Esperanto

31 the reason for the invention of Esperanto

32 examples of situations where Esperanto has been used

33 a reason why English should not be the main international language

34 the results of a study which compared learning Esperanto to learning another language

Questions 35–40

Do the following statements agree with the information given in the text above?

In Boxes 35–40 on your answer sheet, write

TRUE	*if the statement agrees with the information*
FALSE	*if the statement contradicts the information*
NOT GIVEN	*if there is no information on this*

35 Ludovic Zamenhof was a doctor by profession.

36 Zamenhof spent several years learning Latin and Greek.

37 All nouns in Esperanto end in *-o*.

38 One way of making a new word is to add more letters to an existing word.

39 Idioms in Esperanto are rare.

40 Esperanto represents a true world language.

WRITING

WRITING TASK 1

You should spend about 20 minutes on this task.

> ***You have recently moved to a different town.***
>
> ***Write a letter to an English-speaking friend. In your letter***
> - ***explain why you have moved***
> - ***describe the new town***
> - ***invite your friend to come and visit***

Write at least 150 words.

You do **NOT** need to write any addresses.

Begin your letter as follows:

Dear .... ,

WRITING TASK 2

You should spend about 40 minutes on this task.

Write about the following topic:

> ***Some people believe it is good for children to do chores. Others, however, say that children should not be asked to do household tasks.***
>
> ***Discuss both these views and give your own opinion.***

Give reasons for your answer and include any relevant examples from your own knowledge or experience.

Write at least 250 words.

Academic Test 3

LISTENING

SECTION 1 *Questions 1–10*

Complete the form below.

Write ***NO MORE THAN TWO WORDS AND/OR A NUMBER*** *for each answer.*

New Password

Example	*Answer*
Call taken by:	Natasha

Customer's full name:	Michael **1** ....
Date of birth:	27 March 1988
Previous address:	319 **2** ....
	East Providence
Phone number:	0492 48002
Data allowance:	**3** ....
Current payment plan:	**4** ....
Mother's maiden name:	**5** ....
First pet:	**6** ....
New password sent on:	**7** ....
Extra services requested:	New **8** ....
	Cancel **9** ....
	10 .... pack

SECTION 2 *Questions 11–20*

Questions 11–16

Where can each of the following items be found?

*Choose **SIX** answers from the box and write the correct letter, **A–I**, next to Questions 11–16.*

Locations

A on washing machine
B in hallway cupboard
C in hot water cupboard
D next to back door
E in bathroom
F on top of television
G in shoebox
H under kitchen sink
I above front door

11 alarm

12 other keys

13 laundry detergent

14 beach towels

15 bath towels

16 light bulbs

Questions 17–20

Complete the notes below.

*Write **NO MORE THAN TWO WORDS AND/OR A NUMBER** for each answer.*

Difficult parking in town at the weekend because of so many **17** ....

Museum is closed on **18** ....

Recommended places to eat:

- **19** .... for Chinese food
- Pizzeria for Italian food

Phone number for takeaway pizza – **20** ....

SECTION 3 *Questions 21–30*

Questions 21–25

*Choose the correct letter, **A**, **B** or **C**.*

21 Why did Diana accept the offer from Gregory Associates?

A It covered her travel expenses.
B It was from a well-known company.
C It was the only offer she received.

22 Diana was disappointed because

A she found the work routine repetitive.
B the staff were not very helpful.
C the work was not related to her studies.

23 What did Diana like best about her internship?

A Observing how the workplace operates
B Being responsible for completing projects
C Working closely with the project managers

24 What was the hardest part of the internship?

A Combining it with her studies
B Living on so little money
C Working such long hours

25 During the internship, Diana

A changed her mind about her career.
B received a job offer from the company.
C decided not to continue her studies.

Questions 26–30

Complete the flow chart below.

Write ***NO MORE THAN TWO WORDS*** *for each answer.*

How to apply for an internship

Organise your **26** .... in advance

Research a variety of companies

Create a **27** .... of appropriate positions

28 .... the applications for each position

29 .... the companies after one week

Prepare for the interview

30 .... during the interview

SECTION 4 *Questions 31–40*

Complete the notes below.

*Write **ONE WORD ONLY** for each answer.*

Development Studies

Development Studies attempts to understand:

- how societies change and progress over time
- what **31** .... help to make these changes

Two approaches:

- theoretical (understand how change occurs)
- applied (examine particular **32** .... and how they can be applied)

Areas of focus:

Asia-Pacific region; urbanisation (including employment and **33** ....); migration and trade

You will develop the skills to:

- understand key development issues in detail
- gather data (both **34** .... and textual data)
- carefully **35** .... findings
- **36** .... on a research project

Brief history of Development Studies:

1950s — The discipline emerged. **37** .... issues were the major consideration.

1970s — Development Studies became more critical of common **38** .... and underlying assumptions. Questions were raised about power, environmental sustainability and unequal **39** .... issues.

1980s–today — National governments were no longer as important. Growing interest in small-scale practices such as giving very small **40** ....

READING

READING PASSAGE 1

*You should spend about 20 minutes on **Questions 1–13**, which are based on Reading Passage 1 below.*

Knighthoods

An ancient tradition

A Knighthoods are one of the oldest and most prestigious forms of honouring individual citizens in the United Kingdom. Although initially conferred upon members of the armed forces solely on the basis of their performance in combat, the award now recognises all contributions to national life. Some of the most notable knighthoods of recent times have been bestowed on musicians or entertainers such as Sir Elton John and Sir Paul McCartney, and the fields of finance, industry and education are also represented. Citizens of non-Commonwealth[1] countries are eligible for an 'honorary' knighthood for which they are not permitted to use the titles 'Sir' or 'Dame'. Perceived to be a British tradition, the legacy of knighthoods actually dates back to ancient Rome, from where it spread throughout a number of European countries in the Middle Ages and acquired certain features. A would-be knight had to undergo strict military instruction from a young age, which included spending time as an assistant (known as an esquire) to an existing knight, and participating in battle. He had to learn how to equip his knight for battle, and to help him with putting on the heavy and cumbersome armour of the time. He was responsible for keeping this armour in good condition, polishing and cleaning it. He also had to demonstrate chivalrous behaviour such as generosity, selflessness, fearlessness and skill in battle. Finally, the potential knight also required the financial means to purchase horses, weapons and armour for himself, and then make himself available to serve the ruling monarch for a minimum period each year.

B In modern times, the process is very different. Instead of relying on formalised military training or political patronage, a nominations system is used. This way, a person's name can be put forward for a knighthood by any institution such as a school or business, or even just a fellow member of society. After this, an advisory panel, acting on behalf of the sovereign, deliberates and selects the future knights and dames from the pool of applications. Those selected are contacted discreetly before announcements are made to ensure that they wish to accept the honour.

C In rare cases, knighthoods can be revoked through a process known as forfeiture. This most often occurs when the recipient is convicted of a criminal offense. Terry Lewis, a police officer in Queensland, Australia, was stripped of his knighthood after being implicated in a string of illegal activities that included accepting $700,000 worth of bribes from bookmakers and casinos, and forging the signature of an Australian politician on a police document in 1981. Lewis has repeatedly protested his innocence and suggested that he was falsely accused of these crimes, but his appeals failed in court. In a more serious incident, British art historian and intelligence officer, Anthony Blunt, lost his knighthood after it was discovered that he was working as a double agent and handing confidential material over to the Soviet Union.

D Knighthoods have also been forfeited for reasons of incompetence rather than outright illegality or treason. Having been knighted for 'services to banking' in 2004, CEO of the Royal Bank of Scotland, Fred Goodwin, presided over a 24-billion-pound loss at the bank just four years later. Although retaining a 16-million-pound pension, to which he was legally entitled, Goodwin had his knighthood annulled as the Queen's advisory panel deemed him 'the chief decision maker at the time'. Scandals such as these have contributed to spirited debates regarding the role and relevance of knighthoods in 21st-century society.

[1] The Commonwealth is an international association consisting of the UK together with states that were previously part of the British Empire and dependencies.

Questions 1–6

Do the following statements agree with the information given in Reading Passage 1?

In Boxes 1–6 on your answer sheet, write

TRUE	*if the statement agrees with the information*
FALSE	*if the statement contradicts the information*
NOT GIVEN	*if there is no information on this*

1 The knighthood was first awarded only for military service.

2 Most knights now come from the arts and entertainment industries.

3 People from outside the Commonwealth cannot be awarded any type of knighthood.

4 The knighthood began in Great Britain.

5 Esquires, or trainee knights, were usually related to the knights they served.

6 An esquire needed money to buy his own equipment.

Questions 7–10

Complete the summary below.

Choose ***NO MORE THAN THREE WORDS*** *from the passage for each answer.*

Write your answers in Boxes 7–10 on your answer sheet.

Knighthood Selection: Then and Now

The process of becoming a knight has changed over time. In the Middle Ages, people began training to become a knight at **7** .... They had to show they were brave and skilled fighters, and were required to work for **8** .... for part of the year. Today, potential recipients of the knighthood are selected through **9** .... A final decision is made by **10** ....

Questions 11–13

Choose ***THREE*** *letters,* ***A–F****.*

Write the correct letters in Boxes 11–13 on your answer sheet.

Which **THREE** of the following are reasons given in the text for people losing their knighthoods?

A Punishing someone for a crime he or she did not commit
B Using another person's name on an important paper
C Poor management of a company
D Wrongfully accepting pension payments
E Gambling on horseracing or card games
F Giving secret information to a foreign government

READING PASSAGE 2

*You should spend about 20 minutes on **Questions 14–26**, which are based on Reading Passage 2 below.*

'Just do it!'

Or – the subtle art of procrastination

A Procrastination, a kind of chronic time-wasting, has long been dismissed as an innocuous human foible. Researchers are now beginning a more sober examination of this practice, however, and there may be good reason for doing so: twenty per cent of Americans now admit to suffering from procrastination, a fifteen per cent jump from 1970. Researchers are bemused as to what explains this sharp rise in the figures, but there is no doubt that procrastination is wreaking havoc on people's lives. One side effect is perhaps the most predictable: procrastination hampers academic and work commitments as sufferers fail to meet deadlines or achieve their goals. But there are other costs too. In shifting burdens of responsibility onto others and reneging on their promises, procrastinators undermine relationships both in the workplace and in their private lives, all of which takes a toll on their well-being. In one study, over the course of a semester, procrastinating university students were noted to be suffering from notably weaker immune systems, more gastrointestinal problems, and higher occurrences of insomnia than their non-procrastinating peers.

B Is there hope for procrastinators? Everyone admits it's a difficult demon to beat, but a few self-styled procrastination coaches have developed strategies to that end. Although evidence for their efficacy is largely anecdotal at this stage, some of these strategies at least offer promising avenues for future research.

C Career counsellor Amy Sykes focuses on the basics. Firstly, she says, embrace peer pressure. Many weight loss and self-help groups encourage individuals to hold themselves accountable to a wider circle of their peers, and Sykes believes this social safety net can be harnessed just as successfully by procrastinators. A change in perspective is also considered vital. 'When we want people to do something for us, we really sell it to them,' Sykes observes. 'But when we need to do it ourselves, we focus on all the reasons we don't want to.' Instead, she argues, we should pique our own interest and find ways to make our important projects more attractive – by turning them into little competitions or fact-finding missions, for example. If all else fails, Sykes believes we must recompense ourselves for our troubles, ideally with little treats upon finishing a task. 'It doesn't need to be big,' she says. 'Pancakes, a hot bath, or an episode of your favourite television show could all do the trick.'

D Though these tips may be a little too garden variety[①] for some, others have thought up more cunning twists on the human psyche. One such approach was developed by the crime writer

① Common, usual or ordinary

Raymond Chandler, who built his strategy on a basic yet critical observation: procrastinators rarely sit about completely inactively, but rather tend to engage themselves in useful but less pressing tasks: vacuuming behind the bed, cleaning out the fridge, washing the windows and so on. The result is that they 'cheat' themselves into experiencing feelings of productivity and satisfaction that offer further distraction from the original project. Chandler's method, which he successfully used to help himself write detective stories, involves setting aside a period of time in which the procrastinator may do one of two things: absolutely nothing or work on the project that he or she wishes to complete. Sitting still, without the satisfaction of busying himself with less urgent tasks, Chandler slowly felt the itch of tedious monotony sink in. Within five or ten minutes, this itch had become intolerable, and he felt compelled to begin writing his stories.

E Another procrastinator, professor of philosophy John Perry, developed his strategy against procrastination based on essentially the same insight as Chandler's – that procrastinators are actually quite good at doing 'marginally useful' tasks, just not the tasks they really ought to be doing. He thus surmised that the enemy of successful task completion is not, in fact, that great engine of productive activity – procrastination itself – but rather how we order our projects in the hierarchy of urgency. If a procrastinator needs to finish an assignment before 8 o'clock the following morning, for instance, he is likely to find himself sharpening pencils instead. 'But if all the procrastinator had left to do was to sharpen some pencils,' Perry observes, 'no force on earth could get him to do it.' The key to this approach is to rank one's priorities, then bump the most urgent tasks a little further down and place at the top some potentially daunting and important-sounding projects which are ultimately not all that essential. If the student with the essay deadline can convince himself he absolutely must reorganise his email box, or finish reading that old, dusty novel he only got halfway through, then suddenly the essay deadline is going to seem a far superior option.

F If the Ancient Greeks struggled with it, and all the life coaches, counsellors and motivational speakers in the modern world are unable to erase it from our existence either, it seems unlikely that procrastination will ever truly be put to rest. As these procrastination gurus have shown, however, the right strategies have the potential to minimise its impact – if you ever get around to using them.

Questions 14–18

Do the following statements agree with the information given in Reading Passage 2?

In Boxes 14–18 on your answer sheet, write

TRUE	*if the statement agrees with the information*
FALSE	*if the statement contradicts the information*
NOT GIVEN	*if there is no information on this*

14 Procrastination has always been recognised as a serious problem.

15 The reason for the rise in procrastination is unknown.

16 Students are the most likely group to procrastinate.

17 A range of health problems have been linked to procrastination.

18 Most techniques to stop procrastination are based on scientific study.

Questions 19–25

Look at the following statements (Questions 19–25) and the list of people below.

Match each statement with the correct person, ***A, B*** *or* ***C****.*

Write the correct letter, ***A, B*** *or* ***C****, in Boxes 19–25 on your answer sheet.*

19 Doing housework is a common way of avoiding important work.

20 Get support from other people.

21 Make a list of boring tasks before important ones.

22 Look for ways to make the work more interesting.

23 Lists are powerful tools for reducing procrastination.

24 Use boredom as motivation.

25 Use rewards when a task is completed.

List of People

A Amy Sykes
B Raymond Chandler
C John Perry

Question 26

*Choose the correct letter **A**, **B**, **C** or **D**.*

Write the correct letter in Box 26 on your answer sheet.

What is the writer's conclusion?

A Some procrastination-reducing strategies have had proven success.

B Procrastination will never be completely eliminated.

C Procrastinators should employ a life coach to help them.

D Most procrastinators want to learn how to be more efficient.

READING PASSAGE 3

*You should spend about 20 minutes on **Questions 27–40**, which are based on Reading Passage 3 below.*

When evolution works against us

A Life has changed in just about every way since small tribes of hunter-gatherers roamed the earth armed with nothing but spears and stone tools. We now buy our meat from the supermarket rather than stalking it through the jungle; houses and high-rises shelter us at night instead of caves. But despite these changes, some very basic responses linger on. The short, sharp feeling of heightened awareness that sweeps through us when a stranger passes in a dark alley is no different, physiologically speaking, from the sensation our ancestors experienced when they were walking through the bushes and heard a dry twig snap nearby. It's called the 'fight or flight' response, and it helps us to identify dangerous situations and act decisively by, as the name suggests, mustering our strength for a confrontation or running away as fast as we can.

B This shift to survival mode is often popularly described as a sudden unease, a sense that a situation is 'off' or 'not right'. However, the sense is actually the outcome of an incredibly complex mind-body process which involves the brain's 'fear centre', the hypothalamus, advising the sympathetic nervous system and the adrenal-cortical system to work, at first separately, and then together, to blend a potent mix of hormones and chemicals and secrete them into the bloodstream. Our heartbeat rises, along with our respiratory rate. Skin feels cold (hence the 'shiver' down the spine) as blood supply is redirected to the larger muscles required for a physical confrontation or a hasty retreat. The ability to concentrate on issues of minor importance also suffers, as the brain tends to prioritise 'big picture' thinking at this time.

C Without this instinctive response, the human race would never have survived, but at present it is often more of a hindrance than a help. Although instances of physical threats have decreased over the years, activation of the fight or flight response has actually increased, largely in response to mental frustrations. This poses a problem, however, because the fight or flight mechanism functions most helpfully as a response to something that can cause bodily harm, such as a falling tree or a wild animal, rather than in response to a fulminating boss, a traffic jam, or a spouse who has not returned a phone call. During these instances of mental distress, the physical manifestations of fight or flight, such as an inability to think rationally and calmly, can actually exacerbate the problem.

D A similar case of an evolutionary development overstaying its welcome is the example of 'mind chatter'. Mind chatter is the ceaseless train of scattered thoughts and self-talk that occupies our mind, ensuring we are always 'switched on', searching for danger and threats. This would have been a boon for a solitary caveman on a three-hour hunting expedition, but in a modern world already overloaded with sensory input, it causes us to fret about non-existent predicaments and occasionally needlessly triggers the fight or flight response.

E These twin forces, mind chatter and the fight or flight response, have combined to wreak havoc on the modern psyche and have led to a spike in what some studies have suggested is a cause of up to eighty per cent of all illness today: stress. Stress, erroneously considered by many to be a mere feeling, is actually a physiological condition resulting from a cumulative accrual of certain hormones in the body, hormones that can help us in quick, sharp doses, but which are toxic if they are not properly metabolised. Metabolism of these potentially toxic hormones relies on physical exertion, which originally evolved as part of the fight or flight process – hormone release was usually followed by physical exertion (fighting or running), which returned the body to a state of balance. In present day encounters, however, the vital element of physical exertion is missing: a resentful employee cannot punch his co-worker, for example, and a frustrated driver is unable to simply ram his way through a packed intersection.

F What can be done to restore the balance? Stress researcher Neil F. Neimarck, perhaps not surprisingly, recommends physical exercise as one useful strategy. Fortunately, the brain is not clever enough to realise that this exercise is completely unrelated to the original stress stimulus, and in this way we can effectively 'fool' our bodies into metabolising stress hormones by punching a boxing bag instead of the person who annoyed us in the first place. Another option is the 'relaxation response', discovered by Harvard cardiologist Herbert Benson. Benson found that certain behaviours, such as deep breathing, meditation, and the repetition of simple, affirmative phrases, acted as an antidote to mind chatter and the fight or flight responses, calming the nervous system and inducing a relaxed state of mind and body instead. Integrating these methods into our lives will be important if the cycle of stress accumulation that is so endemic in modern Western society is to be stopped.

Questions 27–32

*Complete the summary using the list of words, **A–O**, below.*

*Write the correct letter, **A–O**, in Boxes 27–32 on your answer sheet.*

The fight or flight response

Modern man still has the **27** .... that were needed in his distant past in the jungle. One of these, the 'fight or flight' response, originally assisted humans to recognise **28** .... and take action. Today, this same response manifests itself mostly as nothing more than a feeling of **29** .... It is the result of the hypothalamus producing and releasing **30** .... into the blood, with subsequent rises in heart rate and breathing, and the sensation of a **31** .... in temperature as the blood is diverted to other organs. Although this **32** .... was once essential to human survival, it now occurs as a result of perceived rather than actual threat.

A plan	**B** strengths	**C** substances
D strangers	**E** warmth	**F** mixtures
G instincts	**H** threats	**I** powers
J system	**K** anxiety	**L** pressure
M drop	**N** problems	**O** rise

Questions 33–36

Choose the correct letter, ***A, B, C*** *or* ***D****.*

Write the correct letter in Boxes 33–36 on your answer sheet.

33 When the fight or flight response is activated, it is difficult to

A increase breathing speed.
B focus on small problems.
C maintain body temperature.
D run for long periods of time.

34 The fight or flight response is less useful today because modern individuals

A encounter fewer physical threats.
B can easily manage small daily difficulties.
C are better at creative problem solving.
D do not need to hunt dangerous animals.

35 One disadvantage of 'mind chatter' is that people may

A talk too much and miss important information.
B spend too much time by themselves.
C become distracted from real threats.
D worry about problems that are not real.

36 The writer suggests stress is increasing because of

A a lack of physical release.
B an increase in the number of threats.
C more health problems.
D the loss of some hormones.

Questions 37–40

Do the following statements agree with the views of the writer in Reading Passage 3?

In Boxes 37–40 on your answer sheet, write

YES	*if the statement agrees with the views of the writer*
NO	*if the statement contradicts the views of the writer*
NOT GIVEN	*if it is impossible to say what the writer thinks about this*

37 Stress is an emotion.

38 Fights in the workplace are increasing.

39 In order to metabolise hormones, exercise must be linked with the original cause of stress.

40 Saying positive words can reduce stress.

WRITING

WRITING TASK 1

You should spend about 20 minutes on this task.

The diagram below shows how a solar powered water pump works. Summarise the information by selecting and reporting the main features, and make comparisons where relevant.

Write at least 150 words.

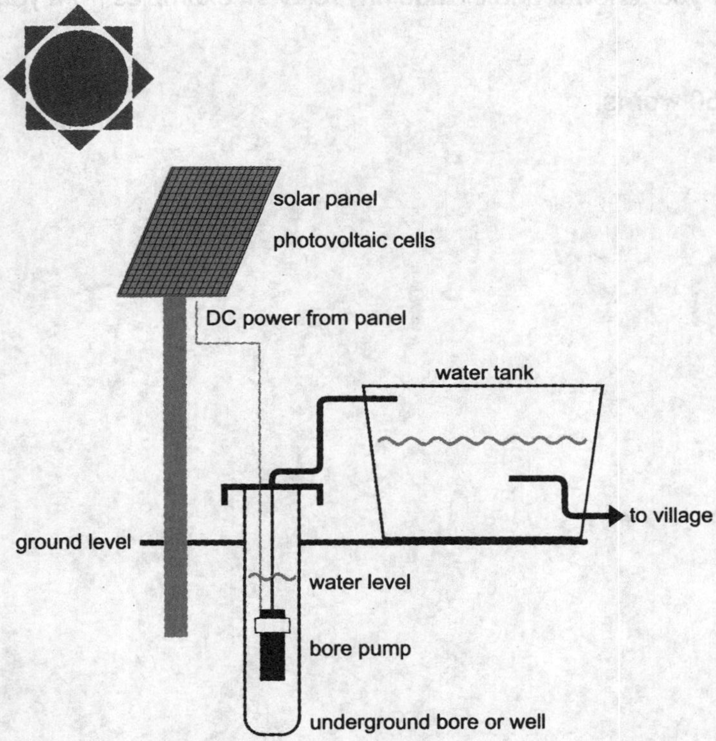

WRITING TASK 2

You should spend about 40 minutes on this task.

Write about the following topic.

> ***Rising university fees and scarce employment prospects for graduates have led some people to say that universities should not teach arts subjects, like philosophy and history, and only offer practical degree courses that maximise chances of employment.***
>
> ***To what extent do you agree or disagree?***

Give reasons for your answer and include any relevant examples from your own knowledge or experience.

Write at least 250 words.

SPEAKING

PART 1

Initial questions about name, where live, work or studies and other personal topics.

Clothes

- What do you like to wear when you are at home? [Why?]
- What do people in your country like to wear to parties? [Why?]
- Do you like to try different kinds of fashion? [Why / Why not?]
- Do people in your country usually like to wear formal or casual clothes? [Why?]

Good manners

- Is it important to be polite in your country? [Why / why not?]
- How do children learn good manners?
- Who do you think is usually more polite, older or younger people? [Why?]
- Do you think more people are more polite at home with family, or with people they don't know? [Why?]

PART 2

Talk about a decision you made that was difficult. You should talk about: • what it was • when you made it • why it was difficult and explain how it has changed your life.

You will be expected to talk about the topic for one to two minutes. You will have one minute to think about what you are going to say in advance. You can make some notes to help you if you wish.

PART 3

Making decisions in general

- What are some decisions that most people need to make these days?
- Who do people think usually gives the best advice in your culture?
- What disadvantages are there when other people give you advice, when you have to make a decision?

Age and decisions

- What are the important things that a teenager has to make decisions about?
- How can your age make a difference to the way you approach decision making?
- How are the kinds of decisions people make today different to life 50 years ago? [Why?]

Academic Test 4

LISTENING

SECTION 1 *Questions 1–10*

Questions 1–6

Complete the flow chart below.

Write ***NO MORE THAN TWO WORDS AND/OR A NUMBER*** *for each answer.*

Making an International Money Transfer

Example

Step 1: Access global payments system
— Log on to Wesley Bank Internet Banking
— Select 'Transfer Money'
— Select 'International Money Transfer' (under International Services)

↓

Step 2: Click on 'Payment Destination **1** ....'
— Scroll down and choose the place

↓

Step 3: Enter '**2** .... Details'
— Name, address, phone number

↓

Step 4: 'Transaction Details'
— Select transaction, savings or **3** .... account
— Enter reason: medical care, **4** ....

↓

Step 5: 'Recipient Account Details'
— Account name and number
(NB: complete the page within **5** .... hours)

↓

Step 6: 'Recipient Bank Details'
— Name, branch, address

↓

Step 7: 'Confirmation Page'
— Press Submit
— Print receipt or write down Transaction **6** ....

Questions 7–10

Answer the questions below.

Write ***NO MORE THAN TWO WORDS AND/OR A NUMBER*** *for each answer.*

7 How long does it take for the Wesley Bank to process a transfer?

....

8 How much does it cost to make each transfer from the Wesley Bank?

....

9 What is the maximum amount of each transfer?

....

10 What is a security token?

....

SECTION 2 *Questions 11–20*

Questions 11–17

Label the plan below.

*Write the correct letter, **A–I**, next to Questions 11–17.*

Plan for upgrade of Bayfield town centre

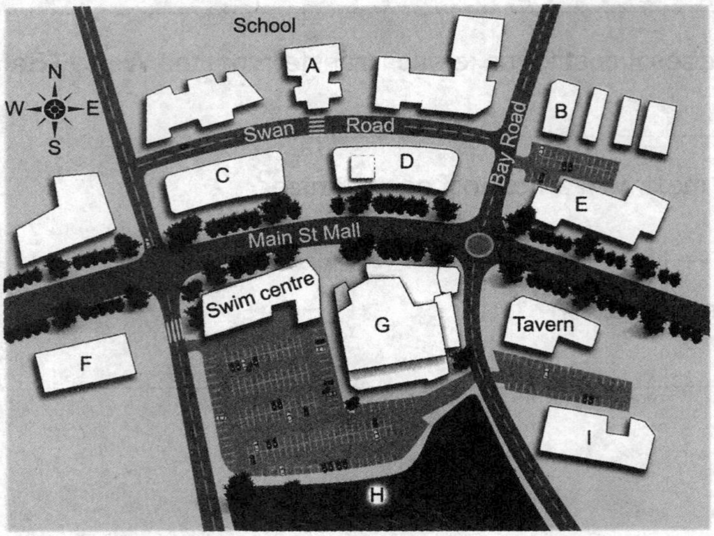

11 supermarket ....

12 park ....

13 market ....

14 office block ....

15 gymnasium ....

16 library ....

17 council ....

Questions 18–20

Complete the sentences below.

*Write **NO MORE THAN TWO WORDS** for each answer.*

18 The key issue for residents is better ....

19 The council needs to buy suitable .... for playgrounds.

20 The council's first choice for controlling the movement of vehicles on Swan Road is to add ....

SECTION 3 *Questions 21–30*

Complete the notes below.

*Write **NO MORE THAN THREE WORDS** for each answer.*

CORPORATE CULTURES

Studies by Quinn and Cameron propose:

'Competing Values Framework'

- **Hierarchy Culture**
  — obeys rules, **21** ______________ and bureaucracy
  — stable, structured **22** ______________
  — leaders use power, **23** ______________, and position to deal with employees
  — common among **24** ______________ organisations and large companies
- **Market Culture**
  — main difference is the importance of **25** ______________ with clients or suppliers
  — this culture produces the best **26** ______________ (due to emphasis on competitiveness and success)
- **Clan Culture**
  — family-like
  — focus on doing things together leads to better morale and a high degree of worker **27** ______________
  — paternalistic, mentoring style of leadership
  — employee training
  — company expects **28** ______________ from workers, with similar ideas and shared goals
- **Adhocracy Culture**
  — workers must be adaptable and accept change
  — focus on flexibility and **29** ______________ with quick responses to outside factors
  — dynamic and entrepreneurial leaders looking for **30** ______________
  — employees encouraged to experiment with new ideas
  — might seem disorganised but inventive and progressive

SECTION 4 *Questions 31–40*

Questions 31–34

Complete the summary below.

*Write **NO MORE THAN TWO WORDS** for each answer.*

Environmental Effects of Pesticide Use

Most pesticides are carried into other environments. They travel along rivers or streams or are carried by the **31** ________________ into unwanted areas. Pesticides can harm animals or remove their **32** ________________ , causing starvation. Those that stay in the soil can cause damage, and also decrease the quality and number of organisms in contrast to **33** ________________. Furthermore, insects can develop immunity to pesticides, and thus **34** ________________ are needed, which create further problems.

Questions 35–40

Complete the table below.

*Write **NO MORE THAN TWO WORDS** for each answer.*

Technique	***Procedure***	***Comment***
Handpicking	Remove insects with gloves	Effective and low-cost; but **35** ________________ so not useful for large farms
36 ________________	Breed 'good' insects to attack pests	Risky due to **37** ________________ outcomes
Companion planting	Use plants with ability to **38** ________________ certain insects	Low risk, but additional plants compete for space and soil nutrients
Crop rotation	Change plant varieties after each harvest – insects must **39** ________________ to access food	Unappealing for big businesses as **40** ________________ are reduced

READING

READING PASSAGE 1

*You should spend about 20 minutes on **Questions 1–13**, which are based on Reading Passage 1 below.*

'Sleep comes more easily than it returns.'

— Victor Hugo, *Les Misérables*

A It is estimated that one in three adults in westernised countries regularly wakes up in the middle of the night and has difficulty getting back to sleep. Physicians often diagnose 'insomnia' and prescribe sleeping pills, but these often have side effects such as negative interactions with food, drink or other drugs, and most are habit-forming. Cessation of the medication frequently causes unpleasant withdrawal symptoms, too, including panic attacks, mood-swings, and even heightened sleep disturbance. Is there a way to treat insomnia without such debilitating consequences?

B The historian A. Roger Ekirch takes a different approach to nocturnal awakening. He maintains it is biologically instinctive and innate and that it is the ideal of the modern-era condensed eight-hour sleep regime that is exceptional. Those people who have so-called insomnia may just be sleeping in the biphasic mode that was the norm for their ancestors: eight hours of sleep split into two chunks by a period of wakefulness which lasted an hour or longer. According to Ekirch, during this sleepless phase, some people might have stayed in bed and prayed, recalled their dreams, or chatted to their partners, while others may have got up to do chores or drop in on the people next door.

C Archives from the pre-industrial era mention segmented sleep as 'first sleep' or 'deep sleep' and 'second sleep' or 'morning sleep'. The change in sleep routines, which started during the Industrial Revolution, mainly came about through the invention of the incandescent bulb. This invention, cheap and available to even the poorest residences, lengthened our daytime activities, such as reading and playing games, and reduced the period of time for sleep. As a result, the modern worker or student tries to squeeze sleep into a continuous period of seven or eight hours, even though this does not conform to natural circadian rhythms. Anthropologists confirm Ekirch's hypothesis by reporting that inhabitants of undeveloped regions of the world that are without the benefit of electric lighting still follow the natural rhythm of a divided sleep pattern.

D Ekirch's hypothesis was corroborated by sleep expert Thomas Wehr in the 1990s. His study kept volunteers in the dark for 14 hours each night (a simulation of wintertime exposure to light and darkness in bygone days). The subjects moved progressively towards a biphasic sleep pattern, taking a couple of hours to doze off and then sleeping in two distinct segments of four hours each with an interval of wakefulness in the middle. He construed from this that bifurcated sleep is not only completely natural but also beneficial, because this kind of sleeping facilitates the recall of dreams, which 'afford people a pathway to their subconscious'. Our predecessors actually considered their dream life to be a crucial component of their lives.

E Sleep is essential and it is by no means a passive state. Sleep scientists have revealed that there are two fundamental cycles of activity, classified as rapid eye movement (REM) sleep and non-rapid eye movement (NREM) sleep. The latter consists of four phases. The first phase, which lasts five to ten minutes, is the 'falling asleep' stage and sometimes there is actually a sense of falling, which often causes a sudden muscle contraction or jerk. One is easily awoken during this stage. Then comes an interlude of light sleep where the heart rate slows and body temperature drops – the body is getting ready for the deep sleep, which occurs in the third and fourth stages of NREM slumber. This is slow-wave or 'delta' sleep and a person woken at this stage may feel quite disorientated. This period of deep sleep is vital for the body to restore itself. During this time, not only does the body carry out repair and regeneration of nerves, bones and muscles, but it also fortifies and repairs the immune system.

F The eyes can be seen to move rapidly beneath the eyelids during REM sleep, which ensues after approximately an hour and a half of NREM sleep cycles. A faster and more erratic heart rate and shallow breathing are typical of this state, and brain activity intensifies, giving rise to vivid dreaming; paradoxically, the major voluntary muscle groups are immobilised, albeit for good reason – thrashing about while asleep could result in serious injury. Although the purpose of dreaming is not yet fully comprehended, the hypothesis is that it is vital for learning and memory (as these regions of the brain are stimulated); indeed, studies have shown that when candidates are denied REM sleep, their memory of recent learning is impaired. Deprivation of REM sleep also leads to anxiety and migraine headaches.

G Sleep specialists agree that without adequate REM and NREM sleep, people's thought processes are likely to be compromised, and they may suffer from impaired memory, fatigue, depression, a weakened immune response, and heightened susceptibility to pain, amongst other negative consequences. Yet modern-day humans remain chronically sleep deprived, notwithstanding the results of this research and its acceptance by many psychiatrists and sleep consultants. Why is the general populace so loath to relinquish its monophasic sleep schedule and enjoy the benefits of a biphasic schedule? It is certain that attitudes to employment responsibilities and social commitments would have to be altered before such a huge behavioural paradigm shift could occur and individuals could allot more time to restful, restorative sleep.

Questions 1–5

Choose the correct letter, ***A, B, C*** *or* ***D****.*

Write the correct letter in Boxes 1–5 on your answer sheet.

1 What can happen if someone stops taking insomnia medication?

A Their sleeping problems improve.
B They experience unstable emotions.
C They begin using other drugs instead.
D There is no change in their behaviour.

2 How does A. Roger Ekirch feel about waking in the night?

A It is the result of our modern lifestyles.
B It is less healthy than uninterrupted sleep.
C It is a rare and problematic condition.
D It is a completely natural sleep pattern.

3 The shift away from biphasic sleep happened mainly because of

A changes in work hours.
B factory and industrial employment.
C new lighting technology.
D less time for sleep in the mornings.

4 What happened to the volunteers in Thomas Wehr's study?

A They began to wake up during the night.
B They slept much longer than before.
C They had a longer winter than normal.
D They experienced more vivid dreams.

5 Why did Thomas Wehr feel that bifurcated sleep can help us?

A The quality of sleep improves.
B We can access hidden thoughts.
C We tend to have more dreams.
D It takes longer to fall asleep.

Questions 6–12

Complete the notes below.

Choose **NO MORE THAN THREE WORDS** *from the passage for each answer.*

Write your answers in Boxes 6–12 on your answer sheet.

Rapid Eye Movement and Non-Rapid Eye Movement Sleep

- NREM Stage 1 = transition to sleep
  — may experience a feeling of **6** ....
  — easy to wake
- NREM Stage 2 = **7** ....
  — decrease in heartbeat and temperature
- NREM Stages 3 & 4 = deep (slow-wave or delta) sleep
  — confusion on waking
  — necessary for healing soft and hard tissue and strengthening **8** ....
- REM = dream sleep
  — Occurs after 90 minutes of NREM
  — Fluctuations of **9** .... , lighter respiration
  — Eyes move, brain more active but arms and legs **10** ....
  — Reason for dreams unknown but important for **11** ....
  — Lack of REM sleep → mood disorders and **12** ....

Question 13

Choose the correct letter, ***A**, **B**, **C** or **D**.*

Write the correct letter in Box 13 on your answer sheet.

What is the writer's conclusion?

A Our lifestyles must change before our sleep can.

B Lack of sleep is harming our work and social lives.

C We will sleep better if our health improves.

D Sleep researchers are frequently misguided.

READING PASSAGE 2

*You should spend about 20 minutes on **Questions 14–27**, which are based on Reading Passage 2 below.*

Theories of Accident Causation in the Workplace

A Herbert Heinrich, a pioneer in workplace safety philosophy, originally suggested that workplace accidents followed a sequence of five contributing causes, and he used the image of a set of dominos to illustrate the cause and effect chain reaction that was central to his theory. Heinrich maintained that eliminating one contributing cause, like taking away one domino from the row, would prevent the chain from collapsing.

B His original theory was published in 1931 and has since been updated and modified. In the original theory, which was later extended, the end result, or final domino in the series, was injury or damage. He stated that the immediate cause of this was an accident in the workplace. As would be expected from the 1930s worldview, Heinrich was inclined to place the blame for accidents fairly and squarely on the shoulders of the workers. A workplace accident, in his theory, was immediately attributable to unsafe acts. Although he did acknowledge that these unsafe acts might take place in a hazardous situation, he stated that these situations were generally created by, and the responsibility of, the workers. He labelled this factor as 'fault of person'. Heinrich suggested that 'fault of person' had its roots in the workers' ancestry, or genetic factors, combined with the social environment they lived or worked in.

C This theory was very popular, and was later updated by several other researchers in the field. The updated theory became known as the International Loss Control Institute or ILCI model. This model included two new concepts; the initial cause of workplace accidents became lack of control. This idea took some of the blame for workplace accidents away from the workers and attributed it to fundamental mistakes made at executive or management level. In keeping with a more holistic view of workplace accidents, loss of production was added as the final outcome of the chain of events. Domino theories tend to be one-dimensional, however, and nowadays, we tend to believe that accidents have manifold causes.

D The multiple causation theory assumes that there are numerous influential elements in the workplace, and that it is various permutations of these that cause accidents. The causative factors are classified as being either behavioural or environmental. Once again, behavioural influences related to the employee, and examples of such influences included an unsuitable mindset, lack of relevant knowledge or skills and/or a poor physical or mental state.

E Perhaps the simplest theory is that of pure chance, that is, that everyone is equally likely to have an accident and that there is apparently no particular identifiable cause for these;

subsequently, there is no possibility of intervention. This theory seems to imply that accidents are inevitable, and that we have to accept this fact in the workplace. There are other theories with little credibility, mainly because of contradictory or inconclusive findings. The accident proneness theory is one of these. In essence, this theory states that there are always a few of us who are more susceptible to suffering mishaps, whether at work or at home, perhaps because of inattention or clumsiness.

F There is, however, a lot of credence given to the human factors theory, which, like the domino theory, ascribes accidents to a chain of events that will lead to human error. There are three main considerations that result in human error: overload; inappropriate responses; and inappropriate activities.

G Overload can arise from the worker's competence, or rather lack thereof, which depends on his proficiency, training, physical or mental condition, fatigue, and so on. Environmental factors also play a part in overload, for instance, excessive noise, heat or cold, insufficient lighting and distractions in the surroundings. There are internal factors which may contribute to overload as well, such as stress or anxiety from family or non work-related issues. Finally, there are situational factors, which include the level of risk inherent in the workplace, or such factors as imprecise instructions.

H Inappropriate responses take into account that workers may overlook possible dangers or safety procedures, or be mismatched to the workstation. Physical factors, such as the size of the worker in relation to the load he is lifting, the force required to lift that load, and how far the worker is required to reach, are all contributing factors. Trying to carry out a workplace assignment without the necessary training, or miscalculating the degree of risk, constitutes an inappropriate activity.

I Dan Petersen added to the inappropriate activity idea from the human factors theory by noting that pressure of deadlines, or the ingestion of drugs or alcohol, could contribute to worker overload, and that a 'superman syndrome' of 'It won't happen to me' should be considered as another inappropriate activity. Some workers believe themselves to be invincible or indestructible, and this results in carelessness and an unwillingness to follow safety precautions.

J Obviously accident causation in industrial settings is a very complex issue and, although a number of theories have been put forward, there is not as yet one that is deemed comprehensive enough to be universally acknowledged as the 'correct' one.

Questions 14–19

Complete the summary using the list of words and phrases, ***A–O****, below.*

Write the correct letter in Boxes 14–19 on your answer sheet.

Updated domino model —— ILCI

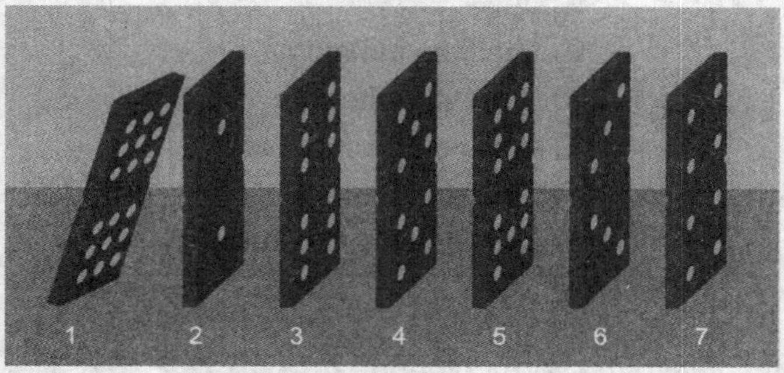

The ILCI model of workplace safety is a revision of Herbert Heinrich's original domino model. In Heinrich's model, the final event was **14** ...., and this was the result of a workplace accident. He believed that the **15** .... of the workers were primarily to blame for accidents, and he called this factor **16** .... He stated that the underlying cause, or first domino in the series, was **17** .... plus the culture of the workers' home or work life.

His model was later modified to the ILCI model. The new model took a wider perspective of workplace accidents. Thus, the first factor was called **18** .... , reflecting error at management level, and the last domino was **19** .... for the workplace.

A hazardous situation	**B** injury or damage	**C** lack of control
D end result	**E** the workers' shoulders	**F** chain reaction
G management mistakes	**H** genetic factors	**I** unsafe acts
J new concepts	**K** fundamental mistakes	**L** loss of production
M workplace accident	**N** fault of person	**O** blame

Questions 20–27

Look at the following statements (Questions 20–27) and the list of theories below.

List of Theories

A Domino
B ILCI
C Multiple causation
D Pure chance
E Accident proneness
F Human factors
G Dan Petersen's theory

Match each statement with the correct theory, ***A, B, C, D, E, F*** *or* ***G.***

Write the correct letter in Boxes 20–27 on your answer sheet.

20 A worker with too much to do or with personal problems may cause accidents.

21 Certain people are more likely to have accidents.

22 Safety problems at work can be avoided by removing just one factor.

23 Some workers don't believe that they will have an accident.

24 All possible causes of accidents can be put into two major categories.

25 Accidents are caused by management as well as by workers.

26 If a worker is too short or too small for the task, this can cause accidents.

27 Accidents cannot be avoided because they are part of life.

READING PASSAGE 3

*You should spend about 20 minutes on **Questions 28–40**, which are based on Reading Passage 3 on the following pages.*

Questions 28–34

*Reading Passage 3 has seven paragraphs, **A–G**.*

*Choose the correct heading for Paragraphs **A–G** from the list of headings below.*

*Write the correct number, **i–x**, in Boxes 28–34 on your answer sheet.*

List of Headings

- **i** Appeals to the public and the media
- **ii** Large promotional budgets endorse trademarks
- **iii** Prevention is better than cure
- **iv** Brand names enter vocabulary with ease
- **v** A changing environment for brand names
- **vi** How brand name loss is decided by law
- **vii** Legal consequences of unlawful use of trademarks
- **viii** Examples of genericide in action
- **ix** Brand names become part of everyday usage
- **x** Taking back the brand name

28 Paragraph **A**

29 Paragraph **B**

30 Paragraph **C**

31 Paragraph **D**

32 Paragraph **E**

33 Paragraph **F**

34 Paragraph **G**

GENERICIDE

(Latin gener-, stem of genus 'kind, origin'
-cide = word-forming element meaning 'killer')

A Occasionally a company's brand name becomes so deeply ingrained in the minds of everyday consumers that it enters the popular lexicon of its time and becomes a catch-all term for the generic product or activity in question. At first glance, this might appear to be the pinnacle of successful marketing. Indeed, companies around the world spend billions of dollars every year conjuring up catchy jingles, memorable catch phrases and cute characters in an effort to ensure their brand is the first to spring into consumers' minds when those consumers realise they require a particular product or service.

B For those companies whose brand names travel too far into the public domain, however, there can be serious repercussions: namely, losing their right to trademark that particular brand. This can occur because in many jurisdictions, such as the United States, companies have a responsibility to ensure their brand names do not pass into broad popular usage, a process known in the legal industry as 'genericisation' or more candidly, genericide. According to a Harvard law school overview on the subject, 'a word will be considered generic when, in the minds of a substantial majority of the public, the word denotes a broad genus or type of product and not a specific source or manufacturer'. In arriving at a conclusion, courts typically examine dictionary definitions, use of the term in the media, and consider whether or not the company has attempted to restrain usage of its trademark. If the court deems the word to be generic, trademark privileges are stripped; no company has an automatic right to continue renewing its trademarks without an end date.

C Over the years, numerous companies have fallen victim to this common and unwanted marketing phenomenon, losing their prized brand names and subsequent loss of trademark status. Otis Elevator Company lost their trademark rights to 'escalator' in a 1950 court case after being found guilty of using the term generically in their own patents and advertising. In 1965, a court ruled that 'yo-yo' was ingrained in common speech, and the Duncan Yo-yo Company subsequently had their trademark revoked. Kerosene, zipper, thermos, and the Philips-head screwdriver round out the list of household goods now in the public domain.

D Genericisation is not an unstoppable process, however, and there are strategies that companies can adopt in order to maintain control of their brand names and avoid them becoming generic. One such strategy is for companies to invent a generic term of their own, which is particularly useful for those businesses that have invented unique products for which no existing terminology is available. In the early 1990s, for example, Nintendo so thoroughly dominated the market for video games that many consumers began referring to all such devices as 'Nintendos'. In response, the company promoted the generic term 'games console', which eventually gained traction and rescued the brand from following the same route as the escalator and the zipper. The Griswold-Nissen company were not so fortunate, however, when they attempted to promote the trampoline as a 'rebound tumbler' – the generic term never caught on and they eventually lost their trademark.

E Other companies have attempted to advise broadcasting services, language authorities and the broader public on the appropriate use of their brand name. The Internet search engine Google, fearing that widespread use of the verb 'to google' could result in future legal trouble, has contacted journalists, dictionaries and even the Swedish Language Council in an effort to avert genericide. In 2006, the company sent out a plea for everyone to 'please only use "Google" when you're actually referring to Google Inc. and our services'. In a similar vein, Xerox corporation was able to successfully encourage users to eschew the verb 'to xerox' in favour of a generic expression, 'to photocopy', and it was helped to its goal by a series of snappy ads including: 'You can't Xerox a Xerox on a Xerox. But we don't mind at all if you copy a copy on a Xerox® copier.'

F Although it is very unusual, it is possible for a trademark that has become generic to be recaptured from the public domain. Two examples of this are the sewing machine manufacturer, Singer and the tyre company, Goodyear. In both cases, however, many years elapsed from the time that the trademark became generic until it was recaptured. In each case, the company was required to prove that their brand name was identified in the minds of the public as belonging to their particular brand, rather than as generic name for all such products.

G In the end, however, language is owned by the community that uses it, and with the growth of the Internet in particular, this community is becoming ever more global. Consequently, it is becoming increasingly difficult for brand managers to monitor and curb inappropriate uses of brand names. 'Things have certainly changed,' says trademark specialist Nigel Jennings, who once wrote hundreds of letters admonishing writers for referring to 'rollerblades' or 'rollerblading' instead of the generic term, inline skating. 'If something becomes generic because everyone ignored your requests, well, that's just fact. You're like King Canute[1], you've failed.'

Question 35

*Choose the correct letter, **A**, **B**, **C** or **D**.*

Write the correct letter in Box 35 on your answer sheet.

Which of the following is **NOT** a legal reason for losing a brand name?

A The name is used to define that kind of product.

B The company has worked hard to keep its brand name.

C Newspapers and TV use the brand name as a generic name.

D People have forgotten that the name refers to just one brand.

---

① In legend King Canute attempted to hold back the tide of the sea.

Questions 36–37

*Choose **TWO** letters, **A, B, C, D,** or **E**.*

Write the correct letters in Boxes 36 and 37 on your answer sheet.

According to the writer, which **TWO** of the following brand names are no longer trademarks?

A Google
B Singer
C Trampoline
D Xerox
E Phillips head screwdriver

Questions 38–39

*Choose **TWO** letters, **A, B, C, D,** or **E**.*

Write the correct letters in Boxes 38 and 39 on your answer sheet.

According to the reading passage, which **TWO** strategies can help to avoid genericide?

A writing dictionary entries for the product

B making a general name for the product

C taking people to court for using the brand name

D creating clever advertising campaigns

E appealing to people via the Internet

Question 40

*Choose the correct letter, **A, B, C** or **D**.*

Write the correct letter in Box 40 on your answer sheet.

What is the main purpose of this reading passage?

A to give advice on how to avoid genericide

B to describe the law about genericide

C to explain genericide with examples

D to argue that genericide is unfair

WRITING

WRITING TASK 1

You should spend about 20 minutes on this task.

> ***The pie chart below shows where energy is used in a typical Australian household, and the table shows the amount of electricity used according to the number of occupants.***
>
> ***Summarise the information by selecting and reporting the main features, and make comparisons where relevant.***

Write at least 150 words.

Household energy use in Australia

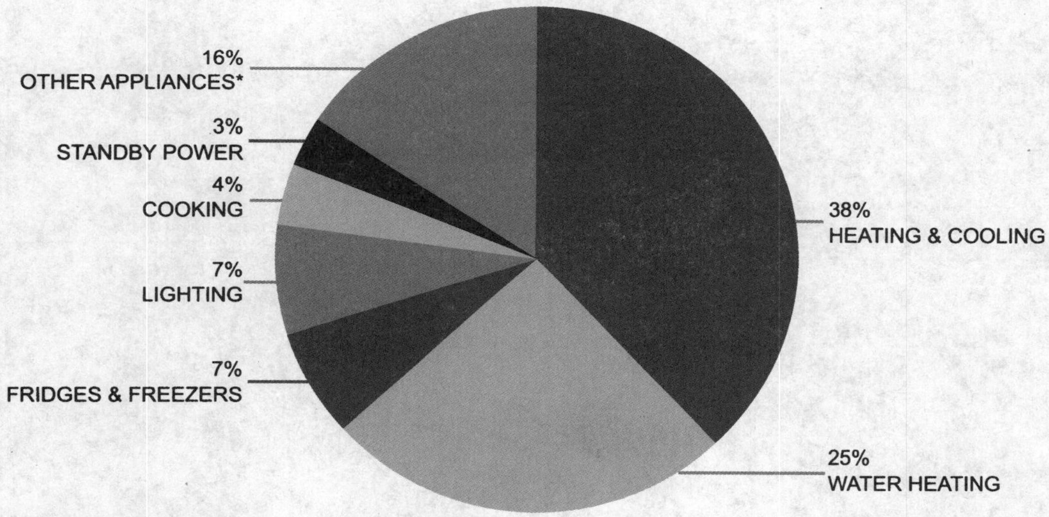

*clothes and dishwashers, entertainment and small appliances e.g. toaster, hairdryer, iron

Amount of electricity used in a typical Australian home	
Number of people in the house	Electricity used: kilowatt-hours (kWh) per year
1	5,000–6,500
2	6,000–8,000
3	7,500–10,000
6 or more	12,000–16,000

WRITING TASK 2

You should spend about 40 minutes on this task.

Write about the following topic:

> ***Most people accept that we now live in a globalised world but not everyone agrees that this is beneficial.***
>
> ***To what extent is globalisation a positive or negative development?***

Give reasons for your answer and include any relevant examples from your own knowledge or experience.

Write at least 250 words.

SPEAKING

PART 1

Initial questions about name, where live, work or studies and other personal topics.

Computers

- Are there a lot of computer shops where you live? [Why / Why not?]
- What do most people in your family use a computer for?
- Do you think people spend too much time using computers in your country?
- What are the most popular computer programmes that people use in your country? [Why?]

Children

- Do you enjoy spending time with children? [Why / Why not?]
- What sort of activities do children enjoy doing? [Why?]
- Do you think children often enjoy stories with animals? [Why?]
- Do you think cities are a good place to bring up children? [Why / Why not?]

PART 2

Talk about someone you met who was interesting. You should talk about: • where he/she was • who he/she was • what you did together and explain why you think this person was interesting.

You will be expected to talk about the topic for one to two minutes. You will have one minute to think about what you are going to say in advance. You can make some notes to help you if you wish.

PART 3

Age and meeting people

- Where do young adults and teenagers usually meet their friends?
- How has the Internet changed the way that people have relationships with each other?
- Do older people enjoy meeting new people as much as the younger generation? [Why?]

Globalisation and relationships

- Increasing numbers of people today are forming relationships on social network sites. Why might this happen?
- It is often said that we live in a global village. How true is this really?
- Some people fear that globalisation will result in societies becoming increasingly similar. Is this an advantage or a disadvantage?

Transcripts

IELTS Listening Test

01 A-B-C-D-E-F-G-H-I-J-K-L-M-N-O-P-Q-R-S-T-U-V-W-X-Y-Z

02
1 A-E-I-O-U
2 G-H-I-J
3 D-T-P
4 B-V-W

03
1 My name? Oh, Suzanne, Suzanne Prentice, that's P-R-E-N-T-I-C-E.
2 I live at 139 Harrison Drive. H-A-R-R-I-S-O-N Drive.
3 That's in the town of Grantham. G-R-A-N-T-H-A-M.
4 I work at Quills Publishing House. I'll spell that for you: Q-U-I-L-L-S.
5 We are part of a larger company called Albatross Publishers. Their web address is: www.A-L-B-A-T-R-O-S-S.com.

04
1 And you leave on the first of June.
2 You are booked into Room Number 804.
3 The room costs a hundred and forty-six euros per night.
4 Breakfast is an extra eleven euros fifty per day.
5 You require a storage facility for a case weighing 23 kilogrammes.
6 And you have requested a late check-out time. That will be 2.30 pm.
7 You will also require a car park for your vehicle, registration number: YXW 6069 AK.

05
1 It's a fairly old car – a dark blue Ford Festiva.
2 I went into town in the morning and parked outside the library at ten o'clock. I was away for about two and a half hours and, when I came back at around twelve thirty, the car was gone.
3 First I went to the dry cleaner's and then the bakery; I saw the car was still there when I went into the library so it must have been taken while I was at the dentist.

06
MAN: Good morning. Can I help you?
WOMAN: Yes. I would like to join the library.
MAN: Has your membership expired or will you be a new member?
WOMAN: I'd be a new member. I've just recently moved here.
MAN: That's fine. Are you a permanent resident?
WOMAN: No, actually I'm only here for a year ... on an **exchange**.
MAN: In that case we'll need the visitor's application form. Ah, here we are. Okay. Firstly, can you tell me why you are here? Oh, you've already said, haven't you? You're on an exchange. Now, can I have your name please?
WOMAN: Sophia Sunderland.
MAN: So, Sunderland is your family name?

WOMAN: Yes. S-U-N-D-E-R-L-A-N-D.

MAN: And your first name is Sophia? Can you spell it for me, please?

WOMAN: Of course. It's **S-O-P-H-I-A**.

MAN: And where do you come from, Sophia?

WOMAN: I was born in Italy. I'm **Italian**.

MAN: Just let me write that down. Now, I need your address.

WOMAN: In Italy?

MAN: No, where you are living here.

WOMAN: Oh. **521 Ashdown** Road – that's A-S-H-D-O-W-N.

MAN: And that's in Winton, right?

WOMAN: Correct.

MAN: Have you got something with you that shows you live at that address? A utility bill, for example?

WOMAN: I've got a **bank statement**. Will that do?

MAN: Wonderful. What about a contact phone number? A mobile number perhaps?

WOMAN: Oh yes. Let's see, it's new, um ... it's oh-4-oh-5-4-9-2-4-5-1.

MAN: Just a couple more questions ... How long are you here for? Sorry, you've told me that; what I really mean is when do you plan to leave?

WOMAN: I arrived on the first of January and I will be returning to Italy on **the thirtieth of December**.

MAN: Do you have any identification documents on you – your passport, for example ... ?

WOMAN: Yes, sure, here it is.

MAN: Thank you. I'll just make a note of the number. **DJG 1-2-zero-4-5-9**.
Now I can issue you with a borrower's card. You'll receive the proper card with your own barcode in the mail in a few days' time but I can give you a temporary card with your membership number on it now. Just present it at the desk if you want to borrow items today.

WOMAN: Thank you.

MAN: Now, let me explain something about our lending policies and charges. Resident members may check out up to 50 items at a time with their library card. For visitors, however, that number is reduced to **15** items at any time including a maximum of 10 DVDs.

WOMAN: I see.

MAN: Loan periods vary according to the type of materials. Books (both fiction and non-fiction), recorded books, CDs and periodicals may all be borrowed for 3 weeks; but recent releases – those are our new books – are limited to 2 weeks; and what we call our 'hot books' – those on current best-seller lists – can only be borrowed for **one week**. DVDs are also lent out for a week at a time. All items are issued free of charge but a fully refundable deposit of **$45** is required for wireless laptops which are for in-library use only. Oh, and there's a time restriction of 90 minutes on those.

WOMAN: Oh, I shouldn't think I'd ever need to borrow a laptop. With the other items you mentioned ... can the loan time be renewed?

MAN: Yes, unless it has been requested by another borrower, an item can be renewed but we recommend that you don't wait until the last minute before renewing.

WOMAN: How can I do that?

MAN: The easiest way is **online** or through the library's **automated telephone** renewal service. Otherwise, you can do it **in person** at the library or through the **self-service checkout**.

WOMAN: Well, that sounds easy enough. Thank you very much for your help.

07 Thank you for volunteering to help out at the athletics festival. For ease of identification and to divide up the duties I have assigned each of you to a colour coded squad or team. You will be given a coloured cap to wear. **Green** caps are in charge of communications so they will answer any enquiries from the public over the phone or in person. They will also be the team on the gate **taking entrance tickets** and handing out programmes. Those of you who will be stationed outside the stadium at the booths selling tickets will wear blue caps. The blue team is also responsible for directing traffic in the car park. **Red** caps will be inside the stadium **taking and relaying messages** between officials. I hope those of you on the red team are very fit because I can guarantee that, by the end of the day, you'll be very tired from all that running around. **Black** caps will be working behind the scenes. I have stationed you in the **food preparation area**. It's important that the black team remember to wear clean white shirts because you'll be working with food, helping to make sandwiches and pouring refreshments, that kind of thing.

08 **1** If you aren't feeling well, it isn't always necessary to see a doctor. This is the season of coughs and sniffles – although the symptoms are unpleasant, sneezing and a runny nose do not merit medical attention. If you have a persistent pain behind the eyes, in the front of your head, go to an optician and get your eyesight assessed – it may be time for new prescription glasses. However, if you are suffering from nausea and vomiting, you should get checked out by your medical practitioner. It may not be a simple case of food poisoning but the first symptom of a particularly severe gastric illness.

2 Jason, one of the participants in my research study, has been experiencing a lot of tension and anxiety at work recently. He has taken on extra work to cover for a sick colleague but he doesn't think this is the cause of the problem. He loves his job and, even with the additional duties, he can easily keep up. I wondered if he might have financial problems but apparently this is not the case either. It seems that the root of the problem is the fact that his company is restructuring and drastically cutting back on the number of employees so Jason is struggling with the idea of facing unemployment.

3 & **4** A senior student, Janice, came in for counselling yesterday. Apparently she is having trouble adjusting to some aspects of what lies ahead of her when she goes to the big city to start university in a couple of months' time. She's not at all worried about leaving her friends and family behind; in fact, she's looking forward to the excitement of the city and making new friends. But she is apprehensive about having to share classes with and relate to boys. She is an only child and has been at this all-girls' school for the last five years. Understandable, really. Her parents are well-off so funds are not an issue and I doubt whether she'll have to look for any evening or weekend work to supplement her finances. I think, however, she is troubled by the thought of how much harder university study will be and whether she will fall behind with the academic work.

09 Welcome to this talk on holidays in New Zealand. To start with, I'll run through six different types of holiday and then, after a show of hands, I'll provide a few more details on the type of tour that the majority of you show an interest in. Okay, first up is freedom walking. As a freedom walker, you have many well-maintained trails to choose from in New Zealand's beautiful wilderness from coastal tracks along golden beaches, pristine rivers and lakes, through ancient native rainforest to snow-capped mountains. You will carry a fully-laden backpack but you can stop and rest whenever you like – **you don't have to keep up** with the fitter walkers up ahead.

On guided walks, you will have the benefit of expert guides to help you understand and enjoy the history and natural beauty of the landscape. These walks can range from one-day excursions to 21-day treks in remote wilderness areas. So, you see, there's **one to suit every budget**. You will carry a light-weight pack with just your daily essentials.

If you lead an active lifestyle and enjoy the outdoors but are not so fond of walking, a cycling tour is for you. All cycling is on the road. Safety is a priority with our guides who will keep you informed of road rules, weather conditions and the type of terrain ahead. The best thing to my mind is that you can **opt out at any time** whether through tiredness, injury or just plain laziness – all tours are accompanied by support vehicles which can uplift you (and your cycle) along the way and take you to the end of the stage.

If you would like to try kayaking, no experience is necessary – you will learn as you go and it's certainly not all hard work – imagine paddling through crystal-clear water and stunning scenery where you will see all manner of wildlife from forest and sea birds to dolphins and seals. At the end of the day, you'll come home to a private beachfront lodge where you will enjoy **a gourmet meal, with the finest seafood and freshest local ingredients**.

Sailing has a lot to offer for those of you who like the ocean but this kind of tour is open only to experienced sailors. The yachts that you hire are fully equipped for exploring the coastline and the beauty of this method of touring is that you will be able to moor off isolated beaches and off-shore islands that very few people ever visit because they are **unreachable** by other means.

If luxury is your thing, however, then consider a cruise. This is **by far the least strenuous option** but that is not to say you have to be inactive. Fishing and snorkel equipment are available and you'd be a fool not to give it a go. It doesn't matter whether you are a novice or a more experienced angler. During each journey, the crew is available to lend a hand with the fishing and share their knowledge of the ocean and local landscapes.

Now that you've heard a quick summary of the tours available, you can vote for the one you are most interested in.

Ah, walking, always popular ... There is a wide variety of walking holidays to suit all levels of fitness on the three main islands that make up New Zealand. We offer **guided** treks over various terrains, from mountainous to flat, throughout the whole of the **South Island**. In the North Island, there are many different trails that you are welcome to walk on your own. There are also some delightful tracks being developed on Stewart Island which will need a guide when they are finished.

At the end of each guided walk, we have a celebration with a buffet meal and then a few days of rest and relaxation before you move on to the next trail. Entertainment is laid on **nearly every night** with the tour guide on hand to arrange interesting talks or local knowledge quizzes and to respond to any special requests from guests.

During long treks you will stay overnight in very basic huts but between treks we have arranged for self-catering accommodation. Each of these units is equipped with a **fridge** and a small stove – gas, not electric – but no dishwasher, I'm afraid. There is a television and a small radio but for access to the Internet you'd have to find a local Internet café. There are two beds per unit and all bedding is provided including **electric blankets** but there isn't any other form of heating in the unit – although the common room where the entertainment goes on does have a log fireplace.

10

A: Could you tell me the way to the station, please?

B: Go straight on until you come to the roundabout. At the roundabout take the second exit into Rose Drive. Go past the hotel on your left and turn right into Iris Street. Then take the first on the left and keep going as far as the traffic lights. Then turn right into Daisy Avenue. At the next junction turn left. Then turn left again into Ivy Lane and take the second on the right. This is Station Road and the station is right at the end. You'll see the car park adjacent to it.

11

1 Which building is on the northwest corner of Oak Avenue and Second Street?
2 Which building is opposite the library?
3 Which building is located on a corner of Elm Avenue and Sixth Street?
4 Which street or avenue lies to the south of Potter Park?
5 In which direction would you walk to go from the shopping plaza to the high school?
6 Which building is almost two blocks east of the library?
7 If you walk out of the church, face west and turn right, then take the second left, what is the first building you come to?
8 If you walk out of the bus station, head east and take the third turning on the right, then turn right again, which building will you see on your right hand side?
9 If you step out of the shopping plaza on Oak Avenue and face east, turn left then right and go straight ahead for two blocks, at what intersection would you be?
10 If you get on the bus outside the high school, travel three blocks south, get off and walk west on Forest Avenue, which store is on your left?

12

IVAN: How are you getting on at university this year, Maria? Is the **coursework** much harder?

MARIA: Actually, Ivan, I don't find it much harder at all. I suppose now that I'm familiar with all the technical terms and special vocabulary, the **workload** isn't so great.

IVAN: I guess the **content** is similar to what you've studied before in your country?

MARIA: Yes, of course, that helps me a lot.

13

GARY: Hi, Zoe. We need to get together to talk about our next assignment.

ZOE: Hi, Gary. What about Saturday?

GARY: Okay, but can you meet me at the public library in town? Say ... at two o'clock? I'll be in the reference section at the back on the ground floor.

ZOE: I haven't used the public library before. How will I find you?

GARY: I'll draw you a quick floor plan. Look, the information desk is just inside the entrance. Stand in front of the desk facing away from it. Then, follow the arrows. The first area you come to is the newspaper section on your left. They have a really good selection of all the national papers there. Anyway, as you continue, you'll pass the new book display on your right.

ZOE: Mmm, I might stop there to browse the latest fiction books – another time, maybe.

GARY: Yeah. Where was I? Ah, new books. Just pass between that display and **the multimedia room** on your left. Actually, we might need to use that at some stage. Next to this room, just around the corner, set back a little bit, is the CD collection. You veer away from that and keep following the arrows around the second corner and you'll go by **junior fiction** on your right. Carry on a bit further and you'll find me in the reference room – it's quite a big room – behind the **journals and magazines**. There are three catalogue computers alongside the reference room, which is very handy, because I think we'll be using them a lot. When we've finished for the day, we can sit back with a cup of coffee in the library **café**. This is it here, at the rear of the reference section. It's rather nice, too – it opens out onto a little enclosed garden.

ZOE: Sounds like a nice way to round off the day; so, the reference section, is that where you'll be waiting?

GARY: Yep.

ZOE: See you there then. Two o'clock.

GARY: Hi, Zoe. Glad you could make it. For this assignment on suspension bridges, have you come up with one that interests you?

ZOE: Yes, it's a fairly old one, started in 1954 and completed in 1957. Have you heard of the Mackinac Bridge?

GARY: It's in Michigan in the USA, isn't it? Across the Straits of Mackinac – it connects Michigan's upper and lower peninsulas.

ZOE: Right. We might be able to find a simple diagram here in one of these reference books.

GARY: Here we are. I've got it.

ZOE: No, that's the Golden Gate in San Francisco Bay. This is the Mackinac, here. See, the main span, in the middle? It's not as long as the Golden Gate or some of the other famous suspension bridges.

GARY: Well, how long is it?

ZOE: The **main span** on the Mackinac is just 1,158 metres – still a considerable distance though, don't you think?

GARY: Uh huh. That reminds me, I heard an amusing story about the bridge – perhaps we can use it in our presentation.

ZOE: Well, go ahead – tell me.

GARY: It happened during the construction of the bridge. Workers had to have a place to work while spinning the main cables; so, they suspended narrow catwalks between the **anchorages**, this one here on the far left and the other here on the far right. Those catwalks followed the same path that the cables do now – up to the top of one tower, curving down to the roadway, or **deck** as it's called, up to the other tower, and back down again. That's all there was – two thin strips of chain-link fence looping over both towers.

ZOE: Those strips of chain-link are not still there, though, are they?

GARY: No, this was just the preliminary work on the bridge, before the cables were strung. Anyway, this one woman saw and she complained to the Bridge Authority demanding to know how they expected a car to climb the high, steep road they had built across the straits!

ZOE: You know, I think we should use that anecdote. But, seriously now, what else can we say?

GARY: Well, obviously we can give a whole lot of **facts and figures** to do with the construction of the bridge.

ZOE: Well, maybe not too many, we don't want to overwhelm the audience, but certainly some of the most important ones.

GARY: You know, in the past, there have been some spectacular collapses of suspension bridges, like the Tacoma Narrows Bridge in 1940.

ZOE: Yes. At the time the Tacoma Bridge was designed and built, suspension bridge engineers and designers thought that lighter bridges with very flexible decks were functionally sound and aerodynamic forces were not well understood at all. A lot was learnt from that failure.

GARY: So they made the Mackinac stiffer and heavier, and all suspension bridges built since 1940 have been designed to move to accommodate wind force, **change in temperature**, and weight of the traffic.

ZOE: The roadway of the Mackinac, at the centre span, could move as much as 10 metres, east or west, but this would happen only under **extreme wind conditions**. And even then, it wouldn't really swing or sway but rather move slowly in one direction according to the force and direction of the wind. And then, after the wind subsides, the weight of the vehicles would slowly move it back into centre position.

GARY: Okay, let's do a bit more research and then go and have that cup of coffee.

ZOE: Good idea.

14

1 One interesting result of this was ...
2 For this reason ...
3 I'd like to start by ...
4 As a consequence ...
5 So far we've covered ...
6 Let's move on to discuss ...
7 Another noticeable feature is ...
8 Amongst these peculiar characters, one was ...
9 Last but not least, ...
10 Take, for instance, ...
11 The root of the problem would seem to be ...
12 Let me wrap up today's lecture by saying ...

15 If you enjoy the hustle and bustle of the city, then sure, this is the place to be. This is where the action is – bars, nightclubs, cafés and restaurants – not to mention the **shopping**! There's everything from your favourite boutique to major department stores. If you're into arts and culture, you've got galleries, museums and theatres on your doorstep. If you work in the city, the best thing about urban living is the proximity to work – imagine a walk or a short bus ride to work instead of hours sitting in traffic jams or packed in trains.

However, if you can't stand the noise of people, traffic and the nightlife, then city living is not the right choice for you. Cities generally have higher rates of **crime** and traffic pollution, too. But one of the biggest arguments against urban living is the cost. If you want a large apartment, it's going to cost you much more than a suburban house.

Suburban living is for those of you who love peace and quiet. There is usually more greenery and more opportunities for children to play. Best of all, in the suburbs you can buy a home with **amenities** like a garage, pool or big back yard.

Suburban life is a long way from all that action in the city and, if you want to enjoy some of that city life, you have to factor in the expense of **transportation** – every excursion to the city adds up. And let's not even think about the wasted time and frustration, not to mention expense, of the daily commute to work.

16 In this country, the process of buying a house is straightforward. When you have found the place you want to buy, you put in a **written offer** – a verbal offer is not legally binding. Your offer is made in writing in the form of a Sales and Purchase Agreement. The offer may be conditional upon a builder's report or mortgage finance, for example. When all the terms of the sale have been agreed to by the buyer and the seller, a **contract** is signed. Once the Sales and Purchase Agreement has been signed and dated by both parties, the buyer is required to give a **deposit**. This is usually 10% of the purchase price. Once all conditions have been met, the sale then becomes unconditional and fully binding. At this point, the deposit is released to the owner and will not be refunded should you fail to settle. Should settlement be delayed for any reason, **interest** is charged on the outstanding amount, until settlement is made in full.

17 The Red Cross is a non-governmental **organisation** operating worldwide that aims to give service to those in need at any time and in any place. It plays a valuable role in wartime assisting **soldiers** in all kinds of ways – sometimes by delivering food parcels, clothing and first-aid supplies or by transferring messages between soldiers and their families into and out of the war zone. It is operational in peacetime too, providing **emergency** relief to survivors in the case of sudden misfortune – sometimes in the aftermath of a serious accident or, more commonly, in the event of natural **disasters**. The Red Cross is quick to respond, often well before governments swing into action, providing **medical** care for the injured, delivering supplies of fresh water and food, and **shelter** for those who have been left homeless. The Red Cross also sponsors community programmes and ...

18 Good afternoon and welcome to the Zoology Department. We're going to consider the effect of introduced species in New Zealand. I'd like to start with a quick look at ancient history. New Zealand is a tiny fragment of the ancient continent of Gondwanaland. Our diverse flora comes from two sources: first, the ancient species present when this country was still part of Gondwanaland, and the second, species which arrived after separation. The vegetation developed without browsing mammals. However, since human settlement, there has been considerable destruction or alteration of the landscape through **fire** and the introduction of mammals and exotic plants ('exotic' here meaning foreign, non-native).

There were three major invasions by humans. First, were the Polynesians and they brought with them the 'kuri' **dog** and the 'kiore' rat. Much later, Captain Cook arrived followed by European sealers and whalers. European rats and **mice** came aboard their ships. Finally, European settlers started arriving from the 1840s onwards introducing all manner of birds, animals and plants into the still fairly pristine environment. Some species were introduced from Australia but most came from the British Isles and Europe.

Let's move on now to look at some of the introduced animals and the reasons for their introduction. The possum, a native of Australia, was introduced to establish a fur industry but is now the greatest wildlife pest of New Zealand. The second in the utility category is of particular interest because it became a pest almost as soon as it was liberated. The **rabbit** was much valued for its meat and fur but was soon out of control. Goats and pigs were brought in as a food supply and the Pacific or kiore rat was used both for food and for its pelt.

Moving on to sport now ... The hare was introduced for food and sport but unlike the rabbit has never become a significant pest. Wallabies were brought from Australia, six species became established and some of those populations are expanding. Both the Himalayan thar and chamois were introduced into the South Island as game animals. Finally, in this category, **red deer** – liberated for sport but responsible for considerable habitat destruction.

What about feral farm animals? Sheep, along with **cattle** and horses were brought by early settlers as domestic stock but, because of a lack of fencing, some escaped and became feral. Unfortunately, ordinary house cats went off into the wild as well and established feral populations.

This brings us to the next section – biological control. The humble **hedgehog** was introduced from England to control insects and other garden pests but the hedgehog also eats native frogs and bird eggs. The three mustelids – the ferret, stoat and weasel – were brought in as biological control for rabbits. Having failed at that, they are busy exterminating rare native birds.

Last, but not least, the stowaways ... The unintentional introduction of rodents has had a huge impact on native birds and reptiles, the black rat alone responsible for the extinction of nine bird species.

So far, we've looked at human impact on the New Zealand environment brought about by the introduction of various animals. I've focussed on some of the worst examples and why they were brought here. Now, let's consider the economic impact and methods of control.

The establishment of introduced mammals is of considerable **ecological** and economic importance. Rabbits, for example, compete with sheep, depleting pasture and causing soil erosion. A virus, myxomatosis, was introduced back in 1951 but it failed to spread. Red deer in the forests prevent the regeneration of native trees but hunting and shooting allows reasonable control. Possums have a devastating effect on all native flora but they also thrive in pine plantations, orchards, pasture and even urban gardens. They pose a particular threat to the **dairy industry** as well because they infect cattle with tuberculosis. Despite enormous sums of money being spent on various means of eradication and control, from trapping to poisoning, the possum population is still unmanageable.

Do introduced species offer any financial benefits, you might ask? Surprisingly, yes. Possums are once again trapped for their fur; rabbit meat is back on the menu; the innovation of hunting deer and goats by helicopter has attracted tourist revenue; wild venison (deer meat) is sold in Europe and deer velvet is sold in Asia.

My concluding words are saved for feral farm animals – an interesting aspect of which is **genetic conservation**. Selective breeding programmes have narrowed the genetic base of domestic animals. However, some of the feral herds display advantageous characteristics that are now highly prized by animal breeders. Unfortunately, many feral herds have been successfully exterminated!

Thank you. Next week we'll look at bird life.

IELTS Speaking Test

Transcript of Audio for Part 1 of the Sample Speaking Test

01

EXAMINER: Now, first, tell me something about yourself. Tell me about where you live in your country. Is the place where you live large or small?

CANDIDATE: I live in Hamilton, which is what I suppose you would call a small city. It's about 140,000 people, and it's a quiet little place which services the local farming community. We don't have any heavy industry in Hamilton, but there is a university.

EXAMINER: Is it a beautiful place?

CANDIDATE: To me it is. There are some people who would say it's not beautiful, but I like it. There aren't any big mountains or anything, but it has lots of green trees and grass, and there's a beautiful big river running right through the centre of it ... flowers everywhere, and lots of gardens. I think it's lovely.

EXAMINER: Is there anything you don't like about this city?

CANDIDATE: Well, the fact that it's small, of course, means that you don't get a lot of the amenities that you'd find in a bigger city. If you're interested in art galleries, or the symphony, or opera, which I am, Hamilton is not exactly a good place to be. You have to jump in a car and drive for an hour or so to the big city for those kinds of things.

EXAMINER: Next we'll talk about numbers. Are any numbers considered to be lucky or unlucky in your culture?

CANDIDATE: I would say there are an awful lot of individual people who consider that some numbers are lucky, or unlucky, but if you mean society-wide, sure, there are a few. The number 13, for example, is widely regarded as being unlucky particularly if it refers to a date when something will happen, and especially if it's Friday the 13th.

EXAMINER: Do you think that some numbers are luckier or unluckier than others?

CANDIDATE: No, I don't think any numbers are lucky or unlucky.

EXAMINER: Why not?

CANDIDATE: Well, it's difficult to imagine any number having any influence at all on the physical world. But, I guess it could affect someone's emotional state if they thought a number was lucky or unlucky.

EXAMINER: Let's talk about motorbikes now. Have you ever owned a motorbike?

CANDIDATE: Well, I haven't actually owned a motorcycle, but I did have possession of one at one time. When I was a younger man, I swapped my 2-seater sports car for my friend's motorbike. He had a girlfriend at the time and he really wanted to take her on a date, so I lent him my car and I had his bike for a while. That was a lot of fun.

EXAMINER: What are some of the advantages of motorbikes in the city?

CANDIDATE: I think there are a lot of obvious advantages: fuel efficiency, easy parking, being able to get around in traffic easily and quickly, but they come with a number of drawbacks too, of course. You are vulnerable not only to the weather but to injury.

EXAMINER: Do you think motorbikes are a safe form of transport?

CANDIDATE: Absolutely not! Not in the society we live in, where people love their cars, and have no respect for others on the roads.

02 Transcript of Audio for Part 2 of the Sample Speaking Test

There are a host of movies I could talk about, but one that comes to mind straight away as a movie I really enjoyed was actually *Avatar*. I went to see it a couple of times, in fact. You know, the movie was released in 2D and 3D. I'm not a big fan of 3D technology, so I went the first time in 2D, and then my kids said, let's go and see it in 3D, so we did. I ... I thought it was a wonderful movie-going experience.

I'm sure you know the plot; it was that movie about the big blue people on another planet, and then the humans arrive and try to take over their world so they can mine the precious ores under the surface. It was called 'Avatar' because the humans used avatars to make contact with the natives. There were so many interesting things that I loved in that movie, especially in the production. The visual imagery of the planet was spectacular; there were all those bioluminescent plants that would light up, and animals that had glowing parts. Then there was the miraculous technology of bringing those giant people to life, with their glowing, cat-like eyes, and their tails, and the wonderful dragon creatures that they rode on after they made that perilous journey up the floating islands to the very top of the world. So, it was such a great spectacle to look at.

And then, layered on top of that, was the story, and the message. I'm sure you remember that. You had the contrast between the people living in harmony with nature in their primitive way, as part of the environment, neither taking anything away nor destroying their ecology, and then the greedy humans, with their mentality of cutting down the trees and destroying everything to make money. I ... I liked that contrast; it was a very satisfying story. And, of course, when you set a story like that on another planet, you can make all sorts of comments about our own world and our own political systems and beliefs.

03 Transcript of Audio for Part 3 of the Sample Speaking Test

EXAMINER: Now we're going to have a more general discussion about movies. Tell me about some of the types of movies that are popular in your culture.

CANDIDATE: In my country, there are several sorts of movies, we call them genres, that are really popular. The ones I can think of are action movies, with Hollywood superstars like Sylvester Stallone or Claude Van Damme. Those are very popular. Then there are romantic comedies, you know boy meets girl in a funny situation and there are some problems with their relationships ...

EXAMINER: And you talked about *Avatar*. Is that genre popular too?

CANDIDATE: Oh, absolutely. There's definitely a large percentage of the population that enjoys that kind of science fiction, and also fantasy, which is a related genre.

EXAMINER: Do you think that men and women enjoy different kinds of movies?

CANDIDATE: Yes, yes and no. There are certainly a lot of movies that both men and women enjoy equally. My wife enjoyed *Avatar*, and so did I, but then there are other movies that she likes a lot and I don't much like, and vice versa. I quite like action thrillers and crime ...

EXAMINER: (interrupting) and do you think most men like those kinds of movies?

CANDIDATE: I don't know about most men, but a lot of men do. But, my wife can't stand them at all ...

EXAMINER: (interrupting) What kind of movies do women like?

CANDIDATE: Well, I don't like to overgeneralise, but if I was pushed, I might say that they do enjoy a romantic comedy. They do enjoy the humour involved when men and women are trying to form a relationship, more than most men do.

EXAMINER: Some people say that movies are becoming very violent and that has a bad influence on young people in particular. Do you agree with that?

CANDIDATE: Not really, no. When I was a child, we used to go downtown to the cinema and pay 20c to watch Godzilla crushing Tokyo. I mean, violence has always been a part of movies. I suppose that what has changed is the realism of the movies and this does make for a stronger emotional connection between the action on the screen and the audience. And for the movie makers, that's part of the creative process. They're experimenting with different ways to portray these violent actions in a more and more realistic way.

EXAMINER: And do you think that this level of realism is more disturbing for young people?

CANDIDATE: It might very well be. I suppose many young people don't have enough life experience to understand a lot of the violence they see.

EXAMINER: Now, let's talk about the modern technology and movie watching. How do you think that modern technology has influenced people's access to movies?

CANDIDATE: I'm sorry, could you repeat that question?

EXAMINER: Well, there are many ways to rent or obtain movies nowadays, aren't there?

CANDIDATE: Oh, yes, there's Blu-ray and online delivery, like downloading from different websites. Yes, I really think this has had an influence on how people watch their movies. There's much more choice and flexibility for the viewer.

EXAMINER: And how do you think that might affect the movie making industry in the future?

CANDIDATE: Well, I don't know. So far they're still managing to make enough money to keep producing movies. I mean the idea of copying a movie without paying for it must have been round at least since the 80's, so making a pirated copy is nothing new in itself. It must be hurting them, though. But, I think people still love the whole experience of going out to a special place to watch a movie on a big screen, and hopefully that won't change.

Academic Test 1

You will hear a number of different recordings and you will have to answer questions on what you hear. There will be time for you to read the instructions and questions and you will have a chance to check your work. All the recordings will be played once only. The test is in 4 sections. At the end of the test you will be given 10 minutes to transfer your answers to an answer sheet. Now turn to Section 1.

SECTION 1

You will hear a telephone conversation between a receptionist at a restaurant and a man who is making enquiries about a job there. First, you have some time to look at Questions 1 to 5.

[20 seconds]

You will see that there is an example that has been done for you. On this occasion only, the conversation relating to this example will be played first.

WOMAN: Hello, Marina Restaurant and Reception Rooms, how can I help you?

MAN: I'm ringing about the advertisement I saw on the Internet. Uh, you were advertising for **casual** staff?

WOMAN: Yes, that's right. Just a moment, I'll put you through to the manager ...

*The woman says the advertisement was for casual staff, so **casual** has been written in the space. Now we shall begin. You should answer the questions as you listen because you will not hear the recording a second time. Listen carefully and answer Questions 1 to 5.*

WOMAN: Hello, Marina Restaurant and Reception Rooms, how can I help you?

MAN: I'm ringing about the advertisement I saw on the Internet. Uh, you were advertising for **casual** staff?

WOMAN: Yes, that's right. Just a moment, I'll put you through to the manager ...

[sound of phone ringing]

I'm sorry, there's no answer on her line. Perhaps I can help you with some of the details and you could talk to her later.

MAN: Yeah, that'd be good. First of all, can you tell me what jobs are available?

WOMAN: Well, we advertised for an assistant cook, a kitchen hand and a cleaner but the cook and the cleaner's positions have been filled already ...

MAN: Not to worry, I'm not qualified to cook anyway. I can barely make toast.

WOMAN: Well, we still have the **kitchen hand** job available. Do you have any experience?

MAN: No, I haven't worked as a kitchen hand before – what would I have to do?

WOMAN: Mainly dishes – lots of dishwashing – and anything the chef tells you to do while he's preparing the meals. We get pretty busy, so you'd have to be able to deal with some pressure, and there's a fair bit of noise and shouting sometimes too. You'd be responsible for making salads and other cold platters.

MAN: I could do that. How many shifts would I have to work every week?

WOMAN: A minimum of two and a maximum of five – we're open seven days a week, and our casual staff are usually asked to do a lot of weekend shifts. You probably won't have to do many Mondays or Tuesdays, but you'll have to be able to work on **Friday** nights – that's our biggest day of the week.

MAN: Mmm, there goes my social life.

WOMAN: Sorry?

MAN: Nothing. I was wondering what the pay is like.

WOMAN: It's very good really. The youth rate is $15 an hour ... Oh, I didn't ask – how old are you?

MAN: 22.

WOMAN: Well, that's an even better rate – **over 18** we pay $**18.50** an hour – and that includes a meal if you work a five-hour shift.

MAN: I like the sound of that. What time is the meal break?

WOMAN: It's very early – before you actually start work – at 5 o'clock. Oh, and I should tell you, if you are even 5 minutes late, you won't get any dinner at all. The chef is very strict about that. You need to start your meal at five because you have to begin work promptly at **5.30** p.m.

MAN: I'll be sure to get there before five then – I'm always starving in the afternoon and I don't mind how early I eat dinner.

Before you hear the rest of the conversation, you have some time to look at Questions 6 to 10.

[20 seconds]

Now listen and answer Questions 6 to 10.

MAN: Aah, I have a question – would I need to wear a uniform of some sort?

WOMAN: Not as such ... but you'll need a good strong pair of shoes, not sneakers (that's in case you drop something on your foot), a clean shirt and trousers ... and the restaurant provides you with a long white apron and **a cap**.

MAN: When can I start?

WOMAN: Not so fast – you'll have to formally apply to the manager first – but I can tell you that the position becomes available on Monday, the 14th of **November** – that's when we really start to get busy – in the lead up to Christmas and the holiday season.

MAN: When can I see the manager?

WOMAN: Umm, let me see, I have her diary here ... What about tomorrow at 11 a.m.?

MAN: Not really, not unless I skip class – is there something later in the day?

WOMAN: 4.30 p.m.? Would that do?

MAN: Yeah, great, so that's 4.30 tomorrow, Thursday, with ... uh, what's her name?

WOMAN: Oh, the manager, yes ... her name is Lola Barrie.

MAN: Just a minute, while I write that down ... B-A-double-R-Y?

WOMAN: There's no 'Y' ... It's **B-A-R-R-I-E**.

MAN: Lola Barrie. I've got it now.

WOMAN: Good. You've got her name but I haven't got yours!

MAN: Jack Lee – that's L-E-E.

WOMAN: Thanks, Jack. When you come to meet with Ms Barrie tomorrow, bear in mind that she'll want to know all about your work history so you'll need to have your CV. If you have one, we'd really like to see **a reference** as well, so bring that with you, if you can. If you haven't got one, then we'll need a referee's name and a phone number instead. Oh, and one more thing ...

MAN: What's that?

WOMAN: She'll probably ask you about your eligibility to work in this country so bring your passport and, if you have one, your **tax** number.

MAN: Thank you, you've been really helpful. Will I see you tomorrow?

WOMAN: Yes, come straight through the front door and you'll see me at Reception. Ms Barrie will meet you there.

MAN: Great. Till tomorrow then ...

That is the end of Section 1. You now have half a minute to check your answers.

[30 seconds]

Now turn to Section 2.

SECTION 2

You will hear a teacher talking to a group of students who are visiting the City Zoo. First you have some time to look at Questions 11 to 16.

[20 seconds]

Now listen carefully and answer Questions 11 to 16.

How many of you have visited the City Zoo before? No one? Well, this is going to be a treat. Before we get off the bus, let me give you a bit of background information. When this city was founded in 1860, it was the intention right from the start to set aside some land for what would become today's zoo. Unfortunately, the plans were lost somewhere in the town planning department and the whole idea was almost forgotten until one of the town's founding fathers died just after the turn of last century – **1902** it was – and he bequeathed to the city a stretch of unused land. He had given the land to the council with the express wish that it be used to build a zoo, but it would be another half century before construction began in 1950. The gentleman who gifted the land simply wanted a place that his grandchildren and future generations would **take pleasure in**, and so, that was the idea behind the design and construction of the zoo. Later, researchers set up a science lab here and started a project to save animal species that are in danger of extinction.

OK, everyone off the bus – please follow me – I'll go through the entrance first because I have all the tickets. Right, is everyone with me? Good. Now, when families come here at the weekend, they normally head straight for the monkey enclosure here on our right but we're going to head north past the nursery – yes, this is where all the zoo babies are born – to the **education block**. Please take note of where we are because we'll come back to this centre after we've had a look at the animals and there'll be a member of the zoo staff to answer your questions and show us a DVD.

Now, if we turn and walk east, you'll see a lake on your right and the polar bears on your left. As you know, they like colder temperatures and the waters of **the Blue Lake** are kept chilly, just for them. See? They can get to the lake by going under this bridge we're standing on. If we go straight on, we'll come to another lake, but that is for the reptiles and amphibians to lounge around in.

Let's head north again – are you all with me? All right, we'll stop here for a quick look at the children's petting zoo on our right – yes, this is one enclosure where the people and the animals can mix. There are lots of small farm animals here and they are all very tame because the idea is that city children can get up really close and touch them if they want. You might like to come back here when we've finished our tour. Okay ... let's step out of the petting zoo now and next up is the **aviary** – right in front of us – it's divided into a roofed-in section in the northern part, and the bigger birds are kept in the southern half.

Let's follow the path to the west now ... Please try to keep up, I don't want to lose any of you ... On our right is the African savannah which, as you can see, is very large so the big cats have plenty of room to roam. You can spend more time here later. Keeping west now, we walk alongside the savannah towards the Asian **rainforest**. Sometimes you have to stay very still if you want to see the animals that live here.

All right, I'm going to leave you now – you can either retrace your steps or continue around the zoo until you get back to where we're scheduled to watch the DVD in exactly one hour's time. See you then.

Before you hear the rest of the talk, you have some time to look at Questions 17 to 20.

[20 seconds]

Now listen and answer Questions 17 to 20.

It's good to see that you all made it here on time. How many of you went back to the petting zoo? All of you! I'm not surprised – it would've been my choice as well. The miniature **pigs** are my absolute favourite! You know, they used to have a larger variety of animals in there but they decided to remove the domestic pets, like cats and dogs, because most kids have access to those in their neighbourhoods, if not at home. The **goats** and **sheep** are always popular and the rabbits used to be too, but they were found to have some kind of disease and had to be taken away. There were farm birds once, as well – hens – but they didn't like being cuddled and they used to peck the children who picked them up, so they were returned to the farm where they came from.

So, time now for the DVD; we've arranged for you to watch it because, as you know, the breeding and **nursery** facility is off limits to the public – for very good reasons – but we all want to see the **zoo babies**, don't we? This DVD, as well as books on exotic and endangered animals and leaflets about the history of the zoo, are all available in the bookshop, which we'll stop and have a look at on our way out.

That is the end of Section 2. You now have half a minute to check your answers.

[30 seconds]

Now turn to Section 3.

SECTION 3

You will hear a conversation between a student called June and her academic counsellor. First you have some time to look at Questions 21 to 24.

[20 seconds]

Now listen carefully and answer Questions 21 to 24.

COUNSELLOR: Thanks for coming to see me, June. I understand that you've been referred to academic counselling because of a rather **poor outcome on your mid-year exams**. Is that right?

JUNE: Yes. I manage quite well with the course assessments but I just seem to go to pieces at exam time. And passing the exam is an essential criterion.

COUNSELLOR: Yours is quite a familiar situation. Exams often trigger stress and anxiety amongst students but, believe me, they're not intentionally designed to do so.

JUNE: I don't know why we have to have exams in the first place.

COUNSELLOR: Well, I guess the main reason is to test students under controlled conditions **so they can demonstrate what they are capable of, themselves, as individuals**, without any outside assistance.

JUNE: But I find them such a strain. And it's not because I don't study.

COUNSELLOR: Well, let me run through some exam preparation tips with you. We'll see if you can learn how to maximise the effectiveness of your preparation and reduce exam anxiety to get a better outcome.

JUNE: All right.

COUNSELLOR: Now, you are given a course outline that tells you when you'll be sitting the exam and how much it will contribute to your overall grade.

JUNE: Yes ... But they give that out in the first week of the course.

COUNSELLOR: Precisely ... Once you have it, you begin to set your exam goals. And from the very first day of lectures, you make sure you take good notes because these are essential for good exam preparation.

JUNE: Oh, I've got heaps of notes.

COUNSELLOR: But ... ah ... did you make summaries?

JUNE: Well, no. Anyway, some lecturers use PowerPoint presentations and they give you a handout with the slides on.

COUNSELLOR: Yes, but slides alone are not sufficient. You still need to write down explanations and examples and add your own notes to the slides.

JUNE: Oh, I see.

COUNSELLOR: As you progress through the semester, it's important to keep up-to-date with your **summaries – not just of the lecture notes** but chapters of any books you've read or **articles in journals**. Be selective though; there is just so much information on the Internet, and it's very difficult to discern what's valuable and what is not, and it's probably not worth the effort to summarise what you read there.

JUNE: Still, that seems like a lot of summarising.

Before you hear the rest of the conversation, you have some time to look at Questions 25 to 30.

[20 seconds]

Now listen and answer Questions 25 to 30.

COUNSELLOR: Yes, June, but that's the key to exam preparation – at revision time, you make a summary of all your summaries! And be sure to start revision before the end of lectures because lecturers often hold a couple of **revision seminars** before the end of the course.

JUNE: Do I need to go to those? I thought they were optional.

COUNSELLOR: They are, but you should attend. It is often in those seminars that you get really useful information to help you with the exams. And, before you go, you must have gone through all the course material. Read critically and carefully, and have **questions** prepared if there is anything you don't understand.

JUNE: Yes, that sounds like a good idea. So the secret is to start revision really early – is that what you're saying?

COUNSELLOR: Yes, but you can also set goals for your exams and, in your case, this is pretty straightforward because, no matter how well you've done on continuous assessment tasks, you still need to get 50% in each exam, right?

JUNE: Yes, passing the exam is compulsory in each of my courses.

COUNSELLOR: Then I suggest you target your **weaker subjects** and focus more effort on them in the lead-up to exams. Get a copy of your exam schedule as … as soon as it's available and make yourself a timetable. Fill in every day from the beginning of study week to the last exam. Write down all the tasks you have to do …

JUNE: You mean like sorting lecture notes, revision and practising past papers?

COUNSELLOR: Yes, although any sorting should be done straight after the last day of lectures … and don't forget to build in some **relaxation** time. I'm glad you practise past papers; that's a really good strategy. You know that different examiners like different styles of exams.

JUNE: Really?

COUNSELLOR: Yes, ah, of course. Multiple choice, essay, short answer, open book, problem solving … all those formats require different strategies, and you need to be aware of the **format** that your examiners prefer. What have you noticed so far?

JUNE: Well, multiple choice is popular …

COUNSELLOR: Ahh, yes. Good old multiple choice! Do you like that style?

JUNE: I'm not sure, really. I sometimes get a bit confused with those ones, and there are always so many questions.

COUNSELLOR: Yes, examiners like those because they are easy to mark, but of course they are harder to write. But from your point of view, you need to remember that multiple choice exams usually rely on recognition rather than **recall**.

JUNE: What does that mean?

COUNSELLOR: Well, you only have to know your subject matter well enough so that you can recognise the right answer when you see it.

JUNE: So that means it's easier?

COUNSELLOR: Not exactly; you can get a lot more questions, which means that you need to cover the breadth of the subject but you don't need to study it in great depth.

JUNE: Thanks, you've been really helpful.

That is the end of Section 3. You now have half a minute to check your answers.

[30 seconds]

Now turn to Section 4.

SECTION 4

You will hear a lecturer giving a talk on feral camels in Australia. First you have some time to look at Questions 31 to 40.

[40 seconds]

Now listen carefully and answer Questions 31 to 40.

Today we're going to be looking at the ecological impact of the feral camel in Australia. As you know, a feral animal is one that survives in the wild even though it originally lived with people, in a **domestic** situation. Camels are not native to Australia, so how did they get here or, more importantly, why?

The importation of camels began in 1840 and continued through to 1907. They were brought here to aid in opening up the arid and semi-arid regions of inland Australia. Initially they provided transport for people and goods involved in exploration or mining in the outback. They were also used to carry **equipment** for the construction of railways and telegraph lines. And often, they were the only way many remote settlements could receive supplies.

Where did they come from? Well, curiously enough, from as far afield as China and Mongolia – that was the large, woolly, two-humped Bactrian camel – and of course there were dromedaries (the typical Arabian camels used primarily for riding); but most of them were from lowland India. These ones, in particular, were very large and powerful and they were used to carry or move **heavy freight**. What we have now are feral camels that are mixtures of these different breeds.

Why are they feral? Well, once the railways were up and running and motor vehicles were becoming more common in the outback, they weren't needed any more. So, many of the 20,000 or so domesticated camels that were around in 1930 were just let go. And because they were so well adapted to desert conditions, they thrived and bred and spread right across **central Australia.**

Pause [2–3 seconds]

What's the problem? You might ask. After all they're just camels living in the desert. The problem is that they are an introduced animal – a very large one at that – and they do extensive damage to the desert eco-system. They wander up to 70 kilometres in one day, grazing on whatever vegetation is available –

that might be grass, shrubs or trees up to 3.5 metres high. In times of drought, when water is scarce, they are capable of drinking up to **200** litres each in three minutes, although if they're consuming a lot of green moist plant material, they don't need that much. They gather around precious water holes to get this water, and the degradation of these water holes is of serious concern. They are crucial for the survival of a wide variety of native animals and plants. Many of these are now threatened to the point of extinction.

Let me also point out that these watering places have a long-standing cultural significance, and many of them are **sacred sites** for the Aboriginal people. Feral camels are literally trampling all over and violating Aboriginal traditions and history. In periods of extreme drought, like Australia has experienced in recent years, there is no limit to their quest for water. Camels are big animals, and they go pretty much wherever they please. They are not primarily interested in hurting people, but it's not advisable to get in their way. They have gone into **remote communities** and damaged domestic infrastructure such as washing facilities in laundries and bathrooms as well as outside bores, taps and tanks.

Let's see: feral camels have a negative impact on native vegetation and animals, water supplies, and Aboriginal and outback communities but they are no friends of the farmers, either. They compete with livestock for pasture and they can wreck the farmer's precious property in the process, knocking down fences, **windmills** and water troughs. Camels also carry some of the same diseases as livestock and are likely to spread infection among cattle and other farm animals. On top of all that, they cause a number of collisions with trains, cars and trucks. Oh, and one more thing, camels are ruminants, which means they emit methane, and they are having a significant impact on climate change.

Feral camels do have some value as a resource. There is a small export market in camel meat, and the **pet meat** trade uses them as well. Although camels have a reputation for being stubborn, and even vicious, they are easy to domesticate once they are captured. We don't use them in industry any more, but sometimes they are used by tourist operators as a novelty form of **transport** for their customers. Even so, it would seem their usefulness is limited and far outweighed by their overall – harmful – economic, environmental, social and cultural impact.

That is the end of Section 4. You now have half a minute to check your answers.

[30 seconds]

That is the end of the Listening test.

Academic Test 2

You will hear a number of different recordings and you will have to answer questions on what you hear. There will be time for you to read the instructions and questions and you will have a chance to check your work. All the recordings will be played once only. The test is in 4 sections. At the end of the test you will be given 10 minutes to transfer your answers to an answer sheet. Now turn to Section 1.

SECTION 1

You will hear a conversation between a hotel receptionist and a woman who wants to make a reservation. First, you have some time to look at Questions 1 to 5.

[20 seconds]

You will see that there is an example that has been done for you. On this occasion only the conversation relating to this example will be played first.

RECEPTIONIST: Good morning, welcome to the Horizon Hotel. How may I help you?
WOMAN: I've come in to make a reservation for a friend.
RECEPTIONIST: And your friend's name is ...?
WOMAN: MacKay, **Sandra MacKay**, that's M-A-C-K-A-Y.
RECEPTIONIST: Thank you.

*The woman says her friend's name is Sandra MacKay, so **Sandra MacKay** has been written in the space. Now we shall begin. You should answer the questions as you listen because you will not hear the recording a second time. Listen carefully and answer Questions 1 to 5.*

RECEPTIONIST: Good morning, welcome to the Horizon Hotel. How may I help you?
WOMAN: I've come in to make a reservation for a friend.
RECEPTIONIST: And your friend's name is ...?
WOMAN: MacKay, Sandra MacKay, that's M-A-C-K-A-Y.
RECEPTIONIST: Thank you. When is she arriving?
WOMAN: She's flying in on the fifteenth but she'll stay with me for the first night because we have an early start on the sixteenth – we're going for a quick trip to the coast – but we should be back on the eighteenth.
RECEPTIONIST: So that's the **18th** of this month?
WOMAN: No, sorry, did I forget to say? It's next month – December.
RECEPTIONIST: Well, that's getting pretty close to Christmas, but we may have something available ... Right, we have one or two nice rooms left ... but how long will she stay for?
WOMAN: A week.
RECEPTIONIST: So, she'd be checking out on ... **Christmas Day – the 25th**.
WOMAN: Is that a problem?
RECEPTIONIST: Well, it depends. We don't have a room available for the whole week, but, if she didn't mind changing rooms mid-way through her stay, we could work something out.

WOMAN:	Oh, I see.
RECEPTIONIST:	And if she wanted to extend her stay, that wouldn't be possible, I'm afraid. We're completely booked out from Christmas Day through to New Year.
WOMAN:	No, she won't want to extend and I don't think she'd have a problem with changing rooms.
RECEPTIONIST:	Good. Well, I'll put her in Room 502 to start with and then she'll have to move to ... 805 ... no, just a minute, let's make that **702** because that's available and it's two floors directly above 502 so the room layout will be identical.
WOMAN:	How much will it cost per night?
RECEPTIONIST:	The basic room rate is **$165**.
WOMAN:	Is breakfast included?
RECEPTIONIST:	No, but a complimentary drink is served every evening at 5 o'clock.
WOMAN:	Oh, that could be quite nice.
RECEPTIONIST:	Shall we make the booking then? We will require a deposit equivalent to one night's stay.
WOMAN:	That's fine – I can pay the deposit.
RECEPTIONIST:	How would you like to do that – in cash or by credit card?
WOMAN:	Credit card, I suppose. Oh, wait a minute – I might have enough money in my purse, yes, let's do it in cash.
RECEPTIONIST:	Hang on, I'll just make a note of that. Deposit paid ... **in cash**.

Before you hear the rest of the conversation, you have some time to look at Questions 6 to 10.

[20 seconds]

Now listen and answer Questions 6 to 10.

RECEPTIONIST:	Just a second while I print a receipt. Who shall I make it out to?
WOMAN:	My name is Zoe **Reed**, R-E-E-D.
RECEPTIONIST:	Thank you Ms Reed. Now, I'll need some contact details for either you or Ms MacKay.
WOMAN:	I'll give you my details, I only live on the other side of town.
RECEPTIONIST:	Can I have your address and phone number, please?
WOMAN:	I live at **14 South Street**, Morning Town. And my phone number is 439 4829.
RECEPTIONIST:	Thank you, 439 4829.
WOMAN:	Yes, that's right.
RECEPTIONIST:	Now, I'll just print the booking form. If you have any questions or need to make any changes, just quote the reservation number on the bottom of the form. That's it there: **AQ459**.
WOMAN:	Thanks very much. Oh, before I go, just a couple of questions. What time does the room get cleaned? I'm only asking because my friend usually has a short nap after lunch and she wouldn't like to be disturbed.
RECEPTIONIST:	Well, the maids are usually finished by 1 p.m. because we have a 2 o'clock check-in

time, you see. They come on duty quite early in the morning ... so they are sure to be finished in your friend's room by lunchtime, yes definitely – I'd say roughly **11 o'clock**.

WOMAN: Thanks ... that's good to know. One more thing ... is there room service for meals?

RECEPTIONIST: Only for breakfast and dinner. Breakfast service finishes at 9 and starts at 5 a.m. **Dinner service starts at 6 p.m.** but the last orders have to be in half an hour before the kitchen closes at 11 p.m. – so full room service **closes at 10.30**. But remember, light snacks – things like toasted sandwiches or muffins – can be ordered at the bar just off the lobby throughout the day and evening – until two in the morning.

WOMAN: Thanks very much. You've been most helpful.

That is the end of Section 1. You now have half a minute to check your answers.

[30 seconds]

Now turn to Section 2.

SECTION 2

You will hear a radio announcer introducing what's on at the local Arts Centre. First you have some time to look at Questions 11 to 16.

[20 seconds]

Now listen carefully and answer Questions 11 to 16.

Hello and thanks for joining me on the Arts Scene tonight brought to you by your local radio station 2ZG and made possible by the generous sponsorship of Bertrand's Music and Video Store.

Firstly, I want to announce that the refurbished Arts Centre downtown is opening soon, with some spectacular visual art displays and performances that you won't want to miss.

In Gallery 1 the Arts Centre will be hosting an extraordinary exhibition of the latest creative works of our regional artists. There'll be landscapes, abstracts, photography, ceramics and sculpture. The exhibition opens on the 4th of March and runs through to the 10th of April. It's free and open to the public from 11 a.m. to 4 p.m. **weekdays** and, by the way, all works on display are for sale, so be sure to bring your credit card with you!

Gallery 2 will put on the annual showcase of the art of school students who take a, sometimes challenging and often emotive, look at the current issues facing youth in particular and society in general. This is the '**Issues** of the 21st Century' exhibition and the dates to keep in mind are 10th of March to the 4th of April – the gallery will be open from 10 till 3 Monday, Wednesday, Friday and weekends. There's no charge but teachers should make bookings if they're bringing large groups.

Let's move on to the performing arts now: Shakespeare season is back again and this year's production is the ever popular *Romeo and Juliet*. Tickets are just **$40** for adults and half price for seniors, and there are rush tickets for students at $15. Performances are in Theatre One at 8 o'clock every evening. Bookings are essential. The show runs from the 5th of March to the 3rd of April, and there is a possibility of more shows if there is a high demand for tickets.

Now, if you like your folk pop with a country twist, you must see Shannon Keel, who is back in town for one night only on the first of April performing for us in the **Basement**. She'll be supported by Ricky Bond's band, which has been touring with her for the last 7 weeks – and show time is **9.15**. Tickets are on sale at the door, just $12.50. Doors open at 8.

Coming to the Arts Centre for 4 performances in the Showroom is Class Act, a quartet who have captivated audiences with their amazing repertoire of **classical** music and who now include top-class cabaret in their programme. They will give matinee performances every Friday in April at 11 o'clock. Tickets are only $14 a single, or better yet, why not get together with a group of six or more friends and pay only $12.

Before you hear the rest of the announcement, you have some time to look at Questions 17 to 20.

[20 seconds]

Now listen and answer Questions 17 to 20.

Now, here's some exciting news. I've just heard that Michael O'Brien is going to perform at the Arts Centre next year but we haven't got any dates finalised as yet. As you know, Michael is **Ireland**'s most popular 'easy listening' entertainer and he's returning from a tour of Canada and the United States where he has enjoyed huge success – even in Nashville: the home of country music – that's a long way from his Irish roots.

Michael is without a doubt a singing superstar – he has had 15 top-ten music videos and is almost a permanent feature in the UK album charts with 18 UK chart albums to date – but he is still as excited and enthusiastic about his work and his fans as he was when he first launched his career **20** years ago.

Perhaps some of you are unaware that Michael's first years were ones of struggle. The family was very poor and his father was forced to go **abroad** to provide for his family. He worked on farms in Scotland and it was very hard, manual labour – very different from the lifestyle Michael enjoys today. Unfortunately, his father died when Michael was only five years old and the burden of raising five children fell on his mother.

Although Michael followed in the footsteps of his **sister** by pursuing a singing career – she was his role model and inspiration – he has attributed much of his success in life to his mother's influence, and he has dedicated his most recent DVD release to her. You can pick up a copy of that DVD, 'Unwavering Devotion', at Bertrand's Music and Video Store.

Well, that's all from me ... it's been nice talking to you – tune in at the same time next week – until then, good night and take care.

That is the end of Section 2. You now have half a minute to check your answers.

[30 seconds]

Now turn to Section 3.

SECTION 3

You will hear a conversation between two second-year students, Steve and Jan, who are planning an assignment together. First, you have some time to look at Questions 21 to 25.

[20 seconds]

Now listen carefully and answer Questions 21 to 25.

STEVE: Hi Jan. Sorry, my tutorial finished late.

JAN: No problem Steve! But let's get straight to work. I've got so many other assignments this week! And we've only got till next Wednesday.

STEVE: Sure, fine by me. So, we've got to do a combined **presentation**, with at least 20 slides and a recommendation at the end. Is that right?

JAN: Yes. And then 5 minutes for questions ...

STEVE: Oh, right, I'd forgotten that.

JAN: So – what shall we choose as a topic? I was wondering about copyright ... or intellectual property law. It's a tricky area though.

STEVE: Well, I've been doing a bit of reading about **digital privacy** and it's actually a really challenging issue now. I mean, the way employers and government departments rely on commercial databases for information on people.

JAN: OK, that sounds like it has potential. Tell me more – I can't say I've read much about it.

STEVE: Um ... well, these databases compile information on all sorts of things, not just birthdates and income. They record people's lawsuits and convictions, employment history, **credit rating,** medical history – a range of statistics and stuff that is often out of date or is only partially true.

JAN: And they get this information from public records on the Internet? You mean it's actually available online?

STEVE: Yes, and that's the problem. We live in such a networked society now. There's so much data on the net, and it's really accessible. Often the company **employees** who compile these databases include dated information or get confused by similar names and list the wrong details for people.

JAN: I'm starting to get the idea. What kind of things can go wrong?

STEVE: Well, for example, a **sales manager** was fired because of a background check by a data company which reported that he'd served a jail term. He protested, but his boss still fired him. All he'd had was something minor like a speeding ticket. He suffered an unjust dismissal plus the stress of trying to find another job. He was out of work for seven months.

JAN: I see. OK, this has really got me thinking now! It's a great topic.

Before you hear the rest of the conversation, you have some time to look at Questions 26 to 30.

[20 seconds]

Now listen and answer Questions 26 to 30.

JAN: Ah ... I'm thinking now about how the search engines apparently compile information on people, based on their online **search habits** ... you know, there's been a bit in the news lately. I guess that's pertinent.

STEVE: That's right; it's all part of this same issue. The search engines actually gather a huge amount of data about computer users, and some of it is definitely sold to other paying customers. The database companies sell lists to direct-marketing companies, for example. That's their core business, so they're always trying to access more information in order to attract new clients and improve their **profitability**.

JAN: Hmm. What about social networking sites? How much of that information is truly private?

STEVE: Not a lot, it seems. And hackers can download sensitive information and misuse it as well. Also, every time you fill out an online form or survey to enter a prize draw, you're compromising your privacy.

JAN: I never thought about that. I often enter those, and give my email address and mobile number.

STEVE: Well, apparently in Europe they have laws controlling the ability of companies to sell or share people's personal data without getting explicit consent. But that's not the case here.

JAN: Then that could be our main **recommendation**.

STEVE: Yes – and then we can advise people to actually purchase their own credit reports and files from a few of the big database companies, to check that the information stored on them is actually accurate.

JAN: It's so frustrating to have to do something like that!

STEVE: For sure. Also bloggers should be very cautious – they can be sued for breaches of privacy and for libel. Even Twitter comments aren't exempt from **legal action**. So that's another area to consider for suggestions. Anyway, we need to decide how to split this up. How about if one of us does an overview of the general issue and the history of it all to date?

JAN: I think I might tackle that. You'd be better on the technical stuff.

STEVE: Great. Then I'll look at new developments and make policy recommendations. For example, there are technology researchers looking at how access to files and information can be restricted. Because, you know, originally the Internet was designed to be as open as possible ...

JAN: That's right. And instead, it's created a real conflict.

STEVE: Already some of the browser companies are working on solutions to this – such as offering a **tracking protection** feature that users can switch on, to restrict how much data can be mined from their computer use. And there are a few other ideas out there as well ...

JAN: And about the question slot ... I seem to remember Professor Duncan suggesting we prepare a couple of questions ourselves, in case no one asks anything.

STEVE: Hmm, I guess that's a good idea.

That is the end of Section 3. You now have half a minute to check your answers.

[30 seconds]

Now turn to Section 4.

SECTION 4

You will hear a lecture on the Antarctic toothfish industry. First you have some time to look at Questions 31 to 40.

[40 seconds]

Now listen carefully and answer Questions 31 to 40.

Good afternoon! As you know ... it's Environment Week, and that seems like a good time to focus on one of the most special places in the world ... the Ross Sea, and its associated fishing industry, which is largely focussed on the Antarctic toothfish.

Now ... back in 2008, this part of the Antarctic, that is the **Ross Sea** – which by the way makes up only about 3% of the Southern Ocean – was rated as being the 'least-changed environment' on the planet. In fact, it's been described by one source as 'a living laboratory, a link with evolution' and it teems with fascinating and unusual sea and mammal life. So there have been urgent pleas for the Ross Sea to be given some kind of permanent protection.

What are the issues facing the area, then? Well, aside from the huge problem of global warming that threatens all of the Antarctic oceans and the ice cap, most of these are associated with the fishing vessels that come into the Ross Sea. As well as the usual things like general rubbish and sewage pollution from these boats, the most significant potential danger is an **oil and diesel spill** from a fishing boat that is either damaged or sunk due to the thick ice. In January 2012, a Korean fishing vessel caught fire in the Ross Sea, with the loss of at least three lives – although luckily an oil spill was averted. In late 2011, another Korean ship, the *In Sung Number 1*, sank with 22 lives lost, although the rest of the crew were saved by other fishing boats in the area.

Again, in December 2011, another vessel, the *Sparta*, caused an international furore when it was holed and stranded in pack ice in the Southern Ocean – that one was **Russian**. New Zealand planes had to fly missions to drop off water pumps and other essential equipment and supplies to the ship – ah ... remember that the crews of such flights are put at extreme risk on such long flights, as the weather can become stormy at very short notice. All in all, it was a miracle that this ship was able to be repaired and moved from the area **without a significant leakage of fuel**. So, apart from the potential for environmental problems from the boats, and the danger to fishermen working in this hostile environment, there's also the matter of the cost and danger of providing support in a crisis.

And ... you know ... there's a lot of pressure on the fishing crews to make the most of the brief weather window during which boats can operate so far south, so they tend to keep fishing no matter what the weather is like ... which means that errors of judgement are more likely. **The officially authorised fishing fleet has a quota or limit** and each boat is hoping to get the biggest share possible of the total allowable catch. Then, of course, there are the illegal boats – that means the boats operating without permits – they just try to catch as much as possible regardless – and the vessels may not even be in a suitable condition to be operating in these icy southern waters.

Pause [2–3 seconds]

Consequently, a key issue is the decimation of the species. Now, how much do we know about this particular fish? The Antarctic toothfish inhabit very cold Antarctic seas, usually between 200 metres to two kilometres deep. They are large creatures ... rather ugly ... and they are slow-growing. Although they live up to approximately **fifty** years, it seems they only reach sexual maturity after about sixteen years. Also, very little is yet known about their life cycle – things like where they spawn, or what happens to the young ones before they are ready to breed. We do know that the adult fish are near the top of the food chain – but we need to know much more about the juvenile forms – things like: what they look like, where they spend those early years and ... ah ... what sort of **predators** go after them.

OK – so the fishing season in the Ross Sea spans December to February. It's estimated that close to three and a half thousand tonnes of Antarctic toothfish have been taken annually since the fishery opened in 1996 – this represents approximately one hundred thousand fish per year. I must add, though, that in the last couple of years overall catches have been reduced due to **overfishing** and the decline in total fish numbers. There's no record, of course, of the numbers of fish caught by illegal fishing boats.

Um ... those in the Antarctic toothfish industry claim that the short fishing season and the difficulties faced by the boats in this inhospitable climate provide their own natural limits on fishing. They say that the industry is concerned to preserve fish stocks, and they assert that, with careful management and monitoring, the fishery is **sustainable**. However, others dispute that this is the case, especially given the distances involved and the difficulties faced in trying to manage and monitor fishing boats in such a remote location.

In the Ross Sea area, a conservative estimate suggests that fish stocks have declined by about 20 per cent over the past 16 years. But in fact there is not enough accurate research to support such claims ... the figure could be even higher. Leading scientists who specialise in this issue are calling for a Marine Protection Area, or MPA, with a total **ban** on fishing, but so far this has not been achieved.

Right – so that's an introduction. Now, let's watch a short video before we discuss your next assignment ...

That is the end of Section 4. You now have half a minute to check your answers.

[30 seconds]

That is the end of the Listening test.

Academic Test 3

You will hear a number of different recordings and you will have to answer questions on what you hear. There will be time for you to read the instructions and questions and you will have a chance to check your work. All the recordings will be played once only. The test is in 4 sections. At the end of the test you will be given 10 minutes to transfer your answers to an answer sheet. Now turn to Section 1.

SECTION 1

You will hear a telephone conversation between a representative of an Internet provider service and a man who wants to get a new password. First, you have some time to look at Questions 1 to 7.

[20 seconds]

You will see that there is an example that has been done for you. On this occasion only, the conversation relating to this example will be played first.

NATASHA: Good evening. This is Web Net and you're speaking with **Natasha**. How can I assist you today?

MICHAEL: Hello, Natasha. I tried to log in to my Web Net account yesterday and I realised I'd forgotten my password. Are you able to help me with that?

*The person answering the call says her name is Natasha, so **Natasha** has been written in the space. Now we shall begin. You should answer the questions as you listen because you will not hear the recording a second time. Listen carefully and answer Questions 1 to 7.*

NATASHA: Good evening. This is Web Net and you're speaking with **Natasha**. How can I assist you today?

MICHAEL: Hello, Natasha. I tried to log in to my Web Net account yesterday and I realised I'd forgotten my password. Are you able to help me with that?

NATASHA: Of course. What I'll need to do is ask you a few questions to check your identity, and then I'll issue you with a new password. Is that okay?

MICHAEL: No problem.

NATASHA: Firstly, can I have your full name please?

MICHAEL: Michael **Simmons, S-I-M-M-O-N-S**. I don't have a middle name.

NATASHA: Great. And your date of birth?

MICHAEL: It's the 27/3/1988.

NATASHA: Right, and I also need to know your previous address.

MICHAEL: I live at 12 Wake Street, and that's in ...

NATASHA: We have that as your current address. What was the address you registered with us before you moved there?

MICHAEL: Oh, yeah. I used to live at 319 **Ocean Drive**. That's in East Providence.

NATASHA: I'll just need your contact phone number as well.

MICHAEL: That's 0492 48002.

NATASHA: And just a few questions about your account. Do you know what your current data allowance is?

MICHAEL: I upgraded to the Gold account not long ago, so it's **unlimited**.

NATASHA: Yes – unlimited data. Right, now can you just tell me about your payment plan? Which plan are you currently on, do you know?

MICHAEL: Oh, hang on a minute while I think. Yes ... I started off with the 12-month automatic renewal, but a few months ago I switched to the **24-month** plan.

NATASHA: That's fine. Now, when you first registered for Web Net, you selected two secret questions and provided us with the answers. In order to issue you with a new password I need you to answer those questions for me. Firstly, what is your mother's maiden name?

MICHAEL: My mother's name is Sarah. That's Sarah with an H.

NATASHA: That sounds like her first name. We're looking for her maiden name – that's her family name before she was married.

MICHAEL: Sorry, I misheard. It's, um ... **White**.

NATASHA: White as in the colour?

MICHAEL: Yes, that's right.

NATASHA: Now, the other question you chose to answer: What was your first pet?

MICHAEL: The first pet I ever had?

NATASHA: Yes.

MICHAEL: It was actually **a goldfish**.

NATASHA: That's what it says on your file! ... Okay, that's all done for you, Mr Simmons. I've sent you a generic password, which should arrive in your e-mail box within a few minutes. I'll just make a note of the date ... **30th of June**. When you log in, I suggest you go to the Member's Details section on the website and change it to something you're going to remember.

MICHAEL: Wonderful, thanks.

Before you hear the rest of the conversation, you have some time to look at Questions 8 to 10.

[20 seconds]

Now listen and answer Questions 8 to 10.

NATASHA: Is there anything else I can help you with today?

MICHAEL: Yeah, there are a few things. I've been having some connection issues recently. I think the problem is with the cable that connects the modem to the computer. Do you supply those?

NATASHA: You need a new **cable**? Not a problem. I'll arrange for that to be sent off tomorrow.

MICHAEL: Thanks. Also, I'm currently signed up for three of your services – home phone, mobile and broadband. I use the Internet a lot, on my computer and on my mobile, but to be honest I never use the home phone and I don't see why I should keep paying for that plan.

NATASHA: Would you like me to cancel that **home phone** for you?

MICHAEL: Yes, please, if you wouldn't mind.

NATASHA: Done. Is there anything else?

MICHAEL: Yes, just one last thing. Do you offer any anti-virus products?

NATASHA: Yes, we have one which offers full protection against viruses, spam and identity theft, which is useful if you're doing any online banking and that kind of thing. It's called the **security** pack.

MICHAEL: Sounds perfect. Sign me up for one of those, please.

NATASHA: And we've got another one – it's called the parenting pack – it prevents your children from accessing harmful websites and downloading things they shouldn't.

MICHAEL: I'm not so worried about that anymore. Both my children are adults and have left home ... so, just the security pack, thanks. That's everything.

That is the end of Section 1. You now have half a minute to check your answers.

[30 seconds]

Now turn to Section 2.

SECTION 2

You will hear a man who owns a holiday home, talking on the phone to a woman who has arranged it. First, you have some time to look at Questions 11 to 16.

[20 seconds]

Now listen carefully and answer Questions 11 to 16.

MAN: Hello, Ron Smith speaking.

WOMAN: Hi. This is Kayla Lawton. I signed up with the Holiday House agency to rent your beach house but the agent isn't available today and I have a problem – I can't remember what she said about the **alarm system**.

MAN: Oh, it's quite simple really. The main thing to remember is to enter **by the back door** which leads into the kitchen because **that is where the alarm is situated** – right next to the light switch **just beside the door**. If you go through the front door into the living room, it will take you longer to reach the alarm and you only have a few seconds to deactivate it. The code is 3498.

WOMAN: Okay, I've got that.

MAN: The agent will have given you the back and front door keys, but there are **other keys** that you may need – for the garage, the laundry and the little garden shed. You'll find them hanging **on a hook inside the cupboard in the hallway** next to the hot water cupboard. The laundry room is outside, next to the garage. It should be kept locked, so please remember to return the key to the hook when you've done your washing. The last tenant lost it somewhere in the garden and I had to have the lock replaced. There should be some **laundry detergent** for the washing machine next to the dishwashing liquid **under the kitchen sink**.

Oh, now about the linen. The sheets are already on the beds and there are lots of towels at the house, too. Of course you'll want to enjoy that lovely, safe swimming beach as much as possible. You'll find a pile of **beach towels** in a basket **on the washing machine**. Feel free to take these to the beach with you. We have lots of them, and they're pretty old, so it doesn't matter if they get a bit dirty or sandy. There are other, newer **towels for use in the bathroom only**; these are **in the hot water cupboard**, on the shelf up above the cylinder – please don't take these ones down to the beach.

Ah, what else? Oh, yes. I should tell you that the electricity supply is generally reliable but sometimes there are power surges which make a few **light bulbs** blow. If that happens, don't worry, there are **spare light bulbs in a shoebox** on the chest of drawers in the bedroom. That reminds me, the main power supply is switched off at the mains box, which is above the front door. The first thing to do when you arrive is to pull down the large lever – it's clearly labelled 'mains switch' – you don't need to touch any of the other switches.

WOMAN: Thank you. Anything else?

Before you hear the rest of the conversation, you have some time to look at Questions 17 to 20.

[20 seconds]

Now listen and answer Questions 17 to 20.

MAN: Oh, one more thing – something that might interest you is a folder of local information – you know the sort of thing, interesting places to visit, opening hours for the shops and services in the town ... plus a little map of local walks. It's on top of the TV along with the remote control. Parking in the town is usually really easy except for weekends when the place is swamped with **tourists**, so I would recommend doing your shopping on weekdays. Oh, one thing though, if you want to combine a shopping expedition with a visit to the Early History Museum, you should know that it's not open on **Mondays**. There are lots of good places to eat in town, too. You'll find a list of menus and takeaway prices for some of the more popular local cafés and restaurants. If you like Chinese, the **Happy Dragon** has excellent food, or I'd recommend the Pizzeria if you prefer Italian – they have a good selection of takeaway pasta and pizza as well. The Happy Dragon is a firm favourite with the locals, though. Both restaurants deliver, free of charge, but note the phone numbers have changed since the menus were printed. Phone **3-2-3-1-1-9-0 for pizza** and 3-2-3-9-9-1-1 for Chinese. You won't be disappointed.

WOMAN: Thanks a lot, I'll do that.

That is the end of Section 2. You now have half a minute to check your answers.

[30 seconds]

Now turn to Section 3.

SECTION 3

You will hear a college professor and a postgraduate student Diana discussing her recent internship experience. First, you have some time to look at Questions 21 to 25.

[20 seconds]

Now listen carefully and answer Questions 21 to 25.

PROF: Thanks for coming in today to discuss your internship experience. Completing some sort of work experience, like an internship, is a core part of our Master's programme, and we want to make sure students are able to make the most of it.

DIANA: That's fine.

PROF: So, as I understand, you were offered an internship by Gregory Associates. Is that correct?

DIANA: Actually, I got offers from a few companies, but Gregory Associates was the only one I seriously considered.

PROF: Was there any reason for that?

DIANA: Yeah. They didn't offer the best conditions – some of the other companies were offering to cover transportation and other living costs, that kind of thing – but I knew Gregory Associates was a **widely recognised leader in the industry**, and that was the big factor for me.

PROF: And were you happy with your choice?

DIANA: Well, yes and no.

PROF: Mixed feelings?

DIANA: Yeah. I mean, don't get me wrong – everyone in the office was great. They didn't talk down to me and they were always happy to assist if I wasn't sure about something.

PROF: Was it the work, then? Some students do find internships a little tedious and boring.

DIANA: It's not that it was boring. I was doing new things every day, and I loved that. They really kept me on my toes. It's just that, I'm studying economics, you know? But most of the projects I was assigned to involved more ... administrative stuff ... **It just wasn't relevant to what I've been studying**.

PROF: I'm sorry to hear that. I'll make a note of it. Let's talk about the good things. What did you particularly enjoy about the experience?

DIANA: Well, as an intern, the managers do tend to keep you at arm's length – they just don't trust you enough to let you take on a lot of responsibility for the big projects.

PROF: That's understandable.

DIANA: Yes, but in a way, I liked that – because **I got to stand back and watch**, and get a real sense of how a company like that runs on a day-to-day basis. And **that was the highlight for me**.

PROF: That's great to hear. How did you find managing the internship alongside your study commitments?

DIANA: Well, because my internship was over the summer break, that wasn't an issue for me at all.

PROF: Okay. What would you say was the biggest struggle then?

DIANA: In the beginning, I might have said the hours. Those 6 a.m. starts were tough! But I quickly got used to that. In retrospect, **the biggest difficulty was getting by on such a tight budget**. As I wasn't earning anything, the whole experience really drained my savings account.

PROF: Yeah, that can be tough. And my last question: what was the outcome of this internship for you? Some of our students are lucky enough to get offers of employment before finishing.

DIANA: At first, I was hoping I would be one of them. In the end I wasn't, but I'm happy about that now.

PROF: Why's that?

DIANA: Well, over the course of the internship, I ended up reconsidering whether this industry is really for me after all. I'm going to finish my degree, because I'm only a semester away from graduation now, but then after that **I've decided to pursue a different line of work**.

PROF: Well, I do hope you're successful with that.

Before you hear the rest of the conversation, you have some time to look at Questions 26 to 30.

[20 seconds]

Now listen and answer Questions 26 to 30.

PROF: Now, we're putting together a step-by-step guide about the process for students who want to apply for internships, and we were wondering if you could help us with it.

DIANA: Sure.

PROF: What would you say is the first step?

DIANA: Before they do anything else, students need to get their **documents** sorted. Companies need to see all sorts of things, such as reference letters and verified copies of academic transcripts. It can take time to get it all together, so applicants need to get onto this as soon as possible.

PROF: Great, we'll put that down as Number One. And then students should begin researching companies?

DIANA: Absolutely. They should look at a wide range of companies and the internships they offer. They really shouldn't limit themselves at that stage.

PROF: It would be time-consuming to apply to them all, though.

DIANA: Yeah, so I think they need to weed out those positions they are not qualified for or that don't meet their own needs and interests, and then put together a **shortlist** consisting only of those positions that are a good match.

PROF: And then?

DIANA: Well, the next part is the applications, of course. I think the big mistake here is that some students just send the same cover letter and the same CV to each company, when in reality every position is a little bit different. They really need to **alter** their applications so that they refer to the individual needs of each position.

PROF: I'll make a note of that. And should students follow up on their applications?

DIANA: I think so. It's best to **call** each company – an e-mail is too easy to ignore or delete. And not too soon, either – a week after the applications have been submitted is probably ideal.

PROF: So if they get an interview, what's next?

DIANA: Obviously they need to prepare. For me this included all sorts of things, like practising my body language in front of the mirror and researching common interview questions online.

PROF: Any tips for the interview itself?

DIANA: Most students are so obsessed with having the right answers, but I think the most important thing is actually to **ask questions**. It shows the employer that you are genuinely interested in their company and in the position.

PROF: That's really helpful advice. Thanks for coming by today.

DIANA: No problem.

That is the end of Section 3. You now have half a minute to check your answers.

[30 seconds]

Now turn to Section 4.

SECTION 4

You will hear the first lecture of a course in Development Studies. First you have some time to look at Questions 31 to 40.

[40 seconds]

Now listen carefully and answer Questions 31 to 40.

Good morning, everyone, and welcome to your first lecture in Development Studies.

Development Studies, as a discipline, can be boiled down to a couple of core objectives. Basically, we are trying to understand how it is that societies experience particular kinds of change and how they progress as they develop. We're also trying to go beyond that, however, and work out how different sorts of **actions** can facilitate or even encourage these changes to happen.

To achieve these objectives, there are two key approaches that underpin Development Studies. Firstly, there's a theoretical approach, which is all about the 'how' of change. With theory we can explore some of the big questions: What kind of change should we aspire to, and how can this be achieved? But we don't just talk; we've also got to apply some of this thinking. So through the applied approach we're looking at specific **policies**, and trying to understand how they can most effectively be put into place.

Although we try not to limit ourselves, we do focus on a few key areas. Due to our location, for example, the Asia-Pacific region is an important area of research for us. At the moment we're doing a lot of work on urbanisation, and there are two elements to this. One is employment, as urbanisation leads to major employment problems, and the other is **housing** – with so many people moving to cities, many of them struggle to find a place to live. Other issues of particular interest to our staff are migration and, of course, trade.

So what will you be able to do with a degree in Development Studies? Well, firstly, you'll develop a full working knowledge of all aspects of development. You'll also learn how to gather data. We include sessions on how to gather **statistics**, but we mostly focus on textual data, that is, policy briefings, research reports, and so on. Once you've done your research, you need to know what it all means; after all, there's not much point in collecting a whole lot of data if you don't know whether it is significant or not – so we're going to teach you how to critically **evaluate** your findings. And finally, teamwork is a big part of development work – your major piece of research work for this class is done in groups of four, so you're going to learn how to **cooperate** as a team in order to plan and conduct this research assignment.

I want to move on now to give you a brief overview of how Development Studies has evolved as a discipline since it was first established.

The first thing to note is that, unlike other subjects, such as mathematics or philosophy, Development

Studies is very young. It began taking shape as a formal discipline only in the 1950s. At that stage, **economic** concerns were at the forefront of nearly all research efforts. Researchers assumed that development in general could be measured by indicators such as Gross Domestic Product (GDP), or unemployment levels.

In the 1970s, a new set of scholars took charge. These researchers, informed by the social movements of the 1960s, brought a new set of issues to the table. At that time, Development Studies grew increasingly critical of established **practices**, and the assumptions that lay behind these practices. Questions were raised in three areas: the role of power in creating policy, the importance of environmentally sustainable change, and problems with inequalities in terms of **gender**.

From the 1980s onwards, the economy staged a comeback as a centrepiece of development practice. A key factor here was the reduced significance of national governments due to a number of market-led reforms in many countries around the world. In contrast to the 1950s, however, researchers have recently shown a heightened interest in smaller-scale economic projects. One significant innovation here is the idea of making tiny **loans**, sometimes only a few dollars, to help women, in particular, to start up a small business.

And that brings us to today. So let's finish now by talking about ...

That is the end of Section 4. You now have half a minute to check your answers.

[30 seconds]

That is the end of the Listening test.

Academic Test 4

You will hear a number of different recordings and you will have to answer questions on what you hear. There will be time for you to read the instructions and questions and you will have a chance to check your work. All the recordings will be played once only. The test is in 4 sections. At the end of the test you will be given 10 minutes to transfer your answers to an answer sheet. Now turn to Section 1.

SECTION 1

You will hear a telephone conversation between a bank representative and a client who wants to make an international money transfer. First, you have some time to look at Questions 1 to 6.

[20 seconds]

You will see that there is an example that has been done for you. On this occasion only, the conversation relating to this example will be played first.

WOMAN: Wesley Bank, how can I help you?
MAN: Oh, hi. Um, I want to know how to send money to my family overseas.
WOMAN: No problem. If you have access to the Internet, I can guide you through the process of how to use our **global payments** system.

*The bank representative says she will tell the man how to use the global payments system, so **global payments** has been written in the space. Now we should begin. You should answer the questions as you listen because you will not hear the recording a second time. Listen carefully and answer Questions 1 to 6.*

WOMAN: Wesley Bank, how can I help you?
MAN: Oh, hi. Um, I want to know how to send money to my family overseas.
WOMAN: No problem. If you have access to the Internet, I can guide you through the process of how to use our **global payments** system.
MAN: That's great. I'm online now.
WOMAN: Good. First, you have to log on to Wesley Bank Internet Banking and select Transfer Money.
MAN: Okay.
WOMAN: Once you've done that, select International Money Transfer.
MAN: Um ... I don't see ...
WOMAN: It's the first option under the heading of International Services.
MAN: Right, I've found it.
WOMAN: Now, click on Payment Destination **Country** and scroll down to the location you wish to send money to. It's all in alphabetical order.
MAN: Oh, yes, Zimbabwe – I've got it, right at the bottom.
WOMAN: Good. Then Step Three is to fill in **your Personal** Details ... name, **address** and contact phone number.
MAN: Uh huh. Done that. When I put in my phone number, my other details popped up

automatically.

WOMAN: Yes, that will happen, but take a moment just to check that everything is correct. Then we'll move on to Transaction Details.

MAN: So this is where I select the account that the money comes out of?

WOMAN: Yes, you have a transaction account, a savings account and a **business** account. Which one did you want to choose?

MAN: It had better be my savings account.

WOMAN: Okay, have you clicked on that?

MAN: Yes, but ... next it says 'enter a payment reason' – why do I have to give a reason?

WOMAN: Ah, well, I'm afraid that's a legal requirement – you can't send money overseas without a valid reason.

MAN: My mother needs to pay for an urgent medical procedure and I have to pay for my sister's **school fees**, as well. Will that do?

WOMAN: Yes. Both are valid reasons.

MAN: Thanks. What now?

WOMAN: The next step is to fill in the Recipient Account Details.

MAN: Sorry?

WOMAN: You need to enter the account name and number of the person who will receive the money.

MAN: Oh, I see, of course. But I haven't got that information with me at the moment. I'm at the office and those details are at home.

WOMAN: Don't worry – you can return to this page and fill it in later – you can save what you've done so far and defer completion. Don't leave it too long, though – the system will hold it for no more than two days. After **forty-eight** hours you'll have to start over again.

MAN: That's fine; I can do it this evening. Is there much more?

WOMAN: After the Account Details, you'll need to fill in the Bank Details of the person you are transferring money to – the name, branch and address of the bank.

MAN: That should be easy enough. Anything else?

WOMAN: No. Once you've completed everything, a confirmation page will appear – just ensure all the information you have entered is correct and press Submit. Then print off the receipt page. If you haven't got a printer at home, just make a note of your Transaction **Reference Number**.

Before you hear the rest of the conversation, you have some time to look at Questions 7 to 10.

[20 seconds]

Now listen and answer Questions 7 to 10.

MAN: When can my family expect the money? Will they get it within the next five days?

WOMAN: It takes **three days** to process but, of course, we can't be responsible for any delays arising from the recipient bank.

MAN: I understand. And, is there a charge for Internet transfers? When I did this through a teller at the bank last year, I was charged forty dollars.

WOMAN: It does cost more to use a teller but the Wesley Bank will only deduct **thirty dollars** from your account per online international transaction. However, we have no control over any fees that may be charged by other financial institutions at the receiving end.

MAN: How much can I send in one transaction?

WOMAN: Well that depends on your bank balance but, assuming you have enough funds, the upper limit is **ten thousand dollars**. By the way, you'll need to use a special security token to transfer more than five thousand dollars.

MAN: You mean my secret password?

WOMAN: You'll definitely need that but you'll also need a security token. That's a **special code** that the bank gives you. Just call into your local branch, with photo ID, and they will arrange it for you. Is there anything else I can help you with or do you have any more questions?

MAN: No, thank you. That's all I need to know for now.

That is the end of Section 1. You now have half a minute to check your answers.

[30 seconds]

Now turn to Section 2.

SECTION 2

You will hear a town chancellor talking about a plan for the re-development of the Bayfield town centre. First, you have some time to look at Questions 11 to 17.

[20 seconds]

Now listen carefully and answer Questions 11 to 17.

Good evening. I've been asked to speak to you about the proposed plan for the improvement of our town centre. As you know, there was extensive community consultation before the designers were engaged. I'm sure you'll agree that a great many of your concerns have been acknowledged and incorporated into the draft plan that you see before you.

Firstly, you'll notice that the existing **supermarket** has been enlarged – it's the biggest building you see on the plan, on the south side of the Main Street Mall. You can see that the part of Main Street in the town centre has been turned into a pedestrian mall. We're planning extensive plantings of shrubs and small trees to provide shade. There'll be plenty of parking for supermarket shoppers on the west side of the building and a few spaces to the south facing the **park**. The **park** will not be touched except for the addition of a small artificial lake, which we hope will attract ducks and other bird-life.

We've taken into account your petition not to expand the tavern. I know some of you wanted it removed from the town centre altogether, so it will be discreetly screened from public view by more trees. The existing car park at the rear of the tavern will remain. Opposite the tavern, on the other side of Main Street, there will be a covered **market**. The Saturday farmers' market is hugely popular but stall holders have suffered from a lot of bad weather recently. We think everyone will be happy with this part of the re-development.

These two rectangular buildings here, in the middle of the plan, are new. We plan to demolish the existing shops, some of which are unsound anyway, and put up these two modern buildings instead. The one across Bay Road from the market will house boutiques, delicatessens and other specialty shops all under one roof. The other one to the west will contain **offices** so you'll have convenient access to all the professionals in town inside one building.

The swimming pool will remain where it is, of course. The school is a major user of the pool so, to make it safer for students to cross Swan Road, a pedestrian crossing will be installed in front of the school **gymnasium**. You can see we've planned a gap in the trees here, on the Main Street Mall, so that students will be able to walk across the Main Street Mall straight to the pool. Another pedestrian crossing to the west of the pool will give students and other users safer access to the new **library**, here. Library users will be able to share the supermarket parking.

We expect that Swan Road may become a busier thoroughfare once the Main Street has been converted to pedestrians only; but we'll address that issue in the second stage of the development. In the meantime, the east end of Swan Road will be converted into a public car park – here, between the **council building** and the market.

Before you hear the rest of the talk, you have some time to look at Questions 18 to 20.

[20 seconds]

Now listen and answer Questions 18 to 20.

I'll deal with any questions you may have at the end of this talk. In the meantime, I'll give you some idea of what the second stage of development will involve. In line with the overwhelming concern of Bayfield inhabitants, improved **public transport** is definitely at the forefront of the next stage. We're planning to develop a modern transportation hub on the outskirts of town. Another issue we want to address is the lack of playgrounds and sporting facilities. These could be part of Stage Two depending on the council's ability to purchase appropriate **sites**. As I mentioned earlier, traffic may become a problem in Swan Road. Once Main Street has been blocked off, the council will study the speed, flow and density of vehicles on Swan Road and decide on appropriate measures. I know the council's preference would be to install **traffic lights** either side of the pedestrian crossing, but they'll consider other options to alleviate traffic problems, like diverting non-essential vehicles to a back road.
Are there any questions?

That is the end of Section 2. You now have half a minute to check your answers.

[30 seconds]

Now turn to Section 3.

SECTION 3

You will hear a conversation between a lecturer in Business Studies and a student Blair who is preparing for a seminar on corporate cultures. First, you have some time to look at Questions 21 to 26.

[20 seconds]

Now listen carefully and answer Questions 21 to 26.

LECTURER: Hello, Blair. Come in and take a seat. Now, are you ready for the seminar on Friday?

BLAIR: I think so.

LECTURER: Good. What aspect of business have you decided on for your presentation?

BLAIR: I thought I'd talk about corporate culture.

LECTURER: There are many facets of corporate culture – you're not going to try to cover them all, are you?

BLAIR: No – I've been reading research by Robert Quinn and Kim Cameron and they put forward a model of just four distinctive corporate cultures – it's called the Competing Values Framework.

LECTURER: Good. Where do you want to start?

BLAIR: I'll start by talking about the Hierarchy Culture. This is found in a business that observes formal rules, **regulations** and bureaucracy.

LECTURER: How do the leaders achieve this?

BLAIR: Well, in such a structured and controlled **environment**, leaders usually take pride in running stable, organised and efficient operations. In fact, this may even be part of their mission statement. They rely on their power, **status** and the importance of their position to manage their workers.

LECTURER: What sort of company is most likely to have a hierarchy culture?

BLAIR: Well, a few smaller firms might have some of the elements of the hierarchy culture in their day-to-day operations, but on the whole I think this culture is typical of **government** bodies and big corporations.

LECTURER: Very good. What's next?

BLAIR: I'd then move on to discuss Market Culture.

LECTURER: Very popular in the 1960s, I believe, and quite similar to the hierarchy culture in that it also emphasises stability and control.

BLAIR: Yes, but the main point of difference is that market culture attaches a great deal of importance to **external relationships** with stakeholders such as customers, suppliers and creditors.

LECTURER: Why are these particular associations important to a market culture?

BLAIR: I suppose because successful interactions with these people would increase the company's productivity.

LECTURER: Do you know whether this practice does have the desired effect?

BLAIR: Well, according to studies carried out by Angelo Kinicki and his colleagues in the School of Business at …

LECTURER: Arizona State University …

BLAIR: Yes, um … where was I? Oh, oh, right, um, Kinicki and the others revealed that this culture type tended to generate the greatest **financial results**, probably as a result of their focus on competition and achievement.

Before you hear the rest of the conversation, you have some time to look at Questions 27 to 30.

[20 seconds]

Now listen and answer Questions 27 to 30.

LECTURER: All right, now, what's next?

BLAIR: Clan Culture ... you know, I think I'd like to work in a clan culture.

LECTURER: Oh, yes? Why's that?

BLAIR: Well, a clan culture is more like a family than a rigid, structured organisation.

LECTURER: What do you mean by 'like a family'?

BLAIR: Well, it's more focussed on teamwork and morale. It's probably not surprising that this type of culture results in the greatest level of **satisfaction** among employees.

LECTURER: What about the internal structure of a clan-type business?

BLAIR: It's quite flat, really, nothing like the hierarchy type we talked about before. There is usually just a single leader or owner whose role is quite paternalistic, and he, although I suppose it could be a she, would act as a mentor, guiding, nurturing and encouraging employees.

LECTURER: I can see that ongoing employee training would be characteristic of this kind of business.

BLAIR: Definitely. And, in a company like this, **loyalty** would be very important. Also, management would want to know that everyone within the company had the same ideas and objectives. You know ... my brother works for a company like this and he absolutely loves his job and puts everything into it. He's extremely loyal and devoted and thinks he's very lucky.

LECTURER: He probably is lucky to have a job he enjoys.

BLAIR: Yes, well, he's better off there than in an Adhocracy Culture.

LECTURER: But adhocracy does appeal to a certain type of person ...

BLAIR: Yes, if you're adaptable and don't mind lots of changes all the time.

LECTURER: What's most important in an adhocracy culture?

BLAIR: It would have to be flexibility and **innovation** and the ability to react swiftly to a changing market, competition or other factors in the external environment.

LECTURER: What kind of leadership would you expect in this culture?

BLAIR: They would be entrepreneurs who welcome change, are not afraid of taking risks, and are always seeking **growth opportunities**. Workers would be urged to try out new ideas and not sit back taking things for granted. To an outsider, especially someone from a hierarchy culture, this kind of culture might look a bit chaotic and disordered but it is innovative, forward-looking and adjusts rapidly to change.

LECTURER: Okay, Blair, I think you've got the basics of a good presentation and you've responded well to my questions. Just one further question, and then I'll let you go ... *[fade]*

That is the end of Section 3. You now have half a minute to check your answers.

[30 seconds]

Now turn to Section 4.

SECTION 4

You will hear a lecture on the environmental effects of pesticides and some alternatives to their use. First you have some time to look at Questions 31 to 40.

[40 seconds]

Now listen carefully and answer Questions 31 to 40.

Good evening. I'm here today to present the findings from our research into pesticides and alternatives to using them.

I'd like to begin by talking about some of the environmental effects of pesticide use. As most of you will be aware, pesticides have proven to be very harmful to our environment. The principal reason for this is because nearly all pesticides travel beyond their target areas. This often happens when rain carries pesticides along water channels such as rivers, where they are then transported downstream. In other situations, particularly when they are dropped by plane, the **wind** blows pesticides into wild areas where they are not wanted. These areas can be up to several kilometres away.

We also need to think about the effects of pesticides on animals. Pesticides can cause illness and even death in many animals, including birds and aquatic life. Animals can also be affected, however, when pesticide use eliminates their **food source** and causes them to starve or migrate to other areas.

When pesticides don't travel into neighbouring environments, they tend to seep into the soil. There they degrade the quality of the soil and in addition, they can weaken biodiversity – studies of pesticide-contaminated soil show a much lower count of organisms compared to **healthy soil**.

There's a final consideration to take into account, and that's the environmental effects of pesticides in terms of pest numbers. In the short term, pesticides significantly reduce the number of pests in an area, as might be expected. After long-term, regular use, however, insects tend to become immune to certain kinds of pesticide and are no longer negatively affected by them. As the number of insecticide resistant pests grows, this creates the need for **new varieties** of pesticide, and further exacerbates the pesticide problem.

Let's move on now to look at some possible alternatives to pesticide use. As I'll explain, although these techniques can help reduce our dependence on pesticides, they do have their own drawbacks too.

The first technique will be familiar to any of you who have even a small vegetable garden at home. You see a slug on a piece of lettuce, and what do you do? Put on some gloves, walk right up to the plant and pick the slug off with your hands. This is called handpicking. Handpicking is remarkably effective and requires little in the way of money to implement. But while it may be sufficient for the home gardener, the **time-consuming** nature of handpicking makes it unsuitable for large-scale operations.

Owners of larger crops and orchards require a more systematic approach to pest management, and they have a few options here. You may be familiar with a technique known as **biological control**. This involves the strategic use of what we call 'good' insects – that is, insects which eat pests, rather than plants. When they eat the pests, they also protect the crop environment. Unfortunately, biological control is always risky because we can never know for sure how insects will behave in a particular environment, and the results are therefore **unpredictable**.

A safer option is companion planting, where certain plants are grown together. Garlic, for example, fends off spider mites and aphids, and basil drives away the tomato hornworm, making it a good companion for tomatoes. This is because some varieties of plant can **repel** specific breeds of insects, so planting them alongside and around more vulnerable vegetables will discourage the insects from coming near. Of course, all these extra plants begin fighting for space and competing with the protected plants for access to water and nutrients in the soil.

A final possibility is crop rotation. This involves alternating plants every harvest, which forces insects to **migrate** in an attempt to locate their food source. Crop rotation is unappealing for large-scale commercial operations, however, because the high cost of constantly changing crops cuts into their **profits**.

As you can see, there's still no easy answer to the question of how to keep plants free from the scourge of pests. I'm happy to take any questions ...

That is the end of Section 4. You now have half a minute to check your answers.

[30 seconds]

That is the end of the Listening test.

Answer Key

IELTS Listening Test

Activity 1

02 1.2

1 A-E-I-O-U
2 G-H-I-J
3 D-T-P
4 B-V-W

03 1.3

1 Prentice
2 Harrison Drive
3 Grantham
4 Quills
5 albatross

04 1.4

1 1(st) June / June 1(st)
2 804
3 €146
4 €11.50
5 23 kilogram(me)s / 23 kg
6 2.30 pm
7 YXW 6069 AK

05 Activity 2

1 dark blue
2 10 am / 10 o'clock
3 at the dentist

06 Test Practice

Section 1 ***Questions 1–10***

1 Sophia
2 Italian
3 521 Ashdown
4 bank statement
5 30(th) December / December 30(th)
6 DJG120459
7 15/fifteen
8 one/1 week
9 $45 / $45.00 / 45 dollars
10 Any **one** of the following: online; automated telephone; in person; self-service checkout

07 Activity 3

1 C
2 D
3 A

08 Activity 4

1 B
2 C
3 D } In Either Order
4 E }

09 Test Practice

Section 2 ***Questions 11–20***

11 C
12 A
13 G
14 D
15 B
16 F

17 B*
18 C**

19 D
20 E
In Either Order

* Did you underline the key words in the question 'with a guide' and 'currently'?
** Did you listen carefully? '**nearly** every night' = most nights, not every night

Activity 5

10 **5.1** Answers in the transcript

11 **5.2**

1 fire station
2 post office
3 shoe store
4 Elm Avenue
5 northeast
6 fire station
7 library
8 bank
9 Elm Avenue & Third Street
10 pharmacy

Activity 6

12

1 coursework
2 workload
3 content

Test Practice

13

Section 3 ***Questions 21–30***

21 H
22 F
23 E
24 A
25 E
26 A
27 D
28 facts and figures
29 change in temperature
30 extreme wind conditions

Activity 7

14

1 e - stating **effect**
2 d - stating **cause**
3 a - **introducing** the topic or a new phase of the talk
4 e - stating **effect**
5 f - concluding or **referring back**
6 a - **introducing** the topic or a new phase of the talk
7 b - **adding** information or developing the topic
8 c - giving an **example**
9 b - **adding** information or developing the topic
10 c - giving an **example**
11 d - stating **cause**
12 f - concluding or **referring back**

Activity 8

15

1 shopping
2 crime
3 amenities
4 transportation

16 Activity 9

1 written offer
2 contract
3 deposit
4 interest

17 Activity 10

1 organisation/organization
2 soldiers
3 emergency
4 disasters
5 medical
6 shelter

18 Test Practice

Section 4 ***Questions 31–40***

31 fire
32 dog
33 mice
34 rabbit
35 red deer
36 cattle
37 hedgehog
38 ecological
39 dairy industry
40 genetic conservation

IELTS Reading Test

Activity 1

1 four/4
2 a menswear store
3 5.15 a.m.
4 the roof collapsed
5 the kitchenette
6 defective wiring

Activity 2

1 **TRUE** The meaning of the question matches the meaning in the text: 'some people do work *faster and more efficiently under time pressure*'.

2 **FALSE** The meaning does not match: '*Most often*, though, procrastination turns out to be a *serious problem*'.

3 **TRUE** The meaning matches: 'costing *big businesses* millions of dollars *every year*'.

4 **NOT GIVEN** The text says: 'Doctors, too, are known for it', but there is no information about whether they procrastinate *more often* or not.

5 **FALSE** The meaning does not match: 'When their superior, *or* subordinate, makes a request ...' The question has not used exactly the same words but it can be understood that a 'superior' is a boss and a 'subordinate' (someone of lower rank) can be an assistant.

Activity 3

15 **FALSE** Compare the statement in the question 'Bullies seldom lack confidence' with the statement in the text 'Bullies are frequently insecure people with low self-esteem '. Although 'lack confidence' matches the meaning of 'insecure' and 'low self-esteem ', the adverbs mean the opposite.

16 **TRUE** The statement in the question 'Bullies generally focus their unwanted attention on capable, decent individuals' **matches the meaning** of the statement in the text 'Their targets are usually competent, honest and independent people'.

17 **TRUE** The statement in the question 'Bullies usually feel powerful when they frighten and upset others' **matches the meaning** of the statement in the text 'Bullies are often most concerned with gaining power and exerting dominance over people by causing fear and distress'.

18 **NOT GIVEN** Although **you** may think (or even know) that insomnia or disrupted sleep is a common symptom, it is **not listed** with the others in the text (stress, anxiety, excessive worry, loss of concentration, and irritability)

19 **FALSE** Compare the statement in the question 'Bullying in the workplace *always* has a negative effect on the organisation' with the statement in the text 'The company *may* suffer'. The adverb 'always' does **not** match the meaning of the modal verb 'may'.

20 **NOT GIVEN** There is **no information** in the text that tells you whether the Human Rights Commission is obliged to act.

Activity 4

1 6,650
2 Lake Victoria
3 Amazon
4 Atlantic Ocean
5 Yangtze
6 Yellow Sea

7 6,275

8 Lake Itasca

Activity 5

28 inferior
29 (fundamentally) misconceived
30 (tight) deadline
31 (completely) eliminated
32 subconscious (mind)
33 coffee
34 snooze/sleep
35 fifteen/15
36 feeling refreshed
37 temperature light
38 pump (button)
39 grouphead
40 on/off switch

Activity 6

1 C 'there is no additional burden on the respondents'
2 B 'the data may not be as precise'
3 A 'A census collects information about every unit in a population.'
4 C 'allows for trend analysis'
5 A 'very expensive to carry out' ... 'and it is a protracted procedure'

Activity 7

1 This technique is much more effective than earlier methods of ... = *comparison*
2 Although the population is rising, the birth rate is declining ... = *contrast*
3 The increase in population is mainly due to immigration ... = *reason/cause*
4 Birds like the kiwi are flightless ... = *example*
5 This feature has led to their decline ... = *result*
6 The decline in numbers can be attributed to predation by dogs ... = *reason/cause*
7 Predators such as stoats and rats are unmanageable ... = *example*
8 This has contributed to the loss of many native species of ... = *result*
9 Biomedical engineering is the application of engineering principles and techniques to the medical field ... = *definition*
10 In spite of their efforts to save the stranded whales, ... = *contrast*
11 Deforestation refers to the cutting and clearing of rainforest ... = *definition*
12 As a direct consequence of changes in microclimates ... = *result*

Activity 8

1 G 'pursuit of perfection ... leads to constant dissatisfaction ...'
2 C 'They might have different origins but they feel the same.'
3 B 'current [= today] assumptions ... all generate [= cause] happiness'
4 A 'His theory of ... "happiness", meant living well, ...'
5 D 'For instance, think of an athlete ...; in the case of the athlete ...'
6 B
7 C
8 D
9 A
10 C

Activity 9

14 B	17 C	20 B
15 A	18 B } In Either Order	21 E
16 D	19 E }	22 C

Activity 10

A ii (Although i and iii are mentioned, they are supporting ideas, not the main theme.)
B ii
C iii

Activity 11

1 **Erratic**: inconsistent, unpredictable, irregular, often changing
2 **Recidivism**: the tendency to relapse into previous undesirable behaviour, especially crime
3 **Affable**: pleasant, good-natured, friendly
4 **Permeate**: to enter something and spread **throughout** it so that **every** part is affected (clue = 'entire')
5 **Conduit**: channel or pathway; pipe or tube; conveyor of information (clue = 'cord', 'messages')
6 **Reimbursement**: repayment, **refund**, return of money paid (clue = 'refunded')

Activity 12

27 iv	33 NO	39 classicist
28 ii	34 YES	40 passionate young love
29 viii	35 NOT GIVEN	
30 i	36 YES	
31 v	37 NOT GIVEN	
32 NO	38 order (and) reason	

IELTS Writing Test

Activity 1

Chart 1 – line graph (changes over time)
Charts 2 & 3 – pie and table
Chart 4 – bar chart (usually used for comparing 2 or more features)
Chart 5 – line graph
Chart 6 – bar chart

Activity 2

2.1

Part 1 – Topic
The line chart illustrates changes in four methods of travel in Metropolis from 1985 to 2010, measured in five-yearly intervals.

Part 2 – Main trends
In general, there was an increase in travel over the period. The use of public transport markedly increased, while private car usage declined slightly.

Part 3 – Significant data points
Light rail and bus usage was approximately the same in 1985, at around 5 million trips, but in 1990 light rail saw a dramatic increase to reach approximately 7.8 million trips by 2000. By 2010, this was the most popular form of transport at just over 8 million trips. Usage of buses remained steady as trains grew in popularity, but in 2000, this also started to grow to a high of just over 7 million trips in 2010. (details, public transport)
In 1985, private cars were the most popular form of transport in Metropolis, at just over 6 million trips. However, there was a small but steady decline in car usage to just under 6 million in 2010. Motorbike usage fluctuated, but overall, there was a small increase from about 3.5 million trips in 1985 to just under 4 million in 2010. (details, private transport)

Part 4 – Conclusion
(There is no conclusion, as this answer is already above length, but this is not needed because there is a main trend sentence at the beginning.)

2.2

1 **Main trends:** In general, there was an increase in travel over the period. The use of public transport markedly increased, while private car usage declined slightly.
2 **Data points:** The writer cannot describe every change in each line. This is not possible in the word limit, and also it would not give a clear picture of the chart. Instead he has given data for the **first** and **last** points for each line and has described the **general shape** of each line. He has also given data for the **dramatic rise in light rail usage**, since this is a **significant feature**.

Activity 3

1 **Topic:** ways that residents of Australia use power in their houses, AND the amount of energy each household used per year
2 **Units of measurement:** percentages AND kWh (kilowatt-hours)
3 **Time scale:** These charts both refer to every year (fact), so use present tense.
4 **Main trends:** Heating and cooling of the air and the water are the biggest users. The more people there are in a house, the less electricity is used **per person**.
5 **Significant data points:** 38% heating and cooling, 25% water heating, the others are similar; 5,000–6,000 kWh per person in a one-person house but only 2,000–3,000 kWh per person in a six-person house

Activity 4

1 The average amount of rainfall is similar, though not identical.
2 Options B and D express the main differences. Option A is not directly given in the chart, and Option C is true but it is a detail, not a main idea.

Activity 5

5.1

Options C and D are the best ones, because:

A This answer is true, but the writer has picked on only one detail from the chart to give an overall statement, rather than giving the main idea.
B This answer is true, but the writer has wasted a lot of time adding up approximate rainfall numbers when there is little difference in rainfall, and there are other, more important features to select.
C This answer is true and it gives a good overall picture of the chart.
D This answer is true and it also gives a good overall picture of the chart.

Activity 6

6.1

Option A is the best, because:

A The lines have a clear shape with few fluctuations or high and low points. Therefore, start and finish points plus the crossover point are the most significant data points. The overall shape of each line is also significant.
B This option and Option C would both result in a mechanical list of data points, which would not indicate the main features of the line graph.
C Both Options B and C would result in a mechanical list of data points, which would not indicate the main features of the line graph.

Activity 7

7.1

A This option would result in a mechanical list of data, and would not indicate trends.
B Although this choice has 3 groups, these do not reflect the trends in the chart. This would result in a confusing and incoherent answer.

C This choice groups the data according to those faculties which have more men, medicine, which is approximately equal, and those faculties which have more women. The writer would need to include more information within this grouping to emphasise the degrees of difference.

D This choice describes the two faculties with the biggest differences, then those which have more men, then those which are equal or have more women. Choosing this option allows the writer to emphasise degrees of difference.

E This choice is very similar to Option B, but putting engineering on its own allows the writer to emphasise the degree of difference in this faculty.

7.2 The writer in the Sample Answer chose Option D. (Any of Options C, D and E above would be suitable. It is important to be aware of grouping data, and to structure your answer to give a clear picture of the data.)

Activity 8

1

'Well over half the total household energy is used for the two main purposes of heating and cooling, at 38%, **and** water heating, which consumes 25%.'

– This is **a compound**/complex **sentence**, with a passive construction, and a relative clause (complex sentence). Some data has been included in commas.

'The other uses are all *much smaller*.'

– This is a simple sentence with *a comparative construction*, to qualify a noun (uses).

'The next category is for fridges and freezers and for lighting, each of which accounts for 7% of the total.'

– This sentence has a relative clause structure; it is a complex sentence.

'Cooking and standby power are responsible for 4% and 3% respectively, **and** then other appliances use 16% all together.'

– This is **a compound sentence**.

'The table shows that energy is used *more efficiently* in *larger* households.'

– This is a simple sentence with *both adverbial and adjectival comparative constructions*.

'Whereas one person living alone uses 5,000 to 6,500 kWh per year, a 6-person household consumes only 2 to 3 times of this, at 12,000 to 16,000 kWh.'

– This is a complex sentence which begins with a subordinating conjunction and which uses referencing to avoid repetition.

2

is used for ... (passive construction)
consumes ...
other uses are ... (noun)
category
accounts for ...
are responsible for ...
appliances use ... (verb)

Activity 9

The bar chart compares the average amount of rain over the year in two cities, San Francisco and Moscow. Overall, although the two cities have approximately the same annual rainfall, the distribution of rain over the year is widely different.

In general, Moscow has a more even yearly rainfall than San Francisco. Rain averages about 50 mm in the months of January to March, dropping to an annual low of just under 40 mm in April. It then rises steadily to a high of about 90 mm in June, and slightly less in July and August, and from that point on it fluctuates, dropping at the end of the year to about 45 mm in December.

In contrast, San Francisco illustrates a different trend. It has a widely fluctuating rainfall, with significantly greater annual variation. December, January and February are by far the rainiest months, averaging just under 120 mm in each of these months. From March onwards, there is a dramatic drop to less than 10 mm in June, and effectively no rain falls in July or August. Rainfall then increases steadily and evenly to the December high of about 110 mm.

The chart shows us that Moscow has the most rain in July and August, at a time when San Francisco is virtually dry.

Activity 10

10.1

1 Over the past twenty years there has been a **big rise** in **international tourism**. What are some of the advantages and disadvantages of this growth? (Task 1)

2 Many people now **travel overseas** for their **holidays**, rather than staying in their own countries. What are some reasons for this change? What problems does the rise in international tourism cause? (Tasks 2 and 3)

3 **Tourism** is becoming increasingly **popular**, and this can **affect** some beautiful **natural places**. Why does this happen? What can we do to prevent further damage? (Tasks 2 and 4)

4 Some people say that holding **huge international events** is a great **advantage** for a country, while others say that this is a **costly mistake**. Evaluate both of these viewpoints and give your opinion. (Task 5)

5 It is often said that **exams** are a **poor way** of **evaluating students' ability**, and that they cause a great deal of **unnecessary stress**. To what extent do you agree with this opinion? (Task 6)

Activity 11

11.1

1

In recent years, it has become harder for **new graduates to find employment**, and many **young people struggle to join the workforce**. Why do you think this situation has occurred? What can you suggest to solve this problem?

topic = young qualified people having problems finding a first job

task = suggest reasons and solutions

Possible plan for Essay 1

Para 1 – Introduce topic and essay structure

Para 2 – Reasons:

– more tertiary institutions, so more graduates
– high, sometimes unrealistic, expectations of graduates
– ageing workforce and global recession, so few vacancies

Para 3 – Solutions:

– career guidance and counselling
– encourage young people into growing areas
– get some work experience and be prepared to start at the bottom

Para 4 – Conclusion:

– difficult problem, economic and social causes, need to be realistic and reduce expectations, the situation will ease as the workforce retires

2

It is often said that **exams** are a poor way of **evaluating students' ability**, and that they cause a great deal of **unnecessary stress**. To what extent do you agree with this opinion?

topic = exams are not a good way of evaluating students

task = agree or disagree

Possible plan for Essay 2

Para 1 – Introduce topic and essay structure – I **partially agree**.

Para 2 – Bad assessment tool:

– one-time test
– cause stress, may not show the true ability of the student
– can only test knowledge, not skills

HOWEVER,

Para 3 – Good assessment tool:

– efficient, easy to administer and mark
– fair to all, not influenced by teachers
– the alternatives (internal assessment) – expensive and complex – may not be fair either

Para 4 – Conclusion:

– Exams not perfect – cause stress, limited. However, the alternatives may be worse. Best solution – have exams and ALSO some internal assessment.

Activity 12

12.1

1 This thesis statement gives the writer's opinion.
2 This thesis statement explains the structure of the essay, but does NOT give an opinion.
3 This thesis statement explains the structure of the essay, but does NOT give an opinion.
4 This thesis statement gives the writer's ideas and opinion: we should spend more money.

12.2 Brief Outlines

1

– Introduction
– Disadvantages of international tourism – examples and details

– Advantages of international tourism – money – examples and details
– Conclusion – International tourism has advantages
(This thesis statement may lead to repetition of ideas.)

2

– Introduction
– Advantages of international tourism – examples and details
– Disadvantages of international tourism – examples and details
– Conclusion – could be for advantages OR disadvantages OR balanced
(This thesis statement is more open, but it shows a clear structure.)

3

– Introduction
– Problems – 2 or 3
– Solutions – 1 or 2
– Conclusion – summary of ideas plus writer's opinion
(This thesis statement is more open, but it shows a clear structure.)

4

– Introduction
– Problems – health care system, younger generation
– Solutions – spend more money – develop facilities
– Conclusion – summarise ideas and restate – develop more facilities
(This thesis statement may lead to repetition of ideas.)

Activity 13

13.1 Possible answers

1

A Young people today are spoiled because of their affluence and their many toys, and their lives are generally easy and privileged.

B This essay will discuss the levels of affluence that many of our young people enjoy, and will also consider the difficulties posed by our modern lifestyle.

2

A I will consider the reasons why solar energy has become a common alternative form of energy, and describe its benefits and drawbacks.

B Solar energy has developed because of our need for alternatives to fossil fuels, and it is a clean and efficient, if somewhat unreliable, source of renewable energy.

Activity 14

1

- **bold = main topic**
- underlined = new idea
- blue = extension of that idea

The **main advantage of solar energy** is that after the initial installation it is entirely free and renewable, so there are no extra costs involved in producing the energy. Solar energy is silent and environmentally friendly as well – it does not destroy or poison the ecosystem. This is because the raw material, sunshine, does not need to be extracted or refined, so there are no pollutants or toxic residue produced. Another major advantage is that it is produced where it is needed so there is no energy wasted on transport. This decentralisation of the power source not only leads to savings on transmission, but also to more self-reliant communities – the ability to produce their own power is a significant advantage for remote populations. There are also employment opportunities in the design and development, manufacture, installation and maintenance of the new technology for solar panels, which are consequently becoming less expensive, more available and much more efficient.

2 Paragraph Plan

Para 2 – Advantages of solar energy

- free and renewable – no extra costs
- silent and environmentally friendly – no poison for ecosystem, because no extracting or refining
- produced where needed – no transport costs – self-reliant communities
- employment opportunities – design, manufacture, maintenance of solar panels – cheaper and more efficient

Activity 15

One of the main reasons that young people have difficulty finding jobs is that, with the growing of tertiary institutions, more and more young people are completing this level of education, and consequently, there is simply a larger pool of graduates available to fill every position. In addition, we no longer have the number of vacancies that there were in the past, due to the global recession and the consequent reduction in new companies and positions. This factor is worsened by the large number of people in their 40s and 50s who are not yet at retirement age. Compounding this problem is the high, often unrealistic expectations of many graduates, who expect to step straight out of training into high-level positions, without having accumulated any practical work experience.

There are no easy solutions to these problems, but there are some things young people, their schools and families can do to help. Firstly, school leavers should be encouraged to take career counselling, to identify areas where there may be a growth in employment opportunities and to consider training in those areas. There is not much point in undertaking expensive tertiary education to produce yet another expert in a field with few employment opportunities. Secondly, graduates may need to reduce their expectations and to accept that they have to start their working careers at the bottom, irrespective of their paper qualifications.

Activity 16

- The adverbial expressions and conjunctions that you are familiar with: as a result, because, so, however, while, whereas, on the other hand, in addition ...
- Referencing expressions: because of this, these ideas ...
- **Repetition of words or the use of synonyms (words with similar meanings) to link ideas together**
- Sentences or phrases to link the paragraphs to the thesis statement and the conclusion.

(NB: Not all of these have been marked – there are too many to do so.)

Globalisation is here to stay, driven by advances in information technology and resulting in scientific, technological and economic progress and increased international trade and investment. It has had wide-ranging positive and negative effects on employment and economic development, scientific research, language and culture, global health and the environment.

One positive result of globalisation is the global distribution of labour. It is now much easier to move to other countries to find work, and this leads to better **employment prospects** for individuals and to more **diverse workplaces.** In addition, capital and industrial resources have migrated to developing countries, thus providing **local jobs** and boosting **local economies.** It has also resulted in greater contact between different cultures, as **travel** has become relatively safer and less expensive than it used to be. Ease of communication has encouraged an unprecedented level of global scientific research and cooperation, and a subsequent explosion of knowledge and information.

A downside of this **global economy** is that when a catastrophe occurs, as **(NB: Example, NOT reason)** in the recent **global financial crisis** that started in the USA, this affects the whole world. Similarly, when a virus emerges in one region of the world, it spreads rapidly, threatening worldwide health. Globalisation affects culture and language, too; minority languages are dying out because of the necessity of learning English for international business, and indigenous cultures are being rejected in favour of a dominant, often USA-based, culture. Finally, levels of pollution are rising as **(NB: Reason, NOT example)** countries strive for **economic growth and a competitive edge** in the **global market.**

In conclusion, globalisation is a double-edged sword that has created jobs and promoted international cooperation but has led to cultural losses, more environmental damage, increased health risks and exposure to economic crises. However, our world will continue to shrink as technology expands, and we need to accept globalisation as a fact of life in the 21st century.

Activity 17

In many countries throughout the world, young people are pushed into careers that they have no aptitude for, or do not want to do, and there are two main reasons for this situation.

The first reason is lack of tertiary study options. In some countries, such as China, there are limited places available for tertiary study, and those who do not manage to earn a place at the institution of their choice often find themselves studying a subject which does not interest them, or which is a poor match for their skills and aptitudes. The other main reason, which is closely aligned to the former point, is parental aspirations. Many parents push their children into a limited set of career options because these choices represent social success, security and money in later life. In many cases, the skills and needs of the children are ignored, as their parents encourage them to earn places in prestigious, if inappropriate, institutions and to study subjects that are acceptable to their friends and extended family.

Some of those children who do manage to jump through all the required hoops find that they are trapped in a career which does not suit their needs or abilities, and that they can see no escape from the life sentence imposed by the well-meaning family. This can have both personal and social consequences. Firstly, unsatisfied workers can suffer from job stress, which drains human potential and may lead to physical and psychological illness. Dissatisfaction and distress also impacts on their chosen profession and on society as a whole, as unhappy and disaffected workers tend not to give their best, and this affects the quality of their work.

Activity 18

A In short, I **wholeheartedly disagree with** the statement that arts subjects should not be taught. I suggest that every student should have instruction in philosophy, history or other arts subjects, even if they elect to major in the sciences, because learning critical thinking skills, and developing a wide background knowledge, will benefit them enormously in later life. In addition to this general training, we need specialist graduates in arts subjects to make their contribution to a well-rounded society.

In this conclusion the writer has expressed a strong opinion (see blue text), and this was also stated in the essay.

B In conclusion, a person who is pushed into uncongenial work because of social constraints or family pressure is not likely to be a productive and happy member of society. We need to ensure that individual talents and skills are recognised and catered for if we are to have a harmonious and well-developed society.

The second sentence in this conclusion expresses the writer's opinion.

C In my view, the government needs to take immediate and drastic action to improve public well-being by legislating against the proliferation of fast food businesses, raising taxes on fast food, removing tax from fruit and vegetables and banning all advertising of food with no or low nutritional value. Appropriately resourced PE and fitness programmes must also be compulsory in all schools. A multifaceted approach, which combines schools and public initiatives, is the best way to improve public health.

This conclusion combines a summary of ideas and the writer's opinion. The phrase 'multifaceted approach' indicates a balanced conclusion, where both schools and governments should support child health.

IELTS Speaking Test

Activity 1

1.1

1 D	**3** E	**5** A
2 C	**4** B	

1.2

1 A (*I think ...*), c (*because ...*)	**3** A, B	**5** B, E
2 D, E	**4** E	**6** B, E

Activity 2

2.2 Extra strategy: Giving extra information that was not specifically requested

2.2 & 2.3

- Blue = strategies
- **Bold = stressed words**

EXAMINER: Now, first, tell me something about yourself. Tell me about where you live in your country. Is the place where you live large or small?

CANDIDATE: I live in **Hamilton**, which is what I **suppose** you would call a **small** city. It's about 140,000 people, and it's a quiet little place which services the local **farming community**. We don't have any **heavy industry** in Hamilton, but there is a **university**. **(adding extra information)**

EXAMINER: Is it a beautiful place?

CANDIDATE: To **me** it is. There are **some** people who would say it's not beautiful, but **I** like it. **(giving an opinion)** There aren't any big **mountains** or anything, but it has **lots of green trees** and **grass**, and there's a **beautiful big river** running right through the centre of it ... **flowers** everywhere, and lots of gardens. **(extending with examples) I** think it's lovely. **(adding emphasis)**

EXAMINER: Is there anything you don't like about this city?

CANDIDATE: Well, the fact that it's **small**, of course, means that you don't get a lot of the amenities that you'd find in a **bigger city**. If you're interested in **art galleries**, or the **symphony**, or **opera**, which **I am**, Hamilton is **not exactly** a good place to be. **(extending with examples)** You have to jump in a car and drive for an hour or so to the big city for those kinds of things. **(adding extra information)**

EXAMINER: Next we'll talk about numbers. Are any numbers considered to be lucky or unlucky in your culture?

CANDIDATE: I would **say** there are an **awful lot** of **individual people** who consider that **some** numbers are **lucky**, or **unlucky**, **(buying thinking time)** but if you mean society-wide, **sure**, there are a few. The number **13**, for example, is **widely regarded** as being unlucky particularly if it refers to a **date** when something will happen, and **especially** if it's **Friday** the 13th. **(extending with examples, adding emphasis)**

EXAMINER: Do you think that some numbers are luckier or unluckier than others?

CANDIDATE: No, I don't think **any** numbers are **lucky** or **unlucky**.

EXAMINER: Why not?

CANDIDATE: Well, it's difficult to imagine any number having any **influence** at all on the **physical world**. **(extending with a reason)** But, I guess it could affect someone's **emotional state** if they **thought** a number was lucky or unlucky.

EXAMINER: Let's talk about motorbikes now. Have you ever owned a motorbike?

CANDIDATE: Well, I haven't actually **owned** a motorcycle, but I did **have possession** of one at one time. When I was a younger man, I swapped my 2-seater sports car for my **friend's motorbike**. He had a **girlfriend** at the time and he really wanted to take her on a **date**, so I lent him **my car** and I had his **bike** for a while. **(telling a story)** That was a lot of fun. **(personal opinion)**

EXAMINER: What are some of the advantages of motorbikes in the city?

CANDIDATE: I think there are a lot of **obvious advantages**: fuel efficiency, **easy parking**, being able to get around in **traffic** easily and quickly, **(reasons)** but they come with a number of drawbacks too, of course. **(adding extra information)** You are **vulnerable** not only to the **weather** but to **injury**. **(reasons)**

EXAMINER: Do you think motorbikes are a safe form of transport?

CANDIDATE: **Absolutely not**! **(strong personal opinion)** Not in the society **we** live in, where people **love** their cars, and have **no** respect for others on the roads. **(reason)**

Activity 3

3.1

1.

Topic Card 1: past experience

Topic Card 2: past event

Topic Card 3: future plan or dream

Topic Card 4: facts about someone PLUS my experience with this person

2.

Topic Card 1: past tense

Topic Card 2: past tense

Topic Card 3: would / would like to go with, would like to visit ...

Topic Card 4: present tense for facts, and past tense for my stories

Activity 4

4.2

- blue = the basic answer to the points on the topic card
- <u>underline</u> = <u>details about a place or a person</u>
- *italics = personal stories*
- **bold = the speaker's opinions or commentary about his/her story**

One of my recent goals was to go on a 4-day walk in the mountains in the South Island. <u>This is one of the famous walks in our country, and it is a very beautiful walk round some bays by the ocean.</u> *We planned to stay in hotels each night, so it was going to be a great holiday for my husband and me,* **but I needed to get fit enough to enjoy it first!**

I did lots of exercise and training to prepare for this goal. **When I started, I was reasonably fit, but I knew**

I needed to get a lot fitter, so I did a lot of walking. *At first, the 8 km circle route near my house was really hard for me, and it took about 2 hours, but by the end I could do it easily in a much shorter time. On the weekends I went for longer walks with my husband. We used to walk to the Botanical Gardens, which was a long way, but we got to have lunch in a café when we got there, so that was fun!* **In fact, preparing for the goal was generally a lot of fun, and I found that I had much more energy as I got fitter, too.** *My feet and legs started to hurt with all the exercise, so I went to swimming classes three times a week. I had to get up at 6 am for this! But it was worth it.* **It really improved my balance and stamina, and it helped those sore muscles, too.**

This goal was important because I really wanted to go on this holiday with my husband. Reaching it also gave me a great sense of personal achievement. **I was very proud of myself! And of course I was a lot fitter by the end of the training. I resolved to keep up my level of fitness, but unfortunately, I haven't managed to do that. Still, at least I know that I can do it again if I want to, now.**

Activity 5

5.3

- blue = intonation
- **bold = important stressed words**
- grey = pause

(**NB:** The changes in intonation are often in the same places as the pauses.)

There are a **host** of movies I **could** talk about (down), but one that comes to mind straight away (down) as a movie I really **enjoyed** was actually ***Avatar*** (up down). (pause) I went to see it a **couple** (up) of times, in fact. (pause) You know, the movie was released in **2D** (down) and **3D** (down). I'm not a **big fan** of 3D technology, so I went the first time in **2D**, (pause) and then my **kids** said, let's go and see it in **3D**, so (up) we **did** (down). I ... I thought it was a **wonderful** (up down) movie-going experience. (pause)

I'm sure you know the **plot** (down); (pause) it was that movie about the big **blue people** (up) on another **planet** (up), and then the **humans** arrive and try to take over their world so they can mine the precious ores under the surface (up). (pause) It was called (pause) 'Avatar' because the humans **used** avatars to make contact with the natives. There were **so many interesting things** (down) that I **loved** in that movie (down), **especially** (up down) in the **production**. (pause) The **visual imagery** of the planet was **spectacular** (up down); there were all those **bioluminescent plants** that would **light up** (up), and **animals** that had glowing parts (down). Then there was the **miraculous technology** of bringing those **giant people** to life, with their **glowing, cat-like eyes**, and their **tails**, and the wonderful **dragon creatures** that they rode on after they (pause) made that perilous journey up the floating islands to the very top of the world (up). So, it was **such** a great **spectacle** (down) to look at (down).

And then, layered on **top** of that, was the **story**, and the **message** (down). I'm sure you remember that (down). You had the **contrast** between the (pause) people living in **harmony** with **nature** in their **primitive way**, as part of the **environment**, (pause) neither taking anything away nor destroying their ecology, and then (pause) the **greedy humans**, with their **mentality** of cutting down the trees and **destroying** everything to make **money**. I ... I **liked** that **contrast** (pause); it was (pause) a **very satisfying story**. (pause) And, of course, when you set a story like that on another **planet**, you can make all **sorts of** comments about our **own world** and our **own political systems** and **beliefs**.

Activity 6

6.1

Answer B is better.

It is more natural and idiomatic. Although the speaker in Answer A has an extensive vocabulary, some of the words he/she uses are inappropriate, e.g. a prestigious city, alluring art works. His/Her style is more suitable for a written, academic essay than for speaking.

6.2

A city I'd like to visit is Rome. I've always wanted to go there, mainly because of the architecture. I'd really like to see the Coliseum. The idea of those ancient gladiators fighting in the arena really captures my imagination. And, of course, like everyone else, I'd want to visit the famous art works, especially the Sistine Chapel. The photos I've seen of that are awe-inspiring, and the food and the wine are a big drawcard, too. I'd have to try …

6.3

There are a host of movies I could talk about, but one that comes to mind straight away as a movie I really enjoyed was actually *Avatar*. I went to see it a couple of times, in fact. You know, the movie was released in 2D and 3D. I'm not a big fan of 3D technology, so I went the first time in 2D, and then my kids said, let's go and see it in 3D, so we did. I … I thought it was a wonderful movie-going experience.

I'm sure you know the plot; it was that movie about the big blue people on another planet, and then the humans arrive and try to take over their world so they can mine the precious ores under the surface. It was called 'Avatar' because the humans used avatars to make contact with the natives. There were so many interesting things that I loved in that movie, especially in the production. The visual imagery of the planet was spectacular; there were all those bioluminescent plants that would light up, and animals that had glowing parts. Then there was the miraculous technology of bringing those giant people to life, with their glowing, cat-like eyes, and their tails, and the wonderful dragon creatures that they rode on after they made that perilous journey up the floating islands to the very top of the world. So, it was such a great spectacle to look at.

And then, layered on top of that, was the story, and the message. I'm sure you remember that. You had the contrast between the people living in harmony with nature in their primitive way, as part of the environment, neither taking anything away nor destroying their ecology, and then the greedy humans, with their mentality of cutting down the trees and destroying everything to make money. I … I liked that contrast; it was a very satisfying story. And, of course, when you set a story like that on another planet, you can make all sorts of comments about our own world and our own political systems and beliefs.

Activity 7

1 C
2 D
3 A
4 E
5 B

Activity 8

8.1

- blue = useful structures

- **bold = useful expressions and language**
- shade = what candidate is asked to do

EXAMINER: We've been talking about a person who you admire, and now we're going to have a more general discussion about this. Let's think about personal qualities. What qualities make a person admirable? (list)

CANDIDATE: Oh, well, um ... first of all, I think honesty is **a very important quality** that most people admire (relative clause), oh, and also, kindness. My friend was very kind to me, and I think that being kind (noun phrase) is one of the most admirable qualities (comparative structure) in a friend, or in anyone, really. Sometimes **it's very hard to put other people first**, especially if it is **inconvenient**, and people who are prepared to do that (relative clause, referencing) are very **rare and special people**.

EXAMINER: I see. Can you think of any other qualities that are considered admirable? (extend the answer)

CANDIDATE: Well, I suppose that **competence is always admirable**.

EXAMINER: Yes, can you tell me any more about that? (give more details)

CANDIDATE: Most people **look up to those** who do things well (relative clause, use of adverb). Successful people are usually admired, aren't they? **It doesn't really matter** what they have succeeded in. Oh, and I suppose that hard work is part of that, so being hard-working (noun phrase) can **make you** an admirable person.

EXAMINER: Do you think that men and women tend to respect different qualities? (compare)

CANDIDATE: Oh, I'm not sure. I think that men probably admire competence more than women do (comparative structure), and maybe (qualifying language) women prefer personal qualities, such as kindness (noun form).

EXAMINER: Why do you think that is? (give a reason)

CANDIDATE: Well I suppose it's because of their **traditional roles**. You know, women **traditionally looked after the children** and men worked to earn the money, so they **grew to admire** different qualities. Oh, and I think women are more prepared to (comparative structure) **acknowledge their feelings**, so maybe (qualifying language) that's why they admire those qualities (referencing). But I also think this is changing (referencing) and that men and women are becoming more similar (comparing) in their work and **attitudes**.

EXAMINER: Right, let's move on to think about the media and admirable people. Do you think that the media has a big influence on the qualities that people admire? (give an opinion)

CANDIDATE: Oh, yes, I do. I think it has a **huge influence, especially with people like** sports stars and movie actors.

EXAMINER: Why is that? (give a reason)

CANDIDATE: Well, we see them **all the time**, and we read about them on the Internet, and so we're all **encouraged to** admire the same people (comparative language), **in fact to think the same way**.

EXAMINER: OK, and do you think this will continue to change in the future? (speculate about the future)

CANDIDATE: Yes, **I'm sure it will**. With **the growth of social media websites**, I think it's going to become (future structure) harder and harder (comparative structure) **to be an individual**, and to **have your own opinions**, unless you **cut yourself off altogether** of course. I think it could become (qualified future reference) **quite a serious problem**, if the media is able to (future conditional) **control and influence global opinions and attitudes**.

Activity 9

9.2

- blue = useful structures
- **bold = useful expressions and language**
- shade = what candidate is asked to do

EXAMINER: Now we're going to have a more general discussion about movies. Tell me about some of the types of movies that are popular in your culture. (list)

CANDIDATE: In my country, there are several sorts of movies, we call them **genres**, that are really popular (relative clause). The ones I can think of (referencing) are **action movies**, with **Hollywood superstars** like (example) Sylvester Stallone or Claude Van Damme. Those (referencing) are very popular. Then there are (listing) romantic comedies, **you know boy meets girl** in a **funny situation** and there are some problems with their relationships ...

EXAMINER: And you talked about *Avatar*. Is that genre popular too? (extend his answer)

CANDIDATE: **Oh, absolutely. (strong agreement)** There's **definitely a large percentage of the population** that enjoys **that kind of** science fiction, and also fantasy, which is a **related genre**.

EXAMINER: Do you think that men and women enjoy different kinds of movies? (compare)

CANDIDATE: **Yes, yes and no. (buying time to think)** There are certainly a lot of movies that both men and women enjoy equally (comparing). My wife enjoyed *Avatar*, and so did I (ellipsis), but then there are other movies that she likes a lot and I don't much like (comparing), and **vice versa**. I **quite like action thrillers and crime ...**

EXAMINER: (interrupting) And do you think most men like those kinds of movies? (get back to general topics, not personal information)

CANDIDATE: I **don't know about** most men, but a lot of men do. But, my wife **can't stand them** at all ...

EXAMINER: (interrupting) What kind of movies do women like? (get back to general topics, not personal information)

CANDIDATE: Well, **I don't like to overgeneralise**, but **if I was pushed**, I might say that (qualifying language) they do enjoy (emphasis) a romantic comedy. They do enjoy (emphasis) the humour involved (reduced relative clause) when men and women are trying **to form a relationship**, more than most men do (comparing, and ellipsis).

EXAMINER: Some people say that movies are becoming very violent and that has a bad influence on young people in particular. Do you agree with that? (give an opinion)

CANDIDATE: **Not really, no. (polite disagreement)** When I was a child, we used to **go downtown** to the cinema and pay 20c to watch Godzilla crushing Tokyo. **I mean**, **violence** has always been a part of movies. **I suppose (qualifying)** that what has changed (relative clause) is the **realism** of the movies and this does **make for** a stronger (comparative) emotional connection **between** the action on the screen **and** the audience. And for the movie makers, that's part of the **creative process**. They're **experimenting with** different ways to **portray** these **violent actions** in a more and more realistic way (comparing).

EXAMINER: And do you think that this level of realism is more disturbing for young people? (give more details)

CANDIDATE: It **might very well be (qualified agreement)**. **I suppose (qualifying)** many young people **don't have enough** life experience **to** understand a lot of the violence they see.

EXAMINER: Now, let's talk about the modern technology and movie watching. How do you think that modern technology has influenced people's access to movies? (give examples)

CANDIDATE: **I'm sorry, could you repeat that question? (ask for clarification)**

EXAMINER: Well, there are many ways to rent or obtain movies nowadays, aren't there? (clarifying by breaking the question down)

CANDIDATE: Oh, yes, there's Blu-ray and online delivery, **like** downloading from different websites. Yes, **I really think** this (referencing) **has had an influence on** how people watch their movies. There's much more **choice and flexibility** for **the viewer**.

EXAMINER: And how do you think that might affect the movie making industry in the future? (speculate)

CANDIDATE: Well, I don't know. **So far** they're still **managing to make enough money** to keep producing movies. I mean the idea of copying a movie without paying for it **must have been round** at least since the 80's, so making a **pirated copy** is **nothing new in itself**. It must be **hurting them**, though. But, I think people still love the whole experience of going out to a special place to watch a movie on a big screen, and hopefully that won't change (speculating).

Activity 10

Personal answers

Practice Tests

Academic Test 1

LISTENING

Section 1 ***Questions 1–10***

1 kitchen hand
2 salads
3 Friday
4 18.50
5 5.30 / five thirty
6 (a) cap
7 November/Nov
8 Barrie
9 (a) reference
10 tax

Section 2 ***Questions 11–20***

11 B
12 C
13 Education Block / education block
14 (the) Blue Lake
15 Aviary/aviary
16 Rainforest/rainforest
17 B
18 D
19 F
(17–19 In Any Order)
20 A

Section 3 ***Questions 21–30***

21 B
22 A
23 B
24 D
(23–24 In Either Order)
25 revision seminars
26 questions
27 weak(er) subjects
28 relaxation
29 format
30 recall

Section 4 ***Questions 31–40***

31 domestic
32 equipment
33 (heavy) freight
34 central Australia
35 200 / two hundred
36 sacred (sites)
37 remote communities
38 windmills
39 pet meat / pet-meat
40 transport

READING

Reading Passage 1 ***Questions 1–13***

1 thalamic neurons
2 male sex hormones
3 (various) stimuli
4 the left hemisphere / the left brain
5 B
6 B
7 A
8 B
9 C
10 A
11 C
12 B
13 D
(12–13 In Either Order)

Reading Passage 2 ***Questions 14–26***

14 C
15 A
16 C
17 satire
18 (the) supernatural
19 Music/music
20 (burgeoning) middle-class audiences
21 a violent force / violent

22 Portraits/portraits
23 Sculpture/sculpture
24 (nationalist) political movements
25 the Enlightenment
26 (dramatic) (movie) soundtracks

Reading Passage 3 ***Questions 27–40***

27 F
28 B
29 A
30 E
31 A
32 F
33 C
34 D
35 NO
36 NO
37 YES
38 NO
39 NOT GIVEN
40 YES

WRITING

Writing Task 1 – Model Answer

The bar chart compares the average amount of rain over the year in two cities, San Francisco and Moscow. Overall, although the two cities have approximately the same annual rainfall, the distribution of rain over the year is widely different.

In general, Moscow has a more even yearly rainfall than San Francisco. Rain averages about 50 mm in the months of January to March, dropping to an annual low of just under 40 mm in April. It then rises steadily to a high of about 90 mm in June, and slightly less in July and August, and from that point on it fluctuates, dropping at the end of the year to about 45 mm in December.

In contrast, San Francisco illustrates a different trend. It has a widely fluctuating rainfall, with significantly greater annual variation. December, January and February are by far the rainiest months, averaging just under 120 mm in each of these months. From March onwards, there is a dramatic drop to less than 10 mm in June, and effectively no rain falls in July or August. Rainfall then increases steadily and evenly to the December high of about 110 mm.

The chart shows us that Moscow has the most rain in July and August, at a time when San Francisco is virtually dry.

(217 words)

Writing Task 2 – Model Answer

Physical activity is widely commended for its health benefits. Apart from increasing physical fitness, it boosts brain function, and thus academic performance, and reduces the likelihood of obesity, cardiovascular disease and other illnesses. However, physical education, although important, is not the only consideration for better public health.

Many people feel that schools should bear the major responsibility for encouraging and promoting healthy lifestyles, especially given the sedentary lifestyle favoured by many school age children. Compulsory PE at school may be the major, or indeed the only, form of physical activity for children who spend their leisure hours travelling round in cars and playing video and Internet games. Exposure to sports such as soccer or basketball has the potential to foster a lifelong interest in these activities, as well as promoting all the physical benefits of activity, such as a general decrease in stress and improvement in academic grades.

However, schools cannot be expected to solve the health problems of society unaided. For example, it is vital that eating behaviour be addressed. In my country, the latest statistics reveal that obesity has overtaken smoking as the major threat to health, and communities are alarmed at the rapid expansion of international fast food outlets that serve energy-dense, nutrient-poor food such as burgers, pizza and pies at relatively cheap prices. Schools have a part to play here in educating children and providing healthy choices at the cafeteria, but society as a whole needs to support these efforts to improve public health.

In my view, the government needs to take immediate and drastic action to improve public well-being by legislating against the proliferation of fast food businesses, raising taxes on fast food, removing tax from fruit and vegetables and banning all advertising of food with no or low nutritional value. Appropriately resourced PE and fitness programmes must also be compulsory in all schools. A multifaceted approach, which combines schools and public initiatives, is the best way to improve public health.

(326 words)

General Training Reading and Writing Test 1

READING

Section 1 *Questions 1–14*

1 A
2 C
3 B
4 (during) winter months
5 (by) (free) bus
6 English with golf
7 D
8 A
9 E
10 B
11 C
12 A
13 A
14 B

Section 2 *Questions 15–27*

15 B
16 G
17 A
18 O
19 H
20 K
21 I
22 FALSE
23 TRUE
24 NOT GIVEN
25 TRUE
26 NOT GIVEN
27 FALSE

Section 3 *Questions 28–40*

28 viii
29 v
30 ii
31 iv
32 vii
33 x
34 a complaint
35 Roman Senate
36 B
37 C
38 D
39 B
40 A

WRITING

Writing Task 1 – Model Answer

Dear Sir or Madam,

I wish to take my family to the seaside for a holiday and we would like to stay in your hotel.

We require adjoining rooms: one with a king-size bed and bathroom and one with twin beds for my two daughters. I would also really appreciate a balcony with a view of the ocean.

I would like to book this accommodation from Saturday 20 July to the following Sunday 28 July. We will arrive quite late on the first day, around 8 p.m., and we will check out at 9.30 a.m. on the last day. I would appreciate it if you would confirm this reservation as soon as possible.

Could you let me know if there is a playroom or indoor recreation centre for rainy days? My wife would also like to use laundry amenities and I will need business facilities such as Internet access, fax and printer.

I look forward to hearing from you.

Yours faithfully,

William Barrow

(163 words)

Writing Task 2 – Model Answer

The way that children spend their leisure hours should always be a concern for their parents. However, it is important to allow children the freedom to interact with classmates and friends, within reason.

Children learn a great deal from their peers and it is vital for their development that they spend time with others of the same age. Research indicates that social skills such as negotiating, turn taking, creative problem solving, and conflict resolution are invaluable in later life, and that these are often best learned in the context of unstructured play.

In addition, young people learn communication skills not only from participation in a game or activity but also while reliving the excitement with friends. This holds true even for relatively passive, or solitary, activities such as watching television shows or YouKu videos; these often form the basis of eager discussions in the playground. This enjoyment and discussion of mutual pursuits is an important part of forming and strengthening the bonds of friendship.

On the other hand, parents must be aware of what their children are doing, and they need to be prepared to put a stop to any free-time pursuits that they consider to be neither healthy nor age-appropriate. For example, if they suspect that their children are accessing inappropriate material online or bullying other children, they may need to intervene. Discretion and judgement are important here. Some parents may not value the ways their children choose to spend their free time, but, provided there is a balance of work and play in their children's life, they should step back and allow youngsters to enjoy their leisure in their own way.

In conclusion, I believe that children should have the freedom to do what their friends do, but that parents need to keep a watchful eye and be prepared to give guidance where necessary.

(306 words)

Academic Test 2

LISTENING

Section 1 ***Questions 1–10***

1 18(th)
2 25(th) / Christmas Day
3 702
4 165
5 in cash
6 Reed
7 14 South Street/St
8 AQ459
9 A
10 B

Section 2 ***Questions 11–20***

11 weekdays
12 Issues
13 40
14 Basement/basement
15 9.15
16 classical
17 B
18 C
19 abroad
20 sister

Section 3 ***Questions 21–30***

21 presentation/assignment
22 digital privacy
23 credit rating
24 employees
25 sales manager
26 (search) habits
27 profitability/profits
28 recommendation
29 legal action
30 tracking protection

Section 4 ***Questions 31–40***

31 A
32 B
33 C
34 C
35 B
36 50/fifty
37 predators
38 overfishing/over-fishing
39 sustainable
40 ban

READING

Reading Passage 1 ***Questions 1–13***

1 C
2 F
3 E
4 D
5 A
6 Emmanuel Chabrier
7 a black bodice
8 an auditorium
9 a trapeze artist
10 a/Manet's private studio
11 E
12 D
13 A

Reading Passage 2 ***Questions 14–26***

14 viii
15 iii
16 i
17 ix
18 iv
19 vi
20 NO
21 YES
22 NOT GIVEN
23 NO
24 NOT GIVEN
25 YES
26 NO

Reading Passage 3 *Questions 27–40*

27 F
28 D
29 E
30 H
31 B
32 G
33 a safety net
34 Albert Mummery
35 unclimbed
36 Clean climbing
37 Nuts
38 rappel bolting
39 technical mastery
40 B

WRITING

Writing Task 1 – Model Answer

The bar chart shows the proportion of men and women who taught in seven different faculties of a particular university in 2012.

There was a large gender disparity in some faculties: engineering was dominated by male academics whereas education had the highest percentage of female academics. Notably, 85% of the engineering teachers were male and only 15% female. Three quarters of the academic staff in education were women, with just 25% males.

However, other faculties were more balanced in their composition. In medicine, gender representation was almost equal, while in arts subjects slightly more than half the academics were female (55%). It is interesting to note that business and science had the same proportions of men and women, with 65% male to 35% female academics in those faculties. Law had a slightly higher percentage of women at 40%.

Although the faculties of engineering, business, science and law were still primarily male-dominated in 2012, women made up half the faculty of medicine and were predominant in education and arts.

(168 words)

Writing Task 2 – Model Answer

Solar power as a source of domestic household energy is becoming more desirable because many individuals and governments are concerned that burning fossil fuels adds carbon to the atmosphere and thus accelerates global warming and climate change. Others feel that nuclear power is potentially unsafe, and do not like its associated pollution from radioactive waste. Therefore, many researchers and consumers have looked at alternative sources of energy and have found that solar power has many benefits and few drawbacks.

The main advantage of solar energy is that after the initial installation, it is entirely free and renewable, and there are no extra costs involved in producing the energy. Solar energy is silent and environmentally friendly as well – it does not destroy or poison the eco-system. This is because the raw material, sunshine, does not need to be extracted or refined, so there are no pollutants or toxic residue produced. Another major advantage is that it is produced where it is needed so there is no energy wasted on transport. This decentralisation of the power source not only leads to savings on transmission, but also to more self-reliant communities – the ability to produce their own power is a significant advantage for remote populations.

There are also employment opportunities in the design and development, manufacture, installation and maintenance of the new technology for solar panels, which are consequently becoming less expensive, more available and much more efficient.

The greatest drawback of solar power is that it is totally reliant on sunlight, which is not always constant; in fact, there are some regions where it may not be practicable. As it does not work at night, power from daytime sunshine must be stored in large batteries. In addition, the panels tend to be big and cumbersome. A major drawback for some is that the initial purchase and installation of the equipment is costly.

In my view, the benefits of a clean, quiet, renewable, eco-friendly source of energy far outweigh the drawbacks, provided that there is sufficient sunlight available to make this source of power feasible.

(342 words)

General Training Reading and Writing Test 2

READING

Section 1 ***Questions 1–14***

1 NOT GIVEN
2 TRUE
3 TRUE
4 TRUE
5 FALSE
6 NOT GIVEN
7 FALSE
8 C
9 E
10 G
11 H
12 F
13 B
14 A

Section 2 ***Questions 15–27***

15 iii
16 viii
17 ix
18 vii
19 i
20 iv
21 insecurity
22 chronic negativity
23 optimists
24 exercise
25 affirmative attitude
26 professional competence
27 job market

Section 3 ***Questions 28–40***

28 E
29 A
30 D
31 B
32 F
33 A
34 C
35 TRUE
36 NOT GIVEN
37 FALSE
38 TRUE
39 TRUE
40 FALSE

WRITING

Writing Task 1 – Model Answer

Dear Marie,

I'm writing to tell you that I have moved away from the hustle and bustle of the city. The apartment in Auckland was too small and too noisy and I was tired of the traffic congestion and exhaust fumes. It was also very expensive to live there.

I have moved to a little farmhouse just outside the town of Wade. What a different lifestyle! The town is quite small but the people are really friendly and welcoming. It has got all the amenities of a city without a lot of the problems. There is a hospital and several medical clinics; the shopping is more than adequate, with three large supermarkets and most of the major retailers; parking is plentiful and there are no parking metres! What's more: it is by the sea. The air is fresh and the climate is a little different too – with much more sunshine even in winter!

Why don't you come and visit me here? I have a spare bedroom and you are welcome anytime. There are flights to the local airport where I could pick you up or, if you come by bus, I can collect you from the depot.

Please say you'll come – it would be great to catch up again.

Love,

Annette

(211 words)

Writing Task 2 – Model Answer

Whether a child should do chores or not has long been a matter of discussion amongst childhood experts and parents. Some think children benefit from being given these tasks while others disagree. There are many compelling reasons offered by both sides.

Some people take the view that younger children should be free to play and that they should not be saddled with chores; besides, it is argued, they do not have the patience or competence required to complete routine tasks and they easily become resistant to helping with repetitive household jobs. Older children should be committed to their studies and ought to spend time on homework, not household assignments. Furthermore, children engaged in extra-curricular activities such as sport and music lessons have enough to do without chores. Much of their after-school time should be spent practising their chosen sport or instrument, not helping out at home.

On the other hand, many parenting experts believe that children benefit from carrying out regular household duties. This regular requirement promotes confidence and a sense of responsibility while preparing the child for independent living later in life. Young children are often keen to help as it makes them feel more grown up. Older children with heavy study schedules could be asked to help only at the weekend or during vacation time.

In my opinion, chores can be regarded as a teaching tool – sooner or later children must learn how to take care of themselves. However, parents should lead by example so that their offspring have good role models to follow. Chores must also be age-related and rotated so that there is a variety and, above all, parents should not expect perfection.

(277 words)

Academic Test 3

LISTENING

Section 1 ***Questions 1–10***

1 Simmons **2** Ocean Drive **3** unlimited

4 24-month
5 White
6 (a) goldfish
7 30(th) June / June 30(th)
8 cable
9 home phone
10 security

Section 2 ***Questions 11–20***

11 D
12 B
13 H
14 A
15 C
16 G
17 tourists
18 Monday(s)
19 Happy Dragon
20 3231190

Section 3 ***Questions 21–30***

21 B
22 C
23 A
24 B
25 A
26 documents
27 shortlist
28 Alter/alter
29 Call/call
30 Ask/ask questions

Section 4 ***Questions 31–40***

31 actions
32 policies
33 housing
34 statistics
35 evaluate
36 cooperate
37 Economic
38 practices
39 gender
40 loans

READING

Reading Passage 1 ***Questions 1–13***

1 TRUE
2 NOT GIVEN
3 FALSE
4 FALSE
5 NOT GIVEN
6 TRUE
7 a young age
8 the ruling monarch
9 a nominations system
10 an advisory panel
11 B
12 C } **In Any Order**
13 F

Reading Passage 2 ***Questions 14–26***

14 FALSE
15 TRUE
16 NOT GIVEN
17 TRUE
18 FALSE
19 B
20 A
21 C
22 A
23 C
24 B
25 A
26 B

Reading Passage 3 ***Questions 27–40***

27 G
28 H
29 K
30 C
31 M
32 J
33 B
34 A
35 D
36 A
37 NO
38 NOT GIVEN
39 NO
40 YES

WRITING

Writing Task 1 – Model Answer

The diagram demonstrates how a solar powered water pump is used to supply water for a village. There are three main components to the system: a solar panel, an underground bore or well with a water pump inside it, and a tank for holding the water after it has been pumped up from the underground source.

The first part of the process involves collecting sunlight to power the pump. A solar panel consisting of photovoltaic cells is mounted facing the sun on a raised pole well above the ground. DC electricity is collected when the panel is exposed to sunlight. This DC current travels from the panel to power a water pump, which is suspended below the water level inside an underground well or bore.

The DC power is used to pump water from the well into an outlet pipe which runs from the pump up the well through the bore cap and into the top of a water tank which is situated on the ground nearby.

The water then runs in a pipe to a village, where it provides fresh water to the residents.

(186 words)

Writing Task 2 – Model Answer

Students spend a great deal of time and money on tertiary study; therefore, vocational subjects would be a better investment in terms of immediate job opportunities. However, not everyone has an aptitude for science, engineering or medicine, and there is a need for graduates with expertise gained from arts courses.

In subjects such as philosophy, students learn a valuable set of skills. They become active thinkers who learn how to solve problems, rather than passive learners who memorise facts and other people's ideas. Philosophy students become proficient at critical and moral thinking, argumentation and debate. The ability to examine and analyse topical issues or challenge the status quo is very important. After all, someone needs to question the results or indeed the usefulness of scientific research, the politician's assertions, and historical events and assumptions in general. What is more, scandals in business and government emphasise the need for ethics in the corporate and public domain.

The sciences and business are clearly very important for our community, and those who have talent should, of course, pursue a university degree and a career in those fields. If, however, they also have training in logic and analytical thinking or a broad general knowledge from studying arts subjects, they are more likely to be able to solve problems, create initiatives, identify bias and avoid major pitfalls as they progress through their careers.

In short, I wholeheartedly disagree with the statement that arts subjects should not be taught. I suggest that every student should have instruction in philosophy, history or other arts subjects, even if they elect to major in the sciences, because learning critical thinking skills, and developing a wide background knowledge, will benefit them enormously in later life. In addition to this general training, we need specialist graduates in arts subjects to make their contribution to a well-rounded society.

(307 words)

Academic Test 4

LISTENING

Section 1 *Questions 1–10*

1 Country/country
2 (Your/your) Personal/personal
3 business
4 school fees
5 48/forty-eight
6 Reference Number / reference number
7 three/3 days
8 $30 / 30 dollars / thirty dollars
9 $10,000 / ten thousand dollars
10 special code

Section 2 *Questions 11–20*

11 G
12 H
13 E
14 C
15 A
16 F
17 B
18 public transport/transportation
19 sites
20 traffic lights

Section 3 *Questions 21–30*

21 regulations
22 environment
23 status
24 government
25 (external) relationships
26 financial results
27 satisfaction
28 loyalty
29 innovation
30 growth opportunities

Section 4 *Questions 31–40*

31 wind
32 food source
33 healthy soil
34 new varieties
35 time-consuming / time consuming
36 biological/Biological control
37 unpredictable
38 repel
39 migrate
40 profits

READING

Reading Passage 1 *Questions 1–13*

1 B
2 D
3 C
4 A
5 B
6 falling
7 light sleep
8 (the) immune system
9 (the) heart rate
10 (are) immobilised
11 learning and memory
12 (migraine) headaches
13 A

Reading Passage 2 *Questions 14–27*

14 B
15 I
16 N
17 H
18 C
19 L
20 F
21 E
22 A
23 G
24 C
25 B
26 F
27 D

Reading Passage 3 *Questions 28–40*

28 ix
29 vi
30 viii
31 iii
32 i
33 x
34 v
35 B
36 C } **In Either Order**
37 E }
38 B } **In Either Order**
39 D }
40 C

WRITING

Writing Task 1 – Model Answer

The pie chart illustrates the proportion of energy consumed by different appliances in an average Australian home. In general, the pie chart shows that temperature control, both for heating and cooling, is the major user, followed by water heating, and the table shows that energy consumed per capita drops as household size increases.

Heating and cooling devices account for almost 40% of total energy, and water heating consumes a quarter of total household power. Other appliances, such as dishwashers, televisions and smaller items, make up 16% of energy consumption. Slightly less than half that amount (7%) is used for both refrigeration and lighting. Standby power comprises a remarkable 3% compared with stoves, ovens and other cooking equipment that expend only 4% of household energy.

The table shows that a single person's electricity usage is 5,000 to 6,500 kWh per annum, whereas two people use a similar amount or not much more. A three-person Australian household typically uses about the same as two people (6,000–8,000) or perhaps up to 10,000 kWh. Six people or more living in the same house only double the consumption of a two-person household.

In summary, all forms of heating and cooling – air temperature, water, refrigeration and cooking – are major consumers of energy in Australian houses, and it is more economical to live in a larger household.

(222 words)

Writing Task 2 – Model Answer

Globalisation is here to stay, driven by advances in information technology and resulting in scientific, technological and economic progress and increased international trade and investment. It has had wide-ranging positive and negative effects on employment and economic development, scientific research, language and culture, and the environment.

One positive result of globalisation is the global distribution of labour. It is now much easier to move to other countries to find work, and this leads to better employment prospects for individuals and to more diverse workplaces. In addition, capital and industrial resources have migrated to developing countries, thus providing local jobs and boosting local economies. It has also resulted in greater contact between different cultures, as travel has become relatively safer and less expensive than it used to be. Ease of communication has encouraged an unprecedented level of global scientific research and cooperation, and a subsequent explosion of knowledge and information.

A downside of this global economy is that when a catastrophe occurs, as in the recent global financial crisis that started in the USA, it affects the whole world. Similarly, when a virus emerges in one region of the world, it spreads rapidly, threatening worldwide health. Globalisation affects culture and language, too; minority languages are dying out because of the necessity of learning English for international business, and indigenous cultures are being rejected in favour of a dominant, often USA-based, culture. Finally, levels of pollution are rising as countries strive for economic growth and a competitive edge in the global market.

In conclusion, globalisation is a double-edged sword that has created jobs and promoted international cooperation but has led to cultural losses, more environmental damage, increased health risks and exposure to economic crises. However, our world will continue to shrink as technology expands, and we need to accept globalisation as a fact of life in the 21st century.

(307 words)

Answer Key Explanation

Academic Test 1

LISTENING

Section 1: MARINA RESTAURANT AND RECEPTION ROOMS

Questions 1–10: Notes completion

MARINA RESTAURANT AND RECEPTION ROOMS

Example Internet advertisement for **casual** staff

You will hear an introduction to the first 5 questions of Section 1 of the Listening test. Then you will have 20 seconds to preview these questions and to predict (guess) the answers you are listening for.

There is an example to introduce this section. The audio for the example will be played first, with an explanation of the answer. After that, the full conversation will be played once only. This includes the example part of the recording.

Example:
Predict to hear: adjective describing staff

[01:22]

WOMAN: Hello, Marina Restaurant and Reception Rooms, how can I help you?

MAN: I'm ringing about the **advertisement I saw on the Internet** (=Internet advertisement). Uh, you were advertising for ***casual*** staff? (Internet advertisement for casual staff)

Jobs available: 1 **kitchen hand**

Predict to hear: a type of job

[02:31]

MAN: Yeah, that'd be good. First of all, can you tell me **what jobs are available**? ('jobs available' – key words for the topic)

WOMAN: Well, we advertised for an **assistant cook, a kitchen hand and a cleaner**, but **the cook and the cleaner's positions have been filled already ...** (three jobs, but two of them have already been taken)

MAN: Not to worry, I'm not qualified to cook anyway. I can barely make toast. (distractor text)

WOMAN: Well, we still have the 1 ***kitchen hand*** job available. Do you have any experience?

Duties: wash dishes
help the chef
2 prepare **salads** and other cold food

[02:53]

MAN: No, I haven't worked as a kitchen hand before – **what would I have to do** (=duties)?

WOMAN: Mainly dishes – **lots of dishwashing** (=wash dishes) – and **anything the chef tells you to do** (=help the chef) while he's preparing the meals (distractor text – the chef is preparing the meals, so this is not the man's duty). We get pretty busy, so you'd have to be able to deal with some pressure, and there's a fair bit of noise and shouting sometimes too. (distractor text) **You'd be responsible for** (=your duty is) making (=preparing) 2 ***salads*** and other cold platters (=cold food).

Availability: 3 Saturday, Sunday and **Friday** nights

Predict to hear: day of the week

[03:16]

MAN: I could do that. **How many shifts would I have to work every week** (=availability)?

WOMAN: A minimum of two and a maximum of five – we're open **seven days a week**, and our casual staff are usually asked to do a lot of **weekend** (=Saturday and Sunday) **shifts**. You probably won't have to do many Mondays or Tuesdays (distractor text – NOT Monday or Tuesday), but you'll have to be able to work on 3 ***Friday*** nights – that's our biggest day of the week.

MAN: Mmm, there goes my social life. (distractor text)

WOMAN: Sorry?

Hourly adult rate: 4 $ 18.50

Predict to hear: number (amount)

[03:43]

MAN: Nothing. I was wondering what the **pay** (key word for 'hourly rate') is like.

WOMAN: It's very good really. The youth rate is $15 an hour ... (distractor – the man is NOT a youth) Oh, I didn't ask – how old are you?

MAN: 22.

WOMAN: Well, that's an even better rate – **over 18** (he is 22) we pay 4 ***$18.50*** an hour ...

Start time: 5 at 5.30 / five thirty p.m. (meal provided beforehand)

Prepare to hear: time

[04:00]

WOMAN: ... and that includes a meal if you work a five-hour shift.

MAN: I like the sound of that. What time is the meal break?

[04:07]

WOMAN: It's very early – before you actually start work – at 5 o'clock. (distractor) Oh, and I should tell you, if you are even 5 minutes late, you won't get any dinner at all. The chef is very strict about that. (distractor) You need to start your meal at five (distractor) because you have to begin work promptly at 5 ***5.30*** p.m.

Uniform: (own) strong shoes, shirt, trousers; 6 (supplied) apron and (a) cap

Predict to hear: noun (piece of clothing)

[05:08]

MAN: Aah, I have a question – would I need to wear a **uniform** (key word in the notes) of some sort?

Note that, in notes, the use of articles is optional. Therefore, you can write 'cap' OR 'a cap'.	WOMAN: Not as such ... but you'll need a good **strong pair of shoes**, not sneakers (that's in case you drop something on your foot), a clean **shirt and trousers** ... and the restaurant **provides you with** (=supplies) a long white apron and 6 ***a cap***.

Start date: 7 14th November/Nov

Predict to hear: date (month)	[05:26] MAN: **When can I start**? (key words for the notes: start date) WOMAN: Not so fast – you'll have to formally apply to the manager first – but I can tell you that **the position becomes available on** (=the start date is) 7 **Monday, the 14th of *November*** – that's when we really start to get busy – in the lead up to Christmas and the holiday season.

Appointment: 8 Lola Barrie 4.30 p.m. Thursday

Predict to hear: last name	[05:43] MAN: **When can I see the manager**? (key words for 'appointment') WOMAN: Umm, let me see, I have her diary here ... What about tomorrow at 11 a.m.? MAN: Not really, not unless I skip class – is there something later in the day? WOMAN: 4.30 p.m.? Would that do? MAN: Yeah, great, so that's **4.30 tomorrow, Thursday** (key words), with ... uh, what's her name? WOMAN: Oh, the manager, yes ... her name is Lola Barrie. MAN: Just a minute, while I write that down ... **B-A-double-R-Y** (distractor – incorrect spelling)? WOMAN: There's no 'Y' ... It's 8 ***B-A-R-R-I-E***.

Bring: 9 CV and **(a) reference**, if available
10 passport and **tax** number

Predict to hear: items/ information

[06:31]

WOMAN: Thanks, Jack. When you come to meet with Ms Barrie tomorrow, bear in mind that she'll want to know all about your work history **so you'll need to have** (=bring) **your CV**. If you have one (=if available), we'd really like to see 9 ***a reference*** as well, so bring that with you, if you can. If you haven't got one, then we'll need a referee's name and a phone number instead. (distractor) Oh, and one more thing ...

MAN: What's that?

WOMAN: She'll probably ask you about your eligibility to work in this country so bring your **passport** (key word in the notes) and, if you have one, your 10 ***tax* number**.

MAN: Thank you, you've been really helpful. Will I see you tomorrow?

Section 2: CITY ZOO

Questions 11–12: Multiple choice

The answers for these first 2 multiple choice questions will be found in the first part of the talk, because the questions follow the order of the audio.

11 The zoo site was gifted to the city in
A 1950.
B 1902.
C 1860.

The key word here is 'gifted' (=given, donated).

You should expect to hear ALL the dates in the audio. Your job is to decide which date shows when the land was given to the city.

[08:46]

How many of you have visited the City Zoo before? No one? Well, this is going to be a treat. (introduction – no questions) Before we get off the bus, let me give you a bit of **background information**. When this city was founded (when the **city** began, not the zoo) in 1860 (distractor date), it was the intention right from the start to set aside some land for what would become today's zoo. Unfortunately, the plans were lost somewhere in the town planning department and the whole idea was almost forgotten until one of the town's founding fathers died (distractor text) just after the turn of last century – **1902** it was – and he bequeathed (=gave, donated) to the city a stretch of (=a piece of) unused land. **He had given the land to the council with the express wish that it be used to build a zoo** (=he gave the land for a zoo), but it would be another half century before construction began in 1950 (distractor date – this was the date when the zoo was built, NOT when the land was given to the city).

12 The zoo was originally designed for

A the preservation of endangered animals.

B scientific research.

C entertainment.

The key word here is 'originally' (=the first purpose for the zoo).

You should expect to hear ALL the purposes in the audio. Your job is to decide which purpose was the original (=first) one.

[09:36]

The gentleman who gifted the land simply wanted a place that his grandchildren and future generations **would take pleasure in** (=enjoy, and have fun in), and so, that was **the idea behind** (=the original purpose of) the design and construction of the zoo. Later, researchers set up a science lab here (distractor – later purpose) and started a project to save animal species that are in danger of extinction (distractor – later purpose).

Questions 13–16: Map labelling

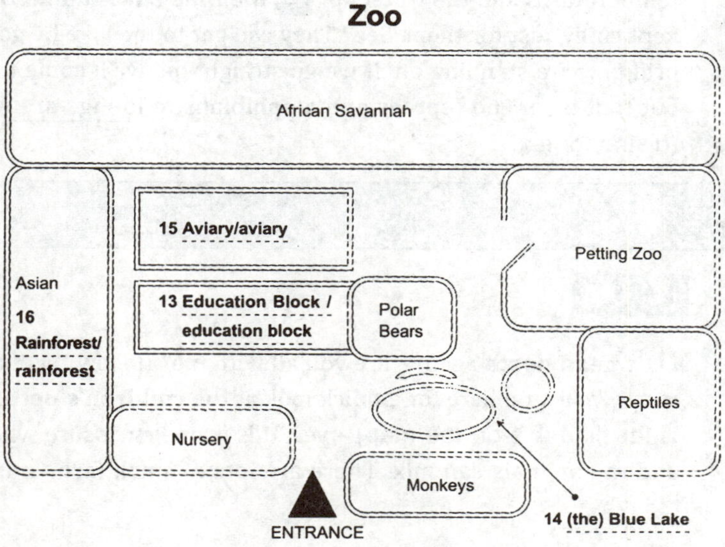

The answers for these map-labelling questions will be found in the next part of the talk, because the questions follow the order of the audio. Listen for key words or linkers to introduce the topic of the zoo layout. Listen carefully for key words from the map: *monkeys*, *nursery*, *reptiles* and so on.

13 Education Block / education block

[09:58]

OK, everyone off the bus – please follow me – I'll go through the **entrance** (find the entrance on the map) first because I have all the tickets. Right, is everyone with me? Good. (context setting introductory text) Now, when families come here at the weekend, they normally head straight for the **monkey enclosure** (find the monkeys on the map) here **on our right** (so now you know you are at the arrow at the entrance, because the monkeys are on the right) but we're going to head north past the **nursery** (find the nursery) – yes, this is where all the zoo babies are born – to the 13 ***education block*** (above the nursery). Please take note of where we are because we'll come back to this centre after we've had a look at the animals and there'll be a member of the zoo staff to answer your questions and show us a DVD. (distractor text)

14 (the) Blue Lake

Note that, in maps, the use of articles is optional. Therefore, you can write 'Blue Lake' or 'the Blue Lake'.

[10:39]

Now, if we turn and walk east (you need to follow this instruction on the map as you hear it), you'll see **a lake** on your **right** and the **polar bears** on your **left** (find them on the map). As you know, they like colder temperatures and the waters of 14 ***the Blue Lake*** (name of the lake) are kept chilly, just for them. See? They can get to the lake by going under this bridge we're standing on. If we go straight on, we'll come to another lake, but that is for the reptiles and amphibians to lounge around in (=lie in). (distractor text)

15 Aviary/aviary

[11:08]

Let's **head north** again – are you all with me? (follow this on the map) All right, we'll stop here for a quick look at the **children's petting zoo** on **our right** (find this on the map) – yes, this is one enclosure where the people and the animals can mix. There are lots of small farm animals here and they are all very tame because the idea is that city children can get up really close and touch them if they want. You might like to come back here when we've finished our tour. (distractor text) Okay ... let's step out of the petting zoo now (see the gate marked on the map) and next up is the **15** ***aviary*** – **right in front of us** (in this context, right = straight ahead, or immediately ahead, **not** to the right) – it's divided into a roofed-in section (=this part has a roof) in the northern part, and the bigger birds are kept in the southern half.

16 Rainforest/rainforest

[11:52]

Let's follow the path **to the west** (follow this on the map) now ... Please try to keep up, I don't want to lose any of you (distractor text) ... **On our right** is the **African savannah** (=open, flat piece of grassland) (find this on the map) which, as you can see, is very large so the big cats have plenty of room to roam (=wander, move). You can spend more time here later. Keeping **west now**, we walk **alongside the savannah** towards the Asian **16** ***rainforest*** (this is ahead of you on the map). Sometimes you have to stay very still if you want to see the animals that live here. (distractor text)

Questions 17–20: Multiple choice

17–19 Which **THREE** animals can be found in the children's petting zoo?

A cats
B goats
C hens
D pigs
E rabbits
F sheep
G dogs

These three questions are all options from one list. You can put them in any order on your answer sheet.

You should expect to hear ALL of the animals mentioned in the audio. Your job is to decide which ones are NOT in the zoo, and which ones ARE in the zoo.

[13:16]

It's good to see that you all made it here on time. How many of you went back to **the petting zoo** (key words for the question)? All of you! I'm not surprised – it would've been my choice as well. The miniature **pigs** are my absolute favourite! (they are the speaker's favourite animal in the petting zoo, therefore they must be in the petting zoo) You know, they used to have a larger variety of animals in there but they decided to **remove the domestic pets** (key word – remove), like **cats and dogs** (therefore, cats and dogs are NOT in the petting zoo), because most kids have access to those in their neighbourhoods, if not at home. The **goats** and **sheep** are always popular (therefore, they are also in the zoo) and the **rabbits** used to be too, but they were found to have some kind of disease and **had to be taken away** (so they are no longer there). There **were farm birds once** (=in the past but not now), as well – **hens** – but they didn't like being cuddled and they used to peck the children who picked them up, so **they were returned to the farm** where they came from (so they are no longer there).

20 The DVD will show

A the young zoo animals.

B the history of the zoo.

C endangered animals.

You should expect to hear ALL of the items in the audio. Your job is to decide which one is shown on the DVD.

[14:07]

So, time now for the **DVD** (key word for the answer); we've arranged for you to watch it because, as you know, the breeding and **nursery** (=a place for young creatures) facility is off limits to the public – for very good reasons – but we all want to see the **zoo babies** (=young zoo animals), don't we? This DVD, as well as **books on exotic and endangered animals** and **leaflets about the history of the zoo** (distractor text – these are written material, not a DVD), are all available in the bookshop, which we'll stop and have a look at on our way out.

Section 3: ACADEMIC COUNSELLING SESSION

Questions 21–24: Multiple choice

21 June is with the counsellor because

A she is under stress from course work.

B she didn't do well in her exams.

C she is struggling with course assessment.

You should expect to hear ALL of the items in the question. Your job is to decide which one is the purpose of June's visit.

[16:06]

COUNSELLOR: Thanks for coming to see me, June. I understand that you've **been referred to academic counselling** (key words for the question topic: June has come to see the counsellor) because of a rather **poor outcome** (=bad results, she didn't do well) **on your mid-year exams.** Is that right?

JUNE: Yes. **I manage quite well with the course assessments** (therefore Options A and C are incorrect, because June is NOT under stress or struggling with course assessment) but I just seem to go to pieces at exam time. And passing the exam is an essential criterion.

22 The counsellor suggests that the purpose of exams is

A to test students' personal ability.

B to test students' self-control.

C to assist students in the outside world.

You should expect to hear ALL of the purposes in the question. Your job is to decide which one is the purpose of exams.

[16:37]

JUNE: I don't know **why** we have to have exams in the first place. (June is asking an indirect question about the purpose of exams – key word for the question is 'why' = purpose)

COUNSELLOR: Well, I guess the main reason is to test students **under controlled conditions** (distractor for 'self-control', Option B) **so they can demonstrate what they are capable of, themselves, as individuals** (=the students can show the examiner their personal ability), without any outside assistance (distractor for 'outside world', Option C).

23–24 June should make summaries of which **TWO** of the following sources?

A PowerPoint presentations
B lecture notes
C information from the Internet
D journal articles
E explanations and examples

You should expect to hear ALL of the items in the list. Your job is to decide which ones are negative, that is, you should NOT do this, or these are NOT summary activities.

There is quite a long section of audio before the first answer appears here.

You can write the answers in either order on the answer sheet.

[16:56]

COUNSELLOR: Well, let me run through some exam preparation tips with you. We'll see if you can learn how to maximise the effectiveness of your preparation and reduce exam anxiety to get a better outcome.

JUNE: All right.

COUNSELLOR: Now, you are given a course outline that tells you when you'll be sitting the exam and how much it will contribute to your overall grade.

JUNE: Yes ... But they give that out in the first week of the course.

COUNSELLOR: Precisely ... Once you have it, you begin to set your exam goals. And from the very first day of lectures, you make sure you take good notes because these are essential for good exam preparation.

JUNE: Oh, I've got heaps of notes. (all of this is distractor text)

COUNSELLOR: But ... ah ... did you make **summaries** (key word)?

JUNE: Well, no. Anyway, some lecturers use **PowerPoint presentations** (distractor – there is no mention of summarising these) and they give you a handout with the slides on.

COUNSELLOR: Yes, but slides alone are not sufficient. You still need to write down explanations and examples and **add your own notes to the slides.** (distractor text – adding your own notes, explanations and examples is not summarising the slides)

JUNE: Oh, I see.

COUNSELLOR: As you progress through the semester, it's important to keep up-to-date with your **summaries – not just of the B lecture notes** (therefore you **should** summarise the lecture notes) but chapters of any books (distractor text) you've read or **D articles in journals** (you should also summarise journal articles). Be selective though; there is **just so much information on the Internet, and it's very difficult to discern what's valuable and what is not, and it's probably not worth the effort to summarise what you read there**. (the counsellor suggests NOT summarising notes from the Internet)

Questions 25–30: Notes completion

To prepare for exams:

- make summaries of summaries
- begin revising before lectures end
- attend 25 **revision seminars**

[19:04]

COUNSELLOR: Yes, June, but that's the key to exam preparation – at revision time, you **make a summary of all your summaries** (key words for the notes)! And **be sure to start revision before the end of lectures** (key words for the notes) because lecturers often hold a couple of 25 ***revision seminars*** before the end of the course.

JUNE: Do I need to **go to** (=attend) those? I thought they were **optional** (=there is a choice).

COUNSELLOR: They are (optional), but you should **attend**. (in this case the key word, 'attend', comes AFTER the answer)

- ... (prepare 26 **questions** beforehand)
- set goals (50% pass in everything)

[19:24]

COUNSELLOR: They are, but you should attend. It is often in those seminars that you get really useful information to help you with the exams. And, **before you go** (=beforehand), you must have gone through all the course material. Read critically and carefully, and have 26 ***questions*** prepared (=prepare questions beforehand) if there is anything you don't understand.

...

COUNSELLOR: Yes, but you can also **set goals** (key words in the notes) for your exams and, in your case, this is pretty straightforward because, no matter how well you've done on continuous assessment tasks, you still **need to get 50% in each exam**, ...

- focus on 27 **weak(er) subjects**

[20:05]

JUNE: Yes, passing the exam is compulsory in each of my courses.

COUNSELLOR: Then I suggest you **target** (=focus on) your 27 ***weaker subjects*** and **focus more effort on them** in the lead-up to exams.

- get exam schedule & make study plan for each day but also plan time for 28 **relaxation**

[20:17]

COUNSELLOR: ... **Get a copy of your exam schedule** (key words for the notes) as ... as soon as it's available and make yourself **a timetable** (=a study plan). Fill in every day from the beginning of study week to the last exam. Write down all the tasks you have to do ...

JUNE: You mean like sorting lecture notes, revision and practising past papers?

COUNSELLOR: Yes, although any sorting should be done straight after the last day of lectures ... and **don't forget to build in** (=plan time for) some 28 ***relaxation*** time.

- familiarise myself with the 29 **format** of each exam

[20:44]

COUNSELLOR: ... I'm glad you practise past papers; that's a really good strategy. You know that different examiners like **different styles of exams** (key words for the question, 'style' = format).

JUNE: Really?

COUNSELLOR: Yes, ah, of course. Multiple choice, essay, short answer, open book, problem solving ... all those **formats** require different strategies, and you need to **be aware of** (=familiarise yourself with) the 29 ***format*** that your examiners prefer. What have you noticed so far?

NB Multiple choice relies on recognition, not **30** **recall**, so study the subject extensively, not intensively.

[21:10]

JUNE: Well, **multiple choice** (key words for the question) is popular ...

COUNSELLOR: Ahh, yes. Good old multiple choice! Do you like that style?

JUNE: I'm not sure, really. I sometimes get a bit confused with those ones, and there are always so many questions.

COUNSELLOR: Yes, examiners like those because they are easy to mark, but of course they are harder to write. (distractor text) But from your point of view, **you need to remember that** (=note that=NB) multiple choice exams usually **rely on recognition rather than** (=rely on recognition, not ...) **30** ***recall***.

Section 4: FERAL CAMELS IN AUSTRALIA

Questions 31–34: Summary completion

A feral animal lives in the wild after coming from a **31** **domestic** environment.

[23:46]

Today we're going to be looking at (signpost words for the introduction: look at=learn about, discuss) the ecological impact of the **feral camel in Australia**. (introduction to the topic – feral camels) As you know, a **feral animal** (key words for Question 31) is one that **survives in the wild** (=lives in the wild) even though it originally lived with people, in a **31** ***domestic*** situation (=environment). Camels are not native to Australia, so how did they get here or, more importantly, why? (introduction to the next part of the talk)

Camels were brought to Australia primarily for transport. They carried people, supplies and construction **32** **equipment** into the arid inland areas.

[24:07]

The importation of camels began in 1840 and continued through to 1907.

They were brought here to aid in opening up the **arid and semi-arid regions** (key words for Question 32 – BUT the summary is not in the same order as the audio) of inland Australia. Initially they **provided transport for people and goods** (=carried people and supplies) involved in exploration or mining in the outback. (distractor text) They were also used to carry 32 ***equipment*** **for the construction of railways and telegraph lines** (key words for Question 32 – BUT the summary is not in the same order as the text). And often, they were the only way many remote settlements (=places difficult to get to) could receive supplies. (distractor text)

The camels were imported from China, Mongolia, Arabia and India. Because of their size and strength, the Indian ones were used specifically for transporting 33 **(heavy) freight**.

[24:39]

Where did they come from? (key words for the summary) Well, curiously enough, from as far afield as **China and Mongolia** (key words for the summary) – that was the large, woolly, two-humped Bactrian camel – and of course there were dromedaries (distractor text) (the typical **Arabian camels** used primarily for riding); but most of them were from lowland **India** (key word for the summary). **These ones, in particular, were very large and powerful** (because of their size and strength) and they were used to **carry or move** (=transport) 33 ***heavy freight***. What we have now are feral camels that are mixtures of these different breeds. (distractor text)

Eventually, the camels were replaced by trains and cars and so they were released into the wild. Now they are very common in 34 **central Australia**.

[25:12]

Why are they feral? Well, once the **railways** were up and running and **motor vehicles** (=cars) were becoming more common in the outback, they weren't needed any more. So, many of the 20,000 or so domesticated camels that were around in 1930 **were just let go** (=were released into the wild). And because they were so well adapted to desert conditions, **they thrived and bred and spread** (=became very common) right across 34 ***central Australia***.

Questions 35–40: Notes completion

In this section you need to wait for the answer to the first question, which comes quite late in the audio. Therefore, you need to be able to follow the notes and relate them to the audio.

Problems caused by feral camels

– roam over large areas eating all kinds of plant material
– can drink enormous amounts of water: 35 **200 / two hundred** litres in 3 minutes

[25:38]

What's the **problem**? You might ask. After all they're just camels living in the desert. The **problem** (key word) is that they are an introduced animal – a very large one at that – and they do extensive damage to the desert eco-system. (distractor text) They **wander** (=roam over) **up to 70 kilometres** (large areas) **in one day, grazing on** whatever vegetation is available – that might be **grass, shrubs or trees up to 3.5 metres high** (eating all kinds of plant material). In times of drought, when water is scarce, they **are capable of drinking** (=can drink) up to 35 ***200*** **litres** each in three minutes, although if they're consuming a lot of green moist plant material, they don't need that much (distractor text).

– damage sensitive areas and threaten the survival of native species
– damage water holes that are 36 **sacred (sites)** for Aboriginals

[26:16]

They gather around **precious water holes** to get this water, and **the degradation of these water holes** (=damage water holes) is of serious concern. They are crucial for the survival of a wide variety of native animals and plants. Many of these are now threatened to the point of extinction. (distractor text)

Let me also point out that these watering places have a **long-standing cultural significance** (key words for Question 36), and many of them are 36 ***sacred sites*** for the **Aboriginal** (key word for Question 36) people. Feral camels are literally trampling all over and violating Aboriginal traditions and history. (distractor text)

– enter 37 **remote communities** and destroy domestic facilities such as bores and tanks

[26:50]

In periods of extreme drought, like Australia has experienced in recent years, there is no limit to their quest for water. Camels are big animals, and they go pretty much wherever they please. They are not primarily interested in hurting people, but it's not advisable to get in their way. (distractor text) They have **gone into** (=entered) 37 ***remote communities*** and **damaged domestic infrastructure such as washing facilities in laundries and bathrooms as well as outside bores, taps and tanks** (=destroyed domestic facilities such as bores and tanks).

– damage farm property e.g. fences, 38 **windmills** and water troughs

[27:20]

Let's see: feral camels have a negative impact on native vegetation and animals, water supplies, and Aboriginal and outback communities (summary of previous points) but they are no friends of the **farmers** (key word for the topic), either. They compete with livestock for pasture and they can **wreck the farmer's precious property** (=damage farm property) **in the process**, knocking down **fences** (key word). 38 ***windmills*** and **water troughs** (key words).

– carry disease and cause accidents
– produce methane

[27:41]

Camels also carry some of the same diseases as livestock and are likely to **spread infection** (=carry disease) **among cattle and other farm animals**. On top of all that, they **cause a number of collisions** (=cause accidents) **with trains, cars and trucks**. Oh, and one more thing, camels are ruminants, which means they **emit methane** (=produce methane), and they are having a significant impact on climate change.

Feral camels as a resource

Camel meat is exported and also used by the **39** **pet meat / pet-meat** trade.

They can be captured, domesticated and used in tourism for **40** **transport**.

[28:04]

Feral camels do have some value as **a resource** (key words for the notes). There is a small **export market in camel meat** (=camel meat is exported), and the **39** ***pet meat* trade** uses them as well. Although camels have a reputation for being stubborn, and even vicious, they are easy to **domesticate once they are captured** (key words). We don't use them in industry any more, but sometimes **they are used by tourist operators** (=used in tourism) as a novelty form of **40** ***transport*** for their customers. Even so, it would seem their usefulness is limited and far outweighed by their overall – harmful – economic, environmental, social and cultural impact.

READING

Reading Passage 1: MAKING SENSE

Questions 1–4: Summary completion using words/numbers from the text

In this practice test, the summary question is the first set of questions, so it is likely that the answers will be found at the beginning of the passage. The summary is taken from Paragraph A and the first part of Paragraph B. Notice that, while the meaning is the same, the order of information in many sentences has changed.

Experimental evidence from studies of gender differences in vision shows that the 1 **thalamic neurons** that control vision in the brain are different in men and women. These differences happen very early in life, and are affected by 2 **male sex hormones**. In addition, women's hearing and smell generally respond more to 3 **(various) stimuli** in their surroundings. Whereas women use their entire brain to process noise, most men use 4 **the left hemisphere / the left brain** to do this.

A According to the results of new research (=experimental evidence) into vision carried out at the City University of New York (CUNY), there are marked differences in the way that men's and women's brains process visual data. (... from studies of gender differences in vision shows that the ...) Israel Abramov of CUNY stated that the experiments relate to specific sets of 1 ***thalamic neurons*** in the brain's primary visual cortex (thalamic neurons that control vision in the brain), which appear to be gender related (are different in men and women). The development of these neurons is influenced by the 2 ***male sex hormones*** during foetal growth early in pregnancy. (these differences happen very early in life, and are affected by male sex hormones)

B ... there are also differences in the senses of hearing and the olfactory system (=senses of hearing and smell). Previous studies have revealed that in women, these senses are more sensitive to (=respond more to) 3 ***various stimuli*** in the environment (=in their surroundings) than in men. (in addition, women's hearing and smell generally respond more to various stimuli in their surroundings) Women can hear higher-pitched sounds and, when listening, they show activity in the temporal lobe across their whole brain (women use their entire brain to process noise), whereas men generally show activity exclusively in the **4** ***left hemisphere of the brain***. (whereas women use their entire brain to process noise, most men use the left hemisphere OR the left brain to do this)

Questions 5–11: Matching features

In this set of questions, the options are comparisons that generally come from research results. Therefore, after you have located the correct place in the text, you need to ask yourself, is this more common among men, among women or equally common? This part of the test continues directly from where Questions 1–4 ended, in the middle of Paragraph B.

5 B They can tell the difference between similar smells. **more common among women**

B Likewise, research indicates that odours activate a larger region of the brain in females, and **they** (females/women) **are more sensitive to and are able to differentiate and categorise subtle distinctions in aromas** (tell the difference between similar smells) **better than males** ...

6 B They are able to identify minor variations in colour. **more common among women**

C At CUNY ... it was discovered that the males needed a slightly longer wavelength of a colour to detect the same shade as females, and that **men were not as good at discriminating between shades** (=minor variations in colour) (men are not as good, so women are better than men).

7 A They are more easily distracted when listening to someone. **more common among men**

D Earlier studies ... revealed that males and females **focus differently** as well. ... when focussing on a speaker (=listening to someone), a man will fixate on (=look at, stare at) the lips of the person, but he is liable to **divert his focus** (=become distracted) **to any action taking place behind the person**, for instance a passing pedestrian or vehicle.

8 B They focus on body language and what it means. **more common among women**

D Former studies showed that **women are better able to interpret nonverbal communication** (=focus on the meaning of body language) ...

9 C They misunderstand the intention of simple gestures. **equally common among men and women**

D It could be said that women pay more attention to the social nature of the setting whereas men are more drawn to shifts in motion and speed. The fact that men do not discern, or have trouble decoding, nonverbal cues leads to **each sex constantly misconstruing the other's signals.** (misunderstanding the intention of body language – both sexes do this) (examples follow) A man may ...

10 A They can see something from all sides without touching it. **more common among men**

E ... Diane Halpern believes that many of the cognitive differences are biologically innate (=we are born with differences in our brains). For instance, even looking at different age groups and cultures, it has been proved that **men have better visual-spatial skills – such as rotating an object in their minds** (they can see something from all sides without touching it) ...

11 C They have the potential to excel at mathematics. **equally common among men and women**

F In fact, there are a fair few myths (=untrue beliefs) out there with regard to gender differences. **You might have heard it said that boys are better at mathematics, but** Halpern explains that any difference is context dependent. In more gender-equal societies, **'the male advantage in math disappears'**, she says. (=Some people believe that boys are better at maths but if society is equal, the two sexes are the same.)

Questions 12–13: Multiple choice – researcher's opinion

In this reading passage, the answers are found in Paragraphs E, F and G, where the main researcher, Diane Halpern, comments on the research results that she has described in the article.

12–13 B, D (in either order) Halpern claims that:

B Gender differences in the brain lead to different sets of skills.

E ... but psychologist Diane Halpern believes that many of the cognitive differences are **biologically innate** (=we are born with differences in our brains). ... it has been proved that men have better visual-spatial skills – such as rotating an object in their minds, judging angle orientation, and navigating by points of the compass. (skills for men)

F On the other hand, it is also acknowledged that women are more fluent verbally (=speak better), and they are better at remembering objects and therefore navigate by landmarks. (skills for women)

D Men usually work longer hours in their jobs than women.

G Halpern explains that **women** do most of the nurturing in society, such as looking after children and taking care of the elderly; therefore, they **tend to opt for paid jobs that require less investment of time.** (therefore, men usually make more investment of time, or work longer hours)

Distractors for Questions 12–13

A Intelligence is related to the ability to work well with numbers.

This is directly contradicted in the text:

F Halpern is at pains to point out that having different skills is **not the same as** having different levels of intelligence.

C Men are not as good as women at taking care of children.

This is also directly contradicted in the text:

G (Halpern says that) ... fathering is very important and **many men would make great caregivers.**

E The same skills are required for employment and housework.

There is no information or opinion on this topic in the text.

Reading Passage 2: THE ROMANTIC MOVEMENT

Questions 14–16: Multiple choice

14 C 19th century Romantics celebrated **unrestrained feelings and environments.**

Since this is the first set of questions for this text, the answer is likely to be found near the beginning of the text. Search for '19th century Romantics' as your starting point.

A **Romanticism** ... Contrary to a commonly held misconception (=wrong or erroneous belief), Romanticism had little to do with 'romance' in the modern, popular sense of the word, and **Romantics of the nineteenth century** (19th century Romantics) were generally not concerned with questions of infatuation (=love, passion) and heartbreak. **What interested them** more **was a** different **kind of Romantic vision**, one **that** rebelled against caution and reason and **praised** (celebrated) **the intensity and ferocity of wild landscapes and reckless human emotion** (unrestrained feelings and environments).

Distractors for Question 14

A ... (celebrated) emotions related to love between men and women.

This is directly contradicted in the paragraph:

A **Romantics of the nineteenth century** were generally **not** concerned with questions of infatuation and heartbreak.

B ... (celebrated) careful limits and logical thinking.

This is mentioned in Paragraph B but in the context of Enlightenment thinking, not of Romanticism.

D ... (celebrated) rebellion against all forms of state power.

This is mentioned in Paragraph B and also relates to Enlightenment thinking.

15 A The exchange of ideas in a public forum was important in the Enlightenment because **it helped society to reach its full potential.**

The word 'Enlightenment' is a clue that the answer will be found in Paragraph B of the text.

B ... Europe ... was dominated by the ideals of the **Enlightenment**, which were firmly grounded in ... a belief that **polite intellectual discourse in such institutions as coffee houses and debating societies** (exchange of ideas in a public forum) constituted **the most sophisticated expression of humanity's capacity for development** (helped society to reach its full potential).

Distractors for Question 15

B ... (because) it was the highest form of human conversation.

This is a misreading of the text. Enlightenment thinkers wanted to encourage the development of ideas, not conversation.

C ... (because) it encouraged popular interest in science.

This is also a misreading of the text. Enlightenment thinkers valued scientific method, but this was separate from public debate.

D ... (because) it provided a safe place for political discussion.

This is not mentioned in the text.

16 C According to the writer, Enlightenment thinkers **disliked people showing their feelings.**

B Enlightenment thinkers **loathed the expression of emotion, particularly of fiery, uncontrollable feeling** (disliked people showing their feelings), perceiving it to be a threat to order and democracy. They also fought against irrationality and dogmatism (=unreasonable strict rules) of all kinds, having witnessed how despotic (=bad) kings and other manipulative leaders used folk wisdom and superstition to stir discontent and gain power in their countries.

Distractors for Question 16

A ... (Enlightenment thinkers) believed that kings made the best rulers.

This is directly contradicted in the text.

B (Enlightenment thinkers believed that) ... despotic kings and other manipulative leaders used folk wisdom and superstition to stir discontent and gain power in their countries. (they did not like the rule of kings because kings were too powerful)

B ... (Enlightenment thinkers) had strongly held religious beliefs.

This is contradicted in the text by implication.

B They also fought against irrationality and dogmatism (=strict rules) of all kinds, ...

D ... (Enlightenment thinkers) disapproved of the rule of law in society.

This is contradicted by implication.

B Enlightenment thinkers loathed the expression of emotion, particularly of fiery, uncontrollable feeling, **perceiving it to be a threat to order and democracy**. (By implication, Enlightenment thinkers approved of order and democracy. Therefore, they would not disapprove of the rule of law.)

Questions 17–23: Table completion using words/numbers from the passage

Locating the correct paragraph for the answers for these questions is not difficult, because they follow on directly from the previous set of questions. Look for key words such as names or types of art.

ROMANTICISM IN THE ARTS	
Literature	Poets prefer to use regular spoken language.
	Writers are less interested in politics. As a result, 17 **satire** is not as popular as before.
	New topics are explored, such as harmful feelings and 18 **(the) supernatural**.

C Romantic artists resisted the Enlightenment fixation with calmness, order and reason, although the nature of their rebellion varied from one art form to another. **Romantic poets**, for example, dismissed the sculpted, austere prose of their forebears, **favouring styles that focussed on the role of ordinary people and their language** (=preferring to use regular spoken language). As interest in governance and civic affairs waned (=decreased), **writers** (key word to locate Question 17) began to reject the once-respected literary format of 17 ***satire***. (so satire became less popular) Instead, they turned their attention to those areas of human life that were previously downplayed or taboo (=they explored new topics). In *Wuthering Heights*, for example, Emily Brontë describes the effects of **intense, destructive emotions** (=harmful feelings) such as jealousy and vengeance. Elements of 18 ***the supernatural*** are introduced in the short stories of Edgar Allan Poe.

19 **Music/music**	The most appropriate art form for the expression of Romantic ideas. No longer paid for by rich individuals, but by **20** **(burgeoning) middle-class audiences** who wanted to see their favourite artists perform.

D **Composers and soloists** (=musicians) reached new levels of prominence during the Romantic Movement. This was partly because, freed from the constraints of the Enlightenment era, **19** ***music*** was perceived to be the ideal form through which to explore the Romantic notion of a free spirit (=the most appropriate art form for the expression of Romantic ideas). Economic shifts also facilitated music's newfound dominance. Whereas musicians had hitherto been required to source financial support from **a wealthy patron** (=a rich individual) (usually from the royal court), they now earned their living by performing for **20** ***burgeoning*** (=rapidly growing) ***middle-class audiences*** ...

Painting	Nature is shown to be **21** **a violent force / violent** through depictions of extreme weather and landscapes. **22** **Portraits/portraits** are used to show more unpleasant aspects of human life.

E Romanticism also made its mark on **painting**, in two notable ways. The first change can be seen in landscape representations. **In Enlightenment-era paintings**, (the next part describes Enlightenment paintings, not Romantic paintings) nature was usually neglected in favour of human subjects. Where nature was shown, it was typically in the form of manicured (=tidy and well kept) hedges and lawns, as in the style of estates and palaces of the time. **Romantic artists**, however (=in contrast), depicted (=showed) nature as **21** ***a violent force***, rather than as something to beautify gardens and walkways. Windswept mountaintops, dense bush and fogs, and stormy, dark red skies were all popular with such artists.

F The Romantics also revolutionised **the painting of human subjects** (=portraits). Previously considered a staid (=serious), sedate form of painting, whose principle objective was simply to achieve a lifelike representation of the subject, **22** ***portraits*** became a vehicle for **examining the darker side of the human experience** (showing more unpleasant aspects of human life). (example follows)

23 **Sculpture/sculpture** Not affected by the Romantic movement.

G By the mid-nineteenth century, **Romanticism had hugely influenced** (=affected) every art form **with the exception of** 23 ***sculpture*** (therefore, sculpture was not affected), which **remained stubbornly impervious to** (=was not affected by) Romantic influences due to the practical constraints of the discipline.

Questions 24–26: Sentence completion using words/numbers from the passage

Peak, decline & legacy

24 The Romantic Movement brought about changes in science and education, and led to the growth of **(nationalist) political movements**.

G Its influence had extended far beyond the arts; **scientists** reconfigured (=changed) their ideas about nature, and **educators** reconsidered their curriculum priorities. Most significantly, 24 ***nationalist political movements*** were proliferating (=growing quickly) across Europe, inspired by the celebration of folklore and indigenous customs (=local culture) in many Romantic art works.

25 Even as Realism grew in popularity, some artists felt that ideas from **the Enlightenment** were still relevant.

H Toward the end of the nineteenth century, however, Romanticism's dominance waned (=popularity decreased) considerably. What was once revolutionary and provocative began to seem phony (=unreal) and melodramatic (=exaggerated). **Many authors and artists** turned toward **Realism**, a newer movement that advocated (=supported) artistry without exaggeration or contrivance. **Others** (other authors and artists) saw a need to begin taking social and political affairs seriously again, and sought to retrieve (=wanted to revive) some of the values of 25 ***the Enlightenment***, such as the need for dialogue and reasoned debate.

26 Romantic ideas are currently used in **(dramatic) (movie) soundtracks**, and also in stories of people overcoming problems in their lives.

H Romanticism never faded away completely, however. **26** ***Dramatic movie soundtracks*** and plotlines in which men fight adversity to achieve great triumphs (overcome problems in their lives) show that the Romantic spirit (=Romantic ideas) remains with us to the present day (=currently).

Reading Passage 3: THE UPSIDE OF FEELING DOWN

Questions 27–34: Matching features

In this set of questions, the options are researchers' names. These are listed in the order that they appear in the text. Therefore, you need to find **Joe Forgas** first. The statements that match each researcher are NOT in the order of the passage, so you need to read the paraphrases of research findings associated with each researcher carefully, and match this to the researcher. Note that there are 6 researchers and 8 findings, so some researchers will match more than one finding.

27 F Modern ideas about happiness are not helpful. **Steven Hayes**

F With an array of studies indicating that sadness plays a constructive and significant role in human affairs, what are we to make of the current fervour (=enthusiasm, great interest) surrounding the pursuit of happiness? Are we being led toward an illusion (=a false idea) by false prophets of positivity? (=Are modern ideas not helpful?) According to **Steven Hayes**, a psychology professor at the University of Nevada, we are. (we are being told unhelpful things by modern researchers)

28 B Medication is being used unnecessarily. **Astrid James**

C In an editorial in the esteemed medical journal *The Lancet*, deputy editor **Dr Astrid James** warned that psychiatrists are **in danger of** (= ... is a bad idea) pathologising (=naming ... as a disease) normal human experiences by **prescribing anti-depressant pills** (=giving patients medication) instead of acknowledging (=recognising) the superior role of prolonged sadness in naturally rehabilitating sufferers (=helping sufferers to recover). (therefore sadness is helpful, not bad)

29 A Sad people can remember things better. **Joe Forgas**

B Professor **Joe Forgas** discovered that people experiencing negative moods are less gullible, and less likely to make judgemental errors than their happy counterparts. He also found that sad people **had better recall** (=memory) **of past events and feelings** (=could remember things better), were better able to communicate their thoughts, and were less likely to judge someone based solely on their appearance.

30 E Art can help teenagers to express their feelings. **Laura Young**

E **Laura Young**, a researcher at Boston College, has found that **adolescents** (=teenagers) **or young adults who participate in arts programmes** are more likely to experience sadness than their peers, a finding that is also true for older adult artists. Young emphasises, however, that painting and drama are not themselves catalysts for depression (=causes of the depression). Rather, she suggests, they (the arts programmes) are a chance for some people to **vocalise their anger** (=express their feelings) and can provide a therapeutic space for those with emotional troubles (=help people feel better).

31 A Sad people are more careful and alert than happy ones. **Joe Forgas**

B **Forgas** notes that a positive mood indicates comfort and familiarity, whereas a negative mood (=sadness) alerts the brain to be vigilant (=alert). As a result, he believes, sadness encourages a **'more attentive and externally focused, information-processing style'** (=a more careful, alert style) whereas happiness prompts us to switch off, making us prone to deception.

32 F People should focus on what is important to them. **Steven Hayes**

F He (Hayes) believes we need to set aside the idea of happiness altogether, or at least any notion of 'pursuing' it (=trying to find it). ... What is more important than experiencing the transient flush (=brief experience) of happy feelings, he suggests, is **moving through life in accordance with our core values** (focussing on what is important to us).

33 C Sadness can stop us repeatedly making bad decisions. **Jerome Wakefield**

D According to **Jerome Wakefield**, clinical social worker at New York University, ... In this way, the memory of sadness – and of taking time out to be sad – imprints itself on our mind as a **psychological deterrent for the future** (=helps us to learn what not to do). ... Without the prodding of sadness upon our memory of these situations, we might **endlessly repeat these follies** (=make the same mistakes, or bad decisions, many times) with no reason to alter our behaviour.

34 D Thinking about sadness can help people produce original material. **Modupe Akinola**

E ... Harvard University, **Modupe Akinola**, experimented with the connection between depression and creativity. She asked depressed people to perform creative tasks and gave them feedback that was designed to reinforce (=strengthen) their negative feelings. Akinola speculates that this feedback encouraged research participants to **dwell on their negativity** (=think about sadness), and that this unearthed hidden feelings and **bolstered their creative output** (=made them more creative, or original).

Questions 35–40: Yes, no, not given

The structure of this text is that some paragraphs, especially the first and third ones, give the author's opinion and then he uses examples from research evidence to support those opinions. The answers for this set of questions are likely to be found in the authorial comments rather than in the information about research findings.

35 People are becoming less interested in happiness. **NO**

A Over the past couple of decades, public imagination has been captured by the notion of 'happiness' in an unprecedented way (=a new way). There is now a *Journal of Happiness Studies*, a burgeoning (=quickly growing) field of study known as 'happiness economics', and everyone from self-help gurus to sociological researchers to public policy makers is trying to understand what happiness is and how everyone can get more of it. (more and more people are becoming interested in happiness)

36 Sadness is an undesirable state. **NO**

undesirable = unwanted

A ... during a three-month period this year, over one thousand books on the subject were released. In our frantic pursuit of good feelings, however, some researchers worry that we may have overlooked the flipside (=other side) of the coin – sadness. By **framing sadness as solely a negative condition** (=making sadness sound undesirable), a fetter to free ourselves from (=a condition to avoid), these scholars believe that we may be neglecting an important facet of the human experience (sadness is an important part of our lives).

37 Sadness makes it easier to deal with events that cause psychological pain. **YES**

C In other contexts, **sadness** allows us to **cope with traumatic occurrences** (=deal with events that cause psychological pain) and, ultimately, move on from them (=recover from them).

38 People feel more energetic when they are sad. **NO**

C **Unlike** (key word) other negative emotions such as anger or fear, which temporarily spike energy levels (=make us very energetic) and impel (=force) the person experiencing them to act decisively, **sadness drains energy** (therefore, sad people have less energy).

39 Grief is not experienced very often in most people's lives. **NOT GIVEN**

Paragraph C mentions grief but there is no information given about how often people suffer from grief.

C In doing so it draws the sufferer away from the activities of other people and encourages them to reflect on their feelings and the importance of what caused them. This process, known as **grief**, serves an important role in helping humans to adjust to loss and to integrate it into their lives.

40 Sadness is a necessary and important part of human experience. **YES**

This idea is expressed throughout the reading passage. See the end of Paragraph A and the beginning of Paragraph B, for example.

A ... these scholars believe that we may be neglecting an important facet (=part) of the human experience.

B Much evidence suggests that sadness plays an important and constructive role in our lives.

General Training Reading and Writing Test 1

READING

Section 1: ENGLISH WITH A DIFFERENCE

Questions 1–3: Matching features

Note that, although this set of questions has one answer which matches each package, or option, this kind of question can sometimes have 2 or more answers which match one option, and/or no answer which matches an option.

1 **A** This package does not cater for people who can't swim. **English with surfing**

does not cater for = won't accept

You will find the answer in the 'Comments' section of the table.

Must prove ability to swim (=you must show that you can swim) before enrolment (=joining the course). (therefore, the company won't accept people who can't swim on this package.)

2 **C** This package requires you to supply your own equipment. **English with tennis**

You will find the answer in the 'Comments' section of the table.

Must provide own racquets (tennis racquets) (So, you must bring your own racquet. The other packages have equipment for hire, or rent.)

3 **B** This package involves a travel cost. **English with golf**

You will find the answer in the 'Transport to & from sporting facility' section of the table.

½ hour by minibus to golf course ($2 each way) (so, you must pay $2 for each trip on the minibus.)

Questions 4–6: Short answers

4 When will one of the packages not be offered? **(during) winter months**

You will find the answer in the 'Comments' section of the table. Look at 'English with surfing'.

Note: this package is not available (=not offered) during winter months.

5 Which is the faster way to get to the tennis facility? **(by) (free) bus**

Note that you can write: 'by free bus', 'by bus' or 'bus'.

You will find the answer in the 'Transport to & from sporting facility' section of the table. Look at 'English with tennis'.

5 minutes by (free) bus or ½ hour on foot to tennis courts (so the free bus is faster than walking)

6 Which package offers a meal at no extra cost? **English with golf**

You will find the answer in the 'Price' section of the table. Look at 'English with golf'.

Packed lunch included (=you will get a packed lunch as part of the package)

Section 1: ATLANTIC PRIVATE DAY HOSPITAL

Questions 7–14: Matching features

Note that this set of questions has more answers than options, so some options will be used more than once.

Reading the headings will help you to answer this set of questions. It is most likely that:

- **Pre-Admission Information** = **A** you must do before admission day
- **On the Day of Admission** = **B** you must do on admission day
- **Discharge Information** = **C or D** you must do on the day you leave hospital OR you must **not** do on the day you leave the hospital

However, you still need to read the information carefully, and look for time expressions, such as 'prior to' (=before).

7 D drive a car = **you must not do on the day you leave the hospital**

You will find the answer in the 'Discharge Information' section.

- You must not drive a car until at least 24 hours following your operation.

8 A fill out a patient history form = **you must do before admission day**

You will find the answer in the 'Pre-Admission Information' section.

To ensure that we can confirm your admission and financial and other arrangements, we ask that you complete (=fill out) the following forms in full and return them to the hospital **immediately** (before you come to the hospital for your operation):

- consent forms
- **patient history form**

9 E tell the hospital which day you will have your operation = **your doctor must do**

You will find the answer in the 'Pre-Admission Information' section.

Your doctor will notify (=tell) the hospital of the date (=which day) of your procedure/operation and inform you of the day of admission.

10 B have the contact details of your driver = **you must do on admission day**

You will find the answer in the 'On the Day of Admission' section.

Please ensure that you bring the following with you to the hospital:

- ...
- phone number or email (=contact details) of the person taking you home (=your driver)

11 C talk to your doctor about any pills you need = **you must do on the day you leave hospital**

You will find the answer in the 'Discharge Information' section.

- You must check with your doctor (=talk to your doctor) about medication (=pills) and follow-up appointments.

12 A give insurance details to the hospital = **you must do before admission day**

You will find the answer in the 'Pre-Admission Information' section.

If your account is subject to Private Insurance Cover, forward (=send on) full details of the claim including a letter from your insurance company ... to our Pre-Admission Office at least 48 hours prior to (=before) your procedure.

13 A take a shower = **you must do before admission day**

You will find the answer in the 'On the Day of Admission' section. CAREFUL! Remember that 'prior to' = *before*.

Please

- shower the day prior to (=before) coming to the hospital

14 B take off any expensive watches or rings = **you must do on admission day**

You will find the answer in the 'On the Day of Admission' section.

Do not

- ...
- wear jewellery
- wear make-up
- bring any valuables with you

(Therefore, you must take these items off on admission day.)

Section 2: SETTING UP A SAFE HOME WORK BASE FOR TELECOMMUTING

Questions 15–21: Summary completion with options supplied

Since this summary is the only set of questions for this reading passage, you should expect that the summary will cover most of the passage. In this set of questions, the introduction paragraphs are not included in the summary. All of the options are paraphrases of the original text.

To make the home a safer place to work in, any **15** **B furniture** that restricts freedom of movement should be moved. Any **16** **G rugs** and items that clutter floor space should be removed. Attach **17** **A electrical cables** to the wall in the work area. Where steps and stairs are concerned, have **18** **O uneven steps** repaired, and get new handrails fitted if any are missing or not firmly attached. Make a **19** **H checklist** before arranging for all needed repairs.

It is also important to have a family conference to encourage **20** **K safety awareness** and observance of the rules for a clean and tidy house. Finally, arrange a check with your **21** **I employer**.

15 B furniture

- Minimise the risk – falls are the most common household accident but are easily prevented. Start with the floor: shift **chairs, desks or cabinets** (=furniture) that impede progress (=restrict freedom of movement) from one area to another, ...

16 G rugs

- Get rid of (=remove) loose floor coverings such as **small carpets** (=rugs), or use only those with a non-slip backing.

17 A electrical cables

- Carefully examine your workplace environment, and ensure that **lamp, telephone or extension cords and computer leads** (=electrical cables) are off the floor to avoid the chance of tripping and falling. Taping (=attaching) these (electrical cables) along the edge of the wall above the skirting board and over doorways is one option, ...

18 O uneven steps

- Next, look at the **stairs and steps** both inside and outside your home. Keep steps and stairs clear; fix (=repair) any steps that are loose or not level (=uneven); if carpeted, ensure the carpet is firmly attached, or attach non-slip rubber treads to uncarpeted steps; where there are loose (=not firmly attached) or absent (=missing) **handrails**, install new ones; ...

19 H checklist

- Create a comprehensive **inventory** (=checklist) of necessary repair work and/or new installations and follow through on your risk controls (=arrange for all needed repairs).

20 K safety awareness

- Hold a forum with your household members (=family conference) to promote (=encourage) safety consciousness and **hazard awareness** (=safety awareness) and run through safety drills; get household members' compliance (=observance of the rules) on issues of tidiness, cleanliness, etc.

21 I employer

After the risk assessment and fixes have been completed (=finally), the **workplace manager** (=employer) must inspect (=check) the workplace with the employee ...

Section 2: STARTING A NEW BUSINESS

Questions 22–27: True, false, not given

Remember that the questions will follow the order of the reading passage.

22 Successful businesses generally copy from previous ideas. FALSE

previous ideas = businesses that other people have done before

B Firstly, you must be able to offer something unique (=different) that people want. Why unique? Well, if you are simply following the trends (copying from previous ideas), there is no reason for people to buy from your new business. Be creative – design or discover something that is exceptionally good or different (=unique) in a specific domain or sector (=in one area) rather than going down the same track as (=copying) all the other vendors (=sellers).

23 Good surveys can use a variety of styles and sizes. TRUE

C Before you begin, you have to identify what people want and whether and how much they would be prepared to pay for it. **Customer questionnaires, or surveys,** are an often-used method of testing the market, ... **Some people say that** the best survey should contain fewer than 20 questions, or that all questions should be answerable with one or two words (these are rules for good surveys), **but** (important word) each business is different and you need to tailor (=change) the size and format of a survey to your own situation (so you should use the style and size that is best for your business).

24 Training in business management is important for success. **NOT GIVEN**

There is no mention of business management training in the passage. Paragraph D mentions expertise, but not training.

D Finally, to ensure the success of your enterprise, you must have a passion for what you are doing and a certain expertise or particular strength in that field.

25 Older people can cope with change because they are confident. **TRUE**

START-UP VENTURES BY OLDER PEOPLE

E If you have got what it takes to compete in the modern world, **maturity** (=being older) is a plus (=an advantage); ...

F Older people are also more likely to recognise the true extent of their capabilities ... Although they are not often credited with this, older people are actually very good at adjusting to changing circumstances (=coping with change) and at problem solving, as they generally have faith in their own decisions (they are confident).

26 Older people are more likely to succeed than younger people. **NOT GIVEN**

The reading passage discusses the advantages that older people have, and then the advantages that younger people have, but it does not compare older and younger people's possible success.

27 It is best for young people to pay someone for business advice. **FALSE**

START-UP VENTURES BY YOUNG PEOPLE

G If you are still a bit wet behind the ears (=you are young and inexperienced), can you start a new business? Of course you can! ... Lack of experience can be a problem, and one way to overcome this is to use the services of a business mentor (=advisor). This person **could** be a paid professional **or** a family friend (=the advisor could be paid, or unpaid), but in either case (paid or unpaid) their suggestions are likely to be invaluable (=very helpful) in helping the young entrepreneur to succeed.

Section 3: SERENISSIMA REPUBBLICA DI SAN MARINO

Questions 28–33: Matching paragraph headings

28 Paragraph **A = viii Geography**

Paragraph A describes the location, size, land and climate of San Marino. This is the geography. It begins:

A The Republic of San Marino is a landlocked microstate or enclave, the third smallest state in Europe, situated on the Italian peninsula.

29 Paragraph **B = v Historical background**

Paragraph B describes how San Marino was founded (=started) and some of the problems it faced in keeping its independence. This is the history of the country. It begins:

B San Marino is perhaps the world's oldest constitutional republic, founded in the year 301 AD by a stonemason fleeing religious persecution.

30 Paragraph **C = ii How the governance system works**

Paragraph C describes how the government operates, or works. It begins:

C San Marino today is a multi-party democratic republic, but political parties have to align themselves with one of the two opposing coalitions: the right or the left.

31 Paragraph **D = iv The currency of San Marino**

The topic of Paragraph D is the money system, or currency of San Marino. This topic is introduced in the second sentence of the paragraph.

D Modern-day San Marino belongs to the Council of Europe and the United Nations but is not a member of the European Union although it is permitted to use the euro as its legal tender (=money); it is even allowed to have its own designs on the national side of the euro coins.

32 Paragraph E = vii The economy

Paragraph E describes where San Marino gets its income from. This is the economy of the country. It begins:

E Chief sources of income arise from the industries of tourism, banking, ceramics and electronics together with the manufacture and export of furniture, paints, fabrics and wearing apparel (=clothes).

33 Paragraph F = x The people of San Marino

Paragraph F talks about the people of the state. It begins:

F For such a tiny, geographically inhospitable country with few natural resources, apart perhaps from building stone, **residents** (=the people) **of San Marino** nevertheless enjoy a relatively high standard of living equivalent to (=the same as) that of Danes or Germans.

Distractors for Questions 28–33

In this type of question the distractors (=unused headings or incorrect answers) are often found somewhere in the text, but either:

1. they are *not the main idea* of the paragraph, or
2. *the information* in the paragraph *does not match the heading*.

i Relationship with Italy

The relationship with Italy is briefly mentioned in Paragraph B (history) and Paragraph D (money), but this is not the main idea of either paragraph.

iii Agricultural produce

Paragraph E mentions agriculture but this is not the main idea of the paragraph.

vi Climate in the enclave

This is part of Paragraph A, but it is not the main idea.

ix Natural life

There is no mention of animal or bird life in this reading passage.

xi Current and future problems

There is no mention of problems in this reading passage.

Questions 34–35: Sentence completion using words/numbers from the passage

These sentences are about government, and the answers come from Paragraph C of the text. You should know this because of the matching-heading questions that you have already completed.

34 If the people of San Marino make **a complaint**, the Heads of State are answerable.

answerable = responsible for answering the complaint

C Twice a year, the legislature (=government), known as the Grand and General Council, elects two **Heads of State** (key words for this question). ... After their six-month term in office is up (=finished), if the people are unhappy with their performance in any way, they may lodge (=make) **34** ***a complaint*** within three days, and if any of their grievances are justified, the ex-heads of state will be held to account (=answerable).

35 The Grand and General Council is the equivalent of the old **Roman Senate**.

is the equivalent of = does the same job as

C Twice a year, the legislature (=government), known as the **Grand and General Council** (key words for this question), elects two Heads of State. ... This system of government, as unusual as it may seem to many of us today, originates from (=comes from) the principles (=ideas) of the ancient Roman Republic. The Council (=Grand and Central Council) performs the role of (=does the same job as) the **35** ***Roman Senate*** and the Captains Regent are comparable to the consuls of early Rome.

Questions 36–40: Multiple choice

These questions start at the beginning of the passage, and follow on in order.

36 **B** Which of the following does NOT describe San Marino? **It has many beaches.**

Remember that you are looking for **false** information here.

A The Republic of San Marino is a landlocked (=surrounded by land) (therefore no beaches, therefore Option B is false) microstate or enclave, the third smallest state in Europe, situated on the Italian peninsula. ... (It is) completely surrounded by Italy (so there are no beaches) ...

Distractors for Question 36

A It is very hilly.

A Its total area is no more than 61 square kilometres of rugged terrain (=hilly ground) (there is no natural level ground at all) **(therefore the whole country is hilly)** ...

C It is an old state.

A **(It is)** completely surrounded by Italy with a border just thirty-nine kilometres long. ... Although it is a small state with a small population, estimated to be 32,448 in July 2013, it has a very long history **(so it is an old state)**.

B San Marino is perhaps the world's oldest constitutional republic ...

D It has pleasant (=nice) weather.

A The climate is typically Mediterranean with warm, sunny summers and mild (=not too cold), sometimes cool, winters **(so the weather is pleasant)**.

37 C In Paragraph B we are told that **there were two threats to San Marino's independence.**

B San Marino is perhaps the world's oldest constitutional republic, ... A community was established which managed to flourish (=grow and prosper) and maintain its sovereignty (=stay independent) over the many succeeding centuries, even surviving a potential invasion from Napoleon's army in the 18th century **(the first threat to independence)** and the period of Italian political unification in the 19th century **(the second threat to independence)**.

Distractors for Question 37

A ... San Marino was established (=started) to start a new religion.

B San Marino is perhaps the world's oldest constitutional republic, founded in the year 301 AD by a stonemason fleeing (=running away from, escaping from) religious persecution. **(The man was escaping from people who didn't like his religion, or who wanted him to join their religion. There is no mention that he wanted to start a new religion.)**

B ... the original founder (=the person who started this state) came from Rome.

B The stonecutter, Marinus (from whom the settlement derived its name), came from the Roman colony of Arba, which is an island off the coast of present-day Croatia. (he came from a Roman colony, but not from Rome itself)

D ... the Italian army wanted to invade San Marino.

B ... even surviving a potential invasion from Napoleon's army in the 18th century and the period of Italian political unification in the 19th century. (Napoleon wanted to invade San Marino, but the Italians wanted to unify (=take over the government of) San Marino)

38 D Paragraph D states that **many collectors want to buy San Marino coins.**

D Modern-day San Marino belongs to the Council of Europe and the United Nations but is not a member of the European Union although it is permitted to use the euro as its legal tender (=money); it is even allowed to have its own designs on the national side of the euro coins (=money). ... Because limited numbers of both the euro and lira coins are/were minted, they are eagerly sought (=often looked for) by coin collectors around the world (=many collectors want to buy the coins).

Distractors for Question 38

A ... nowadays, San Marino uses its own currency (=coins and notes).

D Modern-day San Marino belongs to the Council of Europe and the United Nations but is not a member of the European Union although it is permitted to use the euro as its legal tender; it is even allowed to have its own designs on the national side of the euro coins. **Before** moving to the euro, it used the San Marino lira for money (so nowadays it uses the euro, not its own money), ...

B ... San Marino uses the Italian euro coins.

D ... Before moving to the euro, it used the San Marino lira for money, and this was linked in value and exchangeable with the Italian lira (so the Italians use lira, not euros).

C ... there are a great many San Marino coins.

D ... Because limited numbers (=only a small number) of both the euro and lira coins are/were minted (=made), they are eagerly sought by coin collectors around the world.

39 B The main source of overseas income in San Marino comes from **tourism.**

E Chief sources of income arise from the industries of tourism, banking, ceramics and electronics together with the manufacture and export of furniture, paints, fabrics and wearing apparel. About a third of San Marino's GDP comes from the manufacturing industry **but tourism is the key player** (=the biggest source of income).

Distractors for Question 39

A ... agriculture.

E Only about sixteen per cent of land in San Marino is arable (=suitable for farming) and primary agricultural products mainly consist of some wine and cheese (most food is imported from Italy) (therefore, the main source of income will not come from farming); farmers do, however, raise sheep, cows and pigs and produce fruit and grain for local consumption.

C ... manufacturing.

E Chief sources of income arise from the industries of tourism, banking, ceramics and electronics together with the manufacture and export of furniture, paints, fabrics and wearing apparel. About a third of San Marino's GDP comes from the manufacturing industry but tourism is the key player (so manufacturing is important, but tourism is the main source of income).

D ... taxes.

E About a third of San Marino's GDP comes from the manufacturing industry but tourism is the key player and the government makes substantial returns from the taxes and customs imposed on the two to three million annual visitors, who also provide income for many local businesses. (so taxes are part of the income from tourism, but part of the income also comes from the money tourists spend while they are visiting)

40 A Which of the following best describes San Marino's people? **Most people have enough money and live a long time.**

F For such a tiny, geographically inhospitable country with few natural resources, apart perhaps from building stone, residents of San Marino (=San Marino's people) nevertheless enjoy a relatively high standard of living ... the pleasant climate and the general affluence (=a good level of wealth, or money) of the populace (=people) undoubtedly have an impact on life expectancy (=how long people will live), which is amongst the highest in the world, the average lifespan of females in San Marino being in excess of eighty-five years and the average male expecting to reach the age of eighty. (so they live a long time)

Distractors for Question 40

B Most people are of Danish or German origin.

F For such a tiny, geographically inhospitable country with few natural resources, apart perhaps from building stone, residents of San Marino nevertheless enjoy a relatively high standard of living equivalent to (=equal to) that of Danes or Germans. (so they have a similar lifestyle to the Danes and Germans, but they are not Danish or German)

C It is hard to find a job because San Marino is so small.

F Unlike many other European nations, the citizens of San Marino experience a very low level of unemployment. (so there are plenty of jobs)

D The population mostly lives in the country, not the towns.

F The population is predominantly urban (94%) (so most people live in the cities or towns) ...

Academic Test 2

LISTENING

Section 1: HORIZON HOTEL

Questions 1–8: Notes completion

Horizon Hotel

Example

Guest name: **Sandra MacKay**

You will hear an introduction to the first 5 questions of Section 1 of the Listening test. Then you will have 20 seconds to preview these questions and to predict (guess) the answers you are listening for.

There is an example to introduce this section. The audio for the example will be played first, with an explanation of the answer. After that, the full conversation will be played once only. This includes the example part of the recording.

Example:
Predict to hear: a name

[01:24]

RECEPTIONIST: Good morning, welcome to the Horizon Hotel. How may I help you?

WOMAN: I've come in to make a reservation for a friend.

RECEPTIONIST: And your friend's name is ... ?

WOMAN: MacKay, ***Sandra MacKay***, that's M-A-C-K-A-Y.

RECEPTIONIST: Thank you.

Date of arrival: 1 18(th) December

Predict to hear: a number (a date)

Note that you can choose to write the number only – 18 OR the number plus 'th' – 18th.

[02:22]

RECEPTIONIST: Thank you. When is she arriving?

WOMAN: She's flying in on the fifteenth but she'll stay with me for the first night because we have an early start on the sixteenth – we're going for a quick trip to the coast (distractor text) – but we should be back on the eighteenth.

RECEPTIONIST: So that's the 1 ***18th*** of this month?

WOMAN: No, sorry, did I forget to say? It's next month – **December** (key word in the notes).

Date of departure: 2 25(th) / Christmas Day December

Predict to hear: a number (a date)

Note that you can choose to write the number of the date, OR to write 'Christmas Day'.

[02:45]

RECEPTIONIST: Well, that's getting pretty close to Christmas, but we may have something available ... Right, we have one or two nice rooms left ... but how long will she stay for?

WOMAN: A week. (distractor text)

RECEPTIONIST: So, she'd be checking out on (=date of departure) ... 2 ***Christmas Day – the 25th***.

WOMAN: Is that a problem?

Room number: 3 502 and 702

Predict to hear: a room number

[03:05]

RECEPTIONIST: Well, it depends. We don't have a room available for the whole week, but, if she didn't mind changing rooms mid-way through her stay, we could work something out. (distractor text)

WOMAN: Oh, I see.

RECEPTIONIST: And if she wanted to extend her stay, that wouldn't be possible, I'm afraid. We're completely booked out from Christmas Day through to New Year. (distractor text)

WOMAN: No, she won't want to extend and I don't think she'd have a problem with changing rooms. (distractor text)

RECEPTIONIST: Good. Well, I'll put her in **Room 502** (key word and number in the notes) to start with and then she'll have to move to ... 805 ... (distractor text) no, just a minute, let's make that 3 ***702*** because that's available and it's two floors directly above 502 so the room layout will be identical. (distractor text)

Room rate: 4 $**165**

Predict to hear: a dollar amount

[03:47]

WOMAN: How much will it cost per night?

RECEPTIONIST: The basic **room rate** (key words in the notes) is 4 $***165***.

WOMAN: Is breakfast included?

RECEPTIONIST: No, but a complimentary drink is served every evening at 5 o'clock.

WOMAN: Oh, that could be quite nice. (distractor text)

Deposit: 5 Paid **in cash**

Predict to hear: a method of payment

[04:02]

RECEPTIONIST: Shall we make the booking then? We will require a **deposit** (key word in the notes) equivalent to one night's stay.

WOMAN: That's fine – I can **pay the deposit** (key words in the notes).

RECEPTIONIST: How would you like to do that – **in cash or by credit card** (key words to write in the notes)?

WOMAN: **Credit card, I suppose.** (distractor text) Oh, wait a minute – I might have enough money in my purse, yes, let's do it in cash.

RECEPTIONIST: Hang on. I'll just make a note of that. **Deposit paid** (key words in the notes) ... 5 ***in cash***.

Receipt

- in name of: 6 Zoe **Reed**

Predict to hear: a family name (a surname)

[05:07]

RECEPTIONIST: Just a second while I print a receipt. Who shall I make it out to (=in name of)?

WOMAN: My name is Zoe 6 ***Reed***, R-E-E-D.

RECEPTIONIST: Thank you Ms Reed. Now, I'll need some contact details for either you or Ms MacKay.

Contact details

- Address: 7 **14 South Street/St**, Morning Town
- Phone: 439 4829

Predict to hear: a street name

Note that you can choose to write 'Street' in full OR 'St'.

[05:22]

WOMAN: I'll give you my details, I only live on the other side of town. (distractor text)

RECEPTIONIST: Can I have your **address and phone number** (key words in the notes), please?

WOMAN: I live at 7 ***14 South Street***, Morning Town. And my phone number is 439 4829.

RECEPTIONIST: Thank you, 439 4829.

WOMAN: Yes, that's right.

Booking number: 8 **AQ459**

Predict to hear: a number

[05:44]

RECEPTIONIST: Now, I'll just print the booking form. If you have any questions or need to make any changes, (distractor text) just quote the reservation number (=booking number) on the bottom of the form. That's it there: 8 ***AQ459***.

Questions 9–10: Multiple choice

The answers for these 2 multiple choice questions will be found in the last part of the conversation, because the questions follow the order of the audio.

9 The room will be cleaned at around

A 11 a.m.

B 1 p.m.

C 2 p.m.

You should expect to hear ALL of the times mentioned in the audio; your job is to decide which is the room cleaning time.

[05:58]

WOMAN: Thanks very much. Oh, before I go, just a couple of questions. **What time does the room get cleaned?** (key question for Question 9) I'm only asking because my friend usually has a short nap after lunch and she wouldn't like to be disturbed. (distractor text)

RECEPTIONIST: Well, the maids are usually finished by **1 p.m.** (distractor text) because we have a **2 o'clock check-in time** (distractor text), you see. They come on duty quite early in the morning ... so they are sure to be finished in your friend's room by lunchtime, yes definitely (distractor text) – I'd say roughly **9** ***11 o'clock***.

10 Room service for dinner is available from

A 6 p.m. to 2 a.m.

B 6 p.m. to 10.30 p.m.

C 9 p.m. to 11 p.m.

You should expect to hear ALL of the times mentioned in the audio; your job is to decide which ones refer to the start and end of room service for dinner.

[06:28]

WOMAN: Thanks ... that's good to know. One more thing ... **is there room service for meals?** (key question for Question 10)

RECEPTIONIST: Only for breakfast and dinner. Breakfast service finishes at 9 and starts at 5 a.m. (distractor text, not dinner) **Dinner service starts at** **10** ***6 p.m.*** but the last orders have to be in half an hour before the kitchen closes at 11 p.m. (distractor text) – so **full room service closes at** **10** ***10.30***. But remember, light snacks – things like toasted sandwiches or muffins – can be ordered at the bar just off the lobby throughout the day and evening – until two in the morning. (distractor text, not dinner)

WOMAN: Thanks very much. You've been most helpful.

Section 2: ARTS REPORT

Questions 11–16: Table completion

Venue	Event	Date	Time	Admission Price
Gallery 1	Regional Art exhibition – all works for sale	4 March – 10 April	11 a.m. to 4 p.m. **11 weekdays**	No charge
Gallery 2	**12 'Issues** of the 21st Century' exhibition – by students	10 March – 4 April	10 a.m. to 3 p.m. Mon, Wed, Fri & weekends	No charge
Theatre 1	Shakespeare's *Romeo & Juliet*	5 March – 3 April	Daily at 8 p.m.	Adult **13 $40** Senior $20
The **14 Basement/ basement**	Shannon Keel – folk/pop/country	1 April	**15 9.15** p.m.	$12.50
The Showroom	Class Act – **16 classical** music & cabaret	1–30 April	11 a.m. Fridays only	$14 Concession $12

The answers for these table completion questions begin after quite a long introduction. Listen for key words or linkers to introduce each display or performance. Use the table to predict the kind of information you need, and listen for this information. Note that:

1. the information in the audio follows the general order of the events, BUT
2. within each event, information can be presented in a different order

11 11 a.m. to 4 p.m. **weekdays**

Predict to hear: a day or days

[08:35]

Hello and thanks for joining me on the Arts Scene tonight brought to you by your local radio station 2ZG and made possible by the generous sponsorship of Bertrand's Music and Video Store.

Firstly, I want to announce that the refurbished Arts Centre downtown is opening soon, with some spectacular visual art displays and performances that you won't want to miss. (this is all distractor introduction text)

In **Gallery 1** (key words for the table: Venue) the Arts Centre will be hosting an extraordinary exhibition of the latest creative works of our regional artists. There'll be landscapes, abstracts, photography, ceramics and sculpture. (distractor text) The exhibition opens on the **4th of March and runs through to the 10th of April** (key information for the table: Date). It's free and open to the public from **11 a.m. to 4 p.m.** (key information for the table: Time) **11** ***weekdays*** and, by the way, all works on display are for sale, so be sure to bring your credit card with you!

12 '**Issues** of the 21st Century' exhibition – by students	
Predict to hear: the name of an exhibition	[09:29] **Gallery 2** (key words for the table: Venue) will put on the annual showcase of the art of school students who take a, sometimes challenging and often emotive, look at the current issues facing youth in particular and society in general. (distractor text) This is the '**12** ***Issues*** of the 21st Century' (key information for the table: Event – note that the answer comes BEFORE the text given in the table) exhibition and the dates to keep in mind are 10th of March to the 4th of April – the gallery will be open from 10 till 3 Monday, Wednesday, Friday and weekends. There's no charge but teachers should make bookings if they're bringing large groups. (distractor text for Question 12)

13 Adult $**40** Senior $20	
Predict to hear: a dollar amount	[10:04] Let's move on to the performing arts now: Shakespeare season is back again and this year's production is the ever popular ***Romeo and Juliet*** (key words for the table: Event). **Tickets** (key word for the table: Admission Price) are just **13** $***40*** for adults and half price for seniors, and there are rush tickets for students at $15 (distractor text). Performances are in Theatre One at 8 o'clock every evening. Bookings are essential. The show runs from the 5th of March to the 3rd of April, and there is a possibility of more shows if there is a high demand for tickets. (distractor text for Question 13)

14 The **Basement/basement**

Predict to hear: a place name	[10:37] Now, if you like your **folk pop** with a country twist, you must see **Shannon Keel** (key words for the table: Event), who is back in town for one night only on the first of April performing for us in the **14** ***Basement*** (key word for the table: Venue).

15 **9.15** p.m.

Predict to hear: a time	[10:48] She'll be supported by Ricky Bond's band, which has been touring with her for the last 7 weeks (distractor text) – and **show time** (key words for the table: Time) is **15** ***9.15***. Tickets are on sale at the door, just $12.50. Doors open at 8. (distractor text for Question 15)

16 Class Act – **classical** music & cabaret

Predict to hear: the name of a kind of music	[11:03] Coming to the Arts Centre for 4 performances in the **Showroom is Class Act** (key words for the table: Venue and Event), a quartet who have captivated audiences with their amazing repertoire (distractor text) of **16** ***classical*** music and who now include top-class cabaret in their programme. They will give matinee performances every Friday in April at 11 o'clock. Tickets are only $14 a single, or better yet, why not get together with a group of six or more friends and pay only $12. (distractor text for Question 16)

Questions 17–18: Multiple choice

17 Michael's home country is

A Canada.

B Ireland.

C the USA.

You should expect to hear ALL of the countries mentioned in the audio; your job is to decide which one Michael came from.

	[12:11] Now, here's some exciting news. I've just heard that **Michael O'Brien**

(key words for Question 17) is going to perform at the Arts Centre next year but we haven't got any dates finalised as yet. As you know, Michael is 17 ***Ireland's*** most popular 'easy listening' entertainer and he's returning from **a tour of Canada** and the **United States** (distractor text – he toured in these countries but he does not live in them) where he has enjoyed huge success – even in Nashville: the home of country music – that's a long way from his **Irish** roots (therefore he comes from Ireland).

18 Michael has been singing for
- A 15 years.
- B 18 years.
- **C 20 years.**

You should expect to hear ALL of the numbers mentioned in the audio; your job is to decide which one refers to the length of Michael's singing career.

[12:40]

Michael is without a doubt a singing superstar – he has had **15 top-ten music videos** (distractor text – the number refers to music videos, not his singing career) and is almost a permanent feature in the UK album charts with **18 UK chart albums** (distractor text – the number refers to albums, not his singing career) to date – but he is still as excited and enthusiastic about his work and his fans as he was when he first launched (=started) **his career** 18 ***20 years*** **ago.**

Questions 19–20: Sentence completion

19 Michael's father went **abroad** to work.

[13:02]

Perhaps some of you are unaware that Michael's first years were ones of struggle. (distractor text) The **family** was very poor and **his father** (key words for Question 19) was forced to go 19 ***abroad*** to **provide for his family** (=work). He worked on farms in Scotland and it was very hard, manual labour – very different from the lifestyle Michael enjoys today. Unfortunately, his father died when Michael was only five years old and the burden of raising five children fell on his mother. (distractor text)

20 Michael's **sister** was also a singer, and was an inspiration for him.

[13:31]

Although Michael followed in the footsteps of his **20** ***sister*** by **pursuing a singing career – she was his role model and inspiration** (key text for Question 20, which comes after the answer) – he has attributed much of his success in life to his **mother's influence** (distractor text, his mother was not a singer), and he has dedicated his most recent DVD release to her (distractor text). You can pick up a copy of that DVD, 'Unwavering Devotion', at Bertrand's Music and Video Store.

Section 3: STUDENT ASSIGNMENT PLANNING SESSION

Questions 21–25: Sentence completion

21 Jan suggests doing their joint **presentation/assignment** on copyright or IP law.

[15:31]

STEVE: Hi Jan. Sorry, my tutorial finished late.

JAN: No problem Steve! But let's get straight to work. I've got so many other assignments this week! And we've only got till next Wednesday. (introduction text – discussion about assignment)

STEVE: Sure, fine by me. So, **we've got to do** (=task) a **combined** (=joint) (key word for Question 21) **21** ***presentation***, with at least 20 slides and a recommendation at the end. Is that right?

JAN: Yes. And then 5 minutes for questions ...

STEVE: Oh, right, I'd forgotten that.

JAN: So – what shall we choose as a topic? I was wondering about **copyright ... or intellectual property law** (key words – the answer for Question 21 will be BEFORE this point). It's a tricky area though.

22 Steve's suggested topic is **digital privacy**.

[15:56]

JAN: So – what shall we choose as a **topic** (key word for Question 22)? I was wondering about copyright ... or intellectual property law. It's a tricky area though. (these are Jan's suggestions, not Steve's – Steve will make his suggestion next)

STEVE: Well, I've been doing a bit of reading about 22 ***digital privacy*** and it's actually a really challenging issue (=big problem) now. I mean, the way employers and government departments rely on commercial databases (=information stored on computers) for information on people.

JAN: OK, that sounds like it has potential (=could be a good topic). Tell me more – I can't say I've read much about it.

23 A database may collect statistics on your date of birth, income, legal history, previous jobs, **credit rating** or health record.

Note that in this question, the order of the information is the same in the audio and the sentence.

[16:24]

STEVE: Um ... well, these **databases** (key word) **compile information** (=collect statistics) on all sorts of things, not just **birthdates and income** (=date of birth, income) (key words for Question 23). They record people's **lawsuits and convictions** (=legal history), **employment history** (=previous jobs), 23 ***credit rating***, **medical history** (=health record) (therefore the answer must come BEFORE these words) – a range of **statistics** and stuff that is often out of date or is only partially true.

JAN: And they get this information from public records on the Internet? You mean it's actually available online?

24 Inaccurate facts may be recorded by data company **employees**.

Note that in this question, the grammar is different in the audio and in the sentence; therefore the order of the information is reversed.

[16:49]

STEVE: Yes, and that's the problem. We live in such a networked society now. There's so much data on the net, and it's really accessible. Often the company 24 ***employees*** (answer, which comes BEFORE the rest of the key words) **who compile these databases** (=record these statistics) **include dated information or get confused by similar names and list the wrong details for people** (=inaccurate facts).

25 Incorrect information about a **sales manager** led to his unfair dismissal.

Note that in this question, the grammar is different in the audio and the sentence, therefore the order of the information is also different.

[17:10]

STEVE: Well, for example, a **25** ***sales manager*** was **fired** (=dismissed from his job) because of a background check by a data company which reported that he'd served a jail term. He protested, but his boss still fired him. All he'd had was something minor like a speeding ticket (the information on the database was incorrect). He suffered an **unjust dismissal** (=unfair dismissal) plus the stress of trying to find another job. He was out of work for seven months.

JAN: I see. OK, this has really got me thinking now! It's a great topic.

Questions 26–30: Table completion

Jan's comments	Steve's comments
Search engines collect data by analysing people's Internet **26 (search) habits**.	Data collecting companies want to collect extra data to expand business and increase their **27 profitability/profits**.
Getting consent could be the main **28 recommendation** in the presentation.	Not legal in Europe to make money from using someone's private details without their direct consent
Annoying to have to buy your own credit reports to ensure accuracy	People writing blogs and Twitter comments should be careful or they may face **29 legal action**.
The 'free information' nature of the Internet has led to this problem.	Browser companies may solve the problem by introducing a **30 tracking protection** system.

The answers for these table questions will be found in the next part of the conversation, because the questions follow the order of the audio. Note carefully which comments in the table come from Steve, and which from Jan, and then listen for paraphrase as you go.

26 Search engines collect data by analysing people's Internet **(search) habits**.

[18:13]

JAN: Ah ... I'm thinking now about how the **search engines** (key words for Question 26) apparently **compile information** (=collect data) **on people, based on their** (by analysing) online (=Internet) **26** ***search habits*** ... you know, there's been a bit in the news lately. I guess that's pertinent.

27 Data collecting companies want to collect extra data to expand business and increase their **profitability/profits**.

[18:26]

STEVE: That's right; it's all part of this same issue. The search engines actually **gather a huge amount of data** (=collect extra data) **about computer users**, and some of it is definitely sold (by data collecting companies) to other paying customers. The database companies sell lists to direct-marketing companies, for example. (distractor text) That's their **core business** (=main business), so they're always trying to access more information in order to **attract new clients** (=expand business) (key words for Question 27) and improve (=increase) their **27** ***profitability***.

28 Getting consent could be the main **recommendation** in the presentation.

[18:49]

JAN: Hmm. What about social networking sites? (distractor topic – NOT listed in the table) How much of that information is truly private?

STEVE: Not a lot, it seems. And hackers (=people that use computers to access information illegally) can download sensitive information and misuse it as well. Also, every time you fill out an online form or survey to enter a prize draw, you're compromising your privacy.

JAN: I never thought about that. I often enter those, and give my email address and mobile number. (all of this is distractor text)

STEVE: Well, apparently in Europe they have laws controlling the ability of companies to sell or share people's personal data (=laws to stop companies from using personal data) without **getting explicit consent** (=clear and open permission) (key words for Question 28). But that's not the case here.

JAN: Then that could be our main **28** ***recommendation***.

29 People writing blogs and Twitter comments should be careful or they may face **legal action**.

Note that there are cells in the table that have no gaps. Therefore, expect some untested text here.

The next gap comes from Steve's comments – see script below.

[19:27]

STEVE: Yes – and then we can advise people to actually **purchase their own credit reports** (=buy their own credit reports) and files from a few of the big database companies, **to check that the information stored on them is actually accurate** (=to ensure accuracy).

JAN: It's so **frustrating** (=annoying) to have to do something **like that** ('like that' refers BACK to what Steve has just said about having to buy your own reports)!

STEVE: For sure. Also **bloggers** (=people writing blogs) (key word for Question 29) should be very cautious – they can be sued for breaches of privacy and for libel. Even **Twitter comments** (key words for Question 29) aren't exempt from (=people may face) **29** ***legal action***. So that's another area to consider for suggestions. Anyway, we need to decide how to split this up. How about if one of us does an overview of the general issue and the history of it all to date?

JAN: I think I might tackle that (=do that part). You'd be better on the technical stuff.

30 Browser companies may solve the problem by introducing a **tracking protection** system.

[20:08]

STEVE: Great. Then I'll look at new developments and make policy recommendations. For example, there are technology researchers looking at how access to files and information can be restricted. Because, you know, originally the Internet was designed to be as open as possible ...

JAN: That's right. And instead, it's created a real conflict (=problem).

STEVE: Already some of the **browser companies** (key words for Question 30) **are working on solutions** (=may solve the problem) to this – such as offering a **30** ***tracking protection*** feature (=system) that users can switch on, to restrict how much data can be mined from their computer use. And there are a few other ideas out there as well ...

Section 4: THE ANTARCTIC TOOTHFISH

Questions 31–35: Multiple choice

31 Which place has been **termed** 'a living **laboratory**'?

termed = called

laboratory = an excellent place for research

A the Ross Sea
B the Antarctic Sea
C the Southern Ocean

You should expect to hear ALL of the places in the audio; your job is to decide which one has been termed a living laboratory.

[22:40]

Good afternoon! As you know ... it's Environment Week, and that seems like a good time to focus on one of the most special places in the world ... the **Ross Sea** ('Ross Sea' are the key words for Question 31, but this distractor text does not contain the answer to Question 31), and its associated fishing industry, which is largely focussed on the **Antarctic toothfish** (main topic for the talk).

Now ... back in 2008, this part of the **Antarctic** (distractor text – the Ross Sea is part of the Antarctic Sea), that is the **Ross Sea** – which by the way makes up only about 3% of the **Southern Ocean** (distractor text – the Ross Sea is part of the Southern Ocean) – was rated as being the 'least-changed environment' on the planet. In fact, **it's** (refers back to the Ross Sea) been described by one source as **'a living laboratory**, a link with evolution' and it teems with fascinating and unusual sea and mammal life. So there have been urgent pleas for the Ross Sea to be given some kind of permanent protection. (distractor text)

32 What is said to be the worst form of pollution that fishing boats might cause?

A rubbish dropped overboard

B fuel leaked overboard

C sewage leaked overboard

You should expect to hear ALL of the forms of pollution in the audio; your job is to decide which one is the worst, or most dangerous.

[23:37]

What are the issues facing the area, then? (key topic question for Question 32) Well, aside from the huge problem of **global warming** that threatens all of the Antarctic oceans and the ice cap (distractor text), most of **these** (problems, or issues) are associated with the **fishing vessels** (=fishing boats) that come into the Ross Sea. As well as the usual things like **general rubbish and sewage pollution** (distractor text – these are not the main problems) from **these** (fishing) boats, the **most significant potential danger** (=the worst form of pollution) is an **oil and diesel spill** (=fuel leaked overboard) from a fishing boat that is either damaged or sunk due to the thick ice.

33 What was the country of registration of the boat which was stuck in thick ice?

A Korea

B New Zealand

C Russia

You should expect to hear ALL of the countries in the audio; your job is to decide which one was the country of registration of the boat that was stuck in thick ice.

[24:09]

In January 2012, a **Korean fishing vessel caught fire in the Ross Sea**, (distractor text – the Korean vessel caught fire; it was not stuck) with the loss of at least three lives – although luckily an oil spill was averted. In late 2011, **another Korean ship, the *In Sung Number 1*, sank** (distractor text – this Korean vessel sank) with 22 lives lost, although the rest of the crew were saved by other fishing boats in the area.

Again, in December 2011, another vessel, the *Sparta*, caused an international furore (=excited, angry reaction) when it was **holed and stranded in pack ice** (=stuck in thick ice) in the Southern Ocean – **that one** (that fishing vessel) was **Russian**. **New Zealand planes** (distractor text – New Zealand planes not ships) had to fly missions to drop off water pumps and other essential equipment and supplies to the ship ...

34 In the case of the *Sparta* repair mission, what does the speaker term 'a miracle'?

a miracle = a good and surprising event

A No fishermen died.

B The weather was not stormy.

C An oil spill was avoided.

You should expect to hear ALL of the good events in the audio; your job is to decide which one the speaker termed 'a miracle'.

[24:35]

Again, in December 2011, another vessel, the *Sparta*, caused an international furore when it was holed and stranded in pack ice in the Southern Ocean – that one was **Russian**. New Zealand planes had to fly missions to drop off water pumps and other essential equipment and supplies to the ship – ah ... remember that the crews of such flights are put at extreme risk on such long flights, as **the weather can become stormy at very short notice**. (distractor text) All in all, it was **a miracle** (key words for Question 34) that this ship was able to be repaired and moved from the area **without a significant leakage of fuel** (=an oil spill was avoided). So, apart from the potential for environmental problems from the boats, and the danger to fishermen working in this hostile environment, there's also the matter of the cost and danger of providing support in a crisis.

35 What does the term 'total allowable catch' refer to?

A the amount any boat in the Antarctic can catch

B the amount all the legal boats can catch

C the amount all the boats (legal and illegal) can catch

[25:30]

And ... you know ... there's a lot of pressure on the fishing crews to make the most of the brief weather window (=short amount of time each year) during which boats can operate so far south, so they tend to keep fishing no matter what the weather is like ... which means that errors of judgement are more likely. (distractor text) **The officially authorised fishing fleet** (=legal boats) **has a quota or limit** (=the amount they can catch) and each boat is hoping to get the biggest share possible of the **total allowable catch** (key words for Question 35 – note that this comes AFTER the answer). Then, of course, there are the illegal boats – that means the boats operating without permits – they just try to catch as much as possible regardless – and the vessels may not even be in a suitable condition to be operating in these icy southern waters. (distractor text)

Questions 36–40: Summary completion

In this section you need to wait for the answer to the first question, which is not at the beginning of the audio. Therefore, you need to be able to follow the summary and relate this to the audio.

The Antarctic Toothfish

These are big fish, which live in freezing Antarctic waters at depths of 200 to 2,000 metres. They have a life span of roughly 36 **50/fifty** years, and develop only slowly.

have a life span of = live for

[26:17]

Consequently, a key issue is the decimation of the species. Now, how much do we know about this particular fish? The Antarctic toothfish **inhabit very cold Antarctic seas** (=live in freezing Antarctic waters), usually between **200 metres to two kilometres deep** (=at depths of 200 to 2,000 metres). They are large creatures ... rather ugly ... and they are slow-growing. (distractor text) Although they live up to approximately (=have a life span of roughly) 36 ***fifty*** years, it seems they only reach sexual maturity after about sixteen years (develop only slowly).

Little is known about the early stages of life for this fish including the kinds of 37 **predators** that feed on the young.

[26:51]

Also, very **little is yet known about their life cycle** (=little is known about the early stages of life for this fish) – things like where they spawn, or what happens to the young ones before they are ready to breed. We do know that the adult fish are near the top of the food chain – but we need to know much more about the juvenile forms – things like: what they look like, where they spend those early years (all of this is distractor text) and ... ah ... what sort of 37 ***predators*** (that feed on the young) **go after them**.

Since 1996, the December–February fishing season has resulted in catches of about 100,000 fish per year – although recent catches have declined because of 38 **overfishing/over-fishing**.

declined = dropped or reduced

[27:23]

OK – so the fishing season in the Ross Sea spans **December to February** (=the December–February fishing season). It's estimated that close to three and a half thousand tonnes of Antarctic toothfish have been taken annually since the fishery opened in 1996 (distractor text) – this represents approximately one hundred thousand fish per year (=has resulted in catches of about 100,000 fish per year). I must add, though, that in the last couple of years **overall catches have been reduced** (=although recent catches have declined) due to (=because of) 38 ***overfishing*** and the decline in total fish numbers. There's no record, of course, of the numbers of fish caught by illegal fishing boats. (distractor text)

Industry spokesmen claim that the Antarctic toothfish industry is 39 **sustainable** but it has been estimated that fish numbers in the Ross Sea have already been reduced by at least a fifth, if not more.

sustainable = fishing is not reducing overall numbers of fish

a fifth = 20%

[28:00]

Um ... **those in the Antarctic toothfish industry claim that** (=industry spokesmen claim that) the short fishing season and the difficulties faced by the boats in this inhospitable climate provide their own natural limits on fishing. They say that the industry is concerned to preserve fish stocks, and they assert that, with careful management and monitoring (distractor text) the fishery is **39** ***sustainable***. However, others dispute that this is the case, especially given the distances involved and the difficulties faced in trying to manage and monitor fishing boats in such a remote location. (distractor text)

In the Ross Sea area, a conservative (=low) estimate suggests that fish stocks have declined by about 20 per cent over the past 16 years (=it has been estimated that fish numbers in the Ross Sea have already been reduced by at least a fifth, if not more).

A plea has been made by several well-known marine scientists for a **40** **ban** on catching fish in the Ross Sea.

plea = request

[28:52]

But in fact there is not enough accurate research to support such claims ... the figure could be even higher. **Leading scientists who specialise in this issue** (=well-known marine scientists) **are calling for** (=a plea has been made for) a Marine Protection Area, or MPA, with a total **40** ***ban*** on fishing, but so far this has not been achieved.

Right – so that's an introduction. Now, let's watch a short video before we discuss your next assignment ...

READING

Reading Passage 1: A BAR AT THE FOLIES

Questions 1–5: Matching information to the text

Overall text structure:

Understanding the text structure will help you to find each answer. Of course you do not have time during the Reading test to write a list like the one below, but you do need to read and notice the paragraph topics.

Paragraph A – introduction to the painting
Paragraph B – description of the painting
Paragraph C – how the painting was painted
Paragraph D – analysis of the painting – Manet's use of background and foreground
Paragraph E – Manet's possible message; the writer's opinion
Paragraph F – art historians' or scholars' opinions

1 a description of how Manet created the painting = **Paragraph C**

created = made

C Although … , Manet did not attempt to recapture every detail of the bar in his rendition. The **painting was largely completed in a private studio belonging to the painter**, where **the barmaid posed with a number of bottles**, and **this was then integrated with quick sketches the artist made at the Folies itself.**

2 aspects of the painting that scholars are most interested in = **Paragraph F**

aspects = parts of the painting, the way things appear in the painting

scholars = researchers

F Ever since … , **art historians** (=scholars) have … **disputing the positioning of the barmaid and patron** (=arguing about the painting) in *A Bar at the Folies*. **Some** (scholars)have even conducted staged representations of the painting in order to ascertain whether Manet's seemingly distorted point of view might have been possible after all. Yet … .

3 the writer's view of the idea that Manet wants to communicate = **Paragraph E**

view = opinion

communicate = express thoughts/feelings/ideas

E Why would Manet engage in such deceit? (writer's question) **Perhaps for that very reason**: ... . (the rest of the paragraph is the writer's answer to his own question)

4 examples to show why the bar scene is unrealistic = **Paragraph D**

D Even more confounding than Manet's relaxed attention to detail, however, (refers back to previous paragraph), is the relationship in the painting between the activity in the mirrored reflection and that which we see in the unreflected foreground. (new idea – background vs. foreground) ... , Manet uses the mirror to toy with our ideas (=make us think) about which details are **true to life** (=real) and which are not (=unreal). In the foreground, ... (several examples follow). The overall impact on the viewer is one of a dreamlike **disjuncture between reality and illusion** (=unsure of what is real and what is unreal).

5 a statement about the popularity of the painting = **Paragraph A**

popular = renowned, favourite, well-known

A One of the **most critically renowned** (=well-known or famous) **paintings of the 19th-century modernist movement** is the French painter Edouard Manet's masterwork, *A Bar at the Folies*. Originally belonging to the composer Emmanuel Chabrier, it is now in the possession of The Courtauld Gallery in London, where it has also **become a favourite with the crowds** (=people love the painting).

Questions 6–10: Short answers

6 Who was the first owner of *A Bar at the Folies*? = **Emmanuel Chabrier**

Look for a name, since the question begins with 'who'. Paragraph A introduces the painting, so this is the most likely place to find the answer. Check spelling carefully when you write the answer.

A One of the most critically renowned paintings of the 19th-century modernist movement is the French painter Edouard Manet's masterwork,

A Bar at the Folies. **Originally belonging to** (=first owned by) the composer ***Emmanuel Chabrier***, it is **now in the possession of** (=current owner) ... .

7 What is the barmaid wearing? = **a black bodice**

Paragraph B describes the painting.

B The painting is set (=located) late at night in a nineteenth-century Parisian nightclub. A **barmaid** stands alone behind her bar, **fitted out in** (=wearing) ***a black bodice*** that has a frilly white neckline, and with a spray of flowers sitting across her décolletage. (more details follow)

8 Which room is seen at the back of the painting? = **an auditorium**

auditorium = room

Paragraph B describes the painting.

B She rests her hands on the bar ... . Also on the bar are ... , but much of the activity in the room takes place in the **reflection of a mirror behind the barmaid** (at the back of the painting). Through this mirror we see an ***auditorium***, bustling with blurred figures and faces: ... (therefore, an auditorium must be a room of some kind).

9 Who is performing for the audience? = **a trapeze artist**

audience = crowd

'Who' tells you that you are looking for a name, or a person, in this case a person's profession. Paragraph B describes the painting. The information needed for Questions 7, 8 and 9 follows the order of information in the paragraph.

B ... bustling with blurred figures and faces: men in top hats, a woman examining the scene below her through binoculars, another in long gloves, even the feet of ***a trapeze artist*** (who is) **demonstrating acrobatic feats** (=performing for the audience) **above his adoring crowd**.

10 Where did most of the work on the painting take place? = **a/Manet's private studio**

Paragraph C describes **how** the painting was painted. You will NEVER be asked to write more than 3 words, so you do not need to include the word 'in' in your answer. The examiners have allowed you to substitute 'Manet's' for 'a' in this answer.

C Although ... . The painting was largely completed in **a private studio belonging to the painter**, where the barmaid posed with a number of bottles, and this was then integrated with quick sketches the artist made at the Folies itself.

Questions 11–13: Matching sentence endings

The answers to these questions are likely to be found in Paragraphs D, E or F, since the other paragraphs have already been tested.

Question 11 refers to the background and foreground of the painting – images in the mirror – so the answer will likely be found in Paragraph D.

11 **E** Manet misrepresents the images in the mirror because he **wanted to manipulate our sense of reality**.

misrepresents = distorts or changes

manipulate = play with or toy with

D ... the relationship in the painting between **the activity in the mirrored reflection and that which we see in the unreflected foreground.** ... , Manet uses the mirror to **toy with our ideas** (=manipulate our sense of reality) **about which details are true to life and which are not**. In the foreground, **for example,**(example follows) ... , **yet in the mirrored reflection** ... . As a result of this, ...(more examples) . The overall impact on the viewer is one of a **dreamlike disjuncture between reality and illusion**(manipulating our sense of reality) .

Distractor for Question 11

A Manet misrepresents the images in the mirror because he wanted to find out if the painting's perspective was realistic.

This may sound plausible, but it is not logical. It was the critics who wanted to check if the painting was realistic, not Manet.

F ... , art historians have produced reams of books and journal articles disputing the positioning of the barmaid and patron in *A Bar at the Folies*. **Some**(critics) **have even conducted staged representations of the painting in order to ascertain whether Manet's seemingly distorted point of view might have been possible after all.**

12 **D** Manet felt modern workers were alienated because they **felt like they had to become different people**.

alienated = removed from something, not part of something

Paragraph E clearly states this.

E ... Manet seems to be conveying his understanding of the modern workplace, a place – from his perspective – of **alienation** (=being/feeling removed from...), where workers felt **torn from their 'true' selves** and **forced to assume an artificial working identity**(workers felt they had to become different people) .

Distractor for Question 12

B Manet felt modern workers were alienated because they felt they had to work very hard at boring and difficult jobs.

This is plausible (=possible)but it is not mentioned at all in the reading passage.

13 **A** Academics have re-constructed the painting in real life because they **wanted to find out if the painting's perspective was realistic**.

re-constructed = made(conducted staged representations)

perspective = the way in which he showed depth in the painting by painting things that are close bigger and things that are far away smaller

Paragraph F clearly states this.

F ... , art historians have produced reams of books and journal articles disputing the positioning of the barmaid and patron in *A Bar at the Folies*. **Some**(critics) **have even conducted staged representations of the painting** (=re-constructed the painting in real life) **in order to ascertain** (=find out) **whether Manet's seemingly distorted point of view might have been possible after all** (=if the painting was realistic).

Distractor for Question13

F Academics have re-constructed the painting in real life because they wanted to focus on the detail in the painting.

This is plausible, but the main reason for reconstructing the painting was to check if the perspective was possible, not to focus on details.

Reading Passage 2: MILES DAVIS

Questions 14–19: Matching paragraph headings

14 Paragraph **A = viii Davis' unique style of trumpet playing**

unique = special, unusual, distinctive

This paragraph describes Davis' technique, or style, and states several times that it was clear and different, or unique.

A At the age of thirteen, Miles Davis … . These early lessons, paid for and supported by his father, had a profound effect on shaping **Davis' signature sound** (=unique style). Whereas … (example follows). This **clear, distinctive style** (=unique style) never left Davis. He continued playing with it for the rest of his career, once remarking, **'If I can't get that sound, I can't play anything.'**

15 Paragraph **B = iii An education in two parts**

This paragraph describes Davis' formal musical education, and his informal education in jazz clubs = two parts.

B Having graduated from high school in 1944, Davis moved to New York City, where he continued his musical education **both in the clubs and in the classroom.** (2 parts – examples follow)

16 Paragraph **C = i A legacy is established**

legacy = an idea that everyone else follows

This paragraph describes the beginning, or establishment, of Davis' own unique sound, and how this became the beginning of a new style of jazz for everyone.

C In the late 1940s, Davis … , to produce ***The Birth of Cool,* an album now renowned for the inchoate sounds** (=the sound was new and therefore not yet fully developed) **of what would later become known as 'cool' jazz.** (examples follow) … in hindsight, ***The Birth of Cool* has become recognised as a pivotal** (=significant) **moment in jazz history**, cementing – alongside his 1958 recording, *Kind of Blue* – **Davis' legacy as one of the most innovative musicians of his era**.

17 Paragraph D = ix Personal and professional struggles

struggles = problems

The first sentence of Paragraph D states that this paragraph is about Davis' problems, or struggles.

D Though Davis' trumpet playing may have sounded effortless and breezy, **this ease** (=easiness) **rarely** (=hardly ever) **carried over into the rest of his life**. (He had problems in his life. Both personal and musical examples follow.)

18 Paragraph E = iv Branching out in new directions

branching out in new directions = making changes to the old ways of doing things

Paragraph E discusses the changes that Davis made to the jazz sound.

E In the latter decades of his career, Davis **broke out of exclusive jazz settings** and **began to diversify** (=increase the variety of) **his output across a range of musical styles**. (examples of the range of styles follow)

19 Paragraph F = vi Change necessary to stay creative

creative = able to develop new ways of doing something (his ability to develop new ways of producing music)

Paragraph F begins by discussing the criticisms that others had of Davis' new ways of playing. The last sentence summarises the author's opinion that change is necessary to stay creative.

F Not everyone was supportive of (=some people did not like the new style) Davis' change of tune. (examples follow) ... In the face of this criticism, Davis ... firmly believed that remaining stylistically inert (=lifeless, unchanging) would have hampered his ability to develop new ways of producing music. From this perspective, Davis' continual **revamping of genre** (=changing and mixing of styles) was not merely a rebellion, but an evolution, a **necessary path** that allowed him to **release his full musical potential** (=be fully creative).

Distractors for Questions 14–19

In this type of question the distractors (=unused headings or incorrect answers)are often found somewhere in the text, but either:

1. they are **not the main idea** of the paragraph, or
2. the **information** in the paragraph **does not match the heading**.

ii Formal education unhelpful

This idea is mentioned in Paragraph B. However, it is contradicted later in the same paragraph.

B His enrolment in the **prestigious** (=famous) **Julliard School of Music** (=formal education) was short-lived, however – he **soon dropped out** (=quickly left the school), criticising what he perceived as an over-emphasis on the classical European repertoire and a neglect of jazz (=it was too traditional for him). **Davis did later acknowledge, however, that this time at the school was invaluable in terms of developing his trumpet-playing technique** (=but later he admitted that the school helped him to develop his skills) and giving him a solid grounding in music theory.

v Childhood and family life

This is briefly mentioned at the beginning of Paragraph A, but it is not the focus of the paragraph, and there are no details given.

vii Conflicted opinions over Davis' earlier work

Paragraph C mentions that some critics did not like his early work, but there are no contrasting, or conflicting, opinions from those who did like the work at the time.

Questions 20–26: Yes, no, not given

20 Davis' trumpet teacher wanted him to play with vibrato. **NO**

vibrato = small, quick changes made to a musical note you are singing or playing

See Paragraph A.

A **Whereas**(opposite idea is coming) most trumpeters of the era **favoured** (=liked) the use of **vibrato** (=short changes in the pitch of the note – definition of vibrato), Davis was taught to play with a **long,**

straight tone(NOT vibrato) , a preference his instructor reportedly drilled into the young trumpeter with a rap on the knuckles (=hitting his hands (knuckles)) every time Davis began using vibrato.

21 According to Davis, studying at Julliard helped him to improve his musical abilities. **YES**

See Paragraph B. Be careful to read ALL the information about Julliard, not just the first part. Watch for important linking words – **however**.

B His enrolment in the prestigious **Julliard School of Music** was **short-lived** (=he stayed only a short time there), however – he soon **dropped out** (=left), criticising what he perceived as an over-emphasis on the classical European repertoire and a neglect of jazz. Davis did later acknowledge, **however**(important word) , that **this time at the school** (Julliard) **was invaluable** (=very useful) in terms of **developing his trumpet-playing technique** and **giving him a solid grounding in music theory**.

22 Playing in jazz clubs in New York was the best way to become famous. **NOT GIVEN**

Jazz clubs in New York are mentioned in Paragraph B, but there is no information about whether they were the **best** way to become famous. The text states only that some famous musicians played in them.

B Having graduated from high school in 1944, Davis moved to **New York City**, where he continued his musical education both **in the clubs** and in the classroom. ... Much of his early training took place in the form of jam sessions (=practice) and performances in **the clubs of 52nd Street**, where he played alongside both **up-and-coming** (=becoming well-known) **and established members** (=famous players) **of the jazz pantheon** such as Coleman Hawkins, Eddie 'Lockjaw' Davis, and Thelonious Monk.

23 *The Birth of Cool* featured music that was faster and louder than most jazz at the time. **NO**

featured = had/included something

See Paragraph C, where this is directly stated.

C In the late 1940s, Davis ... to produce ***The Birth of Cool***, an album now renowned for the inchoate sounds of what would later become known as 'cool' jazz. **In contrast to** popular jazz styles of the day, which featured **rapid, rollicking beats, shrieking vocals, and short, sharp horn blasts,** (fast and loud) Davis' album was the forerunner of a different kind of sound – **thin, light horn-playing, hushed drums and a more restrained, formal arrangement** (different to 'fast and loud').

24 Davis' personal troubles had a negative effect on his trumpet playing. **NOT GIVEN**

Paragraph D states that Davis had personal problems, but does NOT state how, or if, these affected his playing.

25 Davis felt that his contribution to cool jazz had not been acknowledged. **YES**

his contribution = what he gave

acknowledged = recognised

not been acknowledged = been overlooked

Paragraph D directly states this.

D Davis was also frustrated by **his perception** (=view, opinion) **that he had been overlooked by the music critics** (=the critics did not notice, or acknowledge, him), who were hailing the success of his collaborators (=people working with him) and descendants in the 'cool' tradition, such as Gerry Mulligan and Dave Brubeck, but who **afforded** (=gave) **him little credit for introducing the cool sound in the first place**.

26 Davis was a traditionalist who wanted to keep the jazz sound pure. **NO**

traditionalist = a person who follows existing patterns (who does not create new ways of doing things)

Paragraph E states that Davis liked experimenting with new styles.

E In the latter decades of his career, Davis **broke out of exclusive jazz settings** and began to diversify (=increase the variety of) **his output across a range of musical styles**. In the 1960s, he was influenced by early funk performers such as Sly and the Family Stone, which then **expanded into the jazz-rock fusion genre – of which he was a frontrunner** (=one of the first) – in the 1970s. **Electronic recording effects and electric instruments were incorporated** (=included)

into his sound. By the 1980s, Davis was pushing the boundaries further, covering pop anthems such as Cyndi Lauper's *Time After Time* and Michael Jackson's *Human Nature,* dabbling in hip hop, and even appearing in some movies.

Reading Passage 3: ROCK CLIMBING

Questions 27–32: Matching information to the text

Overall text structure:

Understanding the text structure will help you to find each answer. Of course you do not have time during the Reading test to write a list like the one below, but you do need to read and notice the text structure. If you do this, you will quickly see that the first part of this text (Paragraphs A–E) is a dated history of rock climbing, and the second part (Paragraphs F–H) is the author's opinion about rock climbing.

Paragraph A – introduction to the sport of mountaineering, or rock climbing
Paragraph B – end of 19th century- arguments about fair climbing methods
Paragraph C – 1940s – more arguments
Paragraph D – 1970s – first environmental issues – clean climbing
Paragraph E – 1980s – 2 more techniques – safer, indoor climbing
Paragraph F – the environmental impact of climbing
Paragraph G – the future of rock climbing
Paragraph H – the author's opinion about the future of rock climbing

27 examples of the impact of climbers on ecosystems = **Paragraph F**
impact = effect
ecosystems = the environment

F Given the **environmental damage** rock climbing can cause, ... most rock climbers and mountaineers love the outdoors and have great respect for ... nature ... , **but** that in the pursuit of their goals they inevitably **trample** (=walk on and squash) **sensitive vegetation, damaging and disturbing delicate flora and lichens** (=climbers damage fragile plants) **which grow on ledges and cliff faces.** Two researchers ... , have found that **rock faces that are regularly climbed have lost up to 80% of the coverage and diversity of native plant species. If that were not bad enough, non-native species have also been inadvertently** (=not deliberately) **introduced, having been carried in on climbers' boots** (=climbers destroy up to 80% of native plants and carry in non-native plants on their boots).

28 an account of how politics affected rock climbing = **Paragraph D**

account = description

Paragraph D describes government policies(=rules, guidelines).

D The USA, and much of the western world, was waking up to the damage it had been causing to the planet, and **environmentalist campaigns and new government policies were becoming widespread** (=many countries were introducing environmental laws). This new awareness and sensitivity to environmental issues spilled over into the rock climbing community. **As a result, ... 'clean climbing' became widely adopted** (=more common).

29 a less dangerous alternative to climbing rock faces = **Paragraph E**

alternative = a different way of doing something

E Not everyone embraced the clean climbing movement, however. ... Because of this shift in focus, many amateur climbers have **flocked to** (=gone to) **indoor climbing gyms, where the risk** (=danger) **of serious harm is negligible** (=very small).

30 a recommendation for better regulation = **Paragraph H**

regulation = control

H In any event, ... Like many other forms of recreation, rock climbing has increasingly come under the fold of (=become controlled by) **institutional efforts to curb dangerous behaviour and properly manage our natural environments** (=institutions want to increasingly control and regulate rock climbing). ... , and **governing bodies** would do well to **consider heightening such efforts in the future** (=governments should do more regulation in the future).

31 a reference to a climber who did not use any tools or ropes for assistance = **Paragraph B**

assistance = help, aid

B Toward the end of the nineteenth century, however, developments in technology spurred (=encouraged) debate regarding climbing practices. ... Austrian Paul Preuss went so far as to **eschew** (=avoid) **all artificial aids, scaling astonishing heights using only his shoes and his bare hands** (=Paul Preuss climbed with no help, using only his shoes and hands; he used no aids for climbing) ...

32 examples of different types of people who use the outdoors for recreation = **Paragraph G**

for recreation = as a hobby

G This leaves rock climbing with an uncertain future. **Climbers are not the only user group that wishes to enjoy the wilderness** (=the wild outdoors) **– hikers, mountain bikers and horseback riders visit the same areas**, ... (examples of other users of the mountains)

Questions 33–39: Flow chart completion using words/numbers from the text

Locating the correct paragraph for the answers for these questions is not difficult, because of the dates at the top of each box. Each box corresponds to one paragraph in the history of rock climbing.

A rock climbing time line

Late 19th century

Some climbers discuss whether pitons and ropes should only be considered **33** **a safety net**.

34 **Albert Mummery** calls for guidelines based on unwritten rules which discourage climbing aids.

Paragraph B contains the answers for Questions 33 and 34.

B Toward the end of the nineteenth century (=late 19th century), however, developments in technology spurred debate regarding climbing practices. Of particular concern in this era was the introduction of **pitons** (=metal spikes that climbers hammer into the rock face for leverage) and the use of **belaying** (see footnote = fastening or controlling of a climber's rope by wrapping it around a metal device or another person)techniques. **A few** (climbers) such as Italian climber Guido Ray, supported these methods as ways to render climbing less burdensome and more 'acrobatic'. Others (other climbers) felt that they were **only of value as** **33** ***a safety net*** if all else failed. ... **34** ***Albert Mummery***, ... **developed the notion of 'fair means'** as a kind of **informal protocol** (=guidelines) by which the use of **'walk-through' guidebooks and equipment such as ladders and grappling hooks were discouraged.**

1940s

New equipment becomes controversial. Frank Smythe says that Mt Brussels is effectively 35 **unclimbed** because of the techniques that were used in order to scale the mountain.

scale = climb

Paragraph C contains the answer for Question 35.

C **By the 1940s,** bolts had begun to replace pitons as the climber's choice of equipment, and **criticism surrounding their use was no less fierce** (=bolts were also controversial). In 1948, when two American climbers scaled (=climbed) **Mount Brussels** in the Canadian Rockies **using a small number of pitons and bolts**, climber **Frank Smythe** wrote of their efforts: **'I still regard Mount Brussels as** 35 ***unclimbed***, ...

1970s

36 **Clean climbing** is more environmentally friendly. 37 **Nuts** are introduced as a climbing aid.

Paragraph D contains the answers for Questions 36 and 37.

D Climbing purists aside, it was not until **the 1970s** that the general tide (=popular opinion) began to turn against bolting and pitons. The USA, and much of the western world, was waking up **to the damage it had been causing to the planet** (=environmental damage), and **environmentalist campaigns** and new government policies were becoming widespread. This new **awareness and sensitivity to environmental issues spilled over into** (=was adopted by) **the rock climbing community. As a result,** a stripped-down style of rock climbing known as 36 ***'clean climbing'*** became widely adopted. Clean climbing helped preserve rock faces (environmentally friendly) and, compared with older approaches, it was much simpler to practise. This was partly due to **the hallmark** (=main feature) **of clean climbing** – the use of 37 ***nuts*** – which were favoured over bolts because they could be placed into the rock wall with one hand while climbers maintained their grip on the rock with the other.

1980s – today

Climbers discuss the merits of new techniques for making hand holds, and also of 38 **rappel bolting**. Many say that climbing is now a test of physical strength and 39 **technical mastery** rather than of courage.

Paragraph E contains the answers for Questions 38 and 39.

E Not everyone embraced the clean climbing movement, however. **A decade later** (1980s), debates over **two more developments** were erupting. The first (development) related to the practice of chipping, in which climbers chip away pieces of rock in order to create **tiny cracks in which to insert their fingers** (=hand holds). **The other major point of contention** (development which was a problem) was **a process that involves setting bolts in reverse from the top of the climb down** (definition of rappel bolting). 38 ***Rappel bolting*** makes almost any rock face climbable with relative ease, and as a result of this new technique, the sport has lost much of its risk factor and sense of pioneering spirit; indeed, it has become more about **muscle power** (=physical strength) and 39 ***technical mastery*** than **a psychological trial** (=test) **of fearlessness under pressure** (=courage).

Question 40: Multiple choice – title for the passage

All of the answers will be in the passage. Your task is to choose the one that best expresses the **main idea**.

40 (The most appropriate title for the passage is) **B Ethics and issues in rock climbing**

Ethics and issues (=the right, or correct, or best way) to do rock climbing and discussions about how to achieve this goal. This is mentioned throughout the passage.

Distractors for Question 40

A A history of rock climbing

This is mentioned in the first part of the reading passage, in Paragraphs A–E, but this title does not include any discussion about the best way to do rock climbing.

C Current trends in rock climbing

This is mentioned only at the very end of the reading passage.

D Sport climbers versus traditional climbers

Although sport climbers and traditional climbers are mentioned, the reading passage does not state that these two groups are different; in fact, many sport climbers were also traditional climbers, and vice versa.

General Training Reading and Writing Test 2

READING

Section 1: WHAT TO EXPECT FROM YOUR DELTA BANK CREDIT CARD

Questions 1–7: True, false, not given

Remember that the questions will follow the order of the reading passage.

1 You must report a lost or stolen credit card within 24 hours. **NOT GIVEN**

To report a lost or stolen card, phone the 24-hour toll-free number, 0800 700 007.

The reading passage does not tell you WHEN you should call this number.

2 To get a new card, you should appear in person at the bank. **TRUE**

appear in person at the bank = visit the bank yourself

To order a replacement card, call in at (=visit) your local branch of the Delta Bank.

3 You cannot buy more than $5,000 worth of goods in one day using your card. **TRUE**

Note that the answer to this question is located in the footnote at the bottom of the text. You need to read the heading for the section, the text **and** the footnote to answer this question.

Daily limits

...

Cash advances across the counter — Up to your available credit

Please note: available credit on this account is $5,000. (therefore you cannot spend more than $5,000 a day with this card)

4 If you lose your card, you must pay $25 for a new one. **TRUE**

The answer for this question is located inside the table.

Card replacement fee (=charge for getting a new card)

Charged on the day the card is ordered

$25 per card

5 If you don't use your card for 3 months, the card will be cancelled. **FALSE**

The answer for this question is located inside the table.

Inactivity fee (=charge for not using your card)

Charged after 12 weeks of no card activity

$12.50 (so you will have to pay $12.50, but your card will not be cancelled)

6 There is no charge for withdrawing cash using your card at an ATM. **NOT GIVEN**

The table tells you the fee for getting cash across the counter, that is, in the bank, but there is no cell in this table for ATM charges.

7 Credit card insurance is always charged each month. **FALSE**

The answer for this question is located inside the table.

Credit card insurance

Charged monthly on the statement presentation date when applicable (=when it applies to your account)

Calculated at the rate of 75 cents for every $100 owing on your monthly statement. No fee is charged if the monthly statement balance is zero. (therefore this fee is NOT charged every month)

Section 1: JOB ADVERTISEMENTS

Questions 8–14: Matching features

Note that there are 8 job advertisements and 7 job seekers, so one advertisement will not be used.

8 **C** a person with school-age children who used to sell cosmetics in a department store

cosmetics = make-up

Supremo Cleaning Products

Due to on-going growth of our company, we require an experienced salesperson (the job seeker has previous experience selling cosmetics); approx. 12–15 hours per week – flexible – can be worked around school hours (so this job would suit someone with school-age children). To fulfil this role you will need:

- experience in sales (the job seeker has previous experience selling cosmetics)
- excellent communication skills

Call in at the Supremo office, 15 Fairview Road, anytime between 9 a.m. and 5 p.m. to pick up an application form.

9 **E** a student looking for work over the long vacation

Café Kitchen Assistant required for the summer (=in the school holidays)

No previous kitchen experience necessary but must be a clean worker willing to learn.

We are open every day 7.30 a.m. – 9 p.m.

Apply in person – Teapot Café, the Strand.

10 **G** an ex-baker with some cooking experience who wants a job that finishes before 3.30 p.m. so that she can pick up her children after school

Café Express

Kitchen assistant wanted with experience in baking, cabinet food and short orders (=cooking experience) – must be able to work in an organised and safe manner.

We are looking for someone who has a passion for food and the right attitude towards the workplace.

If you are that person, and can commit to a five-hour working day, early start at 6 a.m. (so this job will finish at 11 a.m., and the job seeker can collect her children from school), please send your CV and a reference to:

The Manager, Café Express, 78 Providence Place

11 **H** a mother with school-age children who only wants to work a few hours per week

Tower Office Suite in the CBD

Reliable cleaner required for the above.

Hours of work (2.5 hours Mon–Fri) (short hours each day) flexible but must take place inside office hours (when the children are at school).

$15.00 per hour

Phone Mabel 025 262 3655

12 **F** a person with ten years' experience in the restaurant business who is looking for a well-paid permanent position

Night Duty Manager

Full-time, **permanent** manager required

Minimum (=at least) 3 years' experience in the restaurant trade (the job seeker has 10 years' experience)

Excellent wages (=well paid), meals provided

Phone Jake on 02 724 4798 at the Night Owl Restaurant after 7 p.m.

13 **B** an active parent who wants afternoons and weekends free to spend with his young children

Cleaner

We are looking for an energetic (=active) person to work night shifts from 11.30 p.m. to 7.00 a.m. Sunday evenings through to Friday mornings (so the weekends and afternoons will be free).

Phone Mr Simpson 027 456 987

14 **A** a person who has spent the last five years looking after her elderly parents but is now eager to get back into the workforce

get back into the workforce = get a job

Health Care Assistant

We are looking to recruit health care assistants for our rest home facility for the aged.

- This is a full-time position with immediate start.

- Relevant work experience an advantage (the job seeker has experience for this job)

If you are honest and reliable and comfortable around old people, this job is for you.

To apply please contact Miss Bridges on 02 566 2805

Section 2: OFFICE PROTOCOL (=how to behave in the office)

Questions 15–20: Matching paragraph headings

Note that the first one is done for you, and that you start with Paragraph B.

15 Paragraph **B = iii Remember your manners**

Paragraph B discusses **polite** office behaviour (=manners).

B You will get along better with your colleagues if you show consideration, courtesy and respect. Greet fellow workers every day by making eye contact and saying 'Hello' or 'Good morning'. Be polite – say 'please'. Be appreciative – say 'thank you'. Apologise if you have to interrupt someone; say 'sorry' if you make a mistake.

16 Paragraph **C = viii Be punctual**

be punctual = be on time

Paragraph C talks about being early or on time.

C To assist the smooth running of the workplace, be sure to get to work early or on time and never arrive late for a scheduled meeting.

17 Paragraph **D = ix Adhere to the dress code**

adhere to = follow

the dress code = the correct clothes for the office

Paragraph D discusses clothes for the office.

D Rules about appropriate attire (=clothes) may be unwritten, even unspoken (people may not talk about these and there may be no written rules), but rest assured (=you can be sure) there will be some. Ask if you are not sure, and only wear office outfits that are neat, clean and pressed (=ironed).

18 Paragraph E = vii Respect other people's property

The topic of Paragraph E is borrowing and returning other people's property.

E To maintain a pleasant working atmosphere amongst your colleagues, ask permission (say, can I please borrow your ... ?) before borrowing any item from another person's desk, no matter how small or insignificant; and, most importantly, **return it immediately** you have finished with it.

19 Paragraph F = i Be tidy

F Keep your work area and communal areas orderly and uncluttered (=tidy). This applies to common rooms like the kitchen, as well. Clean up after yourself and wipe down surfaces in the interests of both hygiene and collegial cooperation (=working happily together).

20 Paragraph G = iv Maintain good personal hygiene

maintain good personal hygiene = wash yourself so you don't smell

G Take a shower and clean your teeth before work (so that you won't smell) but avoid wearing overpowering deodorants, scents or aftershaves (=don't wear strong perfume). Be discreet if you need to re-apply makeup, adjust your clothing or blow your nose – the privacy of the bathroom is the best place for this.

Distractors for Questions 15–20

In this type of question the distractors (=unused headings or incorrect answers) are often found somewhere in the text, but either:

1. they are **not the main idea** of the paragraph, or
2. the **information** in the paragraph **does not match the heading**.

ii Use visual communication

This is briefly mentioned in Paragraph B, but it is not the main idea.

B Greet fellow workers every day by **making eye contact** and saying 'Hello' or 'Good morning'.

vi Use appropriate meeting etiquette

Meetings are mentioned in Paragraph C, but the topic of this paragraph is being on time.

C ... never arrive late for a scheduled **meeting**.

x Be trustworthy

This is a possible answer for Paragraph E, but it does not match the paragraph as well as the title 'Respect other people's property'.

E To maintain a pleasant working atmosphere amongst your colleagues, ask permission before borrowing any item from another person's desk, no matter how small or insignificant; and, most importantly, return it immediately you have finished with it.

Section 2: STAYING POSITIVE IN THE WORKPLACE

Questions 21–27: Summary completion using words from the passage

Remember that the summary will follow the order of the passage, but the grammar of each sentence may be changed so that the word order is different. You can write ONE or TWO words in each gap.

21 In general, people spend around 30% of their lifetime at work but often they are unhappy because of financial **insecurity**.

A On average, people spend about a third of their lives (=30% of their lifetime) at work. That's a lot of time to be miserable or depressed. These days, there is often a general atmosphere of anxiety and despondency at work (=people are unhappy at work) because of **21** ***insecurity***: the economy is depressed and many companies are downsizing, restructuring and making redundancies (people could lose their jobs, resulting in financial insecurity).

22 It may be difficult to stay positive but physical and mental illness can result from **chronic negativity**.

B Staying positive despite this is a challenge (=it may be difficult to stay positive) but it is important not to develop a negative attitude at work, especially if you already have a stressful workload. Beware: **22** ***chronic negativity*** may lead to long-term psychological and physical ill health (=physical and mental illness can result from chronic negativity).

23 In contrast, **optimists** feel better about themselves and enjoy their work more.

B On the other hand (=in contrast), **23** **optimists** have a greater sense of self-worth (=feel better about themselves) and are thus more likely to experience job satisfaction (=enjoy their work more) through an appreciation of their own achievements and productivity.

24 It is essential to eat well, get enough rest and **exercise**. Developing friendships and taking part in leisure activities are also important.

C Firstly, take care of your physical health with a wholesome diet (=eat well), **24** ***exercise*** and sufficient sleep (get enough rest). If work has taken over your life, find a balance: find and nurture friendships (=develop friendships) outside of work and do something in your free time (=take part in leisure activities) that is totally unrelated to your job.

25 Try to always be positive: your **affirmative attitude** could have a good effect on fellow employees.
affirmative attitude = positive attitude

D Focus on the good things rather than the bad (=try to always be positive), and smile more often – your **25** ***affirmative attitude*** may (=could) rub off on your colleagues (=have a good effect on fellow employees).

26 Learning new skills and taking on more responsibility will improve your **professional competence**, ...
professional competence = being good at your job

E If job security is causing anxiety, developing **26** ***professional competence*** is essential. Expand your skill set (=learn new skills) – take a course, become familiar with a new computer programme, tackle new tasks – and consider shouldering more responsibility (=taking on more responsibility) if you are not already overworked.

27 ... which will not only give you more expertise in your current job but also set you up for the **job market** if you need to seek new employment.

E Being pro-active and creative will not only keep you focussed, motivated and more in control of your work life (give you more expertise in your current job) but also <u>prepare you for</u> (=set you up for) the **27** ***job market*** if the worst should happen (if you need to seek new employment).

Section 3: ESPERANTO

Questions 28–34: Matching information to the text

Remember these questions do NOT follow the order of the text, and also that you will not use every paragraph, and you may use some paragraphs more than once.

OVERALL TEXT STRUCTURE:

Understanding the text structure will help you to find each answer. Of course you do not have time during the Reading test to write a list like the one below, but you do need to read and notice the paragraph topics.

Paragraph A – English as a world language

Paragraph B – The reason for developing Esperanto

Paragraph C – The beginning of Esperanto, and grammar rules

Paragraph D – Why Esperanto has not become a world language

Paragraph E – The history of Esperanto

Paragraph F – Places where Esperanto is used

28 the story of the <u>decline</u> of Esperanto as a world language = **Paragraph E**

<u>decline</u> = drop, fall

The story of something is its history.

E Historically, Esperanto has had its ups and downs. <u>Initially</u> (=at first) it was <u>well received</u> (=popular) but certain totalitarian <u>regimes</u> (=governments) became suspicious that people learning the language might be a <u>subversive</u> (=bad) influence (therefore governments did not like Esperanto), and consequently Esperanto groups and materials were <u>banned</u> (=forbidden) in those countries. After the Second World War, Esperanto was accepted and encouraged in East European and Asian countries that were looking for a common language and that wanted to avoid English because of its association with American ideology. It is thought that up to five million people may have learnt the language back then, but **since the 1970s** far fewer people have learned the language, and it is now not commonly used. (so it has declined)

29 examples of the international use of English = **Paragraph A**

Paragraph A is about English, not Esperanto.

A English is the common language (=international language) of science and technology, medicine, the aeronautical industry, banking and investment, movies and music, not to mention the Internet, where over 80% of the websites are in English. (many examples here)

30 two reasons why people do not like Esperanto = **Paragraph D**

D Its detractors (=people who do not like Esperanto) would say that its lack of success is due to the fact that it is an artificial or made-up language. (one reason) ... Another common objection to Esperanto (second reason) is that, despite Zamenhof's laudable (=good) intentions, his invented language is Eurocentric, in that it is based only on a small set of world languages.

31 the reason for the invention of Esperanto = **Paragraph B**

B Esperanto was conceived and created (=invented) by a Polish physician, Ludovic Zamenhof. In 19th-century Poland, Zamenhof saw many violent ethnic clashes (=wars because of different cultures and languages) and decided that language was the root (=the cause) of the problem. ... He had the grand vision (=big idea) of bringing peace to the world by giving people of different ethnic and linguistic backgrounds a standard, neutral language to converse (=talk) in. (so he developed Esperanto)

32 examples of situations where Esperanto has been used = **Paragraph F**

F Esperanto has made an appearance (=been used) from time to time in popular culture such as novels and films, usually when the author or director has wanted to introduce a foreign language without denoting (=representing) a specific ethnic or national group. There have even been a couple of feature films made completely in the language of Esperanto but mostly the language is used in futuristic productions (=movies about the future). There are also lively Esperanto conferences and meetings around the world.

33 a reason why English should not be the main international language = **Paragraph A**

A The argument for learning English would therefore seem quite compelling, but some (people) believe that the predominance (=it is very common) of English and its associated culture and attitudes is endangering, if not destroying, other customs and cultures. (so the use of English language also brings Western culture and ideas)

34 the results of a study which compared learning Esperanto to learning another language = **Paragraph C**

C Research (=a study) carried out in Germany shows that students who spend 1500 hours studying English can reach the same level of proficiency in Esperanto after studying for only 150 hours! (the results of the study)

Questions 35–40: True, false, not given

Remember that the questions will follow the order of the reading passage.

35 Ludovic Zamenhof was a doctor by profession. **TRUE**

B In fact, there has been such a language in existence for over a hundred years. Esperanto was conceived and created by a Polish physician (=doctor), Ludovic Zamenhof.

36 Zamenhof spent several years learning Latin and Greek. **NOT GIVEN**

B His (Zamenhof's) first thoughts were to restore Latin or classical Greek as a lingua franca, but he soon decided that both these languages were too complex and difficult to learn, (but this passage does not state whether Zamenhof studied these languages, nor for how long he studied them) and thus he embarked upon the project of developing an entirely new language.

37 All nouns in Esperanto end in *-o*. **FALSE**

The key word in the question is 'all'.

C A sample of the grammar shows us that all common nouns in the singular (so, not proper nouns, and not plurals) end in *-o*.

38 One way of making a new word is to add more letters to an existing word. **TRUE**

C Zamenhof originally published a list of 900 root words (=base words) which could be increased to make many thousands of words by using prefixes and suffixes (=short combinations of letters at the beginning or end of the word) and joining words together to make compounds.

39 Idioms in Esperanto are rare. **TRUE**

C What is more, because the main aim of Esperanto is to make communication uncomplicated and easy, there are **very few idiomatic expressions** or slang words.

40 Esperanto represents a true world language. **FALSE**

D Another common objection to Esperanto is that, despite Zamenhof's laudable intentions, his invented language is Eurocentric, in that it is based only on a small set of world languages. (so it is not a true world language) Thus, it can still be accused of being culturally biased and narrow (=similar to only some of the world's languages) in its vocabulary, structures and pronunciation.

Academic Test 3

LISTENING

Section 1: NEW PASSWORD

Questions 1–10: Form completion

New Password

Example Call taken by: **Natasha**

You will hear an introduction to the first 7 questions of Section 1 of the Listening test. Then you will have 20 seconds to preview these questions and to predict (guess) the answers you are listening for.

There is an example to introduce this section. The audio for the example will be played first, with an explanation of the answer. After that, the full conversation will be played once only. This includes the example part of the recording.

Example:
Predict to hear: a name.

[01:24]

NATASHA: Good evening. This is Web Net and you're speaking with ***Natasha***. How can I assist you today?

MICHAEL: Hello, ***Natasha***. I tried to log in to my Web Net account yesterday and I realised I'd forgotten my password. Are you able to help me with that?

Customer's full name: Michael 1 **Simmons**

Predict to hear: a surname, or family name

Note that you will need to be familiar with some basic computing/telecommunications vocabulary in order to complete this listening.

e.g. log in, modem, Internet, password, broadband ...

[02:15]

NATASHA: Of course. What I'll need to do is ask you a few questions to check your identity, and then I'll issue you with a new password. Is that okay? (introduction text)

MICHAEL: No problem.

NATASHA: Firstly, can I have your **full name** (key words for the form) please?

MICHAEL: Michael 1 ***Simmons***, **S-I-M-M-O-N-S**. I don't have a middle name.

Date of birth: 27 March 1988
Previous address: 319 2 **Ocean Drive**
East Providence

Predict to hear: a street name after the house number

[02:36]

NATASHA: Great. And your **date of birth** (key words for the form)?

MICHAEL: It's the 27/3/1988.

NATASHA: Right, and I also need to know your previous address.

MICHAEL: I live at 12 Wake Street, and that's in ...

NATASHA: We have that as your current address. (distractor text) What was the address you registered with us before you moved there?

MICHAEL: Oh, yeah. I used to live at **319** (key number for the form) 2 ***Ocean Drive***. That's in East Providence.

Phone number: 0492 48002
Data allowance: 3 **unlimited**

Predict to hear: a number OR a word

[03:00]

NATASHA: I'll just need your contact phone number as well.

MICHAEL: That's 0-4-9-2, 4-8-0-0-2.

NATASHA: And just a few questions about your account. Do you know what your **current data allowance** (key words for the form) is?

MICHAEL: I upgraded to the Gold account not long ago, so it's 3 ***unlimited***.

NATASHA: Yes – unlimited data. (repetition of answer)

Current payment plan: 4 **24-month**

Predict to hear: a length of time

[03:17]

NATASHA: Yes – unlimited data. Right, now can you just tell me about your **payment plan** (key words for the form)? Which plan are you currently on, do you know?

MICHAEL: Oh, hang on a minute while I think. Yes ... I started off with the **12-month** (distractor text) automatic renewal, but a few months ago I switched to the 4 ***24-month*** plan.

Mother's maiden name: 5 White

Predict to hear: a family name, or surname

[03:35]

NATASHA: That's fine. Now, when you first registered for Web Net, you selected two secret questions and provided us with the answers. In order to issue you with a new password I need you to answer those questions for me. Firstly, what is your **mother's maiden name** (key words for the form)?

MICHAEL: My mother's name is Sarah. That's Sarah with an H.

NATASHA: That sounds like her first name. (distractor text) We're looking for her maiden name – that's her family name before she was married.

MICHAEL: Sorry, I misheard. It's, um ... 5 ***White***.

NATASHA: White as in the colour? (repetition of answer)

MICHAEL: Yes, that's right.

First pet: 6 (a) goldfish

Predict to hear: a kind of pet animal

[04:12]

NATASHA: Now, the other question you chose to answer: What was your **first pet** (key words for the form)?

MICHAEL: The first pet I ever had?

NATASHA: Yes.

MICHAEL: It was actually 6 ***a goldfish***.

New password sent on: 7 30(th) June / June 30(th)

Predict to hear: a date

Note all the different options for writing the date

[04:23]

NATASHA: That's what it says on your file! ... Okay, that's all done for you, Mr Simmons. I've sent you a generic (=same for everyone) password, which should arrive in your e-mail box within a few minutes (distractor text). I'll just make a note of the **date** (key word for the form) ... 7 ***30th of June***. When you log in, I suggest you go to the Member's Details section on the website and change it to something you're going to remember. (distractor text)

MICHAEL: Wonderful, thanks.

Extra services requested: New 8 cable

Predict to hear: a noun – computer related

[05:20]

NATASHA: **Is there anything else I can help you with** (=extra services) **today?** (key words for the form)

MICHAEL: Yeah, there are a few things. I've been having some connection issues recently. I think the problem is with the 8 ***cable*** that connects the modem to the computer. Do you supply those?

NATASHA: You need a new cable? (repetition of answer) Not a problem. I'll arrange for that to be sent off tomorrow.

Cancel 9 home phone

Predict to hear: a noun – probably computer related

[05:39]

MICHAEL: Thanks. Also, I'm currently signed up for three of your services – home phone, mobile and broadband. I use the Internet a lot, on my computer and on my mobile, but to be honest I never use the 9 ***home phone*** and I don't see why I should keep paying for that plan.

NATASHA: Would you like me to **cancel** that **home phone** for you? (key word for the form and repetition of answer)

MICHAEL: Yes, please, if you wouldn't mind.

NATASHA: Done. Is there anything else?

10 security pack

Predict to hear: an adjective – some kind of pack

[06:02]

MICHAEL: Yes, just one last thing. Do you offer any **anti-virus products** (=software to stop viruses on the computer)?

NATASHA: Yes, we have one which offers full protection against viruses, **spam** (=unwanted email) and identity theft, which is useful if you're doing any online banking and that kind of thing. It's called the 10 ***security*** pack.

MICHAEL: **Sounds perfect. Sign me up for one of those, please.** (=I would like a security pack)

NATASHA: And we've got another one – it's called the parenting pack – it prevents your children from accessing harmful websites and downloading things they shouldn't.

MICHAEL: I'm not so worried about that anymore. Both my children are adults and have left home ... so, just the security pack, thanks. That's everything. (distractor text)

Section 2: HOLIDAY HOUSE RENTAL

Questions 11–16: Matching features

The items that you need to match to their locations are given in the same order as the audio, but the locations are NOT in the order of the audio. Use your preparation time to carefully read each location.

Remember that most or all of the locations given, including the distractor locations, will be mentioned somewhere in the audio. You need to listen carefully for the item, and then for its location.

11 D alarm = next to back door

[08:02]

MAN: Hello, Ron Smith speaking.

WOMAN: Hi. This is Kayla Lawton. I signed up with the Holiday House agency to rent your beach house (introduction text) but the agent isn't available today and I have a problem – I can't remember what she said about the **alarm** (key word for Question 11) system.

MAN: Oh, it's quite simple really. The main thing to remember is to enter by the **back door** which leads into the kitchen because that is where the alarm is situated– right next to the light switch **just beside the door**. If you go through the front door into the living room, it will take you longer to reach the alarm and you only have a few seconds to deactivate it (=turn it off). The code is 3498. (distractor text)

12 B other keys = in hallway cupboard

[08:45]

MAN: The agent will have given you the back and front door keys (distractor text), but there are **other keys** (key words for Question 12) that you may need – for the garage, the laundry and the little garden shed (distractor text). You'll find them hanging on a hook **inside the cupboard in the hallway** next to the hot water cupboard (distractor – next to the hot water cupboard, not inside it).

13 H laundry detergent = **under kitchen sink**

[09:02]

MAN: ... The laundry room is outside, next to the garage. It should be kept locked, so please remember to return the key to the hook when you've done your washing. The last tenant lost it somewhere in the garden and I had to have the lock replaced. There should be some **laundry detergent** (key words for Question 13) for the washing machine next to the dishwashing liquid **under the kitchen sink**.

14 A beach towels = **on washing machine**

[09:25]

MAN: ... Oh, now about the linen. The sheets are already on the beds and there are lots of **towels** (key word for Questions 14–15) at the house, too. Of course you'll want to enjoy that lovely, safe swimming beach as much as possible. You'll find a pile of **beach towels** (key words for Question 14) in a basket **on the washing machine**. Feel free to take these to the beach with you. We have lots of them, and they're pretty old, so it doesn't matter if they get a bit dirty or sandy (=covered with sand). (distractor text)

15 C bath towels = **in hot water cupboard**

[09:50]

MAN: ... There are other, newer **towels for use in the bathroom only** (=bath towels); these are **in the hot water cupboard** (in the hot water cupboard, not beside it), on the shelf up above the cylinder (=container for the hot water) – please don't take these ones down to the beach (distractor text).

16 **G** light bulbs = **in shoebox**

[10:04]

MAN: ... Ah, what else? Oh, yes. I should tell you that the electricity supply is generally reliable but sometimes there are power surges (=changes in the power level) which make a few **light bulbs** (key words for Question 16) blow (=break). If that happens, don't worry, there are spare **light bulbs in a shoebox** on the chest of drawers (distractor text) in the bedroom. That reminds me, the main power supply is switched off at the **mains box** (=electrical switchboard), which is above the front door. The first thing to do when you arrive is to pull down the large **lever** (=switch) – it's clearly labelled 'mains switch' – you don't need to touch any of the other switches. (distractor text)

Questions 17–20: Notes completion

Difficult parking in town at the weekend because of so many **17** **tourists**

Predict to hear: a plural noun

[11:16]

Oh, one more thing – something that might interest you is a folder of local information – you know the sort of thing, interesting places to visit, opening hours for the shops and services in the town ... plus a little map of local walks. It's on top of the TV along with the remote control. (distractor text) **Parking in the town is usually really easy except for weekends** (key words for Question 17) when the place is **swamped** (=crowded) with **17** ***tourists***, so I would recommend doing your shopping on weekdays.

Museum is closed on **18** **Monday(s)**.

Predict to hear: one or more days of the week

[11:45]

Oh, one thing though, if you want to combine a shopping expedition (=trip) with a visit to the **Early History Museum** (key words for Question 18), you should know that it's **not open** (=closed) on **18** ***Mondays***.

Recommended places to eat:
- 19 **Happy Dragon** for Chinese food
- Pizzeria for Italian food

Predict to hear: a restaurant name

[11:56]

There are lots of **good places to eat** (key words for Question 19) in town, too. You'll find a list of menus and takeaway (=takeout) prices for some of the more popular local cafés and restaurants. (distractor text) If you like **Chinese** (key word for Question 19), the 19 ***Happy Dragon*** has excellent food, or I'd recommend the Pizzeria if you prefer Italian – they have a good selection of takeaway pasta and pizza as well. The Happy Dragon (repetition of answer) is a firm favourite with the locals, though.

Phone number for takeaway pizza – 20 **3231190**

Predict to hear: a phone number

[12:24]

Both restaurants deliver, free of charge, but note the **phone numbers** (key words for Question 20) have changed since the menus were printed. 20 **Phone *3-2-3-1-1-9-0* for pizza** and 3-2-3-9-9-1-1 (distractor text) for Chinese. You won't be disappointed.

Section 3: STUDENT INTERNSHIP FEEDBACK

Questions 21–25: Multiple choice

21 Why did Diana accept the offer from Gregory Associates?

A It covered her travel expenses.

B It was from a well-known company.

C It was the only offer she received.

You should expect to hear ALL of the reasons mentioned in the audio. Your job is to decide which one made Diana choose Gregory Associates.

[14:03]

PROF: Thanks for coming in today to discuss your internship experience (=practical work experience during a course of study). Completing some sort of work experience, like an internship, is a core (=key, central) part of our Master's programme, and we want to make sure students are able to make the most of it. (introduction text)

DIANA: That's fine.

PROF: So, as I understand, you were offered an internship by Gregory Associates. Is that correct?

DIANA: Actually, I got offers from a few companies (therefore Gregory Associates was NOT the only offer she received), but Gregory Associates was the only one I seriously considered.

PROF: **Was there any reason for that?** (key text for Question 21)

DIANA: Yeah. They didn't offer the best conditions – some of the other companies were offering to cover transportation and other living costs (but NOT Gregory Associates), that kind of thing – but I knew Gregory Associates was a **widely recognised leader** (=well-known company) in the industry, and that was the big factor for me.

22 Diana was disappointed because

A she found the work routine repetitive.

B the staff were not very helpful.

C the work was not related to her studies.

You should expect to hear ALL the reasons mentioned in the audio. Your job is to decide which one made Diana disappointed.

[14:47]

PROF: And were you happy with your choice? (key text for Question 22)

DIANA: Well, yes and no.

PROF: Mixed feelings (=both happy and unhappy)?

DIANA: Yeah. I mean, **don't get me wrong** (=don't misunderstand me) – everyone in the office was great. They didn't **talk down to me** (=make me feel small) and they were always happy to assist if I wasn't sure about something (so the staff were very helpful).

PROF: Was it the work, then? Some students do find internships a little tedious and boring.

DIANA: It's not that it was boring. I was doing new things every day (therefore the work routine was not repetitive), and I loved that. They really **kept me on my toes** (=I had to work hard). It's just that, I'm studying economics, you know? But most of the projects I was assigned to involved more ... administrative stuff ... It just **wasn't relevant to** (=wasn't related to) what I've been studying.

23 What did Diana like best about her internship?

A Observing how the workplace operates

B Being responsible for completing projects

C Working closely with the project managers

You should expect to hear ALL the items mentioned in the audio. Your job is to decide which one Diana did, or liked best.

[15:27]

PROF: I'm sorry to hear that. I'll make a note of it. Let's talk about the good things. **What did you particularly enjoy about the experience?** (key text for Question 23)

DIANA: Well, as an intern, the managers do tend to **keep you at arm's length** – they just don't trust you enough to let you take on a lot of responsibility for the big projects (this is an explanation of the term 'at arm's length'). (therefore she was not responsible for completing projects, nor did she work closely with the managers)

PROF: That's understandable.

DIANA: Yes, but in a way, I liked that – because I got to **stand back and watch** (=observe), and get a real sense of how a company like that **runs** (=operates) on a day-to-day basis. And that was **the highlight** (=what I liked best) for me.

24 What was the hardest part of the internship?

A Combining it with her studies

B Living on so little money

C Working such long hours

You should expect to hear ALL the items mentioned in the audio. Your job is to decide which one was the hardest for Diana.

[16:00]

PROF: That's great to hear. How did you find managing the internship alongside your study commitments?

DIANA: Well, because my internship was over the summer break, that wasn't an issue for me at all. (therefore there was no problem with combining the internship with her studies)

PROF: Okay. What would you say was the biggest struggle (=problem) then?

DIANA: In the beginning, I might have said the hours (of work). Those 6 a.m. starts were tough! But I quickly got used to that (so this was not the biggest problem). In **retrospect** (=looking back), the biggest difficulty was **getting by** (=managing) **on such a tight budget** (=little money). As I wasn't earning anything, the whole experience really **drained** (=reduced) my savings account.

25 During the internship, Diana

A changed her mind about her career.

B received a job offer from the company.

C decided not to continue her studies.

You should expect to hear ALL reasons mentioned in the audio. Your job is to decide which one made Diana disappointed.

[16:32]

PROF: Yeah, that can be tough. And my last question: what was the **outcome** (=result) of this internship for you? Some of our students are lucky enough to get offers of employment before finishing.

DIANA: At first, I was hoping I would be one of them. In the end I wasn't (so she did not receive a job offer), but I'm happy about that now.

PROF: Why's that?

DIANA: Well, over the course of the internship, I ended up reconsidering whether this industry is really **for me** (=suitable for me) after all. I'm going to finish my degree (so Answer C is incorrect), because I'm only a semester away from graduation now, but then after that I've decided to pursue a different line of work (so she has changed her mind about her career).

PROF: Well, I do hope you're successful with that.

Questions 26–30: Flow chart completion

Organise your **26** .... in advance

Research a variety of companies

Create a **27** .... of appropriate positions

28 .... the applications for each position

29 .... the companies after one week

Prepare for the interview

30 .... during the interview

Note that you are required to write NO MORE THAN TWO WORDS. You will be penalised if you write three or more words.

Flow charts describe a process. Listen carefully for linking words and expressions that indicate the next stage in the process.

26 Organise your **documents** in advance

[17:43]

PROF: Now, we're putting together a step-by-step guide about the process for students who want to apply for internships (introduction text for a process), and we were wondering if you could help us with it.

DIANA: Sure.

PROF: What would you say is the first step (Stage 1 of the process)?

DIANA: **Before they do anything else** (=in advance), students need to get their 26 ***documents*** sorted. Companies need to see all sorts of things, such as reference letters and verified copies of academic transcripts (examples of documents). It can take time to get it all together, so applicants need to **get onto this** (=organise this) as soon as possible.

27 Create a **shortlist** of appropriate positions

[18:15]

PROF: Great, we'll put that down as Number One. And then (Stage 2) students should begin researching companies?

DIANA: Absolutely. They should look at a wide range of companies and the internships they offer. They really shouldn't limit themselves at that stage.

PROF: It would be **time-consuming** (=take a long time) to apply to them all, though.

DIANA: Yeah, so I think they need to **weed out** (=eliminate) those positions they are not qualified for or that **don't meet their own needs and interests** (=are not appropriate), and then put together (=create) a 27 ***shortlist*** consisting only of those positions that are a good match.

28 **Alter/alter** the applications for each position

[18:47]

PROF: And then? (Stage 3)

DIANA: Well, the next part is the applications, of course. I think the big mistake here is that some students just send the same cover letter and the same CV to each company, when in reality every position is a little bit different. They really need to **28** ***alter*** their applications so that they refer to the individual needs of each position.

29 **Call/call** the companies after one week

[19:09]

PROF: I'll make a note of that. And should students follow up on their applications? (Stage 4)

DIANA: I think so. It's best to **29** ***call*** each company – an e-mail is too easy to ignore or delete. And not too soon, either – a **week** (key word for the flow chart) after the applications have been submitted is probably ideal.

30 **Ask/ask questions** during the interview

[19:28]

PROF: So if they get an interview, what's next? (Stage 5)

DIANA: Obviously they need to prepare. For me this included all sorts of things, like practising my body language in front of the mirror and researching common interview questions online.

PROF: Any tips for the interview itself?

DIANA: Most students are so obsessed with having the right answers, but I think the most important thing is actually to **30** ***ask questions***. It shows the employer that you are genuinely interested in their company and in the position.

Section 4: DEVELOPMENT STUDIES

Questions 31–40: Notes completion

Note that you are required to write NO MORE THAN ONE WORD. You will be penalised if you write two or more words.

Development Studies attempts to understand:

- how societies change and progress over time
- what 31 **actions** help to make these changes

[21:52]

Development Studies, as a discipline, can be **boiled down to** (=reduced to) **a couple of** (=2) core objectives (=main aims). Basically, we are trying to understand how it is that societies experience particular kinds of change and how they progress as they develop (=change and progress over time). We're also trying to go beyond that, however, and work out how different sorts of 31 ***actions*** can **facilitate** (=make possible) or even encourage these changes to happen.

Two approaches:

- theoretical (understand how change occurs)
- applied (examine particular 32 **policies** and how they can be applied)

[22:18]

To achieve these objectives, there are **two key approaches** (key words for the notes) that **underpin** (=form the basis of) Development Studies. Firstly, there's a **theoretical** (key word for the notes) approach, which is all about the 'how' of change. With theory we can explore some of the big questions: What kind of change should we aspire to, and how can this be achieved? But **we don't just talk** (=we are practical as well as theoretical); we've also got to **apply** (key word for the notes) some of this thinking. So through the **applied approach** (repetition of key words) we're looking at specific 32 ***policies***, and trying to understand how they can most effectively be put into place (=applied).

Areas of focus:
Asia-Pacific region; urbanisation (including employment and 33 **housing**); migration and trade

[22:56]

Although we try not to limit ourselves, we do focus on a few key areas. Due to our location, for example, the **Asia-Pacific region** (key words for the notes) is an important area of research for us. At the moment we're doing a lot of work on **urbanisation** (=moving to cities), and there are two elements to this. One is **employment** (key word for the notes), as urbanisation leads to major employment problems, and the other is 33 ***housing*** – with so many people moving to cities, many of them struggle to find a place to live. Other issues of particular interest to our staff are **migration** and, of course, **trade**. (these words indicate that the answer will come before this point)

You will develop the skills to:

- understand key development issues in detail
- gather data (both 34 **statistics** and textual data)
- carefully 35 **evaluate** findings
- 36 **cooperate** on a research project

[23:38]

So what will you be able to do with a degree in Development Studies? Well, firstly, you'll develop a full working knowledge of all aspects of development (=learn skills to understand development issues). You'll also learn how to **gather data** (key words for the notes). We include sessions on how to gather 34 ***statistics***, but we mostly focus on **textual data** (the answer will come before this phrase), that is, policy briefings, research reports, and so on. Once you've done your research, you need to know what it all means; after all, there's not much point in collecting a whole lot of data if you don't know whether it is significant or not (distractor text) – so we're going to teach you how to critically 35 ***evaluate*** your findings (=understand your research). And finally, **teamwork** (key word for the notes) is a big part of development work – your major piece of research work for this class is done in groups of four, so you're going to learn how to 36 ***cooperate*** as a team in order to plan and conduct this **research assignment** (=research project).

Brief history of Development Studies:

1950s – The discipline emerged. 37 **Economic** issues were the major consideration.

[24:37]

I want to move on now to give you a brief overview of how Development Studies has evolved as a discipline since it was first established (a brief history of Development Studies).

The first thing to note is that, unlike other subjects, such as mathematics or philosophy, Development Studies is very young. It began **taking shape** (=emerging) as a formal discipline only in the **1950s** (key word for the notes). At that stage, 37 ***economic*** concerns were **at the forefront of** (=the most important factor in) nearly all research efforts. Researchers assumed that development in general could be measured by indicators such as Gross Domestic Product (GDP), or unemployment levels. (distractor text)

1970s – Development Studies became more critical of common 38 **practices** and underlying assumptions. Questions were raised about power, environmental sustainability and unequal 39 **gender** issues.

[25:18]

In the **1970s** (key word for the notes), a new set of scholars took charge. These researchers, informed by the social movements of the 1960s, brought a new set of issues to the table. (distractor text) At that time, **Development Studies** (key words for the notes) grew increasingly critical of established 38 ***practices***, and the **assumptions** (=ideas) that lay behind these practices. Questions were raised in three areas: the role of power in creating policy, the importance of **environmentally sustainable change** (=working to protect the environment) (key words for the notes), and **problems** (=issues) with **inequalities in terms of** 39 ***gender*** (=unequal gender issues).

1980s–today – National governments were no longer as important. Growing interest in small-scale practices such as giving very small 40 **loans**.

[25:56]

From the **1980s** (key word for the notes) onwards, the economy **staged**

a comeback as a centrepiece of development practice (=became a central focus once more). A key factor here was the reduced significance of **national governments** (key words for the notes) due to a number of market-led reforms in many countries around the world. (distractor text) In contrast to the 1950s, however, researchers have recently shown a heightened interest in **smaller-scale economic projects** (key words for the notes). One significant innovation (=new idea) here is the idea of making tiny (=very small) **40** ***loans***, sometimes only a few dollars, to help women, in particular, to start up a small business.

READING

Reading Passage 1: KNIGHTHOODS

Questions 1–6: True, false, not given

In this practice test, the True / False / Not Given questions are the first set of questions, so it is likely that the answers will be found at the beginning of the passage.

1 The knighthood was first awarded only for military service. **TRUE**

knight = a soldier who had an important position in the army and normally fought on horseback

knighthood = title/name/job of a knight

military service = fighting in wars

A Knighthoods are one of the oldest and most prestigious forms of honouring individual citizens in the United Kingdom. Although **initially conferred upon** (=first awarded to) **members of the armed forces** (=soldiers and the navy) **solely** (=only) **on the basis of their performance in combat** (=for good fighting skills), the award now recognises all contributions to national life.

2 Most knights now come from the arts and entertainment industries. **NOT GIVEN**

A **Some** ('some' is not the same as 'most') of the most notable knighthoods of recent times have been bestowed (=given) on musicians or entertainers such as Sir Elton John and Sir Paul McCartney, and the fields of finance, industry and education are also represented. (we are not told how many knights come from each area, and 'some' is not the same as 'most')

3 People from outside the Commonwealth cannot be awarded any type of knighthood. **FALSE**

A Citizens of non-Commonwealth[1] countries **are eligible for** (=can be awarded) an 'honorary' knighthood for which they are not permitted to use the titles 'Sir' or 'Dame'. (therefore, there is a type of knighthood for people outside the Commonwealth)

4 The knighthood began in Great Britain. **FALSE**

A **Perceived to be a British tradition** (=many people believe that the tradition is British), (BUT) the legacy of knighthoods actually dates back to **ancient Rome** (=the tradition comes from ancient Rome), from where it spread throughout a number of European countries in the Middle Ages and acquired certain features.

5 Esquires, or trainee knights, were usually related to the knights they served. **NOT GIVEN**

esquires = knights who were being trained

A A would-be knight had to undergo strict military instruction from a young age, which included spending time as an assistant (known as an esquire) to an existing knight, and participating in battle. He had to learn how to equip his knight for battle, and to help him with putting on the heavy and cumbersome armour of the time. He was responsible for keeping this armour in good condition, polishing and cleaning it. He also had to demonstrate chivalrous behaviour such as generosity, selflessness, fearlessness and skill in battle. (there is a lot of information about the training of esquires, but nothing is given about whether they were related to their knights)

6 An esquire needed money to buy his own equipment. **TRUE**

A Finally, the potential knight also required (=needed) **the financial means** (=money) **to purchase horses, weapons and armour for himself** (=to buy his own equipment), and then make himself available to serve the ruling monarch for a minimum period each year.

Questions 7–10: Summary completion using words/numbers from the text

In this practice test, the summary question is the second set of questions, so it is likely that the answers will be located near the True / False / Not Given questions. In this summary, there is some overlap between the text used for TFNG and the summary text, and the summary does not follow exactly the same order as the text.

Notice also that, in this set of questions, every answer has THREE words and all answers include an article (a, an, the) as the first word. Remember to take every answer directly from the text; do NOT change the word forms from the text in your answers.

Knighthood Selection: Then and Now

The process of becoming a knight has changed over time. In the Middle Ages, people began training to become a knight at 7 **a young age**. They had to show they were brave and skilled fighters, and were required to work for 8 **the ruling monarch** for part of the year. Today, potential recipients of the knighthood are selected through 9 **a nominations system**. A final decision is made by 10 **an advisory panel**.

A Perceived to be a British tradition, the legacy of knighthoods actually dates back to ancient Rome, from where it spread throughout a number of European countries **in the Middle Ages** and acquired certain features. A would-be knight had to undergo strict military instruction (=training to become a knight) from 7 ***a young age***, which included spending time as an assistant to an existing knight, and participating in battle. He had to ... He also had to **demonstrate** (=show) chivalrous behaviour such as generosity, selflessness, **fearlessness and skill in battle** (=show he was a brave and skilled fighter). Finally, the potential knight also **required** the financial means to purchase horses, weapons and armour for himself, and then (he was also required to) make himself available to **serve** (=work for) 8 ***the ruling monarch*** for a minimum period each year (=for part of the year).

B In modern times (=today), the process is very different. (this sentence relates to the FIRST sentence of the summary) Instead of relying on formalised military training or political patronage, 9 ***a nominations system*** is used. (the information about this answer comes after the key words in the text) This way, a person's name **can be put forward for a knighthood** (=suggested, or nominated, for a knighthood) by any institution such as a school or business, or even just a fellow member of society. After this, 10 ***an advisory panel*** (the information about this answer comes after the key words in the text), acting on behalf of the sovereign, **deliberates and selects** (=makes the final decision) the future knights and dames (=female knights) from the pool of applications.

Questions 11–13: Multiple choice

Note that, in these questions with multiple answers, you can write the answers in any order on your paper. Note also that the options for this question are not written in the same order as in the reading passage.

11–13 Which **THREE** of the following are reasons given in the text for people losing their knighthoods?

A Punishing someone for a crime he or she did not commit

B Using another person's name on an important paper

C Poor management of a company

D Wrongfully accepting pension payments

E Gambling on horseracing or card games

F Giving secret information to a foreign government

The information to answer this set of questions is in the last two paragraphs, which describe how knighthoods can be revoked, or forfeited (=lost).

C In rare cases, knighthoods can be revoked (=taken away, or lost) through a process known as forfeiture. This most often occurs when the recipient **is convicted of a criminal offense** (=commits a crime). (examples of crimes follow) Terry Lewis, a police officer in Queensland, Australia, was stripped of his knighthood after being implicated in (connected to) a string of illegal activities that included accepting $700,000 worth of bribes from bookmakers and casinos, and **forging the signature of an Australian politician on a police document** (=using another person's name on an important paper) in 1981. Lewis has repeatedly protested his innocence and suggested that he was falsely accused of these crimes, but his appeals failed in court. In a more serious incident, British art historian and intelligence officer, Anthony Blunt, lost his knighthood after it was discovered that he was **working as a double agent and handing confidential material over to the Soviet Union** (=giving secret information to a foreign government).

D Knighthoods have also been forfeited for **reasons of incompetence** (=for poor performance) rather than outright illegality or treason. (example follows) Having been knighted for 'services to banking' in 2004, CEO of the Royal Bank of Scotland, Fred Goodwin, **presided over a 24-billion-pound loss at the bank** (=he was the boss when the bank lost 24 billion pounds) just four years later. Although retaining a 16-million-pound pension, to which he was legally entitled, Goodwin had his knighthood annulled as the Queen's advisory panel deemed him 'the chief decision maker at the time'. (therefore he lost his knighthood for poor management of a company)

Distractors for Questions 11–13

These distractors will be included in the paragraph, but the information will not match the M/C option given.

A Punishing someone for a crime he or she did not commit

C Lewis has repeatedly protested his innocence and suggested that he was falsely accused of these crimes, but his appeals failed in court. (The distractor text states that Lewis says he was innocent of his crimes. However, he did not punish anyone; he was punished.)

D Wrongfully accepting pension payments

D Although retaining a 16-million-pound pension, ... (this distractor text mentions pensions, but does not state that Goodwin lost his knighthood for wrongfully accepting a pension payment)

E Gambling on horseracing or card games

C ... after being implicated in a string of illegal activities that included accepting $700,000 worth of bribes from bookmakers and casinos, ... (the crime was accepting bribes, not gambling)

Reading Passage 2: 'JUST DO IT!'

Questions 14–18: True, false, not given

In this practice test, the True / False / Not Given questions are the first set of questions, so it is likely that the answers will be found at the beginning of the passage.

14 Procrastination has **always** been recognised as a serious problem. **FALSE**

The key word in this sentence is 'always'.

procrastinate = to be slow to do something, to put off doing something until later

A Procrastination, **a kind of chronic time-wasting** (definition of procrastination), has **long been dismissed as an innocuous** (=harmless) **human foible** (=minor problem). (=for a long time, people thought procrastination was not a serious problem)

15 The reason for the rise in procrastination is unknown. **TRUE**

A Researchers are now beginning a more sober examination of this practice, however, and there may be good reason for doing so: twenty per cent of Americans now admit to suffering from procrastination, a fifteen per cent jump (=rise) from 1970. **Researchers are bemused** (=unsure) **as to what explains this sharp rise in the figures** (=researchers don't know why there is a rise in procrastination), but there is no doubt that procrastination is wreaking havoc (=causing a lot of trouble) on people's lives.

16 Students are the most likely group to procrastinate. **NOT GIVEN**

A In one study, over the course of a semester, **procrastinating university students** were noted to be suffering from notably weaker immune systems, more gastrointestinal problems (=problems with the stomach (gastro) and the intestines (intestinal)), and higher occurrences of insomnia than their non-procrastinating peers. (the text mentions students but does not state that they are the most likely group to procrastinate; instead it talks about their health problems)

17 A range of health problems have been linked to procrastination. **TRUE**

A range of health problems = many health problems

A But there are other costs too. In shifting burdens of responsibility onto others and reneging on their promises, procrastinators undermine relationships both in the workplace and in their private lives, all of which takes a toll on their well-being. In one study, over the course of a semester, procrastinating university students were noted to be **suffering from notably weaker immune systems, more gastrointestinal** (=stomach and intestines) **problems, and higher occurrences of insomnia** (=inability to sleep) **than their non-procrastinating peers.** (this is a range, or list, of health problems suffered by procrastinators)

18 Most techniques to stop procrastination are based on scientific study. **FALSE**

techniques = methods

B Is there hope for procrastinators? Everyone admits it's a difficult demon to beat (=a hard character trait to overcome), but a few self-styled procrastination coaches (=instructors) have developed strategies to that end. **Although evidence for their efficacy** (=how well they work) **is largely anecdotal** (=based on individual examples, not on research or scientific study) at this stage, some of these strategies at least offer promising avenues for future research.

Questions 19–25: Matching features

In this set of questions, the options are people's names. These are listed in the order that they appear in the text. Therefore, you need to find Amy Sykes first. The statements that match each person are NOT in the order of the passage, so you need to read the advice that each person gives carefully, and match this to the best paraphrase. Note that there are 3 people and 7 statements, so it is likely that each person will match to more than one statement.

19 **B** Doing housework is a common way of avoiding important work. **Raymond Chandler**

D One such approach was developed by the crime writer **Raymond Chandler**, who built his strategy on a basic yet critical observation: procrastinators rarely sit about completely inactively, but rather tend to engage themselves in useful but less pressing tasks: **vacuuming behind the bed, cleaning out the fridge, washing the windows and so on** (=doing housework). (therefore, procrastinators often do housework instead of important tasks)

20 **A** Get support from other people. **Amy Sykes**

C Career counsellor **Amy Sykes** focuses on the basics. Firstly, she says, **embrace peer pressure** (=ask your peers or friends to help you). Many weight loss and self-help groups encourage individuals to hold themselves accountable to a wider circle of their peers, and Sykes believes this social safety net can be harnessed just as successfully by procrastinators.

21 **C** Make a list of boring tasks before important ones. **John Perry**

E The key to this approach is to rank one's priorities, then bump (=move) the most urgent tasks a little further down and place at the top some potentially daunting (=difficult or scary) and important-sounding projects which are ultimately not all that essential. If the student with the essay deadline can convince himself he absolutely must **reorganise his email box, or finish reading that old, dusty novel he only got halfway through** (these are boring tasks), then suddenly **the essay deadline** (this is an important task) is going to seem a far superior option.

22 **A** Look for ways to make the work more interesting. **Amy Sykes**

C Instead, she (Amy Sykes) argues, we should pique (=stimulate) our own interest and **find ways to make our important projects more attractive** (=find ways to make the work more interesting) – by turning them into little competitions or fact-finding missions, for example (2 examples).

23 **C** Lists are powerful tools for reducing procrastination. **John Perry**

E He (John Perry) thus surmised (=guessed) that the enemy of successful task completion is not, in fact, that great engine of productive activity – procrastination itself – but rather **how we order our projects in the hierarchy of urgency** (=how we list our projects in order of importance).

24 **B** Use boredom as motivation. **Raymond Chandler**

D **Chandler's** method ... involves setting aside a period of time in which the procrastinator may do one of two things: **absolutely nothing** (=something very boring) or **work on the project that he or she wishes to complete**. **Sitting still** ... Chandler slowly felt the itch of **tedious monotony** (=boredom) sink in. Within five or ten minutes, this **itch** (=boredom) had become **intolerable** (=unbearable), and he felt **compelled** (=motivated) to begin writing his stories.

25 **A** Use rewards when a task is completed. **Amy Sykes**

C If all else fails, **Sykes** believes we must **recompense ourselves** (=reward ourselves) for our troubles, ideally with little treats upon finishing (=completing) a task. 'It doesn't need to be big,' she says. 'Pancakes, a hot bath, or an episode of your favourite television show could all do the trick.' (examples of rewards)

Question 26: Multiple choice – writer's conclusion

It is likely that the conclusion will be found at the end of the passage.

26 **B** What is the writer's conclusion? **Procrastination will never be completely eliminated.**

F If the Ancient Greeks struggled with it, and all the life coaches, counsellors and motivational speakers in the modern world are unable to erase it from our existence either, **it seems unlikely that procrastination will ever truly be put to rest** (=completely be eliminated). As these procrastination gurus (=counsellors) have shown, however, the right strategies have the potential to minimise its impact – if you ever get around to using them.

Distractors for Question 26

A Some procrastination-reducing strategies have had proven success.

This is not stated in the final paragraph, and in Paragraph B the writer states that:

B Although evidence for their efficacy is largely anecdotal at this stage (there is no proof that they succeed), some of these strategies at least offer promising avenues for future research.

C Procrastinators should employ a life coach to help them.

F If the Ancient Greeks struggled with it, and all the **life coaches**, counsellors and motivational speakers in the modern world are **unable to erase it from our existence** ... (the author is stating that life coaches cannot eliminate procrastination)

D Most procrastinators want to learn how to be more efficient.

This is not stated, and the last sentence implies that most procrastinators delay finding solutions to their problem.

F As these procrastination gurus have shown, however, the right strategies have the potential to minimise its impact – **if you ever get around to using them.**

Reading Passage 3: WHEN EVOLUTION WORKS AGAINST US

Questions 27–32: Summary completion with options supplied

Note that in this set of questions, all possible answers are paraphrases of the original text. The original text for this summary comes at the beginning of the reading passage.

This summary comes from Paragraphs A and B of the text, and the first sentence of Paragraph C.

The fight or flight response

Modern man still has the 27 **G instincts** that were needed in his distant past in the jungle. (But despite these changes, some **very basic responses** (=instincts) linger on.) One of these, the 'fight or flight' response, originally assisted humans to recognise 28 **H threats** and take action. (It's called the 'fight or flight' response, and it helps us to **identify dangerous situations** (=recognise threats) and act decisively (=take action) ...) Today, this same response manifests itself mostly as nothing more than a feeling of 29 **K anxiety**. (This shift to survival mode is often popularly described as **a sudden unease** (=a feeling of anxiety), a sense that a situation is 'off' or 'not right'.) It is the result of the hypothalamus producing and releasing 30 **C substances** into the blood, (However, the sense is actually the outcome of ... the **hypothalamus**, advising the sympathetic nervous system and the adrenal-cortical system to work, at first separately, and then together, to blend a potent mix of **hormones and chemicals** (=substances) and secrete (=release) them into the bloodstream (=into the blood).) with subsequent rises in heart rate and breathing, and the sensation of a 31 **M drop** in temperature as the blood is diverted to other organs. (Our heartbeat rises, along with our respiratory rate (=rises in heart rate and breathing). Skin feels cold (=a drop in temperature) (hence the 'shiver' down the spine) as blood supply is redirected (=diverted) to the larger muscles (=to other organs) ...) Although this 32 **J system** was once essential to human survival, it now occurs as a result of perceived rather than actual threat. (Without this instinctive response (=system), the human race would never have survived, but at present it is often more of a hindrance than a help.)

Questions 33–36: Multiple choice

33 B When the fight or flight response is activated, it is difficult to **focus on small problems.**

The answer for this first multiple-choice question overlaps with the final part of the summary. 'Fight or flight' is first mentioned in Paragraph A, and then explained in Paragraph B. You need to follow this linked chain of meaning to answer this question.

B (When the fight or flight response is activated ...) Our heartbeat rises, along with our respiratory rate. Skin feels cold (hence the 'shiver' down the spine) as blood supply is redirected to the larger muscles required for a physical confrontation or a hasty retreat. **The ability to concentrate on issues of minor importance also suffers** (=it is difficult to focus on small problems), as the brain tends to prioritise 'big picture' thinking at this time.

Distractors for Question 33

A ... (it is difficult to) increase breathing speed.

This is directly contradicted in the text.

B Our heartbeat rises, along with our respiratory rate.

C ... (it is difficult to) maintain body temperature.

B Skin feels cold ... (but this does not refer to internal body temperature)

D ... (it is difficult to) run for long periods of time.

This is not directly stated, but the opposite information is implied. Paragraph A suggests that we are ready to run away as fast as we can, but does not state for how long we can continue to run.

34 A The fight or flight response is less useful today because modern individuals **encounter fewer physical threats.**

The answer is found in Paragraph C.

C Without this instinctive response, the human race would never have survived, but at present it is often more of a **hindrance** (=problem) than a **help**. (therefore, it is less useful today – reasons follow) Although instances of physical threats have decreased over the years, activation of the fight or flight response has actually increased, largely in response to mental frustrations. This poses a problem, however, because **the fight or flight mechanism functions most helpfully as a response to something that can cause bodily harm**, such as a falling tree or a wild animal, rather than in response to a fulminating boss, a traffic jam, or a spouse who has not returned a phone call. (it is implied that we do not often encounter things that can cause bodily harm, or physical threats, because the modern day examples are angry bosses, traffic jams, or communication problems)

Distractors for Question 34

B ... (modern individuals) can easily manage small daily difficulties.

The passage states that fight or flight can make it harder to manage small daily difficulties.

C During **these instances of mental distress** (the modern examples), the physical manifestations of fight or flight, such as an inability to think rationally and calmly, can actually **exacerbate** the problem (=make the problem worse).

C ... (modern individuals) are better at creative problem solving.

This is not mentioned in the reading passage.

D ... (modern individuals) do not need to hunt dangerous animals.

This is most likely true, but it is not mentioned in the reading passage.

35 D One disadvantage of 'mind chatter' is that people may **worry about problems that are not real.**

'Mind chatter' is the topic of Paragraph D.

D A similar case of an evolutionary development overstaying its welcome is the example of **'mind chatter'**. Mind chatter is the ceaseless train of scattered thoughts and self-talk that occupies our mind, ensuring we are always 'switched on', searching for danger and threats. (definition of mind chatter) This would have been a boon for a solitary caveman on a three-hour hunting expedition, but in a modern world already overloaded with sensory input, **it causes us to fret about non-existent predicaments** (=it makes us worry about problems that are not real) and occasionally needlessly triggers the fight or flight response.

Distractors for Question 35

A ... (people may) talk too much and miss important information.

D Mind chatter is the ceaseless train of scattered thoughts and self-talk that **occupies our mind** (this is mental talk, not physical talking), ...

B ... (people may) spend too much time by themselves.

D This would have been a boon (=an advantage) for a solitary (=on his own) caveman on a three-hour hunting expedition (the solitary caveman is our ancient ancestor, not a modern man), ...

C ... (people may) become distracted from real threats.

The text directly contradicts this idea.

D ... it causes us to fret about non-existent predicaments and **occasionally needlessly** (=without any need) **triggers the fight or flight response**. (therefore, there are no real threats)

36 A The writer suggests stress is increasing because of **a lack of physical release.**

'Stress' is the topic of Paragraph E.

E These twin forces, mind chatter and the fight or flight response, (this text links back to the topics of previous paragraphs) have combined to wreak havoc on the modern psyche and have led to a spike in what some studies have suggested is a cause of up to eighty per cent of all illness today: **stress** (this is the new topic). Stress, erroneously considered by many to be a mere feeling, is actually a physiological condition resulting from a cumulative accrual (=a steady increase) of certain hormones in the body, hormones that can help us in quick, sharp doses, but which are toxic if they are not properly metabolised. (definition of stress) Metabolism of these potentially toxic hormones relies on physical exertion, which originally evolved as part of the fight or flight process – hormone release was usually followed by physical exertion (fighting or running), which returned the body to a state of balance. In present day encounters, however, **the vital element of physical exertion is missing** (therefore there is no physical release for stress in fighting or running): a resentful employee cannot punch his co-worker, for example, and a frustrated driver is unable to simply ram (=force) his way through a packed intersection.

Distractors for Question 36

B ... (because of) an increase in the number of threats.

This is not mentioned in the text.

C ... (because of) more health problems.

This is mentioned as the result of stress, not its cause.

D ... (because of) the loss of some hormones.

E Stress, erroneously considered by many to be a mere feeling, is actually a physiological condition resulting from a **cumulative accrual** (=a steady increase) of certain hormones in the body .... (the hormones are accruing (=increasing), not reducing)

Questions 37–40: Yes, no, not given

37 Stress is an emotion. **NO**

E Stress, erroneously (=in error, wrongly) considered by many to be a mere **feeling** (=emotion), is actually a **physiological condition** (=a body reaction, not a feeling) resulting from a cumulative accrual of certain hormones in the body, ...

38 Fights in the workplace are increasing. **NOT GIVEN**

The reading passage mentions workplace fights but there is no information about whether these are increasing or not.

E ... a resentful employee cannot punch (=hit) his co-worker, for example, ...

39 In order to metabolise hormones, exercise must be linked with the original cause of stress. **NO**

F Stress researcher Neil F. Neimarck, perhaps not surprisingly, **recommends physical exercise** as one useful strategy. Fortunately, the brain is not clever enough to realise that this **exercise is completely unrelated to the original stress stimulus**, and in this way **we can effectively 'fool' our bodies into metabolising stress hormones by punching a boxing bag instead of the person who annoyed us in the first place**. (therefore, we can exercise to metabolise hormones although this exercise is not linked to the original cause of the stress)

40 Saying positive words can reduce stress. **YES**

F Benson found that certain behaviours, such as deep breathing, meditation, and **the repetition of simple, affirmative phrases** (=saying positive words), acted as an antidote to (=controlled, stopped) mind chatter and the fight or flight responses, **calming the nervous system and inducing a relaxed state of mind and body** (=reducing stress) instead.

Academic Test 4

LISTENING

Section 1: MAKING AN INTERNATIONAL MONEY TRANSFER

Questions 1–6: Flow chart completion

Note that you are required to write NO MORE THAN TWO WORDS AND/OR A NUMBER. You will be penalised if you write three or more words.

Making an International Money Transfer

Example

Step 1: Access **global payments** system

You will hear an introduction to the first 6 questions of Section 1 of the Listening test. Then you will have 20 seconds to preview these questions and to predict (guess) the answers you are listening for.

There is an example to introduce this section. The audio for the example will be played first, with an explanation of the answer. After that, the full conversation will be played once only. This includes the example part of the recording.

Example:

Predict to hear: a kind of system

[01:17]

WOMAN: Wesley Bank, how can I help you?

MAN: Oh, hi. Um, I want to know how to send money to my family overseas.

WOMAN: No problem. If you have access to the Internet, I can guide you through the process of how to use our **global payments** system.

Step 1: Access **global payments** system
— Log on to Wesley Bank Internet Banking
— Select 'Transfer Money'
— Select 'International Money Transfer' (under International Services)

Step 2: Click on 'Payment Destination 1 **Country/country**'
— Scroll down and choose the place

Predict to hear: a noun

Note that you will need to be familiar with some basic Internet banking and banking vocabulary in order to complete this listening.

Example: Log in, select, click on, enter, transaction ...

[02:15]

MAN: That's great. I'm online now.

WOMAN: Good. First, you have to log on to Wesley Bank Internet Banking and select **Transfer Money** (key words for the flow chart).

MAN: Okay.

WOMAN: Once you've done that, select **International Money Transfer** (=transfer money).

MAN: Um ... I don't see ...

WOMAN: It's the first option under the heading of International Services.

MAN: Right, I've found it. (distractor text)

WOMAN: Now, click on Payment Destination 1 ***Country*** and **scroll down to the location you wish to send money to** (=scroll down and choose the place). It's all in alphabetical order.

MAN: Oh, yes, Zimbabwe – I've got it, right at the bottom. (distractor text)

Step 3: Enter '2 **(Your/your) Personal/personal** Details'
— Name, address, phone number

Predict to hear: an adjective

[02:56]

WOMAN: Good. Then Step Three is to **fill in** (=enter) 2 ***your Personal*** Details ... name, address and contact phone number.

MAN: Uh huh. Done that. When I put in my phone number, my other details popped up automatically. (distractor text)

Step 4: 'Transaction Details'
— Select transaction, savings or 3 **business** account
— Enter reason: medical care, 4 **school fees**

Predict to hear:

3 – a kind of bank account

4 – a reason for making the transaction

[03:10]

WOMAN: Yes, that will happen, but take a moment just to check that everything is correct. Then we'll move on to **Transaction Details** (key words for the flow chart).

MAN: So this is where I select the account that the money comes out of? (explanation of 'transaction details')

WOMAN: Yes, you have a transaction account, a **savings account** (key words for the flow chart) and a 3 ***business*** account. Which one did you want to choose?

MAN: It had better be my savings account. (distractor text)

WOMAN: Okay, have you clicked on that?

MAN: Yes, but ... next it says 'enter a payment reason' – why do I have to give a reason?

WOMAN: Ah, well, I'm afraid that's a **legal requirement** (=required by the law) – you can't send money overseas without **a valid reason** (=a reason that is accepted by the bank).

MAN: My mother needs to pay for an urgent **medical procedure** (key words for the flow chart) and I have to pay for my sister's 4 ***school fees***, as well. Will that do?

WOMAN: Yes. Both are valid reasons.

Step 5: 'Recipient Account Details'
— Account name and number
(NB: complete the page within 5 **48/forty-eight** hours)

Predict to hear: a number

[04:01]

WOMAN: The next step is to fill in the **Recipient Account Details** (key words for the flow chart).

MAN: Sorry?

WOMAN: You need to enter the account name and number of the person who will receive the money. (explanation of 'recipient account details'

– key words for the flow chart)

MAN: Oh, I see, of course. But I haven't got that information with me at the moment. I'm at the office and those details are at home. (distractor text)

WOMAN: Don't worry – you can return to this page and fill it in later – you can save what you've done so far and **defer completion** (=complete it later). Don't leave it too long, though – the system will hold it for no more than two days. After 5 ***forty-eight*** hours you'll have to start over again (=complete it again from the beginning).

MAN: That's fine; I can do it this evening. Is there much more?

Step 6: 'Recipient Bank Details'
— Name, branch, address

Step 7: 'Confirmation Page'
— Press Submit
— Print receipt or write down Transaction 6 **Reference Number / reference number**

Predict to hear: some information about your transaction

[04:40]

WOMAN: After the Account Details, you'll need to fill in the **Bank Details of the person you are transferring money to** (=recipient bank details) – the name, branch and address of the bank.

MAN: That should be easy enough. Anything else?

WOMAN: No. Once you've completed everything, a confirmation page will appear – just ensure all the information you have entered is correct and **press Submit** (key words for the flow chart). Then **print off the receipt page** (key words for the flow chart). If you haven't got a printer at home, just make a note of your Transaction 6 ***Reference Number***.

Questions 7–10: Short answers

Note that you are required to write NO MORE THAN TWO WORDS AND/OR A NUMBER. You will be penalised if you write three or more words.

7 How long does it take for the Wesley Bank to process a transfer?
three/3 days

[05:47]

MAN: **When can my family expect the money?** (=how long does it take to process a transfer?) Will they get it within the next five days? (distractor text)

WOMAN: It takes **7** ***three days*** to process but, of course, we can't be responsible for any delays arising from the recipient bank (distractor text).

8 How much does it cost to make each transfer from the Wesley Bank?
$30 / 30 dollars / thirty dollars

[06:00]

MAN: I understand. And, **is there a charge for Internet transfers?** (=how much does it cost to make each transfer?) When I did this through a teller at the bank last year, I was charged forty dollars. (distractor text)

WOMAN: It does cost more to use a teller but **the Wesley Bank** (key words for the question) will only deduct **8** ***thirty dollars*** from your account per online international transaction. However, we have no control over any fees that may be charged by other financial institutions at the receiving end. (distractor text)

9 What is the maximum amount of each transfer? **$10,000 / ten thousand dollars**

[06:27]

MAN: How much can I send in one transaction?

WOMAN: Well that depends on your bank balance but, assuming you have enough funds, the **upper limit** (=maximum amount of each transfer) is **9** ***ten thousand dollars***. By the way, you'll need to use a special security token to transfer more than five thousand dollars. (distractor text)

10 What is a security token? **special code**

[06:43]

MAN: You mean my secret password? (distractor text)

WOMAN: You'll definitely need that but you'll also need **a security token** (key words for Question 10). That is a **10** ***special code*** that the bank gives you. Just call into your local branch, with photo ID, and they will arrange it for you. Is there anything else I can help you with or do you have any more questions?

MAN: No, thank you. That's all I need to know for now.

Section 2: PLAN FOR UPGRADE OF BAYFIELD TOWN CENTRE

Questions 11–17: Map labelling

The locations that you need to match to the letters (Questions 11–17) are given in the same order as the audio, but the letters you must write are NOT in alphabetical order. Use your preparation time to carefully read each location given on the map, and to orient yourself to north, south, east and west.

Remember that there will be some distractor locations in the audio. You need to listen carefully for the locations that are listed in Questions 11–17.

Plan for upgrade of Bayfield town centre

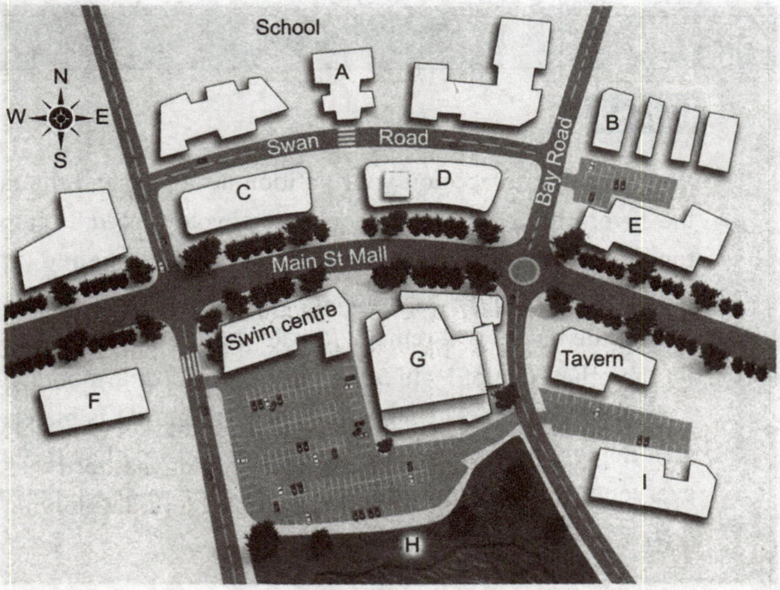

11 supermarket = **G**

[08:27]

Good evening. I've been asked to speak to you about the proposed plan for the improvement of our town centre. As you know, there was extensive community consultation before the designers were engaged. I'm sure you'll agree that a great many of your concerns have been acknowledged and incorporated into the draft plan that you see before you. (introduction text)

Firstly, you'll notice that the existing **supermarket** has been enlarged – it's the biggest building you see on the plan, on the south side of the Main Street Mall. (location is given after the key word) You can see that the part of Main Street in the town centre has been turned into a pedestrian mall. We're planning **extensive** (=a lot of) plantings of shrubs and small trees to provide shade. (distractor text)

12 park = **H**

[09:12]

There'll be plenty of parking for supermarket shoppers on the west side of the building and a few spaces to the south facing the **park**. (so the park is on the south side of the supermarket car park) The **park** will not be touched except for the addition of a small artificial lake, which we hope will attract ducks and other bird-life. (distractor text)

13 market = **E**

[09:30]

We've taken into account your petition not to expand the tavern. (locate the tavern on the map) I know some of you wanted it removed from the town centre altogether, so it will be discreetly **screened** (=hidden) from public view by more trees. (distractor text) The existing car park at the rear of the tavern will remain. (locate the car park) Opposite the tavern, on the other side of Main Street, (location for the market) there will be a covered **market**. The Saturday farmers' market is hugely popular but stall holders have suffered from a lot of bad weather recently. We think everyone will be happy with this part of the re-development. (distractor text)

14 office block = C

[10:08]

These two rectangular buildings here, in the middle of the plan, are new. (locate the buildings) We plan to demolish the existing shops, some of which are **unsound** (=unsafe) anyway, and put up these two modern buildings instead. (distractor text) The one across Bay Road from the market will house boutiques, delicatessens and other specialty shops all under one roof. (locate this building on the map) The other one to the west (location of office building) will contain **offices** so you'll have convenient access to all the professionals in town inside one building. (distractor text)

15 gymnasium = A

[10:42]

The swimming pool will remain where it is, of course. (locate the swim centre) The school is a major user of the pool so, to make it safer for students to cross Swan Road, a pedestrian crossing (locate the pedestrian crossing on Swan Road) will be installed in front of the school **gymnasium**. You can see we've planned a gap in the trees here, on the Main Street Mall, so that students will be able to walk across the Main Street Mall straight to the pool.

16 library = F

[10:58]

Another pedestrian crossing to the west of the pool (locate this crossing) will give students and other users safer access to the new **library**, here. Library users will be able to share the supermarket parking. (extra clue for location of the library)

17 council = B

[11:22]

We expect that Swan Road may become a busier thoroughfare once the Main Street has been converted to pedestrians only; but we'll address that issue in the second stage of the development. (distractor text) In the meantime, the east end of Swan Road (locate this) will be converted into a public car park – here, between the **council building** and the market.

Questions 18–20: Sentence completion

18 The key issue for residents is better **public transport/transportation**.

[12:18]

I'll deal with any questions you may have at the end of this talk. In the meantime, I'll give you some idea of what the second stage of development will involve. (distractor text) In line with the **overwhelming concern of Bayfield inhabitants** (=key issue for residents), improved **18** ***public transport*** is definitely **at the forefront** (=the most important thing) of the next stage. We're planning to develop a modern transportation hub (=central area) on the outskirts of town. (distractor text)

19 The council needs to buy suitable **sites** for playgrounds.

[12:44]

Another issue we want to address is the lack of **playgrounds** (key word for the question) and sporting facilities. These could be part of Stage Two depending on the council's ability to **purchase appropriate** (=buy suitable) **19** ***sites***.

20 The council's first choice for controlling the movement of vehicles on Swan Road is to add **traffic lights**.

[12:56]

As I mentioned earlier, traffic may become a problem in Swan Road. Once Main Street has been blocked off, the council will **study the speed, flow and density of vehicles on Swan Road and decide on appropriate measures** (=find ways of controlling the movement of vehicles on Swan Road). I know the council's **preference** (=first choice) would be to install **20** ***traffic lights*** either side of the pedestrian crossing, but they'll consider other options to alleviate (=improve) traffic problems, like diverting (=rerouting) non-essential vehicles to a back road.

Section 3: CORPORATE CULTURES

Questions 21–30: Notes completion

Studies by Quinn and Cameron propose:

'Competing Values Framework'

- Hierarchy Culture
  — obeys rules, 21 **regulations** and bureaucracy

[14:54]

LECTURER: Hello, Blair. Come in and take a seat. Now, are you ready for the seminar on Friday?

BLAIR: I think so.

LECTURER: Good. What aspect of business have you decided on for your presentation?

BLAIR: I thought I'd talk about corporate culture. (introduction text)

LECTURER: There are many facets (=parts, or areas) of corporate culture – you're not going to try to cover (=describe) them all, are you?

BLAIR: No – I've been reading research by **Robert Quinn and Kim Cameron** (key words for the notes) and they put forward a model of just four distinctive corporate cultures – it's called the **Competing Values Framework** (key words for the notes).

LECTURER: Good. Where do you want to start?

BLAIR: I'll start by talking about the **Hierarchy Culture** (key words for the notes). This is found in a business that observes formal rules, 21 ***regulations*** and bureaucracy.

— stable, structured 22 **environment**

[15:36]

LECTURER: How do the leaders achieve this?

BLAIR: Well, in such a **structured and controlled** 22 ***environment*** (=with many rules and regulations), leaders usually take pride in running stable, organised and efficient operations. In fact, this may even be part of their mission statement. (distractor text)

— leaders use power, 23 **status**, and position to deal with employees

[15:50]

BLAIR: ... They (leaders) rely on their power, 23 ***status*** and the importance of their position to manage their workers.

— common among 24 **government** organisations and large companies

[15:58]

LECTURER: What sort of company is most likely to have a hierarchy culture?

BLAIR: Well, a few smaller firms might have some of the elements of the hierarchy culture in their day-to-day operations, (distractor text) but on the whole I think this culture is **typical of** (=common among) 24 ***government*** bodies and **big corporations** (=large companies).

- Market Culture
  — main difference is the importance of 25 **(external) relationships** with clients or suppliers

[16:13]

LECTURER: Very good. What's next?

BLAIR: I'd then move on to discuss **Market Culture** (key words for the notes).

LECTURER: Very popular in the 1960s, I believe, and quite similar to the hierarchy culture in that it also emphasises stability and control. (distractor text)

BLAIR: Yes, but the **main point of difference** (key words to indicate that the information for Question 25 is coming next) is that market culture **attaches a great deal of importance to** (=values) 25 ***external relationships*** with stakeholders such as customers, suppliers and creditors.

LECTURER: Why are these particular associations important to a market culture?

BLAIR: I suppose because successful interactions with these people would increase the company's productivity (to improve competitiveness).

— this culture produces the best 26 **financial results** (due to emphasis on competitiveness and success)

[16:51]

LECTURER: Do you know whether this practice does have the desired effect?

BLAIR: Well, according to studies carried out by Angelo Kinicki and his colleagues in the School of Business at ...

LECTURER: Arizona State University ... (distractor text)

BLAIR: Yes, um ... where was I? Oh, oh, right, um, Kinicki and the others (distractor text) revealed that (=showed that) this culture type tended to **generate the greatest** (=produce the best) 26 ***financial results***, probably as a result of their focus on competition and achievement.

- **Clan Culture**
  - — family-like
  - — focus on doing things together leads to better morale and a high degree of worker 27 **satisfaction**

[17:50]

LECTURER: All right, now, what's next?

BLAIR: **Clan Culture** (key words for the notes) ... you know, I think I'd like to work in a clan culture.

LECTURER: Oh, yes? Why's that?

BLAIR: Well, a clan culture is **more like a family** (key words for the notes) (=family-like) than a rigid, structured organisation.

LECTURER: What do you mean by 'like a family'?

BLAIR: Well, it's more focussed on teamwork and morale. It's probably not surprising that this type of culture **results in** (=leads to) **the greatest level of** (=the highest degree of) 27 ***satisfaction*** among employees.

— paternalistic, mentoring style of leadership
— employee training
— company expects 28 **loyalty** from workers, with similar ideas and shared goals

[18:21]

LECTURER: What about the internal structure of a clan-type business?

BLAIR: It's quite flat, really, nothing like the hierarchy type we talked about before. There is usually just a single leader or owner whose role is quite **paternalistic** (key word for the notes) (=like a father), and he, although I suppose it could be a she, would act as a **mentor** (key word for the notes) (=teacher and guide), guiding, nurturing and encouraging employees.

LECTURER: I can see that ongoing **employee training** (key words for the notes) would be characteristic of (=typical of) this kind of business.

BLAIR: Definitely. And, in a company like this, 28 ***loyalty*** would be very important. Also, management would want to know that everyone within the company had **the same ideas and objectives** (=similar ideas and shared goals). You know … my brother works for a company like this and he absolutely loves his job and puts everything into it. He's extremely loyal and devoted and thinks he's very lucky. (distractor text)

LECTURER: He probably is lucky to have a job he enjoys.

- **Adhocracy Culture**
  — workers must be adaptable and accept change
  — focus on flexibility and 29 **innovation** with quick responses to outside factors

[19:17]

BLAIR: Yes, well, he's better off there than in an **Adhocracy Culture** (key words for the notes).

LECTURER: But adhocracy does appeal to a certain type of person …

BLAIR: Yes, **if you're adaptable and don't mind lots of changes all the time** (=workers must be adaptable and accept change).

LECTURER: What's **most important in** (=the focus of) an adhocracy culture?

BLAIR: It would have to be **flexibility** (key word for the notes) (=willingness to change or adapt) and 29 ***innovation*** (=new ideas) and the ability to **react swiftly** (=response quickly) to a changing market, competition or **other factors in the external environment** (=outside factors).

— dynamic and entrepreneurial leaders looking for 30 **growth opportunities**
— employees encouraged to experiment with new ideas
— might seem disorganised but inventive and progressive

[19:44]

LECTURER: What kind of leadership would you expect in this culture?

BLAIR: They would be **entrepreneurs** (key word for the notes) (=a businessman who will take risks) who welcome change, are not afraid of taking risks, and are always **seeking** (=looking for) 30 ***growth opportunities***. Workers would be urged to try out new ideas and not sit back taking things for granted. To an outsider, especially someone from a hierarchy culture, this kind of culture might look a bit **chaotic and disordered** (=disorganised) but it is **innovative, forward-looking** (=inventive and progressive) and adjusts rapidly to change.

Section 4: ENVIRONMENTAL EFFECTS OF PESTICIDE USE

Questions 31–34: Summary completion

Note that you are required to write NO MORE THAN TWO WORDS. You will be penalised if you write three or more words.

Environmental Effects of Pesticide Use

Most pesticides are carried into other environments. They travel along rivers or streams or are carried by the 31 **wind** into unwanted areas.

[22:08]

Good evening. I'm here today to present the findings from our research into pesticides and alternatives to using them. (introduction text)

I'd like to begin by talking about some of the **environmental effects of pesticide use** (key words for the title of the summary). As most of you will be aware, pesticides have proven to be very harmful to our environment. The principal reason for this is because nearly all pesticides **travel beyond their target areas** (=are carried into other environments). This often happens when rain carries pesticides along water channels such as **rivers** (key word for the summary), where they are then transported downstream. **In other situations** (=or), particularly when they are dropped by plane, the **31** ***wind*** **blows** (=carries) pesticides into wild areas where they are not wanted. These areas can be up to several kilometres away.

Pesticides can harm animals or remove their **32** **food source**, causing starvation.

[23:00]

We also need to think about the effects of pesticides on **animals** (key word for the summary). Pesticides can cause illness and even death (=harm) in many animals, including birds and aquatic life. Animals can also be affected, however, when pesticide use **eliminates** (=removes) their **32** ***food source*** and **causes them to starve** (key words for the summary) or migrate to other areas.

Those that stay in the soil can cause damage, and also decrease the quality and number of organisms in contrast to **33** **healthy soil**.

[23:21]

When pesticides don't travel into neighbouring environments, they tend to seep into the soil (so they remain in the soil). There they degrade (=decrease) the quality of the soil and in addition, they can weaken **biodiversity** (this term is explained next) – studies of pesticide-contaminated soil show **a much lower count of** (=fewer) organisms compared to **33** ***healthy soil.***

Furthermore, insects can develop immunity to pesticides, and thus **34** **new varieties** are needed, which create further problems.

[23:40]

There's a final consideration to take into account, and that's the environmental effects of pesticides in terms of pest numbers. In the short term, pesticides significantly reduce the number of pests in an area, as might be expected. After long-term, regular use (=repeated use over time), however, insects tend to become immune to certain kinds of pesticide and are no longer negatively affected by them (definition of 'immune to'). As the number of insecticide resistant pests grows, this creates the need for 34 ***new varieties*** of pesticide, and further exacerbates (=worsens) the pesticide problem.

Questions 35–40: Table completion

Note that you are required to write NO MORE THAN TWO WORDS. You will be penalised if you write three or more words.

Technique	***Procedure***	***Comment***
Handpicking	Remove insects with gloves	Effective and low-cost; but 35 **time-consuming / time consuming** so not useful for large farms
36 **Biological/ biological control**	Breed 'good' insects to attack pests	Risky due to 37 **unpredictable** outcomes
Companion planting	Use plants with ability to 38 **repel** certain insects	Low risk, but additional plants compete for space and soil nutrients
Crop rotation	Change plant varieties after each harvest – insects must 39 **migrate** to access food	Unappealing for big businesses as 40 **profits** are reduced

35 time-consuming / time consuming

Predict to hear: an adjective describing a problem

[24:35]

The first technique will be familiar to any of you who have even a small vegetable garden at home. (introduction text) You see a slug (garden pest) on a piece of lettuce, and what do you do? Put on some gloves, walk right up to the plant and pick the slug off with your hands. (Technique 1 – Procedure) This is called **handpicking** (key word for the table – Technique 1). Handpicking is remarkably **effective** (key word for Comment – Technique 1) and **requires little in the way of money to implement** (=low-cost). **But** (key word) (=however) while it may be sufficient for the home gardener, the 35 ***time-consuming*** nature of handpicking makes it unsuitable for **large-scale operations** (=large farms).

36 Biological/biological control

Predict to hear: the name of a technique

[25:07]

Owners of larger crops and orchards require a more systematic approach to pest management, and they have a few options here. You may be familiar with a **technique** (key word for the table – Technique 2) known as 36 ***biological control***.

37 unpredictable

Predict to hear: an adjective describing a problem

[25:20]

This (biological control) involves the strategic use of what we call **'good' insects** (key words for the table – Procedure) – that is, insects which eat pests, rather than plants. When they eat the pests, they also protect the crop environment. Unfortunately, biological control is always **risky** (key word for the table – Comment) because we can never know for sure how insects will behave in a particular environment, and the **results** (=outcomes) are therefore 37 ***unpredictable*** (=we cannot predict them).

38 repel

Predict to hear: a verb

[25:47]

A safer option is **companion planting** (key phrase – Technique 3), where certain plants are grown together (definition of 'companion planting'). Garlic, for example, fends off (=repels) spider mites and aphids (garden pests), and basil drives away (=repels) the tomato hornworm (a garden pest), making it a good companion for tomatoes. This is because some varieties of plant **can** (=have the ability to) 38 ***repel*** specific breeds of insects, so planting them alongside and around more vulnerable (=easily damaged) vegetables will discourage the insects from coming near. Of course, all these extra plants begin fighting for space and competing with the protected plants for access to water and nutrients in the soil. (so the plants compete for soil and nutrients)

39 migrate

Predict to hear: a verb

[26:24]

A final possibility is **crop rotation** (key phrase – Technique 4). This involves **alternating** (=changing) plants **every harvest** (key words for Procedure), which forces insects to **39** ***migrate*** (=move to a new place) in an attempt **to locate their food source** (=to access food).

40 profits

Predict to hear: a plural noun

[26:36]

Crop rotation is **unappealing** (key word for the table – Comment) for **large-scale commercial operations** (=big businesses), however, because the high cost of constantly changing crops **cuts into** (=reduces) their **40** ***profits***.

READING

Reading Passage 1: 'SLEEP COMES MORE EASILY THAN IT RETURNS.'

Questions 1–5: Multiple choice

All 5 of these questions have 4 options and one correct answer. Since they are the first set of questions, they are likely to begin inside **Paragraph A**.

1 **B** What can happen if someone stops taking insomnia medication?
They experience unstable emotions.

unstable = changing, not stable, not even

emotions = feelings, mood

unstable emotions = mood swings

A It is estimated that one in three adults in westernised countries regularly wakes up in the middle of the night and has difficulty getting back to sleep. Physicians often diagnose '**insomnia**' and prescribe **sleeping pills** (=insomnia medication), but these often have **side effects** such as ... **Cessation of the medication** (=stopping the insomnia medication) frequently causes unpleasant withdrawal symptoms, too, including panic attacks, **mood-swings** (=unstable emotions), and even heightened sleep disturbance.

Distractors for Question 1

A Their sleeping problems improve.

This is directly contradicted in the passage.

A Cessation of the medication frequently causes ... **heightened sleep disturbance** (=sleeping problems).

C They begin using other drugs instead.

Using other drugs is mentioned in the paragraph, but NOT as the result of stopping sleeping pills.

D There is no change in their behaviour.

The paragraph lists **many** changes in behaviour as a result of stopping sleeping medication.

2 **D** How does A. Roger Ekirch feel about waking in the night?
It is a completely natural sleep pattern.

natural = instinctive, innate

Look for Ekirch's name, which is first mentioned in Paragraph B.

B The historian **A. Roger Ekirch** takes a different approach to **nocturnal awakening** (=waking in the night). He maintains it is **biologically instinctive and innate** (=completely natural) and that ... Those people who have so-called insomnia may just be sleeping in the biphasic mode that was **the norm for their ancestors** (=natural for ancient people): eight hours of sleep split (=divided) into two chunks (=pieces) by a period of wakefulness which lasted an hour or longer. (this is a definition of biphasic sleep)

Distractors for Question 2

A It is the result of our modern lifestyles.

This is the opposite of the information in Paragraph B, where Ekirch claims that waking in the night was a natural occurrence for our ancestors.

B It is less healthy than uninterrupted sleep.

This is directly contradicted in Paragraphs B and C.

C It is a rare and problematic condition.

This is also directly contradicted in Paragraph B where it states that waking in the night is completely natural.

3 **C** The shift away from biphasic sleep (defined in Paragraph B above) happened mainly because of **new lighting technology.**

shift = move

happened because of = came about through

new lighting technology = invention of lights

The answer is found in Paragraph C.

C Archives from the pre-industrial era mention segmented (=divided) sleep as 'first sleep' or 'deep sleep' and 'second sleep' or 'morning sleep'. (2 phases, as described in Paragraph B) The **change in sleep routines, ... , mainly came about through** (=happened because of) **the invention of the incandescent bulb** (=new lighting technology).

Distractors for Question 3

A changes in work hours.

B factory and industrial employment.

These are both mentioned as results of the change in lighting, which lead to changes in sleep patterns.

D less time for sleep in the mornings.

This is not mentioned at all.

4 **A** What happened to the volunteers in Thomas Wehr's study?
They began to wake up during the night.

volunteer = someone who agrees to do something for no pay, or money

wake up = be awake

Thomas Wehr is first mentioned in Paragraph D.

D Ekirch's hypothesis was corroborated by sleep expert **Thomas Wehr** in the 1990s. His study kept **volunteers** in the dark for 14 hours each night (a simulation of wintertime exposure to light and darkness in bygone days). The subjects **moved progressively towards a biphasic sleep pattern, taking a couple of hours to doze off** (=go to sleep) and then sleeping in two distinct segments of four hours each with **an interval of wakefulness in the middle** (=they began to wake up during the night).

Distractors for Question 4

B They slept much longer than before.

The paragraph states that they were kept in the dark for 14 hours per night, but not that they slept during this entire time.

C They had a longer winter than normal.

The study simulated (=copied) winter, but did not make a longer winter.

D They experienced more vivid (=real and bright) dreams.

The paragraph mentions the recall (=remembering) of dreams, but not that they were more vivid.

5 **B** Why did Thomas Wehr feel that bifurcated sleep can help us? **We can access hidden thoughts.**

bifurcated sleep = biphasic sleep (bi- = 2)

access hidden thoughts = understand (pathway to) our subconscious mind

The answer is found in the rest of Paragraph D.

D The subjects moved progressively towards a biphasic sleep pattern, taking a couple of hours to doze off and then sleeping in two distinct segments of four hours each with an interval of wakefulness in the middle. He construed (=decided) from this that **bifurcated sleep** (=biphasic sleep) is not only completely natural but also beneficial, because **this kind of sleeping facilitates the recall of dreams**, which **'afford people a pathway to their subconscious'** (=allow us to access hidden thoughts).

Distractors for Question 5

A The quality of sleep improves.

Paragraph D states that the sleep was more natural, but not of better quality.

C We tend to have more dreams.

The amount of dreams is not mentioned.

D It takes longer to fall asleep.

This is mentioned but not as a benefit, rather as an observation.

Questions 6–12: Notes completion using words/numbers from the text

It is likely that the answers to these questions will be found in the second part of the text, since the multiple choice questions tested the first part. Look for key words such as **REM** and **NREM** to help you to locate the beginning of the note taking section. 'Be' verbs are often omitted from notes, so these are optional in the answers for these questions.

Paragraph E contains the answers for Questions 6, 7 and 8.
Paragraph F contains the answers for Questions 9–12.

Rapid Eye Movement and Non-Rapid Eye Movement Sleep

- NREM Stage 1 = transition to sleep
  — may experience a feeling of 6 **falling**
  — easy to wake

transition = movement, change

E Sleep is essential and it is by no means a passive state. Sleep scientists have revealed that there are two fundamental cycles of activity, classified as rapid eye movement **(REM) sleep** and non-rapid eye movement **(NREM) sleep**. (use these acronyms to locate the correct place in the text) **The latter** (NREM sleep) consists of **four phases**. The **first phase** (=Stage 1), which lasts five to ten minutes, is the 'falling asleep' stage and sometimes there is actually **a sense of** 6 ***falling*** (=a feeling of falling), which often causes a sudden muscle contraction or jerk. **One is easily awoken** (=easy to wake) **during this stage**.

- NREM Stage 2 = 7 **light sleep**
  — decrease in heartbeat and temperature

decrease = slow down

E Then comes an interlude (Stage 2) of 7 ***light sleep*** where **the heart rate slows and body temperature drops** (=decrease in heartbeat and temperature) ...

- NREM Stages 3 & 4 = deep (slow-wave or delta) sleep
  — confusion on waking
  — necessary for healing soft and hard tissue and strengthening 8 **(the) immune system**

immune system = system that protects body from diseases

E ... the body is getting ready for the **deep sleep**, which occurs in the **third and fourth stages of NREM slumber**. This is **slow-wave or 'delta' sleep** and a person woken at this stage may feel quite **disorientated** (=confused). This period of deep sleep is **vital for** (=necessary for) the body to **restore itself** (=heal). During this time, not only does the body carry out repair and regeneration of **nerves, bones and muscles** (=soft and hard tissue), but it also **fortifies** (=strengthens) and repairs 8 ***the immune system***.

- REM = dream sleep
  — Occurs after 90 minutes of NREM
  — Fluctuations of 9 **(the) heart rate**, lighter respiration
  — Eyes move, brain more active but arms and legs 10 **(are) immobilised**
  — Reason for dreams unknown but important for 11 **learning and memory**
  — Lack of REM sleep → (leads to) mood disorders and 12 **(migraine) headaches**

fluctuations of = changes in

lighter respiration = light breathing

immobilised = unable to move

F The eyes can be seen to move rapidly beneath the eyelids during **REM sleep**, which ensues after approximately **an hour and a half** (=90 minutes) **of NREM** sleep cycles. A faster and **more erratic** (=fluctuating) 9 ***heart rate*** and **shallow breathing** (=lighter respiration) are typical of this state, and **brain activity intensifies** (=brain more active), giving rise to vivid dreaming; paradoxically, **the major voluntary muscle groups** (=arms and legs) 10 ***are immobilised*** (=cannot move), albeit for good reason – thrashing about while asleep could result in serious injury. Although **the purpose of dreaming is not yet fully comprehended** (=reason for dreams unknown), the hypothesis is that it is **vital for** (=important for) 11 ***learning and memory*** (as these regions of the brain are stimulated); indeed, studies have shown that when candidates are denied REM sleep, their memory of recent learning is impaired. **Deprivation of REM sleep** (=lack of REM sleep) also leads to **anxiety** (=mood disorders) and 12 ***migraine headaches.***

Question 13: Multiple choice – writer's conclusion

13 **A** What is the writer's conclusion? **Our lifestyles must change before our sleep can.**

This opinion is paraphrased in the final sentence of the reading passage.

G Sleep specialists agree that without adequate REM and NREM sleep, people's thought processes are likely to be compromised (=cannot think so clearly), and they may suffer from impaired (=damaged, weakened) memory, fatigue, depression, a weakened immune response, and heightened susceptibility to pain (=feel pain more), amongst other negative consequences. Yet modern-day humans remain chronically sleep deprived, notwithstanding the results of this research and its acceptance by many psychiatrists and sleep consultants. Why is the general populace (=most people) so loath (=reluctant) to relinquish its monophasic sleep schedule and enjoy the benefits of a biphasic schedule? **It is certain that attitudes to employment responsibilities** (=work) **and social commitments would have to be altered** (=be changed) **before such a huge behavioural paradigm shift could occur** (moving to a biphasic sleep pattern) **and individuals could allot more time to restful, restorative sleep** (=sleep more naturally and healthily).

Distractors for Question 13

B Lack of sleep is harming our work and social lives.

This is stated, but it is evidence that leads to the conclusion; it is not the final conclusion.

C We will sleep better if our health improves.

This is backwards; the passage states that our health will improve if we sleep better.

D Sleep researchers are frequently misguided (=wrong).

This is neither stated nor implied in the conclusion.

Reading Passage 2: THEORIES OF ACCIDENT CAUSATION IN THE WORKPLACE

Questions 14–19: Summary completion with options supplied

This **summary** comes from **Paragraphs B and C** of the text. The **ILCI model** is discussed in **Paragraph C**, and **Heinrich's original model** is discussed in **Paragraph B**.

The ILCI model of workplace safety (Paragraph C) **is a revision of Herbert Heinrich's original domino model.** (Paragraph B) **In Heinrich's**

model, **the final event** (=end result, or final domino in the series) was **14** **B injury or damage**, and this was the result of a workplace accident (the immediate cause of this was an accident in the workplace). He believed that the **15** **I unsafe acts** of the workers were primarily to blame for accidents (a workplace accident, in his theory, was immediately attributable to unsafe acts), and he called this factor **16** **N fault of person** (he labelled this factor as 'fault of person'). He stated that the underlying cause, or first domino in the series, was **17** **H genetic factors** (Heinrich suggested that 'fault of person' had its roots in the workers' ancestry, or genetic factors) plus the culture of the workers' home or work life (=combined with the social environment they lived or worked in).

His model was later modified to the ILCI model. (this theory was very popular, and was later updated by several other researchers in the field; the updated theory became known as the International Loss Control Institute or ILCI model) The new model took a wider perspective of workplace accidents. Thus, the first factor was called **18** **C lack of control** (the initial cause of workplace accidents became lack of control), reflecting error at management level, and the last domino was **19** **L loss of production** for the workplace (loss of production was added as the final outcome of the chain of events).

Distractors for Questions 14–19

All of the unused options are also phrases from the text; however, they do not fit with the information in the text and the summary.

Questions 20–27: Matching features

In this set of questions, the options are the names of theories. These are listed in the order that they appear in the text. Therefore, you need to find the Domino theory first. The statements that describe each theory are NOT in the order of the passage, so you need to read the information about each theory carefully, and match this to the best paraphrase. Note that there are 7 theories, and 8 paraphrases, so one theory will be used twice.

20 A worker with too much to do or with personal problems may cause accidents. **F Human factors**

too much to do = overload

F There is, however, a lot of credence (=belief, trust) given to the **human factors** theory, which, like the domino theory, ascribes accidents to a chain of events that will lead to human error. There are three main considerations that result in human error: **overload** (=too much to do); inappropriate (=not acceptable) responses; and inappropriate activities.

G There are internal factors which may contribute to overload as well, such as **stress or anxiety from family or non work-related issues** (=personal problems).

21 Certain people are more likely to have accidents. **E Accident proneness**

more likely to have accidents = more susceptible to suffering mishaps

prone = like to have

E The **accident proneness** theory is one of these (theories). In essence, this theory states that there are always **a few of us** (=some people) who are **more susceptible to suffering mishaps** (=more likely to have accidents), whether at work or at home, perhaps because of inattention or clumsiness.

22 Safety problems at work can be avoided by removing just one factor.
A Domino

removing = eliminating

factor = cause

A Herbert Heinrich, a pioneer in workplace safety philosophy, originally suggested that workplace accidents followed a sequence of five contributing causes, and he used the image of a set of **dominos** to illustrate the cause and effect chain reaction that was central to his theory. Heinrich maintained that **eliminating one contributing cause** (=removing just one factor), ... , **would prevent the chain from collapsing** (=could avoid safety problems at work).

23 Some workers don't believe that they will have an accident.
G Dan Petersen's theory

I **Dan Petersen** added to the inappropriate activity idea from the human factors theory by noting that ... a **'superman syndrome' of 'It won't happen to me'** should be considered as another inappropriate activity. **Some workers believe themselves to be invincible** (=powerful) **or indestructible** (=cannot be hurt, therefore, they don't believe that they will have an accident), ...

24 All possible causes of accidents can be put into two major categories.
C Multiple causation

two = either ... or

D The **multiple causation theory** assumes that there are numerous influential elements in the workplace (=many things that affect the workplace), and that it is various permutations (=combinations) of these that cause accidents. The causative factors are classified as being **either behavioural or environmental** (=two major groups, or categories).

25 Accidents are caused by management as well as by workers. **B ILCI**

C The updated theory became known as the International Loss Control Institute or **ILCI model**. This model included two new concepts; ... This idea **took some of the blame for workplace accidents away from the workers and attributed it to fundamental mistakes made at executive or management level** (=accidents are caused by management as well as workers).

26 If a worker is too short or too small for the task, this can cause accidents.
F Human factors

short/small = physical

F There is, however, a lot of credence given to the **human factors theory**, which, like the domino theory, ascribes accidents to a chain of events that will lead to human error. There are three main considerations that result in human error: overload; **inappropriate responses**; and inappropriate activities.

H **Inappropriate responses** take into account that workers may overlook possible dangers or safety procedures, or be mismatched to the workstation. **Physical factors, such as the size of the worker in relation to the load he is lifting** (=the worker may be too small or too short for his task) ...

27 Accidents cannot be avoided because they are part of life.
D Pure chance

E Perhaps the simplest theory is that of **pure chance**, that is, that **everyone is equally likely to have an accident and that there is**

apparently no particular identifiable (=known) **cause for these; subsequently, there is no possibility of intervention** (=taking action). (we cannot avoid accidents because there are no identifiable causes for accidents)

Reading Passage 3: GENERICIDE

Questions 28–34: Matching paragraph headings

28 Paragraph **A = ix Brand names become part of everyday usage**

Paragraph A is the introduction, which explains the problem.

A Occasionally a company's brand name becomes so deeply ingrained in the minds of everyday consumers (=becomes very well-known to everyone) that it **enters the popular lexicon** (=common vocabulary) **of its time** (becomes a new, common word in the language) and becomes a catch-all term for the generic product or activity in question. (everybody with a similar product uses that name)

29 Paragraph **B = vi How brand name loss is decided by law** (=how lawyers decide that a brand name can no longer be used as a brand name because it has become a general word)

Paragraph B contains legal definitions of trademark law.

B For those companies whose brand names travel too far into the public domain, however, there can be serious repercussions (=consequences): namely, **losing their right to trademark that particular brand** (=companies lose their legal claim to a trademark). ... According to a **Harvard law school overview on the subject** (=the rule about this process is explained by the Harvard law school), ... **courts** (of law) typically examine dictionary definitions, use of the term in the media, and consider whether or not the company has attempted to restrain usage of its trademark (=stop people from using the trademark as a general term). If the court deems the word to be generic, trademark privileges are stripped (=taken away); **no** company has an automatic right to continue renewing its trademarks without an end date. (explanation of how courts decide that a trademark is now a common word)

30 Paragraph **C = viii Examples of <u>genericide</u> in action**

<u>genericide</u> = a legal term for making something general

Paragraph C gives examples of companies that lost their trademarks. In this paragraph, the first sentence is the key sentence, followed by examples.

C Over the years, numerous companies have **<u>fallen victim to</u>** (=suffered from) this common and unwanted marketing phenomenon, **losing their prized brand names and subsequent <u>loss of trademark status</u>** (=companies have lost their trademarks). Otis Elevator Company lost their trademark rights to 'escalator' in a 1950 court case after being found guilty of using the term generically in their own patents and advertising. (An example of what happened to one company which lost their trademark. Other examples follow.)

31 Paragraph **D = iii Prevention is better than cure**

Paragraph D explains how companies can avoid the process of genericisation. In this paragraph, the first sentence is the key sentence, followed by examples.

D Genericisation is not an unstoppable process, however, and **<u>there are strategies that companies can adopt in order to maintain control of their brand names and avoid them becoming generic</u>** (=ways that companies can avoid, or prevent genericisation). (examples follow)

32 Paragraph **E = i <u>Appeals</u> to the public and the media**

<u>appeals</u> = is attractive

Paragraph E contains other examples of how companies have avoided genericisation. In this paragraph, the first sentence is the key sentence, followed by examples.

E Other companies have attempted to advise **<u>broadcasting services</u>** (=the media), language authorities **and the broader public** on the appropriate use of their brand name. (=they have appealed to the public and the media) (examples follow)

33 Paragraph F = x Taking back the brand name

taking back = recapturing

Again, the first sentence is the key sentence here, followed by examples.

F Although it is very unusual, it is possible for a trademark that has become generic **to be recaptured** (=taken back) **from the public domain**. (Sometimes, a trademark can be used again by the company. Examples follow.)

34 Paragraph G = v A changing environment for brand names

Paragraph G explains how the Internet has affected brand names.

G In the end, however, language is owned by the community that uses it, and **with the growth of the Internet in particular, this community is becoming ever more global**. (the Internet is changing the world environment for brand names) (the results of this change follow)

Distractors for Questions 28–34

In this type of question the **distractors** (unused headings or incorrect answers) are often found somewhere in the text, but either:

1. they are **not the main idea** of the paragraph, or
2. the **information** in the paragraph **does not match the heading**.

ii Large promotional budgets endorse (=support, promote) trademarks

There is no mention in the passage of companies supporting or promoting their trademarks.

Paragraph A discusses the topic of promotional budgets for products, but it is not the main idea of the paragraph. The paragraph is discussing what happens when companies are too successful at promoting their trademark.

iv Brand names enter vocabulary with ease (=brand names easily become part of our vocabulary)

Paragraphs A and B both mention this topic, but it is not the focus of either paragraph.

vii Legal consequences of unlawful use of trademarks

Paragraphs B and C discuss the law, but they focus on the process of losing a trademark, not on the consequences (=results) of this loss.

Questions 35–40: Multiple choice

35 **B** Which of the following is NOT a legal reason for losing a brand name?
The company has worked hard to keep its brand name.

The information to answer this question is in Paragraph B, which describes the law about genericisation.

The question is: Which of the following is NOT a legal reason for losing a brand name? Answer B is the only one that is NOT mentioned here.

B For those companies whose brand names travel too far into the public domain, however, there can be serious repercussions: namely, **losing their right to trademark that particular brand** (=losing a brand name). This can occur because ... According to a Harvard law school overview on the subject, 'a word will be considered generic when, ... '. **In arriving at a conclusion** (=in making a decision)**, courts typically examine dictionary definitions, use of the term in the media, and consider whether or not the company has attempted to restrain usage of its trademark.**

Distractors for Question 35

You are looking for information that is NOT included in the passage. A, C and D are all mentioned in Paragraph B.

A The name is used to define that kind of product.

... courts typically examine **dictionary definitions**, ...

C Newspapers and TV use the brand name as a generic name.

... use of the term in **the media** (=newspapers and TV), ...

D People have forgotten that the name refers to just one brand.

... 'a word will be considered generic when, in the minds of a substantial majority of the public (=most people think that), the word denotes (=means) a broad genus or **type of product** and **not** a specific source or manufacturer' (=not one brand).

36–37 According to the writer, which TWO of the following brand names are no longer trademarks?

C Trampoline

E Phillips head screwdriver

(in either order)

Paragraphs C, D, E and F all contain examples of companies and their brand names, or trademarks. You need to scan the reading passage, find each brand name, and check if the company has lost its trademark.

D The Griswold-Nissen company were **not so fortunate** (=unlucky), however, when they **attempted to** (=tried to) promote the **trampoline** as a 'rebound tumbler' – the generic term never caught on and **they** eventually **lost their trademark** (therefore, trampoline is no longer a trademark).

C In 1965, a court ruled that 'yo-yo' was ingrained in common speech, and the **Duncan Yo-yo Company subsequently had their trademark revoked** (=Yo-yo's lost their brand name status). Kerosene, zipper, thermos, and the **Philips-head screwdriver** round out the list of household goods now **in the public domain**. (these companies also lost their trademark status, so they are no longer brand names)

Distractors for Questions 36–37

A Google, B Singer, and D Xerox are all still brand names.

E The Internet search engine **Google**, fearing that widespread use of the verb 'to google' could result in future legal trouble, has contacted journalists, dictionaries and even the Swedish Language Council **in an effort to avert genericide** (Google is fighting against genericide, but it is still a brand name). In 2006, the company sent out a plea for everyone to 'please only use "Google" when you're actually referring to Google Inc. and our services'. In a similar vein, **Xerox** corporation was able **to successfully encourage users** to **eschew** (=not use) the verb 'to xerox' in favour of a generic expression, 'to photocopy', (Xerox was successful, so it is still a brand name) ...

F Although it is very unusual, it is possible for a trademark that has become generic to be recaptured from the public domain (=some companies get their trademark back). Two examples of this are the sewing machine manufacturer, **Singer** (Singer is one example of this; therefore it is still a trademark) and ...

38–39 According to the reading passage, which TWO strategies can help to avoid genericide?

B making a general name for the product
D creating clever advertising campaigns
(in either order)

Paragraphs D and E describe strategies for avoiding genericide.

D Genericisation is not an unstoppable process, however, and **there are strategies that companies can adopt in order to maintain control of their brand names and avoid them becoming generic.** (topic sentence) **One such strategy** (=one example) is for companies to **invent a generic term of their own** (=make their own general name for the product), which is particularly useful for ... (examples follow)

E In a similar vein, Xerox corporation was able to successfully encourage users to eschew the verb 'to xerox' in favour of a generic expression, 'to photocopy', and **it** (Xerox) **was helped to its goal by a series of snappy ads** (Xerox created a clever advertising campaign) including: 'You can't Xerox a Xerox on a Xerox. But we don't mind at all if you copy a copy on a Xerox® copier.'

Distractors for Questions 38–39

A writing dictionary entries for the product

Dictionaries are mentioned in Paragraph B, but there is no suggestion that companies write dictionary entries for their products.

B In arriving at a conclusion, courts typically examine dictionary definitions, ...

C taking people to court (=suing) for using the brand name

In Paragraph B, the court is mentioned but not companies suing consumers. In Paragraph E there is mention of companies trying to persuade consumers, but not to sue them.

E appealing to people via the Internet

Paragraph G mentions the Internet, but not as a strategy for companies to use to avoid genericide. Paragraphs D and E mention strategies, but do NOT include the use of the Internet.

40 **C** The main purpose of this reading passage is **to explain genericide with examples**.

The main purpose is found throughout the reading passage.

Paragraphs A and B introduce and define genericide. Paragraph C gives examples of companies which have lost their trademarks. Paragraphs D, E, F and G give strategies for avoiding genericide and examples.

Distractors for Question 40

A to give advice on how to avoid genericide

B to describe the law about genericide

Options A and B are both mentioned, but only in one or two paragraphs of the article, not throughout the article.

D to argue that genericide is unfair

Option D is not mentioned at all.

Appendix: IELTS Writing Band Descriptors (Public Version)

Task 1

Band	Task Achievement	Coherence and Cohesion	Lexical Resource	Grammatical Range and Accuracy
9	▪ fully satisfies all the requirements of the task ▪ clearly presents a fully developed response	▪ uses cohesion in such a way that it attracts no attention ▪ skilfully manages paragraphing	▪ uses a wide range of vocabulary with very natural and sophisticated control of lexical features; rare minor errors occur only as 'slips'	▪ uses a wide range of structures with full flexibility and accuracy; rare minor errors occur only as 'slips'
8	▪ covers all requirements of the task sufficiently ▪ presents, highlights and illustrates key features / bullet points clearly and appropriately	▪ sequences information and ideas logically ▪ manages all aspects of cohesion well ▪ uses paragraphing sufficiently and appropriately	▪ uses a wide range of vocabulary fluently and flexibly to convey precise meanings ▪ skilfully uses uncommon lexical items but there may be occasional inaccuracies in word choice and collocation ▪ produces rare errors in spelling and/or word formation	▪ uses a wide range of structures ▪ the majority of sentences are error-free ▪ makes only very occasional errors or inappropriacies
7	▪ covers the requirements of the task ▪ (Academic) presents a clear overview of main trends, differences or stages ▪ (General Training) presents a clear purpose, with the tone consistent and appropriate ▪ clearly presents and highlights key features / bullet points but could be more fully extended	▪ logically organises information and ideas; there is clear progression throughout ▪ uses a range of cohesive devices appropriately although there may be some under-/over-use	▪ uses a sufficient range of vocabulary to allow some flexibility and precision ▪ uses less common lexical items with some awareness of style and collocation ▪ may produce occasional errors in word choice, spelling and/or word formation	▪ uses a variety of complex structures ▪ produces frequent error-free sentences ▪ has good control of grammar and punctuation but may make a few errors
6	▪ addresses the requirements of the task ▪ (Academic) presents an overview with information appropriately selected ▪ (General Training) presents a purpose that is generally clear; there may be inconsistencies in tone ▪ presents and adequately highlights key features / bullet points but details may be irrelevant, inappropriate or inaccurate	▪ arranges information and ideas coherently and there is a clear overall progression ▪ uses cohesive devices effectively, but cohesion within and/or between sentences may be faulty or mechanical ▪ may not always use referencing clearly or appropriately	▪ uses an adequate range of vocabulary for the task ▪ attempts to use less common vocabulary but with some inaccuracy ▪ makes some errors in spelling and/or word formation, but they do not impede communication	▪ uses a mix of simple and complex sentence forms ▪ makes some errors in grammar and punctuation but they rarely reduce communication
5	▪ generally addresses the task; the format may be inappropriate in places ▪ (Academic) recounts detail mechanically with no clear overview; there may be no data to support the description ▪ (General Training) may present a purpose for the letter that is unclear at times; the tone may be variable and sometimes inappropriate ▪ presents, but inadequately covers, key features / bullet points; there may be a tendency to focus on details	▪ presents information with some organisation but there may be a lack of overall progression ▪ makes inadequate, inaccurate or over-use of cohesive devices ▪ may be repetitive because of lack of referencing and substitution	▪ uses a limited range of vocabulary, but this is minimally adequate for the task ▪ may make noticeable errors in spelling and/or word formation that may cause some difficulty for the reader	▪ uses only a limited range of structures ▪ attempts complex sentences but these tend to be less accurate than simple sentences ▪ may make frequent grammatical errors and punctuation may be faulty; errors can cause some difficulty for the reader

Band	Task Achievement	Coherence and Cohesion	Lexical Resource	Grammatical Range and Accuracy
4	▪ attempts to address the task but does not cover all key features / bullet points; the format may be inappropriate ▪ (General Training) fails to clearly explain the purpose of the letter; the tone may be inappropriate ▪ may confuse key features / bullet points with detail; parts may be unclear, irrelevant, repetitive or inaccurate	▪ presents information and ideas but these are not arranged coherently and there is no clear progression in the response ▪ uses some basic cohesive devices but these may be inaccurate or repetitive	▪ uses only basic vocabulary which may be used repetitively or which may be inappropriate for the task ▪ has limited control of word formation and/or spelling ▪ errors may cause strain for the reader	▪ uses only a very limited range of structures with only rare use of subordinate clauses ▪ some structures are accurate but errors predominate, and punctuation is often faulty
3	▪ fails to address the task, which may have been completely misunderstood ▪ presents limited ideas which may be largely irrelevant/ repetitive	▪ does not organise ideas logically ▪ may use a very limited range of cohesive devices, and those used may not indicate a logical relationship between ideas	▪ uses only a very limited range of words and expressions with very limited control of word formation and/or spelling ▪ errors may severely distort the message	▪ attempts sentence forms but errors in grammar and punctuation predominate and distort the meaning
2	▪ answer is barely related to the task	▪ has very little control of organisational features	▪ uses an extremely limited range of vocabulary; essentially no control of word formation and/or spelling	▪ cannot use sentence forms except in memorised phrases
1	▪ answer is completely unrelated to the task	▪ fails to communicate any message	▪ can only use a few isolated words	▪ cannot use sentence forms at all
0	▪ does not attend ▪ does not attempt the task in any way ▪ writes a totally memorised response			

Appendix: IELTS Writing Band Descriptors (Public Version) (Chinese Version)

写作任务 1

分数	写作任务完成情况	连贯与衔接	词汇丰富程度	语法多样性及准确性
9	▪ 完全满足所有的写作任务要求 ▪ 清晰地呈现充分展开的写作内容	▪ 衔接手段运用自如，行文连贯 ▪ 熟练地运用分段	▪ 使用丰富的词汇，能自然地使用并掌握复杂的词汇特征；极少出现轻微错误，且仅属笔误	▪ 完全灵活且准确地运用丰富多样的语法结构；极少出现轻微错误，且仅属笔误
8	▪ 写作内容充分地涵盖了所有的写作任务要求 ▪ 就主要内容 / 要点进行清晰和恰当的呈现、强调以及阐述	▪ 将信息与观点进行有逻辑的排序 ▪ 各种衔接手段运用得当 ▪ 充分且合理地使用分段	▪ 流畅和灵活地使用丰富的词汇，达意准确 ▪ 熟练地使用不常用词汇，但在词语选择及搭配方面偶尔出现错误 ▪ 拼写及 / 或构词方面错误极少	▪ 运用丰富多样的语法结构 ▪ 大多数句子准确无误 ▪ 只在极偶然情况下出现错误或存在不当之处
7	▪ 写作内容涵盖写作任务的要求 ▪（学术类）清晰地呈现关于主要趋势、区别或不同阶段的概述 ▪（培训类）清晰地呈现写作目的，行文语气一致且恰当 ▪ 能就主要内容 / 要点进行清晰的呈现与强调，但未能更为充分地展开	▪ 符合逻辑地组织信息及观点；清晰的行文推进贯穿全文 ▪ 恰当地使用一系列衔接手段，尽管有时使用不足或过多	▪ 使用足够的词汇，体现一定灵活性及准确性 ▪ 使用不常见词汇，对语体及搭配有一定认识 ▪ 在选择用词、拼写及 / 或构词方面可能偶尔出现错误	▪ 运用各种复杂的语法结构 ▪ 多数句子准确无误 ▪ 对语法及标点符号掌握较好，但有时出现少许错误
6	▪ 根据写作任务要求作文 ▪（学术类）选择恰当的信息进行概述 ▪（培训类）写作目的基本清晰；行文语气有时未能保持前后一致 ▪ 呈现并充分地强调了主要内容 / 要点，但有时含有不相关、不恰当或不准确的细节信息	▪ 连贯地组织信息及观点，总体来说，能清晰地推进行文发展 ▪ 有效地使用衔接手段，但句内及 / 或句间的衔接有时有误或过于机械 ▪ 有时无法保持一贯清晰或恰当地使用指代	▪ 使用足够的词汇开展写作任务 ▪ 试图使用不常用词汇，但有时使用不准确 ▪ 在拼写及 / 或构词方面有错误，但不影响交流	▪ 综合使用简单句式与复杂句式 ▪ 在语法及标点符号方面有一些错误，但这些错误很少影响交流
5	▪ 基本上能就写作任务作文，但某些地方写作格式有时存在不当之处 ▪（学术类）机械地描述细节，缺乏清晰的概述；有时未能提供数据支持所描述的内容 ▪（培训类）信函有时能体现特定的写作目的，但有时目的不清晰；行文语气变化不定，且有时不得体 ▪ 呈现但不能充分地涵盖主要内容 / 要点；有时出现着重表述细节的倾向	▪ 有一定组织性地呈现信息，但总体来说有时缺乏清晰的总体行文推进 ▪ 衔接手段不足、不准确或过度使用 ▪ 由于指代和替换不足显得行文重复	▪ 使用词汇范围有限，但能达到进行写作任务的最低限度 ▪ 在拼写及 / 或构词方面可能出现明显的错误，且可能会对读者造成一定的阅读困难	▪ 仅能使用有限的语法结构 ▪ 试图使用复杂句，但复杂句的准确性常不及简单句的准确性 ▪ 可能经常出现语法及标点符号使用的错误；这些错误会对读者造成一定的阅读困难
4	▪ 试图就写作任务要求行文，但未能包含所有主要信息 / 要点；写作格式有时不恰当 ▪（培训类）未能清晰地说明信件的写作目的；行文语气有时不恰当 ▪ 有时混淆主要信息 / 要点与细节信息；部分写作内容有时不清晰、不相关、重复或不准确	▪ 呈现了信息及观点，但未能连贯地组织这些信息及观点，且未能清晰地推进行文发展 ▪ 使用了一些基本的衔接手段，但有时出现不准确或重复的使用	▪ 只使用基本词汇，且有时重复使用这些词汇或使用对于写作任务不恰当的词汇 ▪ 对构词及 / 或拼写掌握有限； ▪ 错误可能对读者造成阅读困难	▪ 仅能使用非常有限的语法结构，只能偶尔使用从句 ▪ 一些语法结构使用正确，但错误占多数，且标点符号经常出错
3	▪ 可能因完全曲解写作任务而未能根据写作任务行文 ▪ 所表达的观点有限，可能大部分并不相关或重复	▪ 不能有逻辑地组织观点 ▪ 所用衔接手段有时非常有限，且有时未能体现观点之间的逻辑性	▪ 只使用非常有限的词汇及表达方式，对构词及 / 或拼写掌握也非常有限 ▪ 错误可能严重地影响信息的传达	▪ 尝试造句，但语法及标点符号错误占多数，意思被扭曲
2	▪ 写作内容与写作任务几乎无关	▪ 在内容组织方面能力非常有限	▪ 词汇的使用极其有限；基本上未能掌握构词及 / 或拼写	▪ 除了使用预先背诵的短语外，无法造句
1	▪ 写作内容与写作任务完全无关	▪ 未能传达任何信息	▪ 仅能孤立地使用少数单词	▪ 完全无法造句
0	▪ 缺考 ▪ 未以任何方式尝试写作 ▪ 写作内容完全是预先背诵的内容			

*** 评分标准以英文版本为准，中文翻译仅供参考。**

Appendix: IELTS Writing Band Descriptors (Public Version)

Task 2

Band	Task Achievement	Coherence and Cohesion	Lexical Resource	Grammatical Range and Accuracy
9	▪ fully addresses all parts of the task ▪ presents a fully developed position in answer to the question with relevant, fully extended and well supported ideas	▪ uses cohesion in such a way that it attracts no attention ▪ skilfully manages paragraphing	▪ uses a wide range of vocabulary with very natural and sophisticated control of lexical features; rare minor errors occur only as 'slips'	▪ uses a wide range of structures with full flexibility and accuracy; rare minor errors occur only as 'slips'
8	▪ sufficiently addresses all parts of the task ▪ presents a well-developed response to the question with relevant, extended and supported ideas	▪ sequences information and ideas logically ▪ manages all aspects of cohesion well ▪ uses paragraphing sufficiently and appropriately	▪ uses a wide range of vocabulary fluently and flexibly to convey precise meanings ▪ skilfully uses uncommon lexical items but there may be occasional inaccuracies in word choice and collocation ▪ produces rare errors in spelling and/or word formation	▪ uses a wide range of structures ▪ the majority of sentences are error-free ▪ makes only very occasional errors or inappropriacies
7	▪ addresses all parts of the task ▪ presents a clear position throughout the response ▪ presents, extends and supports main ideas, but there may be a tendency to overgeneralise and/or supporting ideas may lack focus	▪ logically organises information and ideas; there is clear progression throughout ▪ uses a range of cohesive devices appropriately although there may be some under-/over-use ▪ presents a clear central topic within each paragraph	▪ uses a sufficient range of vocabulary to allow some flexibility and precision ▪ uses less common lexical items with some awareness of style and collocation ▪ may produce occasional errors in word choice, spelling and/or word formation	▪ uses a variety of complex structures ▪ produces frequent error-free sentences ▪ has good control of grammar and punctuation but may make a few errors
6	▪ addresses all parts of the task although some parts may be more fully covered than others ▪ presents a relevant position although the conclusions may become unclear or repetitive ▪ presents relevant main ideas but some may be inadequately developed / unclear	▪ arranges information and ideas coherently and there is a clear overall progression ▪ uses cohesive devices effectively, but cohesion within and/or between sentences may be faulty or mechanical ▪ may not always use referencing clearly or appropriately ▪ uses paragraphing, but not always logically	▪ uses an adequate range of vocabulary for the task ▪ attempts to use less common vocabulary but with some inaccuracy ▪ makes some errors in spelling and/or word formation, but they do not impede communication	▪ uses a mix of simple and complex sentence forms ▪ makes some errors in grammar and punctuation but they rarely reduce communication
5	▪ addresses the task only partially; the format may be inappropriate in places ▪ expresses a position but the development is not always clear and there may be no conclusions drawn ▪ presents some main ideas but these are limited and not sufficiently developed; there may be irrelevant detail	▪ presents information with some organisation but there may be a lack of overall progression ▪ makes inadequate, inaccurate or over-use of cohesive devices ▪ may be repetitive because of lack of referencing and substitution ▪ may not write in paragraphs, or paragraphing may be inadequate	▪ uses a limited range of vocabulary, but this is minimally adequate for the task ▪ may make noticeable errors in spelling and/or word formation that may cause some difficulty for the reader	▪ uses only a limited range of structures ▪ attempts complex sentences but these tend to be less accurate than simple sentences ▪ may make frequent grammatical errors and punctuation may be faulty; errors can cause some difficulty for the reader

Band	Task Achievement	Coherence and Cohesion	Lexical Resource	Grammatical Range and Accuracy
4	▪ responds to the task only in a minimal way or the answer is tangential; the format may be inappropriate ▪ presents a position but this is unclear ▪ presents some main ideas but these are difficult to identify and may be repetitive, irrelevant or not well supported	▪ presents information and ideas but these are not arranged coherently and there is no clear progression in the response ▪ uses some basic cohesive devices but these may be inaccurate or repetitive ▪ may not write in paragraphs or their use may be confusing	▪ uses only basic vocabulary which may be used repetitively or which may be inappropriate for the task ▪ has limited control of word formation and/or spelling; errors may cause strain for the reader	▪ uses only a very limited range of structures with only rare use of subordinate clauses ▪ some structures are accurate but errors predominate, and punctuation is often faulty
3	▪ does not adequately address any part of the task ▪ does not express a clear position ▪ presents few ideas, which are largely undeveloped or irrelevant	▪ does not organise ideas logically ▪ may use a very limited range of cohesive devices, and those used may not indicate a logical relationship between ideas	▪ uses only a very limited range of words and expressions with very limited control of word formation and/or spelling ▪ errors may severely distort the message	▪ attempts sentence forms but errors in grammar and punctuation predominate and distort the meaning
2	▪ barely responds to the task ▪ does not express a position ▪ may attempt to present one or two ideas but there is no development	▪ has very little control of organisational features	▪ uses an extremely limited range of vocabulary; essentially no control of word formation and/or spelling	▪ cannot use sentence forms except in memorised phrases
1	▪ answer is completely unrelated to the task	▪ fails to communicate any message	▪ can only use a few isolated words	▪ cannot use sentence forms at all
0	▪ does not attend ▪ does not attempt the task in any way ▪ writes a totally memorised response			

Appendix: IELTS Writing Band Descriptors (Public Version) (Chinese Version)

写作任务 2

分数	写作任务完成情况	连贯与衔接	词汇丰富程度	语法多样性及准确性
9	▪ 全面地回应各部分写作任务 ▪ 就写作任务中的问题提出充分展开的观点，并提出相关的、得以充分延伸的以及论据充分的论点	▪ 衔接手段运用自如，行文连贯 ▪ 熟练地运用分段	▪ 使用丰富的词汇，能自然地使用并掌握复杂的词汇特征；极少出现轻微错误，且仅属笔误	▪ 完全灵活且准确地运用丰富多样的语法结构；极少出现轻微错误，且仅属笔误
8	▪ 充分地回应各部分写作任务 ▪ 就写作任务中的问题进行较为充分展开的回应，并提出相关的、得以延伸的以及含有论据的论点	▪ 将信息与论点进行有逻辑的排序 ▪ 各种衔接手段运用得当 ▪ 充分且合理地使用分段	▪ 流畅和灵活地使用丰富的词汇，达意准确 ▪ 熟练地使用不常用词汇，但在词语选择及搭配方面偶尔出现错误 ▪ 拼写及 / 或构词方面错误极少	▪ 运用丰富多样的语法结构 ▪ 大多数句子准确无误 ▪ 只在极偶然情况下出现错误或存在不当之处
7	▪ 回应各部分写作任务 ▪ 回应写作任务过程中始终呈现一个清晰的观点 ▪ 呈现、发展主要论点并就其进行论证，但有时出现过于一概而论的倾向及 / 或论点缺乏重点的倾向	▪ 符合逻辑地组织信息及论点；清晰的行文推进发展贯穿全文 ▪ 恰当地使用一系列衔接手段，尽管有时使用不足或过多 ▪ 每个段落均有一个清晰的中心主题	▪ 使用足够的词汇，体现一定灵活性及准确性 ▪ 使用不常见词汇，对语体及搭配有一定认识 ▪ 在选择用词、拼写及 / 或构词方面可能偶尔出现错误	▪ 运用各种复杂的语法结构 ▪ 多数句子准确无误 ▪ 对语法及标点符号掌握较好，但有时出现少许错误
6	▪ 回应了各部分写作任务，但某些部分的论证可能比其他部分更为充分 ▪ 提出了一个切题的观点，尽管各种结论有时不甚清晰或重复 ▪ 提出了多个相关的主要论点，但某些论点可能未能充分展开进行论证或不甚清晰	▪ 连贯地组织信息及论点，总体来说，能清晰地推进行文发展 ▪ 有效地使用衔接手段，但句内及 / 或句间的衔接有时有误或过于机械 ▪ 有时无法保持一贯清晰或恰当地使用指代 ▪ 使用段落写作，但未能保持段落间的逻辑	▪ 使用足够的词汇开展写作任务 ▪ 试图使用不常用词汇，但有时使用不准确 ▪ 在拼写及 / 或构词方面有错误，但不影响交流	▪ 综合使用简单句式与复杂句式 ▪ 在语法及标点符号方面有一些错误，但这些错误很少影响交流
5	▪ 仅回应了部分写作任务；写作格式有时在某些地方不甚恰当 ▪ 表述了一个观点，但展开论证过程未能保持一贯清晰，且可能缺乏结论 ▪ 提出一些主要论点但十分有限，且未能充分展开论证；有时出现无关细节	▪ 有一定组织性地呈现信息，但总体来说有时缺乏清晰的总体行文推进 ▪ 衔接手段不足、不准确或过度使用 ▪ 由于指代和替换不足显得行文重复 ▪ 没有使用段落写作，或者分段不足	▪ 使用词汇范围有限，但能达到进行写作任务的最低限度 ▪ 在拼写及 / 或构词方面可能出现明显的错误，且可能会对读者造成一定的阅读困难	▪ 仅能使用有限的语法结构 ▪ 试图使用复杂句，但复杂句的准确性常不及简单句的准确性 ▪ 可能经常出现语法及标点符号使用的错误；这些错误会对读者造成一定的阅读困难
4	▪ 仅最低限度地回应了写作任务，或所答相关性不大；写作格式有时不甚恰当 ▪ 提出了一个观点但并不清晰 ▪ 提出了一些主要论点但难以在文中确认，且这些观点可能重复、不相关或缺乏论据支持	▪ 呈现了信息及论点，但未能连贯地组织这些信息及论点，且未能清晰地推进行文发展 ▪ 使用了一些基本的衔接手段，但有时出现不准确或重复的使用 ▪ 没有使用段落写作，或段落使用混乱	▪ 只使用基本词汇，且有时重复使用这些词汇或使用对于写作任务不恰当的词汇 ▪ 对构词及 / 或拼写掌握有限；错误可能对读者造成阅读困难	▪ 仅能使用非常有限的语法结构，只能偶尔使用从句 ▪ 一些语法结构使用正确，但错误占多数，且标点符号经常出错
3	▪ 未能充分回应任一部分的写作任务 ▪ 未能表达一个清晰的论点 ▪ 提出极少论点，且基本上未能就其展开论证或观点不切题	▪ 不能有逻辑地组织论点 ▪ 所用衔接手段有时非常有限，且有时未能体现论点之间的逻辑性	▪ 只使用非常有限的词汇及表达方式，对构词及 / 或拼写掌握也非常有限 ▪ 错误可能严重地影响信息的传达	▪ 尝试造句，但语法及标点符号错误占多数，意思被扭曲
2	▪ 几乎未回应写作任务 ▪ 未能表达一个观点 ▪ 可能试图提出一两个论点，但未能展开论证	▪ 在内容组织方面能力非常有限	▪ 词汇的使用极其有限；基本上未能掌握构词及 / 或拼写	▪ 除了使用预先背诵的短语外，无法造句
1	▪ 写作内容与写作任务完全无关	▪ 未能传达任何信息	▪ 仅能孤立地使用少数单词	▪ 完全无法造句
0	▪ 缺考 ▪ 未以任何方式尝试写作 ▪ 写作内容完全是预先背诵的内容			

*** 评分标准以英文版本为准，中文翻译仅供参考。**

Appendix: IELTS Speaking Band Descriptors (Public Version)

Band	Fluency and Coherence	Lexical Resource	Grammatical Range and Accuracy	Pronunciation
9	▪ speaks fluently with only rare repetition or self-correction; any hesitation is content-related rather than to find words or grammar ▪ speaks coherently with fully appropriate cohesive features ▪ develops topics fully and appropriately	▪ uses vocabulary with full flexibility and precision in all topics ▪ uses idiomatic language naturally and accurately	▪ uses a full range of structures naturally and appropriately ▪ produces consistently accurate structures apart from 'slips' characteristic of native speaker speech	▪ uses a full range of pronunciation features with precision and subtlety ▪ sustains flexible use of features throughout ▪ is effortless to understand
8	▪ speaks fluently with only occasional repetition or self-correction; hesitation is usually content-related and only rarely to search for language ▪ develops topics coherently and appropriately	▪ uses a wide vocabulary resource readily and flexibly to convey precise meaning ▪ uses less common and idiomatic vocabulary skilfully, with occasional inaccuracies ▪ uses paraphrase effectively as required	▪ uses a wide range of structures flexibly ▪ produces a majority of error-free sentences with only very occasional inappropriacies or basic/non-systematic errors	▪ uses a wide range of pronunciation features ▪ sustains flexible use of features, with only occasional lapses ▪ is easy to understand throughout; L1 accent has minimal effect on intelligibility
7	▪ speaks at length without noticeable effort or loss of coherence ▪ may demonstrate language-related hesitation at times, or some repetition and/or self-correction ▪ uses a range of connectives and discourse markers with some flexibility	▪ uses vocabulary resource flexibly to discuss a variety of topics ▪ uses some less common and idiomatic vocabulary and shows some awareness of style and collocation, with some inappropriate choices ▪ uses paraphrase effectively	▪ uses a range of complex structures with some flexibility ▪ frequently produces error-free sentences, though some grammatical mistakes persist	▪ shows all the positive features of Band 6 and some, but not all, the positive features of Band 8
6	▪ is willing to speak at length, though may lose coherence at times due to occasional repetition, self-correction or hesitation ▪ uses a range of connectives and discourse markers but not always appropriately	▪ has a wide enough vocabulary to discuss topics at length and make meaning clear in spite of inappropriacies ▪ generally paraphrases successfully	▪ uses a mix of simple and complex structures, but with limited flexibility ▪ may make frequent mistakes with complex structures, though these rarely cause comprehension problems	▪ uses a range of pronunciation features with mixed control ▪ shows some effective use of features but this is not sustained ▪ can generally be understood throughout, though mispronunciation of individual words or sounds reduces clarity at times
5	▪ usually maintains flow of speech but uses repetition, self-correction and/or slow speech to keep going ▪ may over-use certain connectives and discourse markers ▪ produces simple speech fluently, but more complex communication causes fluency problems	▪ manages to talk about familiar and unfamiliar topics but uses vocabulary with limited flexibility ▪ attempts to use paraphrase but with mixed success	▪ produces basic sentence forms with reasonable accuracy ▪ uses a limited range of more complex structures, but these usually contain errors and may cause some comprehension problems	▪ shows all the positive features of Band 4 and some, but not all, the positive features of Band 6
4	▪ cannot respond without noticeable pauses and may speak slowly, with frequent repetition and self-correction ▪ links basic sentences but with repetitious use of simple connectives and some breakdowns in coherence	▪ is able to talk about familiar topics but can only convey basic meaning on unfamiliar topics and makes frequent errors in word choice ▪ rarely attempts paraphrase	▪ produces basic sentence forms and some correct simple sentences but subordinate structures are rare ▪ errors are frequent and may lead to misunderstanding	▪ uses a limited range of pronunciation features ▪ attempts to control features but lapses are frequent ▪ mispronunciations are frequent and cause some difficulty for the listener
3	▪ speaks with long pauses ▪ has limited ability to link simple sentences ▪ gives only simple responses and is frequently unable to convey basic message	▪ uses simple vocabulary to convey personal information ▪ has insufficient vocabulary for less familiar topics	▪ attempts basic sentence forms but with limited success, or relies on apparently memorised utterances ▪ makes numerous errors except in memorised expressions	▪ shows some of the features of Band 2 and some, but not all, the positive features of Band 4
2	▪ pauses lengthily before most words ▪ little communication possible	▪ only produces isolated words or memorised utterances	▪ cannot produce basic sentence forms	▪ speech is often unintelligible
1	▪ no communication possible ▪ no rateable language			
0	▪ does not attend			

Appendix: IELTS Speaking Band Descriptors (Public Version) (Chinese Version)

分数	流利性与连贯性	词汇多样性	语法多样性及准确性	发音
9	▪ 表达流利，极少出现重复或自我纠正的情况；出现犹豫是基于思考内容，而非寻找合适的词汇或语法 ▪ 表达连贯，衔接手段的使用完全恰当 ▪ 完全且恰当地展开话题	▪ 准确自如地使用词汇来谈论任何话题 ▪ 自然且准确地使用习语	▪ 自如得体地使用语法结构 ▪ 除了出现英语为母语者也会犯的口误外，始终使用准确的语法结构	▪ 准确运用丰富多样的发音特点，能表达微妙的差异 ▪ 表达过程中始终灵活地使用各种发音特点 ▪ 听者理解毫无障碍
8	▪ 表达流利，偶尔出现重复或自我纠正的情况；出现犹豫通常是基于思考内容，仅在少数情况下是寻找合适的语言 ▪ 连贯且恰当地展开话题	▪ 词汇使用丰富，运用灵活自如，表达意思准确 ▪ 熟练地使用非常见的词汇及习语，偶尔欠准确 ▪ 按需进行有效的改述	▪ 灵活地使用多种语法结构 ▪ 除极其偶然情况下出现的不当或简单的 / 非系统性错误外，大部分语句准确无误	▪ 使用多样的发音特点 ▪ 表达过程中灵活地使用多种发音特点，但偶尔出现偏差 ▪ 表达过程中始终易于听者理解；母语的口音对听者理解的影响极小
7	▪ 表达详尽，并无明显困难，不失连贯 ▪ 有时出现与语言相关的犹豫或出现重复及 / 或自我纠正 ▪ 具有一定灵活性地使用一系列连接词和语篇标记	▪ 灵活地使用词汇讨论各种话题 ▪ 使用一些非常见的词汇及习语，对语体及词汇搭配有所认识，但有时词语选择不甚恰当 ▪ 有效地进行改述	▪ 较灵活地使用一系列复杂的语法结构 ▪ 虽然反复出现一些语法错误，但语句通常正确无误	▪ 表现出 6 分水平中所有积极表现，也表现出 8 分水平中部分积极表现
6	▪ 表现出充分交流的意愿，但有时由于偶尔的重复、自我纠正或犹豫而缺乏连贯性 ▪ 能使用一系列连接词及语篇标记，但无法保持一贯恰当	▪ 有足以详尽讨论各种话题的词汇量，虽然有时使用不当但意思表达清晰 ▪ 基本上能成功地进行改述	▪ 结合使用简单与复杂的句型，但灵活性有限 ▪ 使用复杂结构时经常出现错误，尽管这些错误极少造成理解困难	▪ 使用多种发音特点，但掌握程度不一 ▪ 展现出某些有效使用发音特点的能力，但不能持续表现这一能力 ▪ 表达过程中听者基本能理解，但部分单词或音发音不准确导致有时清晰度下降
5	▪ 通常能保持语流，但需通过重复、自我纠正及 / 或降低语速来维持表达 ▪ 过度使用某些连接词及语篇标记 ▪ 能用简单的语言进行流利的表达，但在进行更为复杂的交流时则表达不畅	▪ 能谈论熟悉和不熟悉的话题，但使用词汇的灵活性有限 ▪ 尝试进行改述，但有时成功有时失败	▪ 能使用基本的句型，且具有合理的准确性 ▪ 使用有限的复杂句式结构，但通常会出错且会造成某些理解困难	▪ 表现出 4 分水平中所有积极表现，也表现出 6 分水平中部分积极表现
4	▪ 作答有明显停顿，且语速有时缓慢，出现频繁重复及自我纠正 ▪ 能连接简单句子，但重复使用简单的连接词，有时缺乏连贯性	▪ 能谈论所熟悉的话题，但对不熟悉的话题仅能表达基本意思，且经常用词不当 ▪ 很少尝试改述	▪ 能使用基本句型并正确使用一些简单句型，但极少使用从句 ▪ 常出现错误，且会造成误解	▪ 使用有限的发音特点 ▪ 尝试表现多种发音特点，但频繁出现偏差 ▪ 经常出现发音错误，对听者理解造成一些困难
3	▪ 表达过程中出现长时间停顿 ▪ 连接简单句的能力有限 ▪ 仅能简单作答，且经常无法表达基本意思	▪ 使用简单词汇表达个人信息 ▪ 讨论不熟悉的话题时词汇匮乏	▪ 尝试使用基本句型，但准确度有限，或依赖预先背诵的几句话 ▪ 除预先背诵的内容外，错误很多	▪ 表现出 2 分水平中部分表现，以及 4 分水平中部分积极表现
2	▪ 大部分词汇间出现长时间停顿 ▪ 几乎无法进行沟通	▪ 仅能说出零散的单词或预先背诵的几句话	▪ 不能使用基本的句型	▪ 表达通常无法理解
1	▪ 无法进行沟通 ▪ 无可供评分的语言			
0	▪ 缺考			

* 评分标准以英文版本为准，中文翻译仅供参考。